Reward Management

This thoroughly revised edition adopts a critical and theoretical perspective on remuneration policy and practices in the UK, from the decline of collective bargaining to the rise of more individualistic systems based on employee performance. It tackles the conceptual issues missing from existing texts in the field of reward by critically examining the latest academic literature on the topic.

Fully updated to cover the Chartered Institute of Personnel and Development's reward syllabus, and offering a less prescriptive alternative to current texts for HR practitioners and MBA students, this new edition includes:

- new chapters on executive reward, pensions and benefits
- clear routes to assist the student reader in the journey through this complex area
- a strong contextual framework to enable better understanding.

The second edition of *Reward Management* is an essential read for all those studying or with an interest in human resource management, performance management and reward.

Geoff White is Professor of Human Resource Management and Director of Research at the University of Greenwich Business School, UK. He has written widely on reward issues, especially public sector pay and the national minimum wage.

Janet Druker is Professor of Human Resource Management and Senior Pro-Vice Chancellor at Canterbury Christ Church University, UK. Her previous publications are in the fields of construction management, self-employment and agency workers.

Routledge Studies in Employment Relations
Series editors: Rick Delbridge and Edmund Heery
Cardiff Business School

Aspects of the employment relationship are central to numerous courses at both undergraduate and postgraduate level. Drawing insights from industrial relations, human resource management and industrial sociology, this series provides an alternative source of research-based materials and texts, reviewing key developments in employment research.

Books published in this series are works of high academic merit, drawn from a wide range of academic studies in the social sciences.

Reward Management

A critical text

Second edition

Edited by Geoff White and Janet Druker

Routledge
Taylor & Francis Group

LONDON AND NEW YORK

First published 2009
by Routledge
2 Park Square, Milton Park, Abingdon, Oxon OX14 4RN

Simultaneously published in the USA and Canada
by Routledge
270 Madison Avenue, New York, NY 10016

*Routledge is an imprint of the Taylor & Francis Group, an informa
business*

Typeset in Times New Roman by
RefineCatch Limited, Bungay, Suffolk
Printed and bound in Great Britain by
CPI Antony Rowe, Chippenham, Wiltshire

British Library Cataloguing in Publication Data
A catalogue record for this book is available from the British Library

Library of Congress Cataloging in Publication Data
Reward management: a critical text / [edited by] Geoff White and Janet
Druker. — 2nd ed.
    p. cm.
Includes bibliographical references and index.
1. Employee motivation. I. White, Geoff, 1949– II. Druker, J. (Jan)
HF5549.5.C67R485 2008
658.3′225—dc22
2008018366

ISBN 13: 978–0–415–43188–0 (hbk)
ISBN 13: 978–0–415–43189–7 (pbk)
ISBN 13: 978–0–203–88876–6 (ebk)

ISBN 10: 0–415–431883–4 (hbk)
ISBN 10: 0–415–431891–4 (pbk)
ISBN 10: 0–203–88876–6 (ebk)

Contents

List of figures and tables

Figures

Tables

List of editors and contributors

Editors

Geoff White is Professor of Human Resource Management and Director of Research at the University of Greenwich Business School. Prior to becoming an academic, he worked for the major pay research organisation, Incomes Data Services, and was Managing Editor for Research for several years. Geoff became a university lecturer in 1991 and has acted as an advisor to a number of organisations including the Low Pay Commission, the Local Government Pay Commission, the NHS Staff Council and, most recently, Sir Clive Booth's inquiry into police pay. His previous books include *Managing People in Construction* (IPD 1996), also with Jan Druker, and *Employee Relations in the Public Services* (Routledge 1999), with Susan Corby. He is a Chartered Fellow of the CIPD.

Janet Druker is Professor of Human Resource Management and Senior Pro-Vice-Chancellor at Canterbury Christ Church University. Prior to working in higher education, Jan worked as a project officer at Warwick University where she also read for a PhD. She then worked for seven years with the Union of Construction Allied Trades and Technicians as Head of Research and Organisation. Before her current appointment she was a lecturer in trade union studies at South West London College, Associate Head and later Director of Research at the University of Greenwich Business School and then Head of the University of East London Business School. Jan has researched and written widely on human resource management, especially on the construction industry, on self-employment and agency workers. Her previous books include *Managing People in Construction* (IPD 1996). She is a Chartered Fellow of the CIPD.

Contributors

Sue Hastings is an independent consultant in pay systems, with a particular interest in gender aspects. She previously worked for the Trade Union Research Unit (TURU) at Ruskin College, Oxford and has written widely on the subject of Equal Pay and Equal Value. She has acted as advisor, primarily to unions and Applicants, on many Equal Value cases. She played a major role in the design and implementation of new job evaluation schemes in both local government and the NHS. She was a member of the team which developed and tested the EOC Equal Pay Review tool kit.

Edmund Heery has been Professor of Employment Relations at Cardiff Business School since January 1996 and worked previously at Kingston University, Imperial College, the City University and the London School of Economics. He has published widely on various aspects of industrial relations and human resource management, including reward management. He was until 2007 chief editor of the *British Journal of Industrial Relations*.

Jeff Hyman is Professor and HRM at Aberdeen Business School. Previously at Strathclyde University Business School and then Napier University in Edinburgh, he has published widely in the field of employee financial participation schemes, including a number of books. He is co-author of 'Managing Employee Involvement and Participation' (Sage 1995), 'The Meaning of work in the New Economy' (Palgrave 2007) and co-editor of 'Participation and Democracy at Work' (Palgrave 2005). He has also been a visiting fellow with the International Labour Organisation in Geneva.

Stephen Perkins is Professor of Human Resource Management at London Metropolitan University Business School. He has a D.Phil from Oxford University and before becoming an academic was a FTSE Top-30 company executive. His publications in corporate governance and comparative organisation studies include books/book chapters, conference papers and refereed academic journals. He is a Chartered Fellow of the CIPD and recently completed CIPD-funded research on international employee reward management.

Paul R. Sparrow is Professor of International HRM at Lancaster University Management School where he leads the Centre for Performance-Led HR. Prior to this appointment he was at Manchester Business School and he has also worked at Aston University, Warwick University and Sheffield University. He was also Principal Consultant at PA Consulting Group. He has written widely on business psychology, HR strategy, management competencies and international HRM and was a former editor of the *Journal of Occupational and Organisational Psychology*. He is currently researching the globalisation of human resource management with Chris Brewster for the CIPD.

Stephen Taylor is Senior Lecturer at Manchester Metropolitan University Business School and the CIPD's examiner for its Employment Law and Managing in a Strategic Business Context papers. He teaches and researches in HRM, employee resourcing, reward management and employment law. Stephen has written extensively on occupational pensions. His books include *Human Resource Management* (co-written with Derek Torrington and Laura Hall), *People Resourcing* and *Employment Law: an Introduction* (co-written with Astra Emir). He is a Chartered Fellow of the CIPD.

Marc Thompson is a Fellow in Employment Relations at the Said Business School, University of Oxford and Academic Tutor and Fellow of Templeton College, University of Oxford. He has published over 60 books, articles and papers. His research has explored the adoption and diffusion of innovations in work practices in the aerospace sector, reward practices and their integration with wider HR practices in R&D units, and the impact of HRM on organisational performance. More recently, he has been studying change in inter-governmental organisations and leading a collaborative research programme on the links between innovation and strategic renewal in large firms. He co-directs the MSc programme Consulting and Coaching for Change run jointly by HEC and Oxford.

Angela Wright is Senior Lecturer in Human Resource Management at Westminster University Business School. Prior to her current role she taught at Coventry University and previously worked as a reward specialist for a number of organisations including Incomes Data Services, Industrial Relations Services and the Office of Manpower Economics. She continues to act as a reward consultant. She published her book, *Reward Management in Context*, for the CIPD in 2004. She is currently researching the impact of organisational culture on the design of reward systems.

Acknowledgements

The editors would like to convey their grateful thanks to the contributors to this volume. All of them are very busy people with many and varied responsibilities yet all of them managed to find the time to write the chapters published here. We also thank them for their continued support and enthusiasm through the lengthy editorial process.

We would also like to thank the staff of Routledge for their patience in dealing with the lengthy gestation period, and several unavoidable delays, in the submission of this manuscript. As usual, we should add that any errors, misinterpretations or mistakes are our own! We would particularly like to thank Monique Petit of Canterbury Christ Church University for her excellent help in formatting the text and pointing out errors and omissions.

Lastly, we would like to dedicate this book to our colleagues at the University of Greenwich Business School and Canterbury Christ Church University for their continuing friendship and support. We would also like to acknowledge the vital contribution of all the HRM students we have taught over the years in helping us to frame and develop our ideas about reward and the management of human resources.

1 Introduction

Janet Druker and Geoff White

This book explores the dimensions of reward management and the direction of policy and practice in recent years. It is not intended as a prescriptive text. Rather we aim to analyse the influences shaping reward practices, identifying trends and exploring the rationale for change. Each chapter is written by an academic specialist in the field and provides a survey and critical analysis of recent research on the topic covered. Unlike many prescriptive texts on reward, which tend to concentrate on the techniques and technical details of reward management, this book provides an employee relations perspective on the subject. It takes its starting point from the contested nature of the employment relationship in which different stakeholders will have differing agendas and objectives. The book therefore seeks to challenge the mainstream unitary or normative approaches that typify much of the writing on reward management, especially that emanating from North America. In doing so, we aim to provide the reflective practitioner or student with an understanding of underlying influences impacting on reward management – laying a basis for a more critical and longer-lasting understanding of the subject.

When the first edition was published, eight years ago, the (then) Institute of Personnel and Development in Britain had only recently re-written the professional education syllabus to provide more explicitly for the study of 'reward management'. This now features as a core area of study within the Chartered Institute of Personnel and Development's professional syllabus, acknowledging the significance of reward as an important lever through which business organisations achieve their objectives. This adjustment – which in itself might seem to be a minor change – reflects the importance of this subject in the context of wider changes in work organisations and in the relationships that they engender. The last decade has been one of debate about these issues – not only in the UK and the developed economies but in developing economies too. The chapters that follow draw on recent literature reflecting on these debates, exploring the meaning and implications for reward practice. This edition of the book has two new chapters – executive pay and pensions – to reflect the important debates taking place in those areas of reward.

What is 'fair'?

Pay structures and the dispersion of pay reflect fundamental social values that may differ from one culture to another and which shift over time. There is nothing that can (or should) be taken for granted within prevailing employment structures, without some fundamental questions being considered. Who controls, directs and benefits from business activity? What are the prevailing values against which that activity is undertaken? Should there be a minimum level of reward for work below which no one should fall? If so, how should it be set and who should decide the level?

The notion of 'fairness' also encompasses expectations of the differential that might reasonably be expected between the highest earners and the lowest in society. Narrow pay differentials suggest a society with more egalitarian values, whilst a yawning gulf between the highest earners and the lowest paid points to wide social distinctions between these social groups. A widening of differentials may be taken as a proxy for increasing social inequality. Reward practices may serve to create or to minimise divisions within the workforce. The choices that are made and the underlying values represented by these choices are not simply technical matters. Pay systems are an arena for conflict, wherein norms may be contested and questions of equity and entitlement are posed. Conceptions of skill and social status are important but philosophical and ethical issues – questions of equity and equality – must also be addressed.

Inherent in these considerations are assumptions about access to education and training opportunities as well as about the length of working life and expectations and costs of retirement. Demographic factors influence approaches to state benefits and raise questions about the responsibilities that business organisations should have to the wider community too. How should social costs be shared between employers, the state and the individual? To what extent should employers carry social costs for their employees – for example for training, sickness, medical care, or retirement (Standing 1997)? Will such arrangements disadvantage those who are outside of the labour market or will they encourage labour market participation? Will employer provision for employees permit the state to provide more amply for those who are not employed? To what extent should the state ensure that social benefits are standardised at least to a minimum level? And what impact will state benefits have on labour market participation?

Finally, as we consider the notion of 'fairness' we should also ask what meaning is given to pay by the individual recipient. To what extent can pay systems and pay levels unlock a means to improving performance? Questions of motivation have been extensively explored (e.g. Maslow 1954; Herzberg *et al.* 1957; McGregor 1960; Vroom 1964; Porter and Lawler 1968) but such issues are best understood within their particular social and historical context since questions of culture, class and gender influence social values shaping social values and attitudes toward motivation. How important are pay and benefits as motivational tools when compared with the satisfaction of doing a particular job and doing it well? To what extent does individual recognition outweigh the collective benefits of team achievement? Money rewards are often perceived to be only a part of the real benefit derived from work. Theories of motivation may point to the higher satisfaction that can derive from a job well done. Critics may argue that this is a consideration that is selectively adopted and may be used more frequently to apply to lower paid women's work in the caring professions than to the (typically better paid) senior male executive in corporate life.

Change at work

A discussion of reward management in practice must necessarily be located in the context of wider economic and social change. There is no easy or automatic correlation between forms of production and payment systems but some broad trends are evident. The legacy of (the overwhelmingly male) craft based and hourly paid systems of the nineteenth century was challenged toward the end of that century by management theories and practices that sharpened the division of labour between the planning and organisation of tasks and their execution.

The 'scientific management' theories of the American management writer, Frederick Winslow Taylor (1913), reflected and articulated these developments. He asserted the principles of direct control through which management aggregates to itself the knowledge base that was previously the prerogative of the workforce (Braverman 1974). Through this process an organisational 'brain' is created, responsible for planning and work organisation. This was compounded by assembly line production with management activities increasingly conducted separately from the shop-floor, where workers were to be spurred on to high performance by the use of incentive payments. The distinction between management and production processes that became more marked from the end of the nineteenth century was paralleled by a division within the workforce, with differential treatment in terms of pay and conditions for management, professional and administrative staff on the one hand and production workers on the other. Although time-based payment remained at the core of the employment relationship, payment was defined for employees associated with the management of the enterprise in terms of annual and monthly payments (salaries), whilst for production workers, calculations were often based on the notion of an hourly rate of pay, with associated incentive payments.

From the end of World War One mass production came to be associated in industrial economies with standardised pay arrangements, often negotiated at industry level, through multi-employer bargaining. Pay was set on the basis of a 'rate for the job' and each job was a 'precisely defined aggregate of well-specified tasks and seniority' (Piore and Sabel 1984: 113). As Mahoney (1992: 338) comments, 'the concept of job was the unifying concept in the Scientific

Management approach to organisation and management'. Moreover, the development of such systems led to 'the development and application of a concept of job ownership expressed in the labor movement and collective bargaining' (Mahoney 1992: 339). Trade union representation was based around particular skills or grades and trade unions were engaged in a struggle to defend the interests and to improve the circumstances of those sections of workers – most often men – whose interests they represented. Time rates of pay, often determined through multi-employer collective bargaining, were frequently supplemented at establishment level with incentive payments which, together with shift and overtime pay, contributed significantly to total earnings for manual workers. Arrangements for administrative, professional and managerial staff were less standardised than those for craft or production workers in the private sector, but the principles of equity and public accountability that operated in the public sector encouraged a formalisation and standardisation on the basis of a recognised rate for the job.

These systems applied predominantly, although not exclusively, to men. Working women were at a significant disadvantage because social values emphasised women's domestic role and, outside of specific sectors of employment, such as the textile and garment industries, the social definition of 'skill' tended to exclude them from higher paid work (Pollert 1981). Craft trade unions had, historically, excluded women from membership, adapting only reluctantly during wartime to women's presence in the workplace in higher paid trades. Yet women's growing labour market participation, coupled with changes in the law, encouraged women to challenge traditional patterns of discrimination. The notion of 'fair' employment standards that attached to the internal labour market provided a context for women to claim equality of treatment in terms of employment opportunity and pay – as Sue Hastings demonstrates in Chapter 4 of this volume.

In each country undergoing such development, questions were posed about the role and scope of state support – both for business and for the wider population. To what extent does the state provide a 'safety net' for employees, for the unemployed and their families? Correspondingly, economic and social development poses questions about the role of government and the state in responding to the development of business and the accompanying demands of civil society. These questions have been revived over recent decades, as there has been a fundamental shift in the nature of work and in the management of the employment relationship (Cappelli 1995; Kersley *et al.* 2006). Whilst we cannot equate forms of production and payment systems, there is little doubt about the inevitability that changes in the former will carry with them a necessity that the latter must change in some way too. The era of relatively full employment and social security, based on manufacturing strength, gave way to a rise in unemployment in the 1980s in the USA and Europe. This led to a decline in manufacturing jobs and a growth in the service sector that has continued subsequently. As manufacturing industry is taken up in the newly industrialising economies of Asia and Latin America, so the 'service economy' model increasingly characterises the US, the UK and other European countries too (McGovern *et al.* 2007). This is coupled with increased competition within financial markets, in an era of technological innovation.

The implications for 'reward' at work are fascinating. The pay systems of the 'Fordist' era reflected a segmented workforce, with contrasting experiences between men and women, between white and blue collar, between public and private sector. At the same time it was characterised by social benefits and an expectation of open-ended employment. The decline in male, manufacturing activity called into question prevailing systems of pay determination and pay structures. The application of information and communication technologies (ICTs) blurred some of the distinctions between 'blue-collar' and 'white-collar' workers. Changes in work organisation through lean production (fewer workers) have been associated with changes in job content and in status generating conflicting pressures – both for upskilling and for deskilling and creating the potential for new forms of control in the employment relationship within and across these groups (Crompton *et al.* 1996). Women's labour market participation has challenged traditional assumptions about the benefits that might be valued in the workplace (see Chapter 8 by Angela Wright later in this volume).

Collective bargaining arrangements have been undermined in most developed economies and the scope of bargaining has diminished under the impact of change. Increased product market pressures and the drive for improved performance has encouraged employers to seek to determine pay and conditions in relation to the needs and the performance of the individual business (Streeck 1987; Gospel 1992). In the UK, pay was determined unilaterally in 70 per cent of workplaces for at least some employees, according to the 2004 Workplace Employee Relations survey (Kersley *et al.* 2006: 179). Even where unions continue to be recognised, they are now less likely to be involved in pay bargaining (Brown *et al.* 1998: 69). The percentage of workplaces that engaged in any collective bargaining over pay fell from 30 per cent to 22 per cent between 1998 and 2004 (Kersley *et al.* 2006: 182). Collective bargaining is now largely confined to the public sector and the larger private sector employers.

Changing technologies and new forms of work organisation play an important part in defining the framework for employment (Crompton *et al.* 1996). Information and communication technologies (ICTs) have eroded traditional skills and grading structures associated with apprenticeship training for (mostly) male entrants. Employers now seek new or enhanced skills that facilitate the rapid pace of ICT innovation (Gallie 1996). The reconfiguration of work processes and the demands of knowledge-based technologies mean that employees must adapt rapidly and use their skills and their discretion in the way that tasks are performed (Gallie 1996). Effective business performance relies then on individual performance and seems to give further support to the notion of payment for the person, rather than payment for the job. It may be associated with forms of skill-based payments, with reward for the acquisition of skill or payment intended to mould behaviour and encourage greater responsiveness to change.

Perhaps the most significant changes of the last 25 years in the USA and in Europe reflect and result from the presence of women at all levels within the labour market. Although employment remains significantly gendered, the growth of the service economy has opened up new employment opportunities that have been taken up by women. In the UK, the expansion of part-time work, in conjunction with a framework of legislation that has emphasised equality of opportunity, has prompted awareness of equal pay, equal treatment and family-friendly benefits amongst both employers and employees. Of course these changes have not been straightforward and new rights – and new interpretations of the law – have not been achieved without a struggle. Equal pay remains a goal that has yet to be achieved, but the more visible presence of women within the workforce points the way forward.

Organisational and labour market changes point now to the downloading of risk by employers as they seek, through a variety of means, to integrate employees into the drive to achieve business objectives. Whether the mechanism to be used is constructed on the basis of individual performance or on the basis of a collective (for example team-based or establishment) output arrangement, the implication of change is to minimise risk for the employer.

These changes have led employers to focus increasingly on the pay and performance of individuals, rather than negotiating collectively with representatives of the workforce. Brown *et al.* (1998) identified two possible forms of individualisation of the employment relationship – substantive and procedural. The former assumes that each employee will have his or her own individual employment contract, each with its own unique pay and conditions and with the possibility for individual negotiation of these terms. The latter maintains standardised employment terms and conditions for all employees and these are normally non-negotiable by individual employees. The research by Brown *et al.* (1998) found that few employers had opted for substantive individualisation and most had continued with standardised employment contracts. On the other hand, more recent research (Marginson *et al.* 2007) found that, while there was evidence that individualisation had not necessarily undermined collective bargaining in the sense of delivering base pay increases, the proportion of individual earnings determined outside of collective bargaining had grown. Forms of 'contribution-based pay' (Brown and Armstrong 1999), which link at least part of the pay to appraisals of individual workers, are now common throughout the private sector and to a lesser extent in the public services.

Labour in office: legislative changes

The political context is one of the keys to understanding the changing approaches to reward management over the last twenty years. Writing a second edition of this text after more than a decade of successive Labour Governments in the UK, we are reminded of the impact of the political environment on employer decision taking and on employee voice. Academic debate within this field in the 1990s was concerned with the role of trade unions and the extent to which a recovery in their fortunes might be anticipated if Labour were to take office and reverse some of the legislation of the previous era. Now, more than ten years after Labour's 1997 election success, it is clear that the revisions that have been implemented to the legislative framework in relation to trade union recognition have not led to a fundamental resurgence of trade unions within the workplace. Although the legal framework now offers more support than before the 1997 General Election, trade unionists have been unable to combat the trend away from collective bargaining and diminished workplace influence.

From the point of view of this discussion, more important, perhaps, than legislative support for trade union recognition, has been the Labour Government's adherence to European social legislation opening up the possibility of a floor of individual employment rights. The ending of the previous Conservative Government's opt-out from the Social Chapter of the Maastricht Treaty on Labour's accession to power has led in turn to some important new employee rights. Whilst collective bargaining in relation to pay and benefits has continued to diminish in terms of the number of workplaces and the proportion of employees covered, individual employment rights affect a greater number of employees and impact more significantly on employee expectations than in the past.

The areas first affected by European entitlements, following the 1997 General Election, resulted from the belated implementation of the Working Time Directive of 1993 enacted through the 1998 Working Time Regulations. For the first time employees in the UK benefited from a statutory paid holiday entitlement of 20 days per year. Some 640,000 full-time employees and around 1.7 million part-time employees who previously had no contractual holiday entitlement were affected (White 1999). A further adjustment was brought into effect from October 2007 to increase the entitlement to 24 days, rising to 28 days inclusive of bank holidays from April 2009. Maximum working hours and paid work breaks also resulted, although the scope for bypassing the 48 hour limit to the working week was wide.

The second important change, although this was a result of UK domestic legislation rather than European, was the historic implementation of a national minimum wage for the UK for the first time in 1998 (Low Pay Commission 1998). The minimum wage has been seen as a major success for the Labour Government. Despite previous dire warnings that such a statutory floor to wages would lead to job losses, an increase in business failures and a hike in inflation, when it finally arrived 'it did so with more of a whimper than a bang' (Dickens and Manning 2003: 202). In fact employment growth continued in most low-paid sectors of the economy (clothing and textiles being the only exception) and there was no discernible impact on inflation. This was largely because the number of workers affected at the initial wage level set was significantly over-estimated. Since then the Low Pay Commission has awarded a number of above-average earnings increases which have significantly increased the 'bite' of the minimum wage. Estimates from the latest April 2007 Annual Survey of Hours and Earnings (ASHE) show that the number of jobs paid below the NMW was 292,000 in Spring 2007, or 1.2 per cent of all jobs in the labour market (ONS 2007).

A third legislative development driving change in reward practices was the growth of employee rights to family-friendly benefits. New family-friendly-benefits included extended rights to maternity leave and adoption pay for nine months, effective from April 2007, with a goal of a year's paid leave. New rights also included additional paternity leave, parental leave for parents with a child under the age of six or a disabled child under 18 and time off work to look after dependants (Stanworth *et al.* 2007).

Government concern about the escalating cost of pensions also led to an independent commission which issued three reports identifying the causes of the crisis in pensions provision and advocating particular solutions (Pensions Commission 2004, 2005, 2006). The Government response was the Pensions Act 2007 that will, among other things, increase the state retirement age from its current 65 to 68 for both males and females by 2046. More importantly for employers, the Act will require that by 2012 all employees aged between 22 and state pension age be automatically enrolled into a pension scheme, to which their employer will be required to make a minimum contribution on any earnings between £5,000 and £33,000 per annum (DWP 2007).

One last development since 2000 should be mentioned. Since 2000 the law governing equal pay for equal value continued to be a major influence upon the design of reward systems, especially in the public sector where issues of pay transparency are more evident. In particular the issue of seniority-based remuneration systems and their potential for gender discrimination has been raised. The new age discrimination regulations are creating new challenges to both service-based pay progression and benefits eligibility based on service (CIPD 2008).

Labour in office: economic outcomes

The Labour government was elected with a distinctly different economic agenda to the previous Conservative administrations, with a new emphasis upon investment in public services and an, albeit limited, commitment to some re-distribution of income and wealth. The major instruments to achieve the latter were through both the introduction of a national minimum wage and tax credits for those on low incomes. On the other hand, the Government saw itself also as a force for economic modernisation. In reality much of the economic agenda remained rooted to the same principles that had endured under the Conservatives. There was concern to continue encourage-ment of wealth creation (and hence no real commitment to tackle the issue of escalating executive pay which Labour had condemned in opposition) and a business friendly approach to fiscal matters. There was also a stated object-ive to improve UK labour productivity and 'modernise' labour practices, especially in the public services.

In terms of economic performance, the period since 1997 has been one of continued buoyancy, with employment levels reaching historic high levels and significant labour shortages in key skills. The UK employment rate rose from 71 per cent to over 74 per cent between 1995 and 2006 while the unemploy-ment rate fell from 9 per cent to 5 per cent over the same period, a fall of around a million in the number of unemployed people (Fitzner 2006). Since 2006 both the employment and unemployment rates have continued at these levels. This tight labour market has shaped many of the developments in UK reward practices. These include the increasing emphasis upon the market as the benchmark for pay increases in the private sector, the growth of indi-vidual 'contribution' rewards, and the use of market supplements and house purchase assistance to attract and retain professional workers in the public services.

In terms of the distribution of real income, the pattern changed. In the 1980s, disposable income in real terms for those at the top decile of earners had increased by 38 per cent compared to just 7 per cent for those at the lowest decile. During the economic downturn at the start of the 1990s, how-ever, there was little growth across the income distribution at any level. Between 1994/95 and 2002/03 real income growth remained fairly stable across the distribution, growing by a fifth for those at both the top and the bottom of the distribution (ONS 2004). There was a fall in disposable income inequality between 2001/2 and 2004/5, partly through the introduction of the national minimum wage and partly the provision of tax credits for house-holds with children in the lower part of the distribution. Between 1998 and 2003 there was a clear impact from the minimum wage. The hourly wages of the lowest paid increased by more than the median worker (although the upper end of the earnings distribution continued to have larger increases) and there was a noticeable effect on the gender pay gap (Butcher 2005). In 2005/06, however, income inequality began to increase again (ONS 2007). Income inequality, nonetheless, remains high in the UK by historical stand-ards and the big increase in the gap between the lowest and highest incomes that took place in the 1980s has not yet been reversed. The ratio of the highest to the lowest decile for gross weekly earnings was 3.6 in April 2006, largely unchanged since 3.5 in 1997 (Dobbs 2007). Similarly, despite some small improvement in the gender wage gap, there remains a significant difference between male and female average earnings. The gender pay gap (based on mean full-time hourly earnings excluding overtime) was 20.7 per cent in 1997 when Labour was first elected – 'it narrowed slightly to 20.1 per cent in 2002; fell steadily to 17.1 per cent in 2005 and showed little change at 17.2 in 2006' (Dobbs 2007: 45). In terms of median earnings, the gap fell from 17.4 per cent in 1997 to 12.6 per cent in 2006.

On the basis of Gross Domestic Product (GDP) per worker UK productivity continues to lag behind the G7 countries' average. The UK falls behind all other G7 countries apart from Japan, although it is not far behind Germany, Canada and Italy (ONS 2008). The USA, notably, has productivity 28 per cent above the UK. The UK's productivity lags behind other developed countries for a number of reasons, not least a historic disadvantage from its earlier industrialisation than other countries (leaving less scope for improvement), but five main drivers of productivity have been identified by the Government: investment, innovation, skills, competition and enterprise (Lindsay 2004). The first three of these, especially skills, are particularly important for labour productivity. Compared to the USA, the UK workforce has a smaller proportion of workers with higher skills than the USA and a smaller proportion of those with intermediate skills than Germany or France. UK-owned firms have considerably lower productivity than those UK firms under foreign ownership. The other major problem is the mismatch between the skills available in the workforce and the needs of employers.

Levels of investment in capital by UK employers, also remain problematic. A study of capital per hour worked (O'Mahoney and de Boer 2002 cited in Lindsay 2004) found that the UK is substantially behind its rivals. For example, in 1999 the USA invested 25 per cent more capital per hour worked than the UK, France 60 per cent and Germany 32 per cent.

In conclusion, Labour's policies in office have benefited from a relatively benign economic environment, with relatively full employment overall and a tight labour market in many parts of the UK. Demand for labour has led to consistent growth in above inflation average earnings. Legislative changes concerning new employment rights therefore appear to have had little if any negative economic impact, especially the changes to working time, the national minimum wage and improved family-friendly benefits. At the same time there have been some improvements in income inequality although overall, the wide gap between the highest and lowest paid established under the previous Conservative administration has not changed substantially over the period since Labour entered office, and the gender pay gap has only diminished slightly. Lastly, despite continuing supply side reforms to the labour market, there has been little real improvement in the UK productivity record and capital investment in UK-owned enterprises remains poor in comparison to other developed countries.

Human resource management and reward

The interest in human resource management (HRM) and in 'strategic pay' has accompanied the process of economic and social change. The ideas and the practices associated with HRM can be understood as part of a western, particularly American, response to the success of Japanese business from the 1980s (Legge 1995) as an attempt to challenge the legacy of traditional personnel management and industrial relations. Change was driven by the growing concern with product quality or service delivery and by attempts to streamline work processes. It is not our purpose to repeat here the discussions and debates about what does and does not constitute 'real' or leading-edge human resource management (see Guest 1990; Storey 1992; Sisson 1994; Legge 1995; Hope-Hailey *et al.* 1997). Debates about the meaning and evidence for HRM have focussed on the existence of a 'bundle' of HR initiatives. The composition of the bundle is a matter of debate. Critical factors include the strategic positioning of HR within the organisation; the relationship of the HR function to line management; the use of personnel 'levers', such as recruitment and selection and training and development, and the impact of HR on beliefs and assumption within the organisation (Storey 1992).

Reward management has a key position within HR theory for a number of reasons. Pay is a central organisational concern because questions of financial control and cost management are themselves fundamental to the organisation and to management decisions. Discussion and negotiation about those decisions and about the level and distribution of pay bring personnel or the HR function into a central organisational position. Reward management is one of the key levers to be deployed in pursuit of effective HRM. If pay is to 'deliver the goods' in terms of HR strategy, then it must be structured, it is argued, in order to meet HR objectives.

American 'New Pay' theorists have developed arguments along these lines, pointing to the pivotal link between business strategies and reward management. Lawler (1990) and Schuster and Zingheim (1992) have argued the case for this central relationship and the need for pay to be more explicitly linked to business performance. The 'New Pay' is intended to encourage a more contingent approach to reward, challenging traditional management approaches such as job evaluation, cost-of living pay rises and external referencing (e.g. upper quartile position) for pay norms (Schuster and Zingheim 1992: 25). As Gomez-Mejia states:

> The emerging paradigm of the field is based on a strategic orientation where issues of internal equity and external equity are viewed as secondary to the firm's need to use pay as an essential integrating and signalling mechanism to achieve overarching business objectives.
>
> (Gomez-Mejia 1993: 4)

It follows according to the logic of the 'New Pay' that, as business performance can vary, so too should the levels of pay. In other words the pay package should comprise pay which is 'at risk' as well as pay that is guaranteed. The 'New Pay' writers argue for the continuing need for adaptation in business practice in a dynamic business environment.

There are important qualifications that must be raised in relation to the work of the 'New Pay' theories. First, it might be argued, the 'good for business' case should be questioned for the same reasons that a unitarist approach to HRM is challenged – namely that there are different interests at play within the business organisation and they cannot all be subsumed so easily in pursuit of business goals. The 'New Pay' treats employees as 'important partners' and it also assumes that 'when the organisation does well, employees should do well' (Schuster and Zingheim 1992: 38). Yet it is not clear that employees or their representatives are to be partners in determining the pay system itself or in deciding on the ways in which the benefits of organisational success should be shared. For trade union members this approach may suggest a silencing of employee voice – or at least may seem to pre-empt negotiations. Trade unions have traditionally claimed representation rights around the issues that go to make up the pay package. There is within the collective bargaining process an implicit relationship between pay and benefits (such as sick or maternity pay or pension) or between pay and conditions (hours, holidays, rest breaks, etc.). Whilst trade union membership has declined and collective bargaining has diminished in many industrial economies, trade unions retain the capacity to challenge the hegemony of business interest on behalf of employees. But the last 2004 WERS data indicates that in only 18 per cent of workplaces was there negotiation over pay, in 5 per cent some consultation and in 6 per cent information was provided (Kersley *et al.* 2006: 194). In 70 per cent of workplaces there was neither negotiation nor consultation about pay. In the absence of unions, it is hard to see any genuine alternative avenues for 'employee voice' within the reward system emerging (see Chapter 3 by Heery later in this volume). As Kessler (2007: 174), however, comments, '. . . pay systems are more likely to generate "desired" attitudes and behaviours if an inclusive approach to their design and implementation is adopted'.

Second, it is clear that 'strategic pay' may involve complex and sometimes contradictory objectives. A balance must be found between recognition and reward for the performance of the individual, for the group (and between different groups) and for the business as a whole. Payment 'for the person' which is emphasised by the 'New Pay' puts a premium on rewarding individual performance precisely because individual performance is seen as 'directly controllable' (Lawler 1990: 203). Yet individual performance-related pay may discourage employees from taking risks or from collaborating with others – even though these may be exactly what is required in terms of business development (Herriot 1995: 194). Interestingly, there are signs that a generalised interest in individual performance related pay and particularly in individualised performance management has been challenged more recently by growing concern with team-working and with team-based payments (Pfeffer 1998; Mayo 1995). Furthermore, in the UK employer dissatisfaction with traditional 'pay for performance' systems appears to have led to more hybrid approaches to reward. Brown and Armstrong (1999) have coined the expression 'pay for contribution' to cover this phenomenon. According to them: 'The lessons of applying a relatively homogeneous, rigid, formulaic and top-down approach to our increasingly complex, empowered and rapidly changing organisations have apparently been learned' (Brown and Armstrong

1999: xiii). They characterise the new 'contribution-based' approach as consisting of six elements: paying for how results are achieved as well as the results themselves; paying for future success rather than immediate past results; rewarding a combination of organisational, team and individual performance rather than concentrating wholly on the latter; taking a long-term perspective; using a range of 'reward vehicles'; and addressing all aspects of reward strategy, rather than just the design mechanics (Brown and Armstrong 1999: xiii).

Schuster and Zingheim suggest that group variable pay may be appropriate to reward pre-determined team, business unit or organisational goals, but they have less to say on the ways in which the interests of the business, the team and the individual might be balanced (Schuster and Zingheim 1992). Lawler acknowledges that organisational or group performance is harder to influence than individual performance and so proposes that a larger amount of 'at risk' compensation should attach to group or corporate performance (Lawler 1990: 203). Finding the right compensation mix is clearly a complex process and one which may not easily be understood by those whom it is intended to motivate. It is not surprising that commentators point to the need for 'pay literacy' as a pre-requisite for effective reward management (Stevens 1996: 25). Moreover these complex systems have still to relate to the underpinning terms of the individual employment contract. Here is a critical problem for the 'New Pay', since it is clear that the fundamentals of pay systems are not readily amenable to regular change or adjustment. In terms of the operation of 'New Pay' ideas there is clearly a risk that they will become too sophisticated to be effective and too complex to be easily changed.

There is a growing critique of the contingency approach to reward. For example, according to Pfeffer (1994):

> If we are very well paid, perhaps on a contingent basis, for what we do, we are likely to attribute our behaviour to economic rewards. If, however, we are not particularly well paid, or if pay is less salient, and if it is distributed on a less contingent basis . . ., then we are likely to attribute our behaviour to other, more intrinsic factors, such as inherent enjoyment of the work . . . Thus, pay compression, by helping to de-emphasise pay, can enhance other bases of satisfaction with work and build a culture that is less calculative in nature.
>
> (Pfeffer 1994: 51)

'Employee commitment' is one of the central tenets of HRM since it offers the possibility of something more, in the employment relationship than the simple wage-effort bargain (Walton 1985). 'New Pay' approaches – concerned with pay for the person rather than pay for the job – seem to enhance managerial discretion to reward compliant behaviour patterns or the appearance of commitment. Dickens (1998) has identified the dangers inherent in HRM, with the potential for a 'gender model of commitment' and points to the risks of gender stereotyping by managers. Collective pay determination and job evaluation were established according to principles of 'fair' treatment but they have not delivered equal pay for women. Yet it could be argued that pay for performance offers the potential for more equitable treatment of women because their individual role and contribution will be rewarded. There is nonetheless a risk that the processes through which performance-based pay is determined – including individual objective setting and appraisal – will work to the disadvantage of women. The ways in which skills are perceived and valued underpin pay systems and no one pay system will deliver equal pay (Rubery 1995; Dickens 1998).

It has been recently argued that the strategic model of reward advocated by the US New Pay writers has had limited impact in the UK and the 'suggested primacy of business strategy over internal and external equity in pay practice has failed to emerge' (Kessler 2007: 175). Rather, in the UK developments in pay practices reveal an increasing emphasis upon both internal and external equity. Two main reasons are identified for this failure of a 'strategic reward' paradigm to emerge. First, 'the use of pay systems that seek to relate person and performance are highly problematic' and second there have been other pressures pushing both internal equity and external equity to the top of the reward agenda (Kessler 2007: 175). In the case of internal equity, the increasing legal risk from equal pay legislation has driven a growth in job evaluation, especially in the public services, while in the private sector tight and changing labour markets have driven employers to seek increased alignment with the external market rather than less. Kessler goes further to argue that it may be problematic to view business strategy, internal and external equity as competing principles in pay design and that rather equity, both internal and external, may be seen instead as an integral part of reward strategy.

The declining utility of pay information sources

One common theme throughout some of the chapters that follow is the dearth of good, large-scale, empirical data about reward management policies and practices. In addition the publicly available data sources about both pay levels and pay awards have become more limited in recent years. Apart from the irregular publication of WERS data there is no large-scale survey of reward policies and practices and, by the nature of its wide-ranging remit, WERS coverage of pay and conditions matters is necessarily limited. Since the first edition of this book both the CBI Pay Databank and the OME's inter-quartile survey of pay awards have ceased. Annual surveys of reward policies and practice are conducted by the CIPD but these lack statistical rigour and yield such varying results from year to year that they do not indicate a robust sample. Excellent qualitative research in the form of case study material is provided by Incomes Data Services, Industrial Relations Services and the Labour Research Department but these studies of policies and practice are limited by the volume of organisations covered and the absence of any developed statistical analysis. Government sources of information are also more limited than previously and the ONS Annual Survey of Hours and Earnings is in many ways considerably less useful to both researchers and practitioners than the previous New Earnings Survey. While there has been a growth in the availability of commercial salary surveys these are not generally publicly available and are often largely focused on the highest paid and professional groups of employees. One theme that emerges from this book is a very real need for better publicly available and regularly published sources of information on both pay and conditions and on the distribution of different reward practices.

The contributions

The book is structured into 11 chapters. Following this introduction, Chapters 2 and 3 consider the process of pay determination and the influence of trade union representation. Chapters 4–7 look at grading structures, job evaluation and trends in arrangements affecting wages, salary systems and executive reward. Chapters 8–10 consider other factors in the reward package including benefits, occupational pensions and financial participation schemes. In the final chapter, questions of international reward management are addressed.

In Chapter 2, Geoff White sets the scene by reviewing how the methods and locus of pay determination and the criteria used to set pay levels have changed in recent years. He notes the continued decline of collective bargaining as a means to determining pay – collective bargaining is now largely a phenomenon in the public sector and among the larger private sector employers although the pace of decline has slowed considerably in recent years. It is also the case that collective bargaining outcomes still provide a major influence for more general movements in pay. The alternative to collective bargaining in much of the private sector, however, is now simply management discretion. Employees here have little opportunity to influence the outcomes of the effort-bargain except where they have scarce skills and the economic power to negotiate individually. Changes in the coverage of collective bargaining appear to be related more to the growth of new non-union workplaces than to de-recognition of unions and the ending of bargaining in existing workplaces. On the other hand, even in workplaces where bargaining machinery has remained intact it is often unused. The second key change identified is the decentralisation of pay determination and breakdown of large multi-employer agreements. Even where large multi-employer agreements continue in the NHS, local government and higher education, 'pay modernisation' initiatives have created more opportunities for grading and hence pay to vary at individual institutional level. Comparative research on collective bargaining in different countries appears to indicate that a shift to enterprise level bargaining often heralds the ending of any bargaining at all. There is still some UK evidence to support this view. Multi-employer agreements in the private sector, however, still cover some 1.7 million workers.

White also considers the changing criteria for pay awards. He finds a decreasing emphasis upon individual performance and increasing interest in organisational performance and market benchmarking of jobs as key criteria in the level of pay awards. Inflation remains a modal influence on award levels but appears to be more important in unionised workplaces than in non-union workplaces. This shift to more market-based pay determination has been linked to the tight UK labour market since 2000 and the rise of 'job family' grading structures. Such systems, however, may create a real challenge to notions of reward transparency and a risk of gendered pay structures that simply reproduce inequalities in the wider labour market.

In Chapter 3, Edmund Heery considers the issue of employee voice within the reward system. He argues that reward management is shaped in a number of ways by representative institutions of workers including trade unions, civil society organisations, legal representatives and employer-sponsored systems of employee participation. Despite the decline of collective pay determination, unions continue to play an important role in raising the level of unionised workers' pay, compressing pay inequality, regulating contingent pay systems and expanding the range of benefits available. Non-union systems of employee voice often reinforce union effects but in some cases, such as in the case of 'no-win, no fee' lawyers, they can end in conflict with unions where collective agreements are challenged. In general, non-union vehicles for employee participation in reward matters tend to be rather modest in their influence, compared to trade unions, and their achievements rather limited. Heery argues that the only really effective way for employees to have a guaranteed voice in reward design and processes is to join a union and present a collective voice to management.

In Chapter 4, Sue Hastings offers an account of the history of grading and job evaluation (JE). The chapter exposes the discriminatory values inherent in early grading schemes pointing to the ways in which grading arrangements historically embodied social values that were detrimental to women's position in the workplace. Those values – and the ways in which they were absorbed within JE – have been challenged and more sophisticated approaches to JE have developed, yet the gender imbalance in pay has not been resolved. Sue Hastings illustrates her account through attention to the public sector where JE schemes have been developed and refined to give effect to equal pay legislation. Within the private sector more individualised payment arrangements have discouraged the formulation of systems intended to monitor internal relativities and arrangements are sometimes opaque. Job evaluation has been encouraged by legislation on equal pay and equal value because it provides a line of defence in equal pay claims. Equal value law has provided the terrain over which challenges have been mounted to the institutionalisation of gendered notions of skill and value. The chapter explores changing approaches to grading and the criteria on which it is based. The weightings given to particular types of skill and experience are shown to be important determinants of the outcome in terms of grading and pay.

Sue Hastings concludes that, whilst employers continue to need systems that support internal structure and define relative positions, the future is uncertain. The high costs of detailed and effective JE – especially where it is competence-oriented – may limit the use or application of JE in the future.

Chapters 5 and 6 explore the breakdown in the distinction between wages and salary systems. Contextual changes – both in labour markets and in work processes – are key to understanding this historic division. The difference between waged and salaried workers was bound up with the distinction between task management and execution. Different forms of management control applied to employees in accordance with their relationship to these processes. It is a distinction that has become blurred as manufacturing employment has diminished and technological innovation has encouraged a new alignment of responsibilities within the workplace.

In Chapter 5 Janet Druker points to the importance of hourly rates as a base for wages systems and for calculation of additions to pay. The transformation in economic and labour market context has been a major driver for change and payment by results (PBR) and overtime payments are now less common than they were in the past. In part this is the consequence of the transition from manufacturing to service sector employment but it is a result too of a shift in technology and in processes that is often accompanied by harmonised conditions of service for a smaller number of highly skilled individuals. Hourly-based pay rates, weekly (or fortnightly) pay, and additions to basic pay through payment by results and overtime have not disappeared but traditional output-based bonus schemes contrast with the 'incentive' schemes that often characterise the service sector. The debate about the erosion of the status divide should not be allowed to disguise the continuing disadvantage of the lowest paid within the workforce who are disproportionately likely to be women. The pay differential between women and men is still marked, and change is hampered by continuing occupational gender segregation, with women disproportionately represented in the lower-paid service sector. Low pay remains more common amongst waged workers than salaried employees and the chapter explains the introduction and impact of the National Minimum Wage (NMW) from 1999. Whilst a 'floor' for adult wages is established by the NMW, there is little evidence as yet that the differentials between the highest paid and the lowest paid within the workforce have been eroded.

In Chapter 6, Marc Thompson considers developments in pay progression systems against the various theoretical models of motivation. He finds evidence for a change since the 1980s and early 1990s, which were characterised by a shift to performance-based salary progression, convoluted pay structures and high levels of management control in the context of looser labour markets. In contrast, the last decade or so has been marked by the combination of skill shortages with equal value concerns to challenge this model and re-establish more transparent salary progression systems. A key trend has been the emergence of 'hybrid' salary progression schemes combining behavioural- and output-based metrics, or 'contribution-based' systems as Brown and Armstrong (1999) have termed them. The 'new pay' discourse which has been largely defined by its focus on the strategic alignment of rewards with business priorities has had to adapt to pressures imposed by the so-called 'war for talent' and wider societal pressures to tackle discrimination on gender, age and race. The pendulum has swung back somewhat and notions of 'fairness at work', which characterized New Labour's first term, would appear to have had some impact on salary systems, at least in the public services.

In Chapter 7, Steve Perkins reviews the controversial issue of executive pay systems. He considers executive pay under three explanatory factors – complexity, controversy, and contradiction. The ever-increasing complexity for which executive reward and its management may be judged distinctive is not only subject to controversy, as the interested parties debate approaches and underlying assumptions. Complexity itself creates the conditions for controversy, particularly among simplistically inclined commentators. And complexity may exacerbate concerns about a lack of transparency, fanning the flames of suspicion. Further, the symbolic nature of executive reward in terms of levels of reward for the rest of the workforce augments the scope for a range of viewpoints and 'interpretative gaps'. Agency-based assumptions appear to underpin the regulatory policy that has emerged to date. Given the scope for sending out contradictory messages to the actors, more detailed specification of organisational effectiveness aims, grounded in particular contexts, may be sensible argues Perkins.

Non-pay benefits constitute a significant element of remuneration and in Chapter 8 Angela Wright questions the contribution that they make to the reward package. She notes that non-pay benefits are sometimes regarded as a 'motivator', serving to recruit and retain employees within an organisation and draws on a literature which stresses the importance of employee knowledge and information in affecting their estimations of the value of their benefits package. She shows how the provision of employee benefits has been affected by a range of factors including a growing and competitive insurance market, demographic and labour market changes and social regulation within the European Union (EU). Employers are cutting back on the most costly benefits whilst at the same time enhancing provision of lower-cost lifestyle and voluntary benefits. These initiatives seem to fit with a changing pattern of employment and shifting preference amongst employees since women, particularly mothers, have increased their labour market participation. The future for benefits is uncertain in the light of rising costs and the ageing of the workforce, although continued incremental change seems more likely than radical revisions of benefits provisions.

Provision for retirement income raises important questions concerning the balance of funding that derives from the state, from the employer and from the employee. The low level of state pensions' provision in the UK makes occupational pensions especially significant. In Chapter 9, Stephen Taylor

describes the erosion of occupational pensions since the mid-1990s, pointing particularly to the erosion of defined benefit schemes. The creation of stakeholder schemes is shown to be a hollow provision since employers are unlikely to contribute to such schemes and their value, for the low to middle income earner, is therefore necessarily limited.

In Chapter 10, Jeff Hyman considers the effects of financial participation schemes. Noting the wider global changes that have taken place since Labour's election in 1997, Hyman examines the development of financial participation schemes. He suggests, in the light of the evidence, that under some fairly specific circumstances shared ownership does appear to exert a positive effect on employee behaviour. Further, there is no evidence for any adverse effects of employee share ownership on employees employed by companies with good share prices and trading profitably. Favourable circumstances for such schemes are also associated with high levels of employee ownership, and these are usually coupled with organisational mechanisms to ensure that ownership is matched by some measure of employee influence. Nevertheless, as we have seen, many schemes continue to operate with less generous share provisions, so it would be reasonable to enquire what benefits may be expected to accrue from these schemes. Whilst it is difficult to isolate the effects of financial participation alone on employee motivation and performance, there is convincing evidence that there may be dynamic interaction between employee share schemes and other progressive techniques which influence employee orientations to work.

The pace at which organisations find themselves needing to address issues of international compensation continues to accelerate. In Chapter 11, Paul Sparrow draws on two different approaches to the subject – institutional and cultural – to consider the pace and significance of change in this area. Cultural explanations, he suggests, rely on historically determined notions that are accepted by groups of individuals who share some common historical experience about what is good, right and desirable. A human resources manager in a multinational company with employees in a 'host' country has to consider the cultural dynamic that is in play and the attitudes and expectations of employees in that country. The chapter explores the theoretical links between national culture and rewards and reviews studies that link country-level national culture patterns to patterns of rewards practice, and studies that link national culture to important decision rules and attitudes within rewards systems. Paul Sparrow draws on a wide literature to highlight the dynamic, two-way (i.e. top-down and bottom-up) processes involved when studying national culture. He suggests that any modelling of its impacts on specific behaviours (such as rewards) needs to allow for an understanding of not just *how* national culture exerts an influence on work attitudes, but also of how national culture is enacted within firms and within individuals.

Institutional explanations, by contrast, emphasise social structures (including legal provision, education and training and economic systems that shape incentives). Complex, inter-dependent forces are in operation shaping the

ways in which individuals make sense of and in turn make decisions that will be deemed legitimate, reasonable and appropriate. Narratives around the *Kostenkrise* debate in Germany, and the *Risutora* process in Japan are considered to illustrate this point.

References

Braverman, H. (1974) *Labor and Monopoly Capital: The degradation of work in the twentieth century*, New York and London: Monthly Review Press.

Brown, D. and Armstrong, M. (1999) *Paying for Contribution: Real performance-related pay strategies*, London: Kogan Page.

Brown, W., Deakin, S., Hudson, M., Pratten, C. and Ryan, P. (1998) 'The individualisation of employment contracts in Britain', Department of Trade and Industry, Research paper, London: DTI.

Butcher, T. (2005) 'The hourly earnings distribution before and after the National Minimum Wage', *Labour Market Trends*, October: 427–435.

Cappelli, P. (1995) 'Rethinking employment', *British Journal of Industrial Relations*, Vol. 33 (4): 563–602.

CIPD (2008) *Age Discrimination: Reward policies and procedures*. CIPD Factsheet. London: Chartered Institute of Personnel and Development.

Crompton, R., Gallie, D. and Purcell, K. (1996) 'Work, economic restructuring and social regulation', in R. Crompton, D. Gallie and K. Purcell (eds) *Changing Forms of Employment: Organisation, skills and gender*, London: Routledge.

Department for Work and Pensions (DWP) (2007) http://www.dwp.gov.uk/pensions reform/pensions_act_2007.asp. (accessed 5 April 2007).

Dickens, L. (1998) 'What HRM means for gender equality', *Human Resource Management Journal*, Vol. 8 (1): 23–40.

Dickens, R. and Manning, A. (2003) 'Minimum wage, minimum impact', in R. Dickens, P. Gregg and J. Wadsworth (eds) *The Labour Market Under New Labour*, Basingstoke: Palgrave Macmillan.

Dobbs, C. (2007) 'Patterns of pay: results of the Annual Survey of Hours and Earnings, 1997 to 2006', *Economic & Labour Market Review*, February, Vol. 1 (2): 44–50.

Fitzner, G. (2006) *How Have Employees Fared? Recent UK trends*, Employment Relations Research Series No. 56, London: Department of Trade and Industry.

Gallie, D. (1996) 'Skill, gender and the quality of employment', in R. Crompton, D. Gallie and K. Purcell (eds) *Changing Forms of Employment: Organisation, skills and gender*, London: Routledge.

Gomez-Mejia, L. (1993) *Compensation, Organisation and Firm Performance*, San Francisco: Southwestern.

Gospel, H. (1992) *Markets, Firms, and the Management of Labour in Modern Britain*, Cambridge: Cambridge University Press.

Guest, D. (1990) 'Human resource management and the American dream'. *Journal of Management Studies*, Vol. 27 (4): 378–397.

Herriot, P. (1995) 'The management of careers', in S. Tyson (ed.) *Strategic Prospects for HRM*, London: IPD.

Herzberg, F., Mausner, B. and Snyderman, B. (1957) *The Motivation to Work*, New York: Wiley.

Hope-Hailey, V.V., Gratton, L., McGovern, P., Stiles, P. and Truss, C. (1997) 'A chameleon function? HRM in the 90s', *Human Resource Management Journal*, Vol. 7 (3): 5–18.

Kersley, B., Alpine, C., Forth, J., Bryson, A., Begley, H., Dix, G. and Oxenbridge, S. (2006) *Inside the Workplace: Findings from the 2004 Workplace Employee Relations Survey*, London: Routledge.

Kessler, I. (2007) 'Reward choices: strategy and equity', in J. Storey (ed.) *Human Resource Management: A critical text*, 3rd edn, London: Thomson.

Lawler, E. (1990) *Strategic Pay: Aligning organizational strategies and pay systems*, San Francisco: Jossey-Bass.

Legge, K. (1995) *Human Resource Management: Rhetorics and Realities*, Basingstoke: Macmillan Business.

Lindsay, C. (2004) 'Labour productivity', *Labour Market Trends*, November: 447–454.

Low Pay Commission (1998) *First Report of the Low Pay Commission*, Cm3976, June, London: The Stationery Office.

McGovern, P., Hill, S., Mills, C. and White, M. (2007) *Market, Class and Employment*, Oxford: Oxford University Press.

McGregor, D. (1960) *The Human Side of Enterprise*, New York: McGraw-Hill.

Mahoney, T. A. (1992) 'Multiple Pay Contingencies: Strategic design of compensation', in G. Salaman (ed.) *Human Resource Strategies*, London: Sage.

Marginson, P., Arrowsmith, J. and Gray, M. (2007) 'Undermining or reframing collective bargaining? Variable pay in two sectors compared', Paper for 2007 Performance and Reward Conference (PARC), Manchester, 29 March 2007.

Maslow, A. (1954) *Motivation and Personality*, New York: Harper & Row.

Mayo, A. (1995) 'Economic indicators of HRM', in S. Tyson (ed.) *Strategic Prospects for HRM*, London: IPD.

O'Mahoney, M. and de Boer, W. (2002) *Britain's Relative Productivity Performance: Updates to 1999*, March, London: NIESR.

ONS (1997) 'Low Pay Jobs. 292,000 jobs below national minimum wage in UK', press release, 7 November, London: Office for National Statistics.

ONS (2004) 'Income. Gaps in income and wealth remain large', press release, 7 December, London: Office for National Statistics.

ONS (2007) 'Income Inequality. Rise in inequality in 2005/06', press release, 17 May, London: Office for National Statistics.

ONS (2008) 'International Productivity. USA continues to lead', press release, 19 February, London: Office for National Statistics.

Pensions Commission (2004) *Pensions: Challenges and Choices. The First Report of the Pensions Commission*, London: The Stationery Office.

Pensions Commission (2005) *A New Pension Settlement for the Twenty-First Century. The Second Report of the Pensions Commission*, London: The Stationery Office.

Pensions Commission (2006) *Implementing an Integrated Package of Pension Reforms. The Final Report of the Pensions Commission*, London: The Stationery Office.

Pfeffer, J. (1994) *Competetive Advantage through People. Unleashing the power of the workforce*, Boston Mass.: Harvard Business School Press.

Pfeffer, J. (1998) 'Six dangerous myths about pay', *Harvard Business Review*, 109–119.

Piore, M. and Sabel, C. (1984) *The Second Industrial Divide: Possibilities for prosperity*, New York: Basic Books Inc.

Pollert, A. (1981) *Girls, Wives, Factory Lives*, London: Macmillan.

Porter, L. and Lawler, E.E. (1968) *Management Attitudes and Behaviour*, Homewood SL.: Dorsey.

Rubery, J. (1995) 'Performance related pay and the prospects for gender pay equity', *Journal of Management Studies*, Vol. 32 (5) September: 637–654.

Schuster, J.R. and Zingheim, P. (1992) *The New Pay: Linking employee and organisational performance*, New York: Lexington Books.

Sisson, K. (1994) 'Personnel management paradigms, practice and prospects', in K. Sisson (ed.) *Personnel Management: A comprehensive guide to theory and practice in Britain*, Oxford: Blackwell.

Standing, G. (1997) 'Globalisation, labour flexibility and insecurity: The era of market regulation', *European Journal of Industrial Relations*, Vol. 3 (1): 7–37.

Stanworth, C., Wergin, N.E. and White, G. (2007) 'Work-family integration in the UK – A review', *International Employment Relations Review*, 12 (2). 19–31.

Stevens, J. (1996) 'Pay at the Crossroads', in H. Murlis (ed.) *Pay at the Crossroads*, London: IPD.

Storey, J. (1992) *Developments in the Management of Human Resources*, Oxford: Blackwell.

Streeck, W. (1987) 'The uncertainties of management in the management of uncertainty: employers, labor relations and industrial adjustment in the 1980s', *Work, Employment and Society*, Vol. 1 (3): 281–308.

Taylor, F. (1913) *The Principles of Scientific Management*, New York and London: Harper & Brothers.

Vroom, V. (1964) *Work and Motivation*, New York: Wiley.

Walton, R. (1985) 'From control to commitment in the workplace', *Harvard Business Review*, 63 (2) March–April: 76–84.

White, G. (1999) 'Pay structures and the minimum wage', Occasional Paper No. 3, Low Pay Commission.

2 Determining pay

Geoff White

Summary

This chapter considers how organisations decide pay levels. Three main areas are considered: the method and locus of determining pay; the criteria used by organisations in fixing pay levels; and the changing nature of pay information sources. The chapter points to the growing divide between private sector and public sector pay determination. In the private sector the major method used to determine pay is management discretion alone while in the public sector collective bargaining machinery remains primary. The criteria used to make decisions about pay levels have also changed in recent times, with increasing emphasis upon factors such as organisational performance, 'ability to pay' and recruitment and retention, although inflation retains a modal influence. Finally the increasing difficulty in tracking pay changes is discussed. As collective bargaining has diminished, transparency has reduced and hence the opportunity for employers to obscure the detail of pay decisions has increased. There are now fewer reliable sources of publicly available data available to track both pay levels and the diffusion of new pay practices and those that remain are of decreasing use.

Introduction

The method and level at which decisions are taken and criteria used to determine pay levels are key issues in reward management. As Kersley *et al.* state:

> Methods of pay determination are central to understanding industrial relations in Britain since they are linked to employee pay levels, the distribution of wages between and across workplaces, and the way in which employers seek to recruit, retain and motivate employees.
>
> (Kersley *et al.* 2006: 179)

Various criteria may be used in fixing the overall market position of an organisation's remuneration levels and the pay of an individual, both within the organisation and in relation to the external labour market. While establishing relationships between different jobs and occupations which meet the needs of internal equity is a primary concern in the design of pay systems, linking these pay and grading structures to the external labour market and keeping pay levels competitive is also vital. Robinson (1973: 7) argued that:

> The concept of fairness when applied to wages is inevitably a concept which requires comparisons. It is not possible to decide whether someone is fairly paid until one knows what other people are paid. Differentials and relativities lie at the very heart of the concept of equity as applied to wage determination.

The tension between concerns for internal equity and the external markets for jobs remains one of the key challenges facing organisations in the design of effective reward systems.

As we noted in the first edition of this volume, in the last quarter of the twentieth century there were major changes in the manner in which pay was determined. There was a substantial decline in the use of collective bargaining and its replacement by systems that depend far more on management discretion (Millward *et al.* 1992; Milner 1995; Brown *et al.* 1998; Bland 1999). Even in the sectors where pay remained subject to joint regulation, there had been significant moves away from multi-employer pay determination and towards organisation-based structures (Brown *et al.* 1995; Brown and Walsh 1991; Millward *et al.* 1992). In the public services we have seen 'pay delegation' to individual departments and agencies and in local government, the NHS and Higher Education there have been significant 'pay modernisation' agreements that have simplified bargaining arrangements and devolved some pay decisions, such as grading structures, to institution level. In the private sector there has been increasing emphasis upon the 'market' and the setting of pay levels through market benchmarking for different groups of staff (or 'job families' as they are known) or even individual roles.

This chapter considers the changing nature of pay determination and its impact upon the management of pay. It covers three main areas – the method and locus of pay determination (where and how decisions about pay levels are taken); the criteria used to determine the level of pay increases; and finally the changing nature of pay information sources used in setting remuneration.

The effort bargain

Every employment is made up of two elements – the wage-rate bargain (how much the employee is paid) and the effort bargain (how much work is produced in return for the pay). The employment contract therefore determines the 'terms of exchange of work for money' (Behrend 1957: 505). As Behrend argues, the difficulty with an employment contract, unlike a commercial contract, is that what is being bought from the worker is a 'supply of effort for performing varying work assignments' but this is not only difficult to define but also difficult to measure (Behrend 1957: 505).

In reaching an agreed value for the work done, a number of work contingencies are considered. These, argues Mahoney (1989), consist of performance contingencies; job contingencies; and person contingencies. The first of these is the simplest in that payment primarily relates to the output or outcome – the more the employee produces the more he or she is paid. The second, job contingency, relates primarily to the job held and the time worked. The third, person contingency, relates to the personal qualities of the individual employee, including the value of those tacit skills that they bring to the organisation. There are also non-work contingencies that come into play, such as certain employee benefits that provide various forms of income security for the employee in cases of ill health or in retirement. These, argues Mahoney, reflect more social need than work-based contingencies. Pay will relate to a combination of these contingencies and provide the base upon which differentials are created between different jobs or individuals.

The relative worth of each job or individual employee is subject to various influences. These include both market value and the social value that is placed upon particular skills and duties – both of which can change over time. Government or other forms of regulation (e.g. collective bargaining) also play a part. Achieving internal equity, or the fair distribution of remuneration within an organisation, is a major task for employers (see Chapter 4). The creation of a grading or pay structure provides the basis for differentials and also identifies what is expected from the effort-bargain for different levels of pay. It does not, however, create the basis for pricing individual jobs. The pricing of jobs – as opposed to their internal evaluation or ranking – is usually done by some reference to the external labour market. This normally involves some form of pay comparability with other organisations or occupational norms, or at least some reference to external economic indicators such as the cost of living or average earnings movements. Even where collective bargaining is used to determine pay levels, evidence from the external labour market will normally play an important part in negotiations.

External comparability has been central to pay theory and practice for two reasons. First, as Fay (1989) indicates, jobs have no demonstrable inherent value and hence employers gauge the value of a particular post by reference to external comparators. Second, the pay package is the only part of a job offer which applicants can readily compare with other offers.

Three main approaches to external comparisons have been identified:

1   Setting recruitment rates at market level for entry-level jobs but then basing pay progression on internal career ladders;
2   Setting across-the-board positioning to place an organisation's complete salary structure at some percentage of the market rate; and

3   The selective positioning of specific jobs in the market according to the
    perceived importance of the different jobs.

(Fay 1989: 3–71)

Where collective bargaining is present there may be industry-wide agreed
minimum rates that apply to the organisation or there may be enterprise or
establishment level bargaining over pay levels. In these cases negotiations will
take place against comparator data on pay levels and pay increases in other
industries and organisations, as well as other factors such as company profitability or financial resources available (ability to pay), employee productivity
and the ability to recruit and retain. But the degree of bargaining power
exerted by the union will also clearly affect ultimate levels of pay. A 'union
mark-up' has long been identified in terms of pay levels (Booth 1995), with a
clear advantage for employees covered by collective bargaining but this mark-
up now appears to have been eroded. It is probably still the case, however, that
conditions of service or benefits tend to be more generous and more equally
distributed in unionised workplaces (Forth and Millward 2000a).

Pay levels are therefore determined through both internal and external
factors. But there is a dynamic tension between the needs of the internal
market for equity and fairness and the differential price at which labour can
be purchased in the external labour market. There is, moreover, a continuing
contest between the rates set in the external labour market and the employer's
financial position (the ability to pay). The balance which organisations create
between these factors plays an important role in reward strategy.

The changing nature and locus of pay determination

Two major changes in pay determination over the last 25 years can be
identified. First, the coverage of collective bargaining has diminished and
where it remains, it has become more decentralised. Second, where collective
bargaining is not present the major form of pay determination is now
through unilateral management discretion and the scope for 'employee voice'
in the process has been significantly attenuated (see Chapter 3 for a wider
discussion of this issue). This decline in collective bargaining has been attributed to a range of factors (see Metcalf 2001 for a discussion of the factors).
Millward *et al.* (2000) estimated that around half the decline in collective
bargaining during the 1990s was due to the diminishing coverage in workplaces where unions were recognised and the other half due to the shrinkage
of employment in the unionised sectors of the economy. Brown *et al.* (2003)
argued that the decline was due to a number of factors, including union
de-recognition in the late 1980s; the increasing unwillingness of employers to
grant recognition in new workplaces; and the ending of formal negotiations
over pay in existing unionised workplaces.

More recently it has been argued that, while the broad reasons for the
decline of trade unions in the UK are well known, 'relatively little is known

about the specific causes and consequences of the decline in collective bargaining coverage in the 1990s' (Charlwood 2007: 33). Charlwood indicates that the decline has largely been due to new workplaces choosing not to bargain with unions, rather than that existing workplaces are ceasing to determine pay collectively. Analysis of the 1998 WERS shows that 'of those continuing workplaces that had collective bargaining in 1990, 30 per cent had de-collectivised pay setting by 1998' (Charlwood 2007: 35). But in the overwhelming majority of workplaces that de-collectivised pay determination in the 1990s the machinery of bargaining remained in place, even if unused. Only 2 per cent of workplaces that withdrew from collective bargaining also de-recognised unions (Charlwood 2007: 35). In general workplaces where bargaining took place at workplace level, rather than at organisation or multi-employer levels, were more vulnerable to the ending of pay bargaining. This may be partly due to the small scale of many such bargaining units, as large workplaces (with 500 or more employees) were less likely to abandon pay bargaining.

The main source for information on the changing nature and locus of pay determination in the UK is the series of Workplace Industrial (latterly Employment) Relations Surveys that were conducted in 1980, 1984, 1990, 1998 and 2004. Changes in the survey over the period from 1980 to 2004, not least the change in the method of measurement from workplaces with 25 or more employees to those with 10 or more employees in 2004, make long-term comparisons difficult but some basic data can be presented.

As Milner (1995) indicates, there are both definitional and data problems in estimating the coverage of collective pay setting. The tightest possible definition is the proportion of employees in employment whose pay is directly determined by collective agreement. Bargaining can be at plant, organisation or multi-employer level, but the key issue is whether or not pay is directly determined – i.e. the agreement sets out exactly what each category of employee will be paid. For example, in the civil service there are still negotiations with trade unions about the overall pay budget at departmental and agency level but many civil servants now have their individual pay increase (and hence pay level) determined through individual performance appraisal. A less stringent definition is the proportion of workers affected by collective bargaining through a collective agreement. For example, an employer party to an industry level agreement may decide to top up the nationally agreed award at local level. The difficulty with this second definition is that it is difficult to ascertain whether an employee's pay is actually affected by a collective agreement. This can also lead to double counting of coverage where both a national agreement and a local 'domestic' agreement cover the same employee. The third and loosest definition of coverage includes workers whose employer follows a collective agreement without actually being party to it. For example, some employers in the construction and printing industries follow the relevant industry pay agreements without actually having any members of the signatory unions present in their workplace.

According to Kersley *et al.* (2006: 179), 'by far the most common form of pay determination in 2004 was unilateral pay setting by management, either at the workplace or through individual negotiation with employees'. Around a quarter (27 per cent) of workplaces, however, still set pay for at least some employees through collective bargaining. In the previous edition of this book we pointed to a clear reduction in the numbers of both employees and establishments covered by collective bargaining between 1984 and 1998 as demonstrated through WERS. In Table 2.1 below, we present a re-working of the WERS times series data on collective bargaining coverage which attempts to overcome the methodological problems in comparing data from the various WERS source books. These data have been specially produced for this book by the WERS 2004 information and advice service. According to these re-worked figures, in 1984 in workplaces employing 25 or more workers 70 per cent of employees were covered by collective bargaining. By 1990 this had fallen to 54 per cent and by 1998 to 42 per cent. Millward *et al.* (2000:196) commented that: 'By 1998, collective bargaining . . . had ceased to be the dominant form of wage determination in a majority of British workplaces'. Since 1998, however, the pace of decline appears to have slowed. The comparable figure from the 2004 WERS is that 39 per cent of employees were covered and the change is statistically insignificant.

The different experience of private and public sector workplaces is clearly shown in the table, with collective bargaining remaining the major form of pay determination for public sector employees. According to WERS 2004 data in Table 2.1, the great majority (78 per cent) of employees in the public sector was covered by collective bargaining, compared with 40 per cent of private manufacturing employees and just 21 per cent of employees in private services. It is noteworthy that coverage in the public sector appears to have

Table 2.1 Overall collective bargaining coverage, by broad sector and union recognition, 1984–2004

	Cell percentages			
	Proportion of employees covered by collective bargaining			
	1984	*1990*	*1998*	*2004*
All workplaces	70	54	42	39
Broad sector				
Private manufacturing	64	51	46	40
Private services	40	33	24	21
Public sector	95	78	67	78
Any recognised unions	90	81	69	75

Base: all workplaces with 25 or more employees

Source: ESRC-funded WERS 2004 Information and Advice Service produced for this publication, February 2008. For WERS information see www.wers2004.info.

increased from 1998 to 2004, up from 67 per cent. This largely reflects a change in the classification of employees covered by the NHS Agenda for Change agreement in the WERS methodology. Some NHS staff covered by Pay Review Bodies were reclassified to collective bargaining in 2004 because the Pay Review Bodies were effectively stood down during the three-year pay agreement that accompanied the implementation of the new NHS pay system.

This pattern of decline in collective determination of pay is reinforced by figures from the Labour Force Survey, which surveys employees rather than establishments. In 1993 the LFS began collecting data on the extent to which an employee's workplace recognised trade unions for the purposes of negotiating the pay and conditions of employees. From 1996 a new question was added which established whether an employee was actually covered or not by a collective agreement. Table 2.2 shows the results from 1999 to 2006. In 1999, around 36 per cent of employees had their pay determined by a collective agreement (lower than the 42 per cent shown in the 1998 WERS data). By 2006 this had declined to 33.5 per cent (also lower than the WERS 2004 figure).

The WERS 2004 figures also indicate that there is a clear correlation of collective bargaining with the size of the workplace – almost two-thirds of the larger workplaces (employing 500 or more people) set some pay through collective bargaining. This contrasts with just a fifth of workplaces with fewer than 25 employees (Kersley *et al.* 2006: 179). Similarly, the proportion of employees covered by collective bargaining in larger workplaces (employing 500 or more) was higher at 68 per cent, compared to just 17 per cent in the smallest workplaces (employing below 25). Collective bargaining was also more likely to be found in workplaces that were part of a larger organisation (36 per cent of workplaces) compared to stand-alone workplaces (7 per cent).

In terms of sectors, collective bargaining was most prominent in the public utilities (electricity, gas and water) where 96 per cent of workplaces had bargaining. The public utilities also had the second highest proportion of employees covered by bargaining (87 per cent). This indicates the resilience of trade unions in these industries following the privatisation of the 1980s. Nonetheless, Charlwood (2007) found that de-collectivisation was more likely to take place in the public utilities than elsewhere. Other sectors with high levels of bargaining were public administration (93 per cent of workplaces and

Table 2.2 Employees' pay affected by a collective agreement

Autumn 1999 36.2%	Autumn 2003 35.9%
Autumn 2000 36.3%	Autumn 2004 34.9%
Autumn 2001 35.7%	Autumn 2005 35.3%
Autumn 2002 35.7%	Autumn 2006 33.5%

Source: Grainger and Crowther (2007) *Trade Union Membership 2006.*
DTI/National Statistics

90 per cent of employees); education (67 per cent and 58 per cent respectively) and financial services (63 per cent and 49 per cent respectively) (Kersley *et al.* 2006: 180). In contrast, the lowest levels of bargaining were found in hotels and restaurants (2 per cent of workplaces and 5 per cent of employees) and wholesale and retail (9 per cent and 17 per cent respectively). Surprisingly, only 36 per cent of workplaces (but 60 per cent of employees) in health and social work had collective bargaining, although this is largely explained by the fact that WERS does not classify Pay Review Bodies as collective bargaining.

The LFS data also allow some analysis of industrial variations in collective bargaining coverage (see Table 2.3). The rank order, however, is different to WERS. The highest coverage is found in public administration and defence (73.4 per cent of employees), followed by education (63.3 per cent) and then the public utilities – electricity, gas and water supply (62.6 per cent). The lowest coverage is found in hotels and restaurants (7.6 per cent); agriculture, forestry and fishing (10.1 per cent); and in real estate and business services (11.1 per cent).

Looking at the WERS data for 1998 and 2004, Brown and Nash (2008) note that the overall coverage of collective bargaining has fallen in every

Table 2.3 Collective agreement coverage, 2006. UK employees

All employees	33.5%
Private sector	19.6%
Public sector	69.0%
Industry	
Agriculture, forestry and fishing	10.1%
Mining and quarrying	23.8%
Manufacturing	26.6%
Electricity, gas and water supply	62.6%
Construction	18.8%
Wholesale, retail and motor trade	16.1%
Hotels and restaurants	7.6%
Transport, storage and communication	45.7%
Financial intermediation	31.4%
Real estate and business services	11.1%
Public administration and defence	73.4%
Education	63.3%
Health and social work	43.8%
Other services	24.8%

Source: Grainger and Crowther (2007): 38

sector except transport and communication and for a small minority in 'other business services' (Brown and Nash 2008: 96).

Decentralisation of pay determination

The second major observable trend in pay determination is the increasing decentralisation of decision making about pay. There are three main levels at which collective bargaining takes place – at multi-employer level (either at industry-wide or 'national' level); at the level of the single employer (enterprise or organisation); and at workplace level. Until the 1960s the great majority of UK private sector organisations bargained at multi-employer level but by 1998 the coverage of multi-employer collective bargaining was a fifth of that at organisation or 'enterprise' level (Brown *et al.* 2003: 200).

Milner's (1995) historical study of collective bargaining coverage indicates the importance of multi-employer or industry-wide collective bargaining in the development of UK industrial relations up to the early 1980s and its subsequent shrinkage. The collapse of industry-wide collective agreements in the late 1980s and 1990s had important ramifications for the overall coverage of collective bargaining as a pay determination system. The shift away from multi-employer pay determination began as early as the 1950s (Brown and Walsh 1991) and by the time of the Donovan Commission Report (1968) the effects of such decentralisation were being remarked upon. Donovan commented on the increasing tendency to wage drift (the increasing divergence between the centrally negotiated rates and the actual earnings at company level) resulting from decentralisation. This led some employers to weaken their agreements so that the national agreements simply provided a minimum wage floor upon which company pay structures were erected.

In the 1970s employers increasingly opted out of multi-employer agreements altogether to establish their own company agreements (Brown and Terry 1978). According to Brown and Walsh (1991: 48), 'By 1978 the dominance of single-employer over multi-employer agreements in manufacturing had already become clear' and this process accelerated in the 1980s (Brown 1981; Daniel and Millward 1983; Millward and Stevens 1986; CBI 1988; Booth 1989). So 'by 1986 single employer bargaining was dominant across the whole remuneration package' in the private sector (Purcell and Ahlstrand 1994: 121).

It has been generally assumed, in terms of macro-economic management, that highly centralised bargaining is more efficient than decentralised because the opportunity for wage moderation is higher where 'lowest common denominator' factors are at work. Traxler (2003) identifies two main explanatory positions regarding the economic effects of decentralisation. The first is the corporatist approach (Cameron 1984) that 'contends that a bargaining system's capacity for wage moderation decreases with decentralisation' (Traxler 2003: 3). The second is the 'hump-shape' hypothesis (Calmfors and Driffill 1988) which assumes that the extremes – the most and least decentralised systems – provide the strongest controls over pay growth. However, both theories have been challenged by more recent evidence (OECD 1994) that shows no 'systematic or robust impact by bargaining centralisation on aggregate wage increases, inflation and employment' (Traxler 2003: 3). Others (Soskice 1990; Traxler *et al.* 2001) have argued that the capacity for wage moderation does not depend on the level of bargaining as such but rather the degree of co-ordination between employers and unions in bargaining. Traxler (2003) also points to the key importance of underlying legal support for multi-employer collective bargaining in its continued existence – 'legal support for multi-employer bargaining is an essential determinant of the architecture of a country's overall bargaining structure' (Traxler 2003: 20).

From their study across 20 countries, Traxler *et al.* (2001:10) argue that 'the decay of collective bargaining is not the inevitable outcome of economic forces . . . rather it is the result of special institutional forces'. They note that collective bargaining has dwindled most sharply in countries where institutions supportive of multi-employer bargaining have been dismantled (e.g. the USA, the UK, Australia and New Zealand). In contrast, elsewhere 'inclusive multi-employer bargaining is seen to work as a key mechanism in moderating the destructive economic effects on collective bargaining' (Traxler *et al.* 2001:10). There are thus two observable patterns across the 20 OECD countries examined – the gradual disappearance of single-employer bargaining in some countries on the one hand alongside the continuing stability of multi-employer bargaining in other countries on the other hand. They conclude that from this observation any shift from multi-employer to single-employer bargaining is more likely in the longer term to lead to the demise of collective bargaining. This is borne out by the UK experience. Research by Brown and Nash (2008) indicates that most of the decline in UK collective bargaining coverage has been due to the contraction of single-employer bargaining, rather than to the decline of multi-employer bargaining, which did not change much in coverage between 1998 and 2004. Multi-employer bargaining is now largely a phenomenon found in the public services, construction and a few manufacturing sectors.

As Brown and Nash (2008: 96) comment: 'The locus of private sector pay fixing has been shifting downwards, whether or not firms still bargain with unions'. By 2004 multi-employer bargaining covered just 7 per cent of workplaces but most of these agreements were in the public sector, where 36 per cent of workplaces were still covered by multi-employer agreements (Kersley *et al.* 2006: 184). Only 1 per cent of private sector workplaces followed a multi-employer agreement.

In Table 2.4 we present reworked data on the locus of pay determination supplied by the WERS 2004 information and advice service based on a consistent methodology from 1984 (i.e. on workplaces with 25 or more employees). This shows that multi-employer bargaining remains the most common form of collective bargaining in the UK, albeit for a minority of employees. Research by IDS (2005) indicates that multi-employer industry agreements are still an important force in private sector pay bargaining, covering over 1.7 million employees. This resilience of multi-employer bargaining is also explained by the dominance of national level agreements in the public sector where collective bargaining is much more common. The slight increase from 1998 to 2004 is largely explained by the reclassification of NHS staff covered by PRBs discussed above. However, Kersley *et al.* (2006) note that, while collective bargaining remained the major form of pay determination in the public sector in 2004, there was also an increase in the proportion of pay set unilaterally by employers. It is also noteworthy that, while single-employer bargaining increased between 1984 and 1990, it has now declined to just 9 per cent of workplaces.

The majority of these multi-employer agreements in the private sector fix only a minimum pay level but these agreements may also lay down overtime or shift rates for the industry and core conditions such as hours of work or holiday entitlement. The largest agreements, in terms of coverage, are in the construction sector where the construction industry agreement is said to cover half a million workers and the building and allied trades agreement a further 200,000 workers. Other large industry level agreements include the agricultural wages boards (in England and Wales, Scotland and Northern Ireland) covering 180,000 and the Motor Trade 150,000. The British Clothing Industry Association Agreement covers some 60,000 and the British Printing Industries Agreement 50,000. As IDS (2005) comments, these remaining multi-employer agreements often exist where the sector is composed of many small employers. Their use may also serve as much as a device for setting the price of labour within the contracting process as for industrial relations purposes (Druker 2007).

The outcomes of decentralising pay determination have been identified as twofold: first, increased variations in the size of pay settlements and rates of pay (Jackson *et al.* 1993) and second, increased pay dispersion (OECD 1997). The variation in pay awards is likely to be largest where the employer unilaterally determines pay rates (Jackson *et al.* 1993). Those countries where wage inequality appears to have grown least are those where pay determination remains most centralised (Gottschalk and Smeeding 1997 cited in Bender and Elliott 2003). It has also been argued that centralised bargaining appears to benefit the lowest paid (Flanagan 1999 cited in Bender and Elliott 2003). A study of pay decentralisation in the civil service in Australia, Sweden and the UK (Bender and Elliott 2003) found that pay dispersion had increased as a result, both within grade and between departments, especially in the UK. They noted, however, that in the UK the individualisation of pay (through the introduction of individual performance-related pay) may have played a larger role in this widening within-grade pay dispersion. There was a less clear result for the effect on departmental pay structures. The gender pay gap decreased as a result of decentralisation in Australia but increased in Sweden and the UK. Bender and Elliott also found that decentralisation had different effects upon men and women. Dispersion was most pronounced for males between departments while for females it was greatest within grade.

Pay determination in the non-union workplace

The most common objective for abandoning collective bargaining among management has been the opportunity to 'individualise' reward systems. According to Brown *et al.* (1998) there are two ways in which other forms of pay determination might replace collective bargaining. The first is 'substantive individualisation' where each employee's individual contract is different (i.e. each individual has their own pay and conditions package). The second is 'procedural individualisation' whereby standardised employment contracts continue to apply to all staff, even if these are not negotiated with a union. It would appear from the evidence provided by Brown *et al.* (1998) that few organisations have opted for 'substantive individualisation'. Most have simply continued to operate standardised reward systems without the necessity to discuss these with employees. It is of interest to note that, in workplaces that abandoned collective bargaining, there was actually less likelihood of

Table 2.4 Locus of decision-making within main type of pay determination, 1984–2004

	Column percentages*			
	1984	1990	1998	2004
Collective bargaining	**60**	**42**	**33**	**28**
Most distant level of negotiations:				
Multi-employer bargaining	41	23	13	14
Multi-site, single employer bargaining	12	14	11	9
Workplace bargaining	5	4	3	3
Don't know	1	1	5	2
Not collective bargaining	**40**	**58**	**67**	**72**
Most distant level of decision-making:				
External to organisation	7	9	12	7
Management at a higher level in organisation	11	16	23	30
Management at workplace level	21	30	32	35
Don't know	1	3	0	0
Weighted base	*1977*	*1990*	*1911*	*1915*
Unweighted base	*1990*	*2039*	*1842*	*1560*

Base: all workplaces with 25 or more employees
*subtotals in bold

Source: ESRC-funded WERS 2004 Information and Advice Service produced for this publication. For WERS information see www.wers2004.info.

finding individual performance-related pay rather than more (Charlwood 2007: 41). Marginson *et al.* (2007: 19), in their study of retail banking and machinery and equipment engineering, found that in both sectors unions 'had largely managed to resist the individualisation of pay outcomes and the introduction of variable pay had not undermined collective bargaining in the sense of its core focus on delivering inflation-based increases to basic pay'. Nonetheless they found that the proportion of earnings determined outside of collective bargaining had grown. In other words, the 'at risk' elements of pay had grown.

According to WERS no single pay determination method has replaced collective bargaining in the private sector. The most significant change in the 2004 survey was the growth in the proportion of workplaces where management at workplace level set all pay, increasing to 35 per cent of all workplaces. The second most common approach was for pay to be set by management at a higher level (e.g. at Head Office), increasing to 30 per cent of all workplaces.

The criteria for determining pay changes

A corollary of a move to more organisation-specific pay systems, as advocated by the American 'New Pay' writers (Lawler 1990; Schuster and Zingheim 1992; Gomez-Mejia and Balkin 1992) might also imply less concern with external criteria when deciding increases to pay. There was much management rhetoric about the decline of 'going rates' and the rise of 'ability to pay' as the major criterion for pay increases, especially in the light of low inflation, in the 1990s. Certainly this was the view expounded in much of the practitioner press and was a major feature of the policy agenda of successive Conservative Governments in the 1980s and 1990s. Under Labour too, since 1997 there has been a continuing public rhetoric about the need for pay increases to reflect economic realities and the state of the local labour market, rather than inflation. This has been especially true of public sector pay policy, where the Labour Government changed the terms of reference for four of the five Pay Review Bodies in 1997 (the exception was the School Teachers Review Body because of the continuing statutory nature of teachers' pay). The Government shifted the emphasis from comparability with jobs external to the public sector to other criteria – namely recruitment, retention and motivation; departmental output targets for the delivery of services; expenditure limits; and inflation targets (White 2000). Thomason (2003) suggested that this change reflected the Government's exasperation with the PRBs continuing to make 'over-generous' awards. The Chancellor of the Exchequer has also been keen to stress the need for public sector pay to be more related to regional and local labour markets, with which we deal later.

According to classical labour market theory, under competitive conditions the wage an employer pays is neither under his control nor under that of the workers. As Blanchflower and Oswald (1988: 364) describe this approach: 'The going rate of pay is fixed by conditions in the whole economy, and most especially by the total demand for and supply of labour. Each firm must pay that going rate'. They challenge this deterministic view of the labour market and posit an 'insider–outsider' theory of wages. This approach stresses the importance of the organisation's internal activities and financial performance. Under this framework, wages are determined at least in part by how well the employer is doing. If sales are high, insiders will demand higher pay from their employers, while outsiders (e.g. the availability of replacement labour from the unemployed pool) have little or no influence on this internal market.

Research has suggested that, in reality, there is no such thing as a 'going rate' for a particular job but rather an array of rates. For example, an American study of 21 aerospace firms found that the top-paying firm paid more than 21 per cent above the average pay and the bottom one paid more than 13 per cent below the overall average (Foster 1985 cited in Milkovitch and Newman 1996). In examining how the labour market operates it is important to look at the relative importance of external and internal pressures upon pay levels.

Three main factors affecting the level of pay have been identified (Milkovitch and Newman 1996) – labour market pressures (supply and demand); product markets (level of competition and product demand); and organisational factors (such as the industry, technology, size and business strategies). The top three factors in 1983 were, in rank order, company productivity or labour trends; expected company profits; and local labour market conditions and wage rates. The consumer price index was ranked fifth (Freedman 1985).

Studies in Britain, in contrast, using both WERS data and the (now suspended) pay databank compiled by the Confederation of British Industry (CBI), identified the primacy of inflation as the key criterion. WERS 1990 data showed that the key factor was inflation for both manual and non-manual employees (and for about a quarter of all managers interviewed it was the only influence upon the size of settlement). Ingram *et al.* (1999) similarly found the retail price index to be the modal influence upon the level of pay awards. They also commented that: 'While internal settlement pressures appear to be important features of pay determination, there is little evidence from our sample that internal factors have replaced the role of external factors' (Ingram *et al.* 1999: 42). A study of the data on pay settlements in WERS 1998 (Forth and Millward 2000b) found that inflation continued to be the key factor in pay increases, despite inflation being at historically low levels. They also found that the size of pay awards did not vary between collectively bargained increases and those set through management discretion alone. Arrowsmith and Sisson (1999: 60) concluded that the pay award 'seems to be the outcome of a complex process which simultaneously involves issues of "ability to pay" and assessments of the external "going rate", mediated by labour market pressures'. Most importantly, their work showed that there are strong sectoral patterns in both pay practices and pay movements and that these appear to occur regardless of whether workplaces have collective bargaining or not.

There are currently two main sources of data about the criteria used to determine the size of pay increases. The first is the infrequent WERS data and the second is the annual reward surveys by the Chartered Institute of Personnel and Development (CIPD). Unfortunately the CBI Pay Databank, which asked respondents questions about this issue, was suspended in 2003. The most recently available WERS 2004 data shows that, first, in unionised workplaces inflation remains the key factor in pay awards whereas in non-union workplaces financial performance is most important (Blanchflower *et al.* 2007). Second, the ability to recruit and retain staff also featured as a more important factor in non-union settings. Third, pay increases in unionised workplaces are more likely to follow the 'going rate' for similar workers in the same industry or local labour market. Fourth, financial performance and productivity levels are more likely to be rated as factors in non-unionised workplaces.

The other main source of information about the factors influencing the level of pay awards is the CIPD annual surveys of reward practices. The latest survey in 2008 (CIPD 2008: 4) shows that the most important factor used to determine the size of the overall pay review is organisational performance, followed by inflation and then the movement in market rates (external comparability). Recruitment and retention issues and the 'going rate' were less important. For employers in the public sector the level of government funding and pay guidelines were also important factors.

Market-based pay

It has been observed in recent years that employers have increasingly moved towards determining pay in line with the market (Kessler 2007). 'Benchmarking' salary levels to the market has become more popular as labour markets have tightened and employers have become increasingly disillusioned with individual performance-related pay systems. Another reason is the rise of 'job family' grading structures, where organisations create separate career paths for particular groups of staff with similar knowledge and skills. Under such systems the differing labour market conditions for different types of staff can be met without recourse to general uplifts in pay for all staff by linking pay to the external market for those particular jobs only.

As IDS (2004) argue, linking pay levels to what other organisations pay in the same labour market is nothing new. Its meaning, however, may have changed. According to IDS (2004: 8):

> The extent to which market benchmarking determines pay levels and their subsequent uprating can be very different. At one end of the spectrum organisations use market benchmarking in tandem with other methods of pay setting . . . At the other end, pay levels are set almost wholly in relation to market medians.

Moves to market-based pay determination have been most common in the financial services sector and the civil service. This latter type of market-based pay 'is intended to limit pay increases and the expectation of pay increases, above the market level' (IDS 2004: 8).

A key problem identified with market-based pay is its lack of transparency. Also, as suggested by the CIPD (2007: 3), 'pricing to the external market rate carries the danger of importing into pay structures any gender and other discriminations that exist in the wider labour market'. Such systems also have high transaction costs in terms of the need to regularly review the market and ensure that pay levels are appropriate. IDS comments that such systems may be inherently inflationary and lead to chronic pay drift as employers seek to keep their staff within the upper quartile of pay indicated by survey data. IDS rightly states that in reality it is impossible for all employers to be 'upper quartile' employers and they may end up 'chasing their tail'.

Pay determination in the public sector

Within the public sector there has, as mentioned earlier in this chapter, been an on-going debate about the level at which pay should be determined. Government exhortations to the public services to move away from national level bargaining and towards more regional or local-level arrangements have generally fallen on deaf ears. Multi-employer bargaining at national level has remained the key form of pay determination for most public sector employees, although 'devolved bargaining' to departments and agencies has continued in the civil service since its introduction in the late 1990s (Gagnon 1996; White 1999; Kessler *et al.* 2006). Experiments with decentralised bargaining in the NHS ended with the election of Labour in 1997 and the development of the 'Agenda for Change' agreement. The resilience of multi-employer bargaining in the public services has also been underpinned by the growing influence of pay review bodies, which have increased in both number and coverage.

Nonetheless, the Labour government has continued to urge public service employers to adopt more flexible pay determination systems as part of its agenda of pay 'modernisation'. The Government argument is that more geographic pay variation is needed in the public sector because national pay rates are too inflexible and do not reflect regional differences in labour markets and the cost of living. In 2003 Gordon Brown, then Chancellor of the Exchequer, argued that the economy needed 'to recognise local and regional conditions in pay, such as extra cost for retention and recruitment that arise in London and the South-East'. He went on to warn that pay remits for public sector groups would include 'a stronger local and regional dimension' (Thornton 2003). A cross-cutting review of the public sector labour markets by HM Treasury in 2002 had found that, while average earnings in London and the South-East were markedly higher than elsewhere, there was little variation overall between other regions of the UK. It concluded, however, that 'outside

London, on average pay in the public sector is significantly higher for both males and females than in the private sector' (HM Treasury 2002: 62). The research included work by IDS that considered the impact of private-sector pay structures upon regional earnings. This research indicated that, contrary to common perceptions, large national private-sector firms tended to have UK-wide pay structures although with provision for some variation at regional and/or local level to reflect local labour market circumstances. IDS found that local pay bargaining is not common among national employers and that those with local bargaining have only marginal variation in pay outcomes. They also found that such national organisations tended to have at least two methods to respond to both short-term and long-term labour market difficulties. Many organisations used regional or zonal pay bands or special location allowances to deal with particular recruitment and retention problems but that movement between bands and allowances was strictly controlled from head office. In most national companies, employees are on national pay rates. These pay practices in the private sector partly explained the similarity in earnings between regions (CIPD 2006). Other research, by the Office for National Statistics, on regional price inflation (Wingfield *et al.* 2005), showed that average prices were very similar in most regions with again London and the South-East standing out as high-cost regions (largely explained by higher housing costs). Research conducted for the Office of Manpower Economics in 2005 (OME 2005) concluded that assessing appropriate geographical differences in pay would be complicated. It found that compositional and job responsibility factors probably mean that levels based on aggregate earnings and labour market data would be too blunt an instrument to determine pay levels.

While devolved bargaining operates in the civil service, this is not generally based on geographical pay (except where the agency only operates in one or two locations). Elsewhere, local flexibility is being addressed through either pay supplements within particular geographical boundaries, as under the National Health Service's Agenda for Change agreement, or through allowing local determination of grading structures and the provision of market supplements for hard-to-recruit staff, as with the local government 'Single Status' and the higher education pay modernisation agreements. Under the local government and higher education agreements, a central national pay spine exists to which individual employers match their own grading arrangements. Similar posts are therefore not necessarily placed on exactly the same pay spine points. This allows grading to partly reflect local labour market circumstances if wished.

The changing nature of pay information

Recent changes in payment systems raise some important questions about the pay information systems upon which decisions are based. The literature on the development of pay information systems is limited and certainly there is little data on the use made by employers and unions of such sources (one exception is work by Arrowsmith and Sisson 1999). IDS (2006) point out that there is little published information on organisations' market pricing practices.

It is here worth considering the historical development of pay information sources to put today's changes into context. In a pamphlet entitled *Wages – Fog or Facts*, published over 30 years ago, David Layton (the founder of Incomes Data Services, the major commercial British pay research organisation) argued that there was a strong case for examining the adequacy of published information used for pay determination (Layton 1965). This pamphlet, written against the backdrop of centralised incomes policy and disputes at shop floor level over incentive schemes, suggested that there was a dearth of data on the collective agreements on pay and conditions negotiated at company level, especially at workplace level. In response Layton called for changes in the collection of pay information under the following main headings – pay claims; rates of pay; an informed and regular appraisal of pay and hours statistics; and the systematic study of terms and conditions. Most importantly, Layton argued for the regular publication of such information so that it was available in the public domain. Such data was seen as a basis for economic modelling but, most importantly, it would also provide essential information for those who made the political and industrial decisions on pay and benefits.

This need was prompted by the proliferation of bargaining units and points at which decisions were made about pay. According to Brown and Walsh (1991),

> In the mid-1950s there were probably only a few hundred distinct bargaining units with separate agreements in Britain. Twenty-five years later in 1980 the first Workplace Industrial Relations Survey, covering services as well as manufacturing, permitted a rough estimate that there were 'probably well over 30,000 bargaining units covering twenty-five or more employees'. From the 1980 survey it was estimated that there were 'something of the order of 10,000 pay control points covering twenty-five or more employees . . . 1,000 pay control points covering 1,000 or more employees . . . 100 such points covering 10,000 or more employees'.
> (Brown and Walsh 1991: 48–9)

Given the growth of enterprise level pay structures since 1990 – either collectively bargained or not – it is likely that the number of pay control points will have increased even further since then.

The recognition of the growth of workplace pay bargaining, following the Donovan Commission report (Donovan Commission 1968), in the late 1960s and the growing interest in industrial relations at company and establishment level led to a burgeoning of sources of pay and benefits information. The two major British commercial pay information services – Incomes Data Services

(IDS) and Industrial Relations Services (IRS) – date from 1966 and 1972 respectively (IDS introduced its monthly Pay Chart in 1980 and IRS its monthly databank chart in 1983). These two organisations began to publish wage rates and salary scales from named organisations so that such data came into the public arena for the first time. In 1979 this development was followed by the establishment of the CBI Pay Databank, which collected data from member firms through a regular survey of pay increases. Unlike IDS and IRS, the CBI data was anonymous and presented as survey results. While initially the CBI survey only covered manufacturing, from 1983 the survey included private services. In 1980 the Engineering Employers' Federation established its own survey of engineering firms and in 1983 the trade union-funded Labour Research Department (LRD) began publishing settlement data. Also in 1983 the Office of Manpower Economics (OME), set up in 1971 to service the independent public sector pay review bodies, began surveying pay settlements to inform the civil service pay negotiations from 1984 (and latterly the Police Negotiating Board). The (unpublished) OME survey was, until 2005, conducted on a quarterly basis across a representative sample of non-manual private sector staff pay awards (Charles *et al.* 1998).

Since the 1990s, however, there has been a major shift in the emphasis HR practitioners place on pay information. This change reflects the decline of collectively bargained pay, the increase in enterprise level pay determination and the rise of more market-based pay setting. There remain four main sources of pay award data (and these cover the outcomes of both collective bargaining and not collective bargaining) but the growing emphasis on benchmarking individual jobs to the external market means that other sources such as commercial salary surveys have become increasingly important.

IDS identifies four main sources of pay information: negotiated industry-wide pay rates; company specific data; off-the-shelf salary surveys or consultants' databases; and participatory salary surveys and 'pay clubs'. In addition, organisations are increasingly commissioning bespoke surveys based on job evaluation techniques to ensure that jobs are being compared, as far as possible, on exactly the same basis. The major sources of information about pay awards today are Incomes Data Services, Industrial Relations Services, the Labour Research Department and the Engineering Employers' Federation (although the latter covers only the engineering sector) (see Table 2.5). Since 2000 two further sources of data have ceased to exist – the CBI Pay databank (a rich source for academic research) and the OME survey.

There are also problems stemming from the changing composition of reward. The growth of more 'at risk' pay, either based on individual performance or on organisational profitability, presents increasing difficulties for those monitoring pay. So too does the ending of clear job titles and descriptions (often used to benchmark salaries against the market) and the development of broad banded pay progression systems, which allow greater flexibility in individual pay. In the late 1980s Fay observed:

Table 2.5 Comparisons of main settlement data sources

	EEF	IDS	IRS	LRD
Structured sample	No	No	No	No
Approx. number of awards	1,500	1,000	1,200	1,000
Settlement source	Employers	Employers and unions	Employers and unions	Unions
Basic/Total pay	Basic	Basic	Basic	Basic
Public sector included	No	Yes	Yes	Yes
Manual/non-manual identified separately	No	No	Yes	No
Median/Average/Range	All	Median/ range	All	Median

Source: this material is taken from the CIPD Factsheet, Local pay: approaches and levels (2006) with the permission of the publisher, the CIPD, London (www.cipd.co.uk).

> Base pay is becoming a smaller part of the total compensation package for an increasingly broader range of employees, making it unclear what incumbents in a job actually make. It is certainly more difficult to make comparisons across very different pay systems. When 'at risk' pay may take the form of lump sum bonuses, payments into employee stock ownership or savings plans, or additional time off with pay, comparison of salary figures which may include only base pay or direct cash payouts becomes misleading.
>
> (Fay 1989: 88)

As indicated elsewhere, in the UK the shrinkage in the coverage of collective bargaining and the shift away from multi-employer collective agreements has been accompanied by a growth in discretionary and variable pay systems, particularly the growth of individual performance-related pay. While it has always been the case that a gulf may exist between basic rates of pay and total earnings, the growth of variable pay systems – in which earnings are composed of several separate components – has made the measurement and evaluation of earnings growth increasingly difficult. Many important elements in the total pay and benefits package may be missed if we only concentrate on increases to base rates, such as annual profit-sharing bonuses, profit-related pay, share option schemes, etc. The importance of some of these additions to basic pay was shown by the effect that the annual profit-sharing bonuses had on the Government's Average Earnings Index (IDS 1998: 8).

The UK's annual New Earnings Survey (NES) (now replaced by the Annual Survey of Hours and Earnings – ASHE) reflected the substantial decline in industry-wide collective agreements in 1997 by abandoning its reporting of individual private sector agreements and providing only aggregate information by size of organisation. The new ASHE has abandoned reporting of collective agreements altogether.

These changes mean that, increasingly, both national statistical sources and commercial pay information sources provide only a partial picture. Instead of reporting actual rates of pay, organisations are increasingly quoting scale minima and maxima or average merit increases or indeed total paybill increases. The Government's ASHE survey has attempted to remedy some of the deficiencies in the earlier NES and attempted to make the tracking of pay composition easier but in many ways the new survey is less helpful than the NES. The problems with the new ASHE were highlighted in the most recent Low Pay Commission report (LPC 2008). In a section on the quality of the ASHE data the Commission commented that, despite responding to a consultation exercise by the Office for National Statistics (ONS) in which it had objected to a cut of 10 per cent in the ASHE sample, the cut had still been implemented and, worse, at an even higher level of 20 per cent with no further consultation and 'in the face of strong opposition from the user community' (LPC 2008: 13). The Commission went on to say that:

> Although we remain confident that the ASHE estimates are robust at the aggregate level, this significant reduction in the ASHE sample has reduced the reliability of estimates at detailed industry and occupation level and therefore impaired our ability to analyse what is happening in some individual low-paying sectors.
>
> (LPC 2008: 13)

As indicated earlier, without the ability to check employer estimates with a second party, there is scope for a high degree of mystification by employers. This is problematic for both employees, for Government and for academic research. In particular, as highlighted by Rubery (1995) in a study of the effects of performance-related pay on gender pay equity, opportunities to monitor pay trends will decrease as the spread of such payment systems reduces the transparency of the labour market. Whether the increasing use of equal pay audits by organisations to check their risks of equal pay action will lead to improvements in pay data remains to be seen.

Conclusions

This chapter has discussed the ways in which employers make decisions about pay comparisons. It identified two major changes in pay determination over the last forty years. First, there has been a substantial decline in collective bargaining as the major method of pay determination in the UK labour market and its replacement by an increasingly large segment of non-negotiated pay, where employer discretion rules. Second, there has also been an associated decentralisation of pay determination (in both unionised and non-unionised workplaces) away from industry level and towards enterprise level. As we have noted, the evidence suggests that the demise of multi-employer bargaining has been a significant factor in the demise of collective bargaining of any kind. While the evidence indicates that most moves away from collective bargaining have not been accompanied by 'substantive' individualisation of pay, there has been increasing variability in individual earnings, with a growth of contingent 'at risk' pay components and substantially increased management control over pay progression and promotions.

Despite the growing decentralisation of pay determination, the criteria used by employers in fixing pay levels remain largely unchanged. There is evidence that internal factors such as 'ability to pay' and 'performance/productivity' have become more important but pay comparisons with competitor firms (i.e. benchmarking to the market) appear to be increasing in importance. Inflation remains a central criterion. Most important is the observation that sectoral patterns in pay determination remain strong, despite the decline of multi-employer agreements.

Finally, 'pay intelligence' has become increasingly problematic as collective bargaining has declined and payment systems have become more individualised. The issue of 'pay drift' was a major concern in the 1970s as collective bargaining became more decentralised and the growth of incentive pay was often disguised. This led to the development of many new sources of pay data. The more recent fragmentation of pay and grading systems, the growing absence of co-ordination of pay changes and the degradation of pay monitoring means that it is becoming increasingly difficult to chart, measure and quantify different methods of payment and differences in reward practices. This is especially true of publicly available sources of data. More importantly, to return to the quote from Robinson (1973) cited earlier, the concept of fairness when applied to wages is inevitably tied up with comparisons and transparency. If employees cannot know what others are paid, there can be no assurance that they are fairly paid. The changes to pay determination over the last two decades may have given employers increasing control over employees' remuneration but the outcomes may have important ramifications at the macro-economic level, in terms of pay drift, and for employees in terms of clarity and fairness.

Note

Special thanks to John Forth of the National Institute for Economic and Social Research for provision of specially tailored WERS data used in this chapter.

References

Arrowsmith, J. and Sisson, K. (1999) 'Pay and working time: towards organisation-based systems?', *British Journal of Industrial Relations*, 37 (1): 51–75, March.
Behrend, H. (1957) 'The effort bargain', *Industrial and Labor Relations Review*, Vol. 10 (4): 503–15, July.

Bender, K.A. and Elliott, R.F. (2003) *Decentralised Pay Setting: A study of the outcomes of collective bargaining reform in the Civil Service in Australia, Sweden and the UK*, Aldershot: Ashgate Publishing Ltd.

Blanchflower, D.G. and Oswald, A.J. (1988) 'Internal and external influences upon pay settlements', *British Journal of Industrial Relations*, Vol. 26 (3): 363–70.

Blanchflower, D.G., Bryson, A. and Forth, J. (2007) 'Workplace industrial relations in Britain 1980–2004', *Industrial Relations Journal*, Vol. 38 (4): 285–302.

Bland, P. (1999) 'Trade union membership and recognition 1997–98: an analysis of data from the Certification Officer and the Labour Force Survey', *Labour Market Trends, July*, Vol. 107 (77): 343–53.

Booth, A. (1989) 'The Bargaining structure of British establishments', *British Journal of Industrial Relations*, Vol. 26 (3): 226–34, November.

Booth, A. (1995) *The Economics of the Trade Union*, Cambridge: Cambridge University Press.

Brown, W. (1981) *The Changing Contours of British Industrial Relations: A survey of manufacturing industry*, Oxford: Blackwell.

Brown, W. and Nash, D. (2008) 'What has been happening to collective bargaining under New Labour? Interpreting WERS 2004', *Industrial Relations Journal*, Vol. 39 (2): 91–103.

Brown, W. and Terry, M. (1978) 'The changing nature of national wage agreements', *Scottish Journal of Political Economy*, 25 (2): 119–33, June.

Brown, W. and Walsh, J. (1991) 'Pay determination in Britain in the 1980s: The anatomy of decentralisation', *Oxford Review of Economic Policy*, Vol. 7 (1): 44–59.

Brown, W., Deakin, S., Hudson, M., Pratten, C. and Ryan, P. (1998) 'The Individualisation of Employment Contracts in Britain', Research paper for the Department of Trade and Industry, Centre for Business Research, Department of Applied Economics, University of Cambridge, June.

Brown, W., Marginson, P. and Walsh, J. (1995) 'Management: Pay determination and collective bargaining', in P. Edwards (ed.) *Industrial Relations: Theory and practice in Britain*, Oxford: Blackwell.

Brown, W., Marginson, P. and Walsh, J. (2003) 'The Management of Pay as the Influence of Collective Bargaining Diminishes', in P. Edwards (ed.) *Industrial Relations. Theory and Practice*, 2nd edn, Oxford: Blackwell.

Calmfors, L. and Driffill, K. (1988) 'Centralisation of wage bargaining and macroeconomic performance', *Economic Policy*, No. 6: 13–61.

Cameron, D. (1984) 'Social democracy, corporatism, labour quiescence and the representation of economic interests in advanced capitalist countries', in J.H. Goldthorpe (ed.) *Order and Conflict in Contemporary Capitalism*, Oxford: Clarendon Press.

CBI (1988) *The Structure and Processes of Pay Determination in the Private Sector:1979–1986*, London: Confederation of British Industry.

Charles, G., Bailey, D. and Palmer, S. (1998) *Pay and Earnings Data. An Analysis of the Sources*, Unpublished, Office of Manpower Economics, February.

Charlwood, A. (2007) 'The de-collectivisation of pay setting in Britain 1990–98: incidence, determinants and impact', *Industrial Relations Journal*, Vol. 38 (1): 33–50.

CIPD (2006) *Local pay: approaches and levels*, CIPD Factsheet, September, London: Chartered Institute of Personnel and Development.

CIPD (2007) *Market pricing: approaches and considerations*, CIPD Factsheet, London: Chartered Institute of Personnel and Development.

CIPD (2008) *Reward Management. Survey Report 2008*, London: Chartered Institute of Personnel and Development.

Daniel, W.W. and Millward, N. (1983) *Workplace Industrial Relations in Britain*, London: Heinemann Educational Books.

Donovan Commission (1968) *Royal Commission on Trade Unions and Employers' Associations*, Cmnd 3623, London: HMSO.

Druker, J. (2007) 'Industrial Relations and the Management of Risk in the Construction Industry', in A. Dainty, S. Green and B. Bagilhole (eds) *People and Culture in Construction*, London: Taylor & Francis.

Fay, C.H. (1989) 'External Pay Relationships', in L. R. Gomez-Mejia (ed.) *Compensation and* Benefits, ASPA/BNA Series, Vol. 3, Washington DC: Bureau of National Affairs Inc.

Forth, J. and Millward, N. (2000a) *The Determinants of Pay Levels and Fringe Benefit Provision in Britain*, Discussion Paper No. 171, London: National Institute of Economic and Social Research.

Forth, J. and Millward, N. (2000b) *Pay Settlements in Britain*, Discussion Paper No. 173, London: National Institute for Economic and Social Research.

Freedman, A. (1985) *The New Look in Wage Policy and Employee Relations*, New York: The Conference Board.

Gagnon, S. (1996) 'Promises vs performance: pay devolution to *Next Steps* executive agencies in the British Civil Service', *Employee Relations*, Vol. 18 (3): 25–47.

Gomez-Mejia, L. and Balkin, D. (1992) *Compensation, Organisational Strategy and Firm Performance*, Cincinnati: South Western.

Gottschalk, P. and Smeeding, T.M. (1997) 'Cross-national Comparisons of Earnings and Income Inequality', *Journal of Economic Literature*, Vol. 35 (2): 633–87.

Grainger, H. and Crowther, M. (2007) *Trade Union Membership 2006*, Department of Trade and Industry.

HM Treasury (2002) *Cross-Cutting Review of the Public Sector Labour Market*, November 2002, London: HM Treasury.

IDS (1998) 'What is happening to bonuses and variable pay?', *IDS Report*, 770, October, London: Incomes Data Services.

IDS (2004) 'The pros and cons of market-related pay', *IDS Pay Report*, 907, June: 8–9.

IDS (2005) 'The continuing influence of industry pay agreements', *IDS Pay Report*, 923, February: 10–12.

IDS (2006) *Developments in occupational pay differentiation*, research report for the Office for Manpower Economics by Incomes Data Services, October.

Ingram, P., Wadsworth, J. and Brown, D. (1999) 'Free to choose?, Dimensions of private-sector wage determination, 1979–1994', *British Journal of Industrial Relations*, March, 37 (1): 33–49.

Jackson, M.P., Leopold, J.W. and Tuck, K. (1993) *Decentralisation of Collective Bargaining: An Analysis of Recent Experience in the UK*, London: Macmillan.

Kersley, B., Alpin, C., Forth, J., Bryson, A., Bewley, H., Dix, G. and Oxenbridge, S. (2006) *Inside the Workplace. Findings from the 2004 Workplace Employment Relations Survey*, London: Routledge.

Kessler, I. (2007) 'Reward choices: strategy and equity', in J. Storey (ed.) *Human Resource Management: A Critical Text*, 3rd edn, London: Thomson.

Kessler, I., Heron, P. and Gagnon, S. (2006) 'The fragmentation of pay determination in the British civil service. A union member perspective', *Personnel Review*, Vol. 35 (1): 6–28.

Lawler, E.E. (1990) *Strategic Pay: Aligning Organisational Strategies and Pay Systems*, San Francisco: Jossey-Bass.

Layton, D. (1965) *Wages – fog or facts?*, Eaton paper 7, London: Institute for Economic Affairs.

Low Pay Commission (LPC) (2008) *National Minimum Wage. Low Pay Commission Report 2008*, Cm7333, Low Pay Commission, London: The Stationery Office.

Mahoney, T.A. (1989) 'Employment compensation and strategy', in L. R. Gomez-Mejia (ed.) *Compensation and Benefits*, ASPA-BNA Series (3), 3.1–3.28, Washington DC: The Bureau of National Affairs, Inc.

Marginson, P., Arrowsmith, J. and Gray, M (2007) 'Undermining or Reframing Collective Bargaining? Variable Pay in Two Sectors Compared', Paper for 2007 Performance and Reward Conference (PARC), Manchester, 29 March 2007.

Metcalf, D. (2001) 'British Unions: Dissolution or Resurgence Revisited', in R. Dickens, J. Wadsworth amd P. Gregg (eds) *The State of Working Britain Update 2001*, London: Centre for Economic Performance.

Milkovitch, G.T. and Newman, J.M. (1996) *Compensation*, 5th edn, Burr Ridge, Illinois: Irwin.

Millward, N. and Stevens, M. (1986) *British Workplace Industrial Relations, 1980–1984*, London: Gower.

Millward, N., Stevens, M., Smart, D. and Hawes, W.R. (1992) *Workplace Industrial Relations in Transition. The ED/ESRC/PSI/ACAS Surveys*, Aldershot: Dartmouth Publishing Company.

Millward, N., Bryson, A. and Forth, J. (2000) *All Change at Work: British Employment Relations 1980–1998 as Portrayed by the Workplace Industrial Relations Survey Series*, London: Routledge.

Milner, S. (1995) 'The coverage of collective pay-setting institutions in Britain, 1895–1990', *British Journal of Industrial Relations*, March, 33 (1): 69–91.

OECD (1994) *The OECD Jobs Study. Part 11*, Paris: Organisation for Economic Co-operation and Development.

OECD (1997) *Employment Outlook*, July, Paris: Organisation for Economic Co-operation and Development.

OME (2005) *Recent Research on the Levels of Variation of Geographical Pay Differentials and the Implications for London Weighting Payments for DDRB's Remit Groups*, London: Office of Manpower Economics.

Purcell, J. and Ahlstrand, B. (1994) *Human Resource Management in the Multi-divisional Company*, Oxford: Oxford University Press.

Robinson, D. (1973) 'Differentials and Incomes Policy', *Industrial Relations Journal*, Spring, Vol. 4 (1): 4–20.

Rubery, J. (1995) 'Performance-related Pay and the Prospects for Gender Pay Equity', *Journal of Management Studies*, September, Vol. 32 (5): 637–54.

Schuster, J.R. and Zingheim, P.K. (1992) *The New Pay: Linking Employee and Organisational Performance*, New York: Lexington Books.

Soskice, D. (1990) 'Wage determination: The changing role of institutions in advanced industrialised countries', *Oxford Review of Economic Policy*, Vol. 6: 36–61.

Thomason, G.F. (2003) 'Adjusting the Role of the Pay Review Bodies', *Croner's Human Resource and Employment Review*, Vol. 1 (2): 81–6.

Thornton, P. (2003) 'Pay may reflect regional living costs', *Independent*, 14 November.

Traxler, F. (2003) 'Bargaining (De) centralisation, macroeconomic performance and control over the employment relationship', *British Journal of Industrial Relations*, March, Vol. 41 (1): 1–27.

Traxler, F., Blaschke, S. and Kittel, B. (2001) 'The coverage of collective bargaining', in *National Labour Relations in Internationalised Markets*, Oxford: Oxford University Press.

White, G. (1999) 'The Remuneration of Public Servants. Fair Pay or New Pay?', in S. Corby and G. White (eds) *Employee Relations in the Public Services, Themes and Issues*, London: Routledge.

White, G. (2000) 'The Pay Review Body System: Its Development and Impact', *Historical Studies in Industrial Relations*, No. 9, Spring: 71–100.

Wingfield, D., Fenwick, D. and Smith, K. (2005) 'Relative consumer price levels in 2004', *Economic Trends*, No. 615, February: 36–45.

3 Worker voice and reward management

Edmund Heery

Summary

Much of the debate over reward management is concerned with how best managers can link rewards to business strategy and secure 'strategic pay'. The concern of this chapter is different. It examines the impact of institutions of worker representation on key decisions within reward management, including determining pay levels, pay structures, pay systems and occupational benefits. Central to the chapter is an examination of the impact that trade unions, the traditional institution of worker voice, have on these various aspects of reward management. Unions have been in decline for more than two decades, however, and there is now a more fragmented system of employee representation that includes civil society organisations, legal practitioners taking individual cases and employee participation schemes sponsored by managers. The chapter also considers the impact of these new institutions of worker voice, and traces their emerging role within reward management.

Introduction

Much writing on reward starts from the premise of 'strategic pay' (Lawler 1990): the need for reward systems to complement and reinforce business strategies. The starting point for this chapter is different. It is concerned, not with how business strategy shapes reward practice, but with how employees and their representative institutions influence reward. The level and form of reward are matters of vital interest to employees and are central concerns of the institutions of worker voice that articulate those interests within employing organisations and across the wider labour market. The aim of what follows is to describe and explain how reward management bends to this 'representative contingency'.

The prime institution of worker voice that is considered is trade unions. Unions remain the main institution created by working people to protect their interests at work and bargaining pay and other elements of reward continues to be a central function of unions. It is also the case that there is a large, international research literature that tracks union influence over pay (e.g. Bennett and Kaufman 2007; Bryson 2007). Nevertheless, unions have declined and their influence over management practice has diminished. The proportion of UK employees that are members of trade unions stood at 28.4 per cent in 2006 and in the private sector only 16.6 per cent of employees were union members (Grainger and Crowther 2007). Bargaining coverage, that is the percentage of employees whose pay is affected by a union collective agreement, was higher, at 33.5 per cent for all employees and 19.6 per cent for the private sector. But these figures still indicate that much of the UK economy is now non-union, a feature that represents a sharp break with the relatively recent past.

Accordingly, the chapter also considers forms of non-union worker voice. There is now a more variegated system of worker representation, in which other institutions sit alongside, and sometimes cooperate and sometimes compete with, trade unions. Unions are still the dominant institution of worker voice but other institutions play a significant role and are beginning to attract attention from researchers. Three forms of non-union voice are considered below. First, are systems of worker representation established by employers: company councils and forums and the networks of identity groups (women and minorities) that have been established in many large companies. Second, are civil society organisations (CSOs); voluntary and non-governmental bodies that have become increasingly active in the sphere of employment relations.[1] CSOs include identity-based organisations, like the Fawcett Society, Stonewall and Age Concern, which campaign on behalf of women, lesbians and gays, and older workers respectively. They also include issue-based organisations campaigning on behalf of the lower paid or for improved family-friendly benefits. Third, are private representatives who are hired by individual workers to represent their interests. By far the most important institution here are lawyers who are increasingly active in pursuing equal pay and other cases on behalf of employee clients, often on a no-win, no-fee basis. Much less is known about these three types of institution than is known about unions and for many employers their role is doubtless marginal. In a more fragmented system of industrial relations, however, it is important to consider both traditional and non-traditional institutions.

The process of reward management comprises several critical decisions and the review that follows discusses how five of these are shaped by unions and other representative institutions. It examines the extent to which worker voice raises the pay of workers; compresses pay differentials (including those between male and female and minority and majority workers); influences the use of payment systems which link rewards to performance and thereby place earnings at risk; extends the range of rewards which organisations offer to their employees; and promotes due process and transparency in the management of reward. The majority of evidence is taken from Britain but, where appropriate, data from North America and continental Europe are also used and there is an emphasis throughout on tracking recent trends. The objective, moreover, is not simply to describe trade union and other influences on reward but to offer an explanation in two senses: first by uncovering the rationale that guides the behaviour of worker representatives and, second, by identifying the structural features of organisations which serve to facilitate or constrain the influence of representative institutions.

Reward level

Trade unions classically are bargaining agents which seek to enhance their members' pay and conditions of employment. Research on the union 'wage effect' suggests that historically they have been successful in fulfilling this basic purpose and that the wages of union workers, on average, are higher than those of equivalent non-union employees. The main purpose of this section is to review this evidence and summarise what is known about the size and trend over time of the union effect on wages. It also considers the conditions under which unions are effective in raising pay. A final purpose is to look beyond unions and consider a new form of worker voice that is concerned specifically with raising pay at the lower end of the labour market. These are the living wage campaigns, which have spread across the United States since the early 1990s and which have recently found an echo in Britain, in the East London Communities campaign for a living wage for public service contractors (Wills 2004).

Writing more than a decade ago, Metcalf (1994: 140) observed that there 'is now general agreement that, on average, unionised workplaces pay higher wages than otherwise comparable non-union ones'. Such agreement amongst economists was based on a series of cross-sectional estimates of the union wage-gap which compared the hourly, weekly or annual earnings of individual union members or unionised workplaces with those of their non-union equivalents, while seeking to control for other possible influences on earnings, such as employees' level of human capital. The average estimate of the mean union wage-gap from cross-sectional models was around 15 per cent for the USA and 8 per cent for Britain (Booth 1995: 164–70).

Since these estimates were produced, however, doubts have grown over the continuing capacity of unions to raise wages and a growing body of research suggests that the union wage-gap is declining and, according to some estimates, has disappeared altogether (Metcalf 2005: 90–2). In a longitudinal analysis of trends in the wage gap in the UK and USA, Blanchflower and Bryson (2002) demonstrate that the gap narrowed in both countries in the period from 1994. For many groups of unionised UK workers, they report, the wage premium had disappeared by 2002. However, Blanchflower and Bryson suggest that at least part of this decline is due to the fact that union wage effects are countercyclical: unions protect the wages of their members in hard times but non-union workers catch up in boom periods, such as that since the mid-1990s. Moreover, these same authors report that more recent analysis of the UK Labour Force Survey and the Workplace Employment Relations Survey

(WERS) 2004 produces estimates of the union wage-gap for Britain of 12 per cent and 6 per cent respectively (Blanchflower *et al.* 2007: 291).

On average therefore there is evidence that unions continue to raise pay for their members. But averages can conceal as much as they reveal and it is apparent that union membership is worth more in relative terms to some groups of employees than it is to others. In Britain, the wage-gap is higher for women, manual workers, those with lower education and part-timers. These are 'all groups with traditionally low earnings' (Blanchflower and Bryson 2002: 30), indicating that unions are most effective at raising wages for those most in need.

Another source of variation in union wages is the context in which bargaining over pay takes place. Analysis indicates that two types of condition are important. First, the size of the wage-gap is influenced by union organisation, with research studies reporting a higher premium where there is a closed shop, multi-unionism, high union density or high collective bargaining coverage (Bryson and Forth 2008). Second, the product market conditions faced by the establishment are also important and in 'the vast majority of establishments facing competitive product market conditions, unions are unable to achieve wage levels above those paid elsewhere to comparable non-union workers' (Metcalf 1994: 142). The union effect on reward levels, therefore, is conditional on union organisational power but also on the capacity of employers to yield concessions. It seems where unions possess monopoly power they are in a position to extract a share of economic rents for their members from employers who, themselves, operate in relatively sheltered product markets.

Differences in union organisation and product market conditions appear to determine the size of the union wage-gap *within* national economies. However, if one examines differences between countries, then the structure of collective bargaining appears to be the key. Table 3.1 contains estimates of the union/non-union wage-gap in a series of developed economies (Bryson 2007). It indicates that where bargaining is centralised at national or industry level or where there are mechanisms for extending pay settlements to non-union employers then the union wage premium tends to be lower. These are features of the national system of pay determination in France, Germany, Italy, the Netherlands, Norway, Spain and Sweden, all of which have strong institutions of bargaining co-ordination. Where pay determination is mainly at company or workplace level, however, as is the case in Japan, North America and Britain, then unionised workers are in a position to maximise relative gains.

While co-ordinated bargaining may limit the size of the union wage-gap, it can enable unions to pursue other goals. Within co-ordinated systems, unions operate as 'encompassing' organisations which must have regard to the effects of their bargaining behaviour on the national economy and level of employment and which are in a position to exchange pay restraint for a macro-economic policy and welfare regime beneficial to the broad mass of

Table 3.1 Union wage-gap in developed economies

Country	Years	Union percentage differential
Australia	1994, 8 and 9	12
Austria	1994, 5, 8 and 9	15
Canada	1997–9	8
Denmark	1997–8	16
France	1996–8	3
Germany	1994–9	4
Italy	1994 and 8	0
Japan	1994–6, 8 and 9	26
Netherlands	1994 and 5	0
New Zealand	1994–9	7
Norway	1994–9	7
Portugal	1998–9	18
Spain	1995, 7 9	7
Sweden	1994–9	0
UK	1993–2002	10
USA	1973–2002	17

Source: Adapted from Table 1 (Bryson 2007)

working people (Visser 1998). The motives underpinning union wage bargaining in this kind of system, therefore, are influenced by a complex set of trade-offs between earnings growth, employment and social welfare. Even within decentralised systems, however, there is evidence of unions acting as 'efficient' bargainers, which seek to balance wage, employment and other objectives. Thus, Metcalf (2005: 103–4) reports that the presence of unions not only reduces the incidence of accidents at the workplace but is associated with *lower* compensating wage differentials for hazardous work. 'Organized labour', he notes, 'has chosen the socially responsible accident prevention strategy in preference to squeezing out a bit more pay in dangerous workplaces.'

Living wage campaigns are an example of a non-union voice institution that seeks to raise wages, specifically for those in low-paying jobs, many of whom are migrant workers or members of ethnic minorities. According to Freeman (2005: 17), campaigns have the same redistributive objectives as unions and are a product of union decline: 'as unions have weakened, [living wage campaigns] have stepped forward to champion workers who cannot improve their situation by themselves'. Freeman describes living wage campaigns as 'nonworker organisations', and one of the features of this type of institution is that they speak on behalf of a targeted, client group rather than expressing the interests of members, in the manner of a trade union. Other distinguishing features flow from this characteristic. Campaigns are funded, not by member dues, but typically by charitable grants and donations and rely not on the collective organisation of workers but on a political strategy targeted at public authorities. This uses protest and other tactics, to secure the adoption of an ordinance raising the wages of designated categories of worker employed by sub-contractors. Living wage ordinances, not collective agreements are the prime method of raising wages.

Living wage campaigns have developed into a substantial social movement in the United States, consisting of coalitions of community, faith, student and union organisations (Freeman 2005: 15). Beginning in Baltimore in the early 1990s the movement has grown and in its first ten years led to the adoption of more than 120 living wage ordinances by US cities and other public agencies. In most cases these require contractors or employers receiving public subsidies to pay living wages to particular categories of staff. Living wages themselves are usually defined in terms of the income needs of a family of four and are fixed at levels that are substantially above the US federal minimum wage. The ordinances are highly localised and highly targeted.

The US movement has found an echo in the UK, particularly in the living wage campaign in the East End of London. This began by targeting NHS trusts, pressing them to raise wages for sub-contractors involved in cleaning and ancillary operations, but has since spread to the private sector, where sub-contractors have been targeted at the Canary Wharf office development (Holgate and Wills 2007: 218–22). In the wake of this campaign a number of public agencies, including the Greater London Authority, the Scottish Executive and Wales Assembly Government, have voluntarily adopted living wage policies (Bewley 2006: 357).

The US evidence indicates that living wage campaigns can be highly effective in raising the wages of the low-income workers they seek to represent – by as much as 35 per cent on average. This positive effect, moreover, seems to come at very little cost in terms of job losses or the flight of economic activity from cities with living wage laws (Bernstein 2005). The case study evidence from the UK also points to a positive wage effect (Wills 2004: 277). The problem, however, is that proportionately few workers are affected. Bernstein (2005: 136) estimates that at most 100,000 US workers had gained from living wage campaigns by 2002 in a labour market of 140 million employees, with 30 million on low wages. More recently, living wage advocates have contributed to statewide campaigns to raise minimum wages (Luce 2007: 23) and as the movement develops in the US, and possibly in Britain, it may successfully operate at a broader scale. It remains though that, to date, living wage campaigns have had marginal effects on wages and, perhaps unsurprisingly, have not reproduced the extensive upward lift in pay achieved by trade unions on behalf of their members. As Freeman (2005: 17) notes, '. . . just as local efforts to lower global warming cannot solve the world's climate problem, living wage campaigns cannot solve the problem of low wages broadly.'

Reward structure

A second dimension of reward which representative institutions can influence is the structure or distribution of pay, both within the individual firm and the wider economy. That structure may be relatively extended, with large differentials in pay between the higher and lower paid, or it may be relatively compressed, with a pay floor raising the earnings of the less-skilled relative to the pay of those in better jobs. The purpose of this section is to establish what impact unions and other voice mechanisms have on the distribution of earnings and to review the extent to which they compress pay structures and eliminate low pay. Central to the question of the distribution of rewards is the issue of pay inequality between men and women, white and ethnic minority, and able-bodied and disabled workers. Accordingly, a second purpose is to examine the impact of unions and other institutions on the relative earnings of women and minorities, those who historically have encountered pay discrimination in the labour market.

Potentially, unions can have two effects on the dispersion of pay. First, they can widen pay inequality by raising the earnings of their members relative to those of non-members. Second, they can narrow pay inequality by bargaining for a compressed pay structure in companies where they are recognised. Evidence gathered from Britain, the USA and other countries points strongly to the latter effect (Bryson and Forth 2008; Calmfors *et al.* 2001: 64–5; Card *et al.* 2007; Freeman 1992: 149–50). For the UK, Charlwood and Terry (2007: 333) use WERS 2004 to estimate that wage dispersion is narrowed by on average 6.5 per cent for men and 7.8 per cent for women at workplaces where unions are recognised. Analysis of patterns in Britain, Canada and the USA suggests that, for men, the narrowing of pay dispersion within the unionised sector outweighs the widening of pay dispersion which stems from the union wage-gap, so that the net effect of union wage bargaining is to reduce income inequality. For the same countries, however, this is not the case for women, because of the concentration of women union members in relatively well-paid professional jobs and because the union wage effect is stronger for women than for men (Card *et al.* 2007). The union effect on pay dispersion amongst women therefore is to widen pay inequality. Nevertheless, the broad effect of unions is redistributive and, as a consequence, national economies with relatively high union density have a less unequal wage structure (Freeman 2007b: 619).

Most commentators argue that the union effect on pay structure arises from two separate concerns. The first is a desire to establish standard rates of pay that reduce management's scope to award differential payments to workers in the same occupation or grade: unions 'attach wage rates to jobs rather than to individuals' (Booth 1995: 179). The second is a desire to lift the pay floor and eliminate low pay through bottom-loaded wage agreements; indeed, it is union success in raising the earnings of manual workers relative to non-manual workers which accounts for much of the narrowing of the pay structure in unionised firms (Freeman 2007b: 618). A consistent finding from the WERS series is that there are relatively few low-paid workers in establishments covered by collective bargaining (Cully *et al.* 1998: 25; Kersley *et al.* 2006: 198–9; Millward *et al.* 1992: 364) and for this reason the vast majority of employees affected directly by the National Minimum Wage (NMW) do not work in unionised companies.

Comparative research reveals striking cross-country differences in the extent of pay dispersion, which is high in Britain and the United States but lower in many continental European countries. Much of the explanation for these differences lies, once again, with the structure of collective bargaining. Calmfors *et al.* (2001: 64) report that, 'It is a robust empirical finding in studies trying to explain cross-country variations in pay dispersion that centralization of wage bargaining is conducive to pay compression.' Where bargaining is centralised at national or industry levels, then unions are in a position to even out pay differences between enterprises and industrial sectors. They can pursue a 'solidaristic' wages policy that uses the bargaining power of well-organised workers to lift the pay of the less powerful. The decline of centralised bargaining that has occurred in many countries over the past two decades has been associated with a rise in pay inequality. The latter effect has also been generated by the decline of trade unionism *per se*. Particularly in the USA and Britain, falling union density and declining bargaining coverage have contributed to widening pay dispersion (Card *et al.* 2007; Freeman 2007a: 50). As union influence over the economy has waned, a more unequal society has emerged.

A by-product of the union effect on pay structure is an improvement in the relative earnings of groups who often suffer discrimination. Metcalf (2005: 102–3) describes this as the union 'sword of justice' effect and reports that in the late 1990s British unions closed the earnings gap between men and women, white and non-white and able-bodied and disabled workers. The reduction of the gender pay-gap was particularly marked: women's relative hourly pay was increased by an average of 2.6 per cent by union bargaining. Unions can also influence the gender pay gap more directly through deliberate 'equality bargaining'; that is the inclusion of equal pay and equal treatment in the agenda for collective bargaining with employers. In a range of British industries in the 1980s and 1990s (including local government, gas, electricity supply, banking and supermarket retail) unions negotiated changes to pay and grading structures to combat indirect discrimination against women workers (Colling and Dickens 1998; Gilbert and Secker 1995; Jackson *et al.* 1993: 94). More recent developments have focused on public services, where in the main branches of the UK public sector, unions have negotiated new, job-evaluated grade structures, designed explicitly to provide equal pay for work of equal value (Bewley 2006: 354–6).

Collective bargaining is not the only means through which unions have sought to advance the cause of equal pay. They have also sponsored legal cases, both as a means of putting pressure on employers to negotiate on the issue and to strengthen the law on equal pay itself. Until recently virtually all equal pay cases arose in unionised environments and unions have played an important 'mediating' role in facilitating the enforcement of the legal right to equal pay (Dickens 1989). They have also pressed government for new laws.

For example, in the Warwick Agreement with the Labour Government, concluded before the 2005 General Election, the unions secured a commit- ment to end two-tier wages in public services, in large part because the lower wages paid to workers in contracted-out services primarily affected women and acted as an incentive for public service employers to escape the new job-evaluated grade structures negotiated in health and local government (Bewley 2006: 356; Davies and Freedland 2007: 101–4). Unions have also pressed for compulsory pay reviews and for employers to be given a positive, statutory duty to ensure equal pay. This pressure has been resisted for the private sector but the gender equality duty placed on public authorities by the Equality Act 2006 includes a requirement to ensure equal pay and effectively obliges public sector organisations and private companies and voluntary organisations providing public services to undertake an equal pay review.

Unions have been joined in this pressure to secure equal pay by other representative institutions. Lobbying for a gender equality duty has involved a broad range of campaigning groups, many of which have worked closely with the Trades Union Congress (TUC) to exert pressure on government. Particularly prominent has been the Fawcett Society, a long-established pres- sure group for the cause of sex equality, which commissions research, makes submissions to government, and campaigns actively on the issue of equal pay. Authoritative pressure groups of this kind are accepted as 'insider' organisa- tions by government and play an important part in the policy-making pro- cess. They are part of a network of organisations that includes the TUC and major UK unions, which seeks to use the method of legal regulation to narrow the gender pay gap.

The advocacy work of unions also has a counterpart amongst non-union institutions. The key role here has been played by firms of solicitors, which have been active in seeking out equal pay cases on a no-win, no-fee basis. Following precedents set by union-sponsored cases, which allow the backdat- ing of equal pay claims, solicitors have touted for business amongst low-wage public service workers. Several notable cases have been won against local authorities and there has been a rash of expensive settlements across UK local government (LGE 2006). In one case, moreover, a claim was taken against the GMB union because it had chosen to negotiate a solution to equal pay cases rather than initiating a legal case on behalf of a group of women members at Middlesbrough Council. Unlike the relationship with fellow- lobbyists, like Fawcett, therefore, the relationship between unions and private advocates has been a fraught one. Private solicitors simply seek the best settlement for their individual clients and, unlike unions, do not offer 'effi- cient' representation: there is no regard to the impact of settlements on employment, service levels or the wider pay structure in the employing organ- isations against which cases are taken. Their use of the law differs sharply from that favoured by unions, where its primary function is to act as a lever to open up negotiations (Heery *et al.* 2004: 145–7). The favoured union method remains collective bargaining and there is a desire to seek a collective, negotiated resolution of the equal pay issue across public services.

What evidence is there that non-union representative bodies are themselves bargaining over pay structure? There is certainly potential for them to operate in this way. WERS 2004 revealed that 6 per cent of private sector workplaces and 13 per cent of private sector employees are covered by a non-union representative system. In a further 1 per cent of workplaces and 6 per cent of employees there is dual channel representation, comprising union and non-union representatives (Charlwood and Terry 2007: 324). The evidence suggests that these non-union representative bodies are not effective in shaping employees' pay and, in particular, there is no impact on pay dispersion (Charlwood and Terry 2007: 333). In the private sector, amongst women workers, dual channel representation is associated with a narrower pay dispersion and, indeed, this effect is stronger than that for union representation alone. With this exception, however, non-union representation does not emerge as an effective bargaining agent, producing significant effects on the structure of pay.

Reward systems

A third decision which representative institutions potentially can influence is the selection of reward systems. The latter can be defined as procedures for relating pay to work. They fall into two broad categories: *input-based reward systems* link pay to the skills, competence or time which employees invest in their work while *output-based systems* link pay to measures of worker performance, such as output, productivity, achievement of objectives, sales and profit (Kessler 2001). The measures of worker performance used in the latter category may relate to an individual employee, a work group or team or to all members of a particular enterprise, as occurs with profit-sharing. The bulk of research on this topic deals with the relationship of trade unions to output-based systems and this is the focus of the following section.

The first question to consider is the extent to which unions and other representative institutions shape the incidence of output-based systems. A recent review of the use of individual output-based incentives for manual workers across several countries by Heywood and Jirjahn (2006: 161–6) indicated that there is no common pattern. Incentives are less frequently used in unionised workplaces in Britain but this is not consistently the case in other countries. In Germany, moreover, they are used more frequently where there is a system of employee representation through a statutory works council. Historical accounts of the development of reward systems in industry, however, do show a pattern of union opposition to incentives. The spread of shop-floor incentive schemes in manufacturing was resisted by American unions in the 1950s (Slichter *et al.* 1960: 493–6) and research from Britain in the 1960s reveals an identical pattern (Brown 1973: 13–15; see also Heywood *et al.* 1997).

Unions have also opposed incentive schemes for non-manual workers, particularly those based on performance appraisal (Heery and Warhurst 1994). In Britain and the USA the presence of individual performance-related pay (IPRP) is inversely correlated with union recognition (Blanchflower and Oswald 1990; Freeman 1992: 150), while in Canada, commission is less common for unionised salesworkers (Geddes and Heywood 2003). A number of group-based incentive schemes are also less common in unionised organisations. There is a positive association between union presence and profit-sharing amongst large firms (Kersley *et al.* 2006: 192; Millward *et al.* 1992: 263) but outside the large-firm sector in both Britain and the USA, profit-sharing is found mainly in non-union firms (Eaton and Voos 1992).

The reasons for this recurrent pattern of trade union opposition to contingent payment systems are fivefold.

1   This kind of payment system can pose a threat to union members and particularly to the security and stability of their earnings. This is a factor in union hostility to profit-sharing and profit-related pay and some of the sharpest union resistance to IPRP has arisen where schemes have involved the replacement of cost-of-living with 'merit only' pay increases.

2   Unions have claimed incentives generate perverse effects and can frustrate, rather than promote, effective management. For example, unions of professional workers, such as teachers, lecturers, nurses, doctors and probation officers, have argued that IPRP is likely to erode the commitment that is required for the effective delivery of professional services.

3   Unions have opposed contingent pay because of its impact on pay structure and its tendency to widen the dispersion of pay by generating differences in earnings between individuals, work groups, work-sites and men and women. These differences, moreover, are viewed as 'unfair' because in many cases they reflect not genuine differences in performance but the accidents of job content, job context and management style, and the pernicious effects of gender and race discrimination.

4   Unions have regarded incentives as divisive and threatening to their own capacity to develop collective organisation and purpose amongst employees. IPRP has been opposed because of its potential to detach individuals from union membership and so 'disorganise' the union from within.

5   Unions have opposed contingent pay because it may pose a threat to their procedural role as the collective representatives of employees and be linked to attempts by employers to exclude unions from the process of pay determination. The primary reason for union opposition to profit-sharing has been 'the non-negotiable nature of schemes' (Baddon *et al.* 1989: 45) and opposition to IPRP has been particularly intense because of its association with explicit or tacit moves to derecognise unions (Heery 1997a).

While there is a history of union opposition to contingent pay, this is not the only response and in many cases union policy towards payment systems of this kind is marked by ambivalence. For example, unions have varied in their depth of opposition to IPRP, with many acknowledging the need for pragmatism, and a minority declaring in favour (Arrowsmith *et al.* 2008; Heery and Warhurst 1994). The reason for union acceptance of contingent pay systems is in many cases simple acknowledgement of *force majeure*, that the union is incapable of preventing the introduction of incentives. In other cases, however, contingent pay may be recognised as beneficial for employees and a source of union strength. In the USA in the 1950s, opposition to payment-by-results softened as it became apparent that it provided a 'rich source of indirect wage increases' (Slichter *et al.* 1960: 497). Similar examples are available for more recent payment systems, with unions acceding to IPRP because it provides a means to raise public service salaries or permits members in management jobs to escape from the constraints of a compressed pay structure (Heery and Warhurst 1994). For a range of different contingent pay systems, moreover, there is evidence of union policy moderating over time as the new method of reward is institutionalised within a particular enterprise, sector or occupation. It is notable that the preparedness of unions to accept IPRP is associated statistically with the proportion of members exposed to this system of payment (Heery and Warhurst 1994: 14; see also Baddon *et al.* 1989: 49; Slichter *et al.* 1960: 496).

The primary condition for union acceptance of contingent pay systems appears to be the opportunity to regulate schemes jointly with management through collective bargaining (Kessler 1994). Unions are 'irredeemable bargainers' (Crouch 1982: 117) and their main purpose when faced with contingent pay is to shape its form and operation through collective agreement, essentially to minimise the disadvantages listed above. With regard to IPRP, for instance, unions have sought to reduce the at-risk element in total remuneration and ensure stability of earnings is maintained through parallel cost-of-living awards. Furthermore they have instituted monitoring and appeal procedures to reduce the risk of unfair treatment and have sought to limit management discretion through formal rules governing performance appraisal and procedures which allow for the joint review of IPRP schemes (Brown *et al.* 1998; Heery and Warhurst 1994; Marsden and Belfield 2005).

It remains the case, though, that performance pay systems, particularly when applied to non-manual workers, are associated with non-unionism. Many unions have members covered by IPRP schemes that have not been bargained collectively (Brown *et al.* 1998; Heery 1997a). Necessarily, therefore, unions have had to develop ways of representing members where joint regulation has come to an end. Often this has taken the form of an advisory and representation service for union members on personal contracts with IPRP. The union role in this case becomes one of supporting members who negotiate their own salary, for example, through the provision of pay data, and acting as an advocate on behalf of individuals who believe they have been unfairly assessed. The teaching unions, for example, provide an advisory service for members on how to apply for progression through new performance-based salary scales (Marsden and Belfield 2005: 153–4).

Research on the determinants of union influence over payment systems has identified a range of factors which can allow unions to shape contingent pay. Classic studies of piecework bargaining (Brown 1973) have pointed to the combined influence of buoyant product markets and slack systems of management control in allowing workers to influence the operation of incentive schemes. Other studies have pointed to worker control of key stages of the labour process as a basis for influence (Edwards and Heery 1989) and it is clear that union bargaining power with regard to contingent pay is largely a function of aspects of the economic and organisational context which endow unions with leverage over management.

Research on the determinants of union success in bargaining over IPRP points to additional influences, which include management strategy and the structure of collective bargaining. With regard to the former, it is notable that unions of professional and managerial employees have been less successful in securing collective agreements on IPRP, reflecting the fact that many employers regard joint regulation as illegitimate at higher organisational levels (Brown *et al.* 1998; Heery 1997a). With regard to bargaining structure, it is notable within the public sector that the civil service unions have had most success in securing collective bargaining over IPRP and that this has been secured, at least initially, through the medium of industrywide collective agreements. In local government and the National Health Service, in contrast, IPRP has been introduced largely at the initiative of local managers, who have used the effective decentralisation of pay determination to escape from union influence (Heery 1997a). In the past, locally introduced incentive schemes were a stimulus to workplace trade union activity, but in a period of union decline and weakness, local experiments with contingent pay often take place on management's terms and decentralisation leads effectively to de-recognition.

While influence over pay systems is largely a function of structural context and the 'positional power' which unions possess, it may also be a function of the union's 'organisational power': its ability to shape members' response to contingent pay. Case studies of the introduction of incentives in strongly unionised sectors, for instance, have revealed how workplace union leaders seek a 'disciplined' reaction to the new payment system and enforce norms on effort levels and the distribution of earnings opportunities (Edwards and Heery 1989). In these cases, the union used its collective strength and control over its members to influence the operation of incentives and minimise perceived unfairness and consequent division. Where the local union lacks 'organisational power', however, this kind of disciplined, collective response to contingent pay will be absent. Research on IPRP schemes in local government has revealed quite extensive employee dissatisfaction and a latent demand for union involvement, but also a failure on the part of unions to satisfy that demand through the articulation of grievances (Heery 1997b). Given the substantial weakening of workplace trade unionism in recent years, it is likely that this kind of passive, ineffectual response characterises the reaction to incentive schemes in many other workplaces as well.

While there is evidence of unions shaping the management of pay systems, what of other systems of employee voice? The association between works councils and incentives in Germany was referred to above and has been interpreted as a product of trust relations. Where a works council is present, it is suggested, employees can have confidence that pay for performance will be operated in a fair manner, in accordance with principles of distributive and procedural justice (Heywood and Jirjahn 2006).

The other main finding on non-union representation is an association between the use of employee involvement (EI) and performance pay. McNabb and Whitfield (2007), using the 1998 Workplace Employee Relations Survey, report that performance pay schemes tend to work more effectively when they are reinforced by EI techniques such as quality circles and team briefing. And White and colleagues (2004: 137, 167), using the Change in Employer Practices Survey 2002, note both that performance pay is a typical component of a 'bundle' of high-performance practices and that the spread of teamworking, often classed as a form of EI, has been reinforced by the spread of group incentive schemes. What this research appears to establish, however, is not that EI is used to articulate employee demand for performance pay but that the two types of technique are used in combination by employers to elicit worker effort. The incentive effect of performance pay serves to ensure that the space for discretionary effort allowed by EI is actually used for productive effect.

Reward range

A fourth decision which representative institutions potentially can influence concerns the range of reward. While payment in cash remains the primary reward for work, remuneration for many also embraces benefits, such as pensions, healthcare and paid leave. Accordingly, in this section we first consider the role of unions in broadening the range of rewards and securing employee access to occupational benefits. We also consider the role of non-union agencies in extending benefits, by paying particular attention to identity and issue-based campaigning organisations, which have become increasingly active in this area.

There is a body of evidence stretching back to the early 1980s, which demonstrates that unions increase employee access to benefits. In a summary of this work, Budd (2007) reports that for the USA there is strong and consistent evidence, that unions add occupational pensions and healthcare to the remuneration package. These two benefits are important sources of social welfare and the decline of unions in the USA has been linked to a declining proportion of the population who have access to healthcare and old age support. The evidence also indicates that unions improve the quality of these benefits (e.g. promoting the use of defined benefit as opposed to defined contribution pension schemes) and raise worker knowledge and use of benefit plans. For Britain, successive waves of the Workplace Employment Relations Survey indicate that collective bargaining is associated with the incidence of an occupational pension scheme and sick pay and annual leave in excess of statutory entitlements (Budd 2007: 176; see also Forth and Millward 2000; Kersley *et al.* 2006: 199; White *et al.* 2004: 159). There are exceptions to this pattern and in Britain benefits in kind, company cars and private healthcare are less common in the union sector (Budd 2007: 176; Kersley *et al.* 2006: 199). The probable reasons for this are twofold: that certain benefits may be associated with a paternalist management style that leaves little room for joint regulation or, like private healthcare, may conflict with union support for a high level of state provision.

More recent research has focused on the role of unions in extending benefit provision in two directions. On the one hand, unions have secured the inclusion within benefit schemes of workers who previously were excluded from coverage, particularly those on non-standard contracts. The union campaign to secure sickness, pension, mortgage allowance and other benefits for part-time workers stretches back to the 1970s and has been pursued through political action at European and national levels, the sponsorship of legal cases and collective bargaining with employers (Heery and Conley 2007). In the unionised segment of the economy equal treatment of part-timers on a pro rata basis is now standard practice and has spilt over into many large non-union companies, anxious to avoid union-initiated legal action. Subsequently, unions have campaigned successfully for equal treatment provisions in law for workers on fixed-term contracts and are currently engaged in a drive for similar regulations for agency staff.

On the other hand, unions have pressed for new benefits that allow better work-life integration and support working parents and other carers (Heery 2006; see also Firestein and Dones 2007). Policy here has encompassed attempts to secure enhanced leave and entitlements to flexible working time and, once again, has been developed at multiple levels of the employment system. Unions have negotiated a European framework agreement on parental leave, participated in UK government consultation to develop legislation and included family-friendly practices in collective bargaining. A 2002 survey of paid union officers in Britain found that more than half had negotiated with employers on flexible hours and parental leave in the previous three years (Heery 2006: 51). Other research indicates that work-life policies are more likely to be present at workplaces with union membership and collective bargaining (Bewley and Fernie 2003; Budd and Mumford 2004; White *et al.* 2004: 112–13).

It seems clear therefore that unions have been effective in broadening the range of rewards received by their members. Indeed, if one considers access to training and career development and access to employee involvement programmes that allow workers to exercise greater discretion at work and thereby reap intrinsic rewards, then there is further evidence of union broadening the reward range (Arulampalam and Booth 1998; Kersley *et al.* 2006: 84; McGovern *et al.* 2007: 112–15; White *et al.* 2004: 144, 159). Unions appear to make the reward package more complex.

What are the conditions that underpin this activity? Two types of influence have been identified. First, unions have responded to opportunities afforded by developments in public policy and the strategies of employers. At European level, the Commission's commitment to developing policy through social dialogue has allowed unions to negotiate framework agreements that, *inter alia*, regulate benefit policy, such as those on part-time work, fixed-term contracts and parental leave (Falkner 1998). Developments at European level have also provided a degree of leverage over the British state, allowing unions to press for stronger regulations that transpose European legislation into UK law (Heery and Conley 2007: 20). The UK's own policy of boosting the employment rate, moreover, has provided a further opportunity for unions to influence public policy on family-friendly practices and flexible working; measures that are designed to allow carers to continue in paid work while looking after dependent children and adults (Davies and Freedland 2007: 209–11). Finally, unions have been most able to bargain over work-life and family-friendly policies in the public services, where employers have been more receptive and have themselves adopted a more proactive policy towards these issues (Heery 2006: 52–5).

The other set of influences have arisen largely within unions themselves and are associated with the feminisation of union membership and activism. The development of union policy on part-time work can be taken as a case in point. The drive to secure equal treatment for part-timers in benefit policy, which developed through the 1980s and 1990s, was partly a response to the growth of female-dominated part-time work in the UK economy. It was also a product of the growth of feminist activism within unions, which led in turn to attempts to redirect union policy towards the particular interests of women workers. It was in female-dominated unions with a strong body of women activists and leaders, such as the shopworkers' union USDAW and the banking union BIFU, that the policy on part-time work was first developed (Heery and Conley 2007). For work-life policy, a similarly critical role in formulating policy has been played by the TUC's Equal Rights Department (Heery 2006: 46).

A feature of recent union attempts to extend benefit provision is that they have been pursued through coalitions with other organisations. The TUC campaign on part-time work in the 1990s involved joint work with Citizens Advice and policy on work-life integration has included collaboration with organisations of carers. Quite independently of unions, however, campaigning CSOs have exerted pressure for the broadening of reward policies. Much of this effort has been directed at public policy makers and attempts to secure new law, requiring employers to extend benefit provision. Thus, Working

Families has been a strong advocate of the extension of the right to request flexible working to all parents and not just those of young children.

Increasingly, however, organisations of this type have directly targeted employers and offer advice, consultancy and training services to help employers improve their reward policies. For example, Working Families also provides a broad set of services to employers and operates an Employer of the Year award to reinforce best practice in flexible working. Another example is provided by Stonewall, the gay rights body, which has launched a Workplace Equality Index to help employers ensure they are responsive to the interests of LGBT employees. As part of this policy Stonewall presents standards of good practice in the provision of domestic partner benefits, which are reinforced by monitoring, benchmarking and awards (Stonewall 2008).

In a study of the provision of domestic partner benefits in the USA, moreover, Briscoe and Safford (2008) show that their incidence is related to the presence of activist networks operating within companies. A feature of diversity programmes in many large companies today is the sponsoring of identity-based networks, of women, ethnic minorities, faith groups, LGBT workers and others, and it is likely that these act as a significant internal pressure, ensuring the tailoring of benefit policy to the needs of their specific constituency; for example, pressing for leave policies that meet the needs of particular faith groups or requesting flexible working for those with disabilities. Increasingly, active campaigning bodies outside employing organisations and networks of identity groups within are a combined force that is making reward policy more complex. Acting sometimes in coalition with unions but frequently as an independent source of worker voice, their aim is to extend the range of rewards to meet the needs of a diverse workforce.

Reward processes

The previous four sections have dealt with the influence of representative institutions over substantive issues in reward management, but unions and other bodies also can shape *procedure* and determine the processes through which rewards are managed. It is with the extent and manner of this influence that this final section is concerned. It considers the role of unions and other institutions in providing for employee participation in determining rewards, formalising reward procedures, establishing due process mechanisms for the resolution of disputes, and providing for the transparency of reward practice through monitoring, audit and review.

The main concern of unions with regard to participation has been to secure the right to bargain over reward on behalf of members. Unions, as has been pointed out, are irredeemable bargainers and seek to draw all aspects of reward management within the compass of collective negotiation. As a consequence, they can alter fundamentally the process of decision-making within the field of reward and displace unilateral regulation by employers with a system of union-mediated worker participation or collective joint regulation.

WERS 2004 shows that participation through collective bargaining continues to be a notable feature of unionised workplaces in Britain. The survey indicates that pay is the most frequent subject of collective bargaining and that pay negotiations take place at a majority of workplaces (61 per cent) at which trade unions are recognised. In addition, in 52 per cent of unionised workplaces there is negotiation over holiday entitlement and in 36 per cent negotiation over pensions (Kersley *et al.* 2006: 194).

Although collective bargaining continues to provide for worker participation in reward management, it is declining and across the economy is a feature of fewer than 20 per cent of workplaces (Kersley *et al.* 2006: 194). This raises the question of whether other vehicles of participation are becoming more significant. WERS 2004 revealed that pay is often the subject of management consultation with both union and non-union representatives in the small minority of workplaces (14 per cent) with a consultative committee and is discussed in about a third of team meetings/briefing groups in the much larger (71 per cent) set of workplaces that operate employee involvement. Employer-sponsored forms of worker participation, therefore, do permit some employee influence over reward. Perhaps the key thing to note however is that, in the absence of unions, employers almost universally refuse to concede negotiations over pay (Charlwood and Terry 2007: 322; Kersley *et al.* 2006: 195). The strongest form of participation, based on joint decision-making between worker and employer representatives, is confined almost exclusively to the unionised part of the economy.

Another possible way in which collective bargaining may be replaced is through individual bargaining. McGovern *et al.* (2007: 120) estimate that 29 per cent of workers are able to negotiate pay when entering their job and a slightly higher percentage (31 per cent) negotiate subsequent increases. They also infer that individual bargaining is becoming more common. Individual bargaining, however, does not reproduce the union effect within the economy. It is very much a feature of jobs held by those in higher social classes, performing professional and managerial work, and there is a gender bias, with significantly more men than women making use of personal negotiations. Because of these features, it is likely that individual bargaining widens pay inequality by allowing those with marketable skills to maximise the return on their human capital. Most workers, however, lack the market power to engage effectively in this process. For this majority, the decline of unions is being replaced by unilateral employer regulation of pay and conditions of employment, not individual bargaining (Brown *et al.* 1998; Cully *et al.* 1998: 109).

Evidence of other union effects on reward processes can be seen in Table 3.2, which presents survey responses from trade unions with members covered by IPRP schemes. It indicates, first, that a concern of unions has been to formalise the method of appraisal and the link between appraisal and reward, which lie at the heart of payment systems of this type (see also Marsden and Belfield 2005). A similar process can be seen in the field of reward structure, where union presence is associated with the use of formal job evaluation for estab-

Table 3.2 Union attempts to influence the management of individual performance-related pay (IPRP) schemes

Change in IPRP scheme	Attempted %	Not attempted %
Introduction of 'more' objective method of performance review	74 (55)*	26
Insisting managers follow explicit rules when awarding IPRP	68 (53)	32
Introduction of an appeals procedure	73 (63)	27
Union access to information on the distribution of performance payments	75 (65)	25
Gender monitoring of payments	60 (58)	40
Ethnic monitoring of payments	45 (43)	55
Commitment from management to joint review of IPRP	60 (50)	40

Base equals unions with members covered by IPRP (N=38–41)
* Percentage reporting success in their attempt shown in brackets

Source: Heery and Warhurst (1994)

lishing pay grades and differentials (Kersley *et al.* 2006: 246). Indeed, the growing interest of unions in securing equal pay for work of equal value for women workers has led to the further extension and refinement of job evaluation in a search for procedures that fully capture the relative demands of jobs and eliminate scope for discrimination. Where unions are present analytical, factor-based job evaluation, the kind recommended by equal pay experts, is more likely to be encountered (Kersley *et al.* 2006: 246).

This effect of unions, in formalising or bureaucratising the employment relationship, has been widely noted; indeed, nearly 50 years ago it was identified by Slichter and colleagues (1960) as one of the primary effects of unions on management. It originates in a number of abiding union concerns. Formal rules effectively constrain management decision-making and reduce the scope for arbitrary treatment or favouritism, a concern that has been particularly acute for unions whose members are covered by individualised systems of contingent pay. In limiting management discretion, formal rules also serve to standardise the employment relationship and provide for the consistent treatment of employees who, for example, are paid a standard rate for the job rather than a 'personal' salary fixed by the employer. For this reason, employees are likely to develop a common interest. Moreover, in requiring fair and consistent treatment of its members, the union can also develop its own institutional strength, based upon the shared interests of employees who experience reward management in common.

Table 3.2 also indicates that most unions faced with IPRP have sought to establish an appeals procedure. The table shows that unions have generally been successful in this regard and other research on IPRP has demonstrated that schemes are more likely to include a right of appeal when they have been negotiated with a union (Heery 1997a: 219). Another effect of unions on reward management, therefore, is likely to be the institution of formal procedures for questioning management decisions and resolving disputes over the setting of work standards, the assessment of performance, the grading of individuals, under-payment of wages and so on. General research on industrial relations has demonstrated that procedures of this kind are more common where a union is recognised and also that they are more likely to be used; essentially because individual employees can draw upon representative skills and have more confidence that they will not be penalised for questioning a management decision (Eaton and Voos 1992; Kersley *et al.* 2006: 219).

The scrutiny of management decision-making is one of the central functions of unions within the enterprise and while this function can be discharged through formal appeal mechanisms, it can also be achieved by measures which make the process of management transparent. Unions can pressure managers to provide information about the functioning and outcomes of reward systems and so make it possible to check for inconsistency, unfairness or other problems that are emerging. Table 3.2 demonstrates that making reward management transparent in this way has been a primary concern of unions with members covered by IPRP schemes. Thus, a majority of unions report attempts to gain access to the distribution of performance payments, to establish a system of gender monitoring, and secure management agreement to the joint review of IPRP schemes. A substantial minority also report attempts to institute ethnic monitoring of schemes. Once again, there is confirmatory data from WERS 2004. Monitoring of the relative pay rates of women, ethnic minorities and disabled workers is found in fewer than 10 per cent of UK workplaces but it is significantly more likely to be encountered where there is a union present (Kersley *et al.* 2006: 248). What this suggests is that an important activity of unions is the generation of management information as managers are encouraged to review reward systems and share information with representatives. The effect, once again, is to qualify the management prerogative by making the process and outcomes of management transparent and available for scrutiny.

The extent to which non-union representative bodies contribute to these processes of formalisation, due process and monitoring is uncertain. Nevertheless, it is likely that they do have some effect and that this influence is growing. Perhaps the most potent influence emanates from no-win, no-fee lawyers taking equal pay cases against public service organisations. The potential huge costs of these cases is exerting significant pressure on organisations to audit their pay processes and formalise them in order to demonstrate that remaining gender differences in pay are objectively justified. The activities of groups like Stonewall also appear to be working in this direction. Identity and issue-based organisations of this type encourage employers to adopt formal policies relating to their constituency that embrace but which are not confined to reward management. They may also then seek to monitor and benchmark employers, through instruments like Stonewall's Workplace Equality Index, thereby generating management information. In this case, therefore, union and non-union systems of worker representation seem to be pushing in the same general direction, towards greater review and formalisation of reward processes.

Conclusion

The purpose of this chapter has been to offer a perspective on reward management that is absent from much of the current literature. Instead of focusing on the links between reward and business strategy it has considered the impact on a series of critical reward decisions of representative institutions of workers; examining how reward adapts to a 'representative contingency'. Much of the chapter has been concerned with trade union effects on reward, reflecting the continuing significance of unions in the economy but also the wealth of economic and management research that has analysed union activity. The chapter has also considered new institutions of worker voice, including civil society organisations, legal representatives and employer-supported systems of participation, which have assumed more significance in a context of union decline. The system of worker representation is now characterised by institutional pluralism, with a variety of institutions operating alongside one another.

A primary message that can be drawn from the review is that unions make a difference to reward management. Their impact on reward may be variable and often modest in scope but in aggregate, and with regard to each of the five strategic decisions which have been examined, there is evidence of unions affecting the substance and process of reward management. Thus, unions continue to raise the pay of their members relative to non-union workers; they compress the pay structure and increase the relative pay of women; they restrict and regulate the use of contingent pay systems that place earnings at risk; they extend the range of rewards; and they affect the process of reward management by instituting worker participation through collective bargaining and limiting management discretion through formal rules, due process and transparency.

These effects derive from the main function of unions in employment systems characterised by collective bargaining, namely to engage in distributive bargaining and secure a larger share of the economic surplus for their members. They also derive from other purposes, however, and it is clear from the review that unions pursue a range of objectives within the field of reward. Two deserve particular emphasis. First, unions do not simply want more reward for their members, they also want *fair* rewards and much of their activity is concerned with shaping a moral economy informed by notions of just process and just outcomes. With regard to process, the themes of consistent treatment and the right to protection from arbitrary management loom large. With regard to outcomes, unions tend to stress equality (the rate for the job), equivalence (a fair day's work for a fair day's pay) and redistribution (a compressed pay structure and broad access to benefits). The second objective is reflected in the attempts by unions to 'reposition' themselves as the representatives of women and atypical workers, which were referred to above. What is happening in parts of the labour movement is a process of redefining the interests which unions exist to represent and this, in turn, is shaping the kinds of effect they generate within reward management. In concrete terms, as unions have become more dependent on recruiting women workers and as women have become more active in unions, so unions have tried to negotiate equal value pay structures, have opposed incentive schemes because of the risk of sex discrimination, have pressed for the inclusion of part-timers in benefit programmes, and have tried to institute the gender monitoring of rewards.

While the theme of multiple and evolving purposes runs through the review, so does the theme of multiple and evolving constraints. Again, two deserve emphasis. Echoing a long line of industrial relations research, the review has pointed to the importance of the structure of collective bargaining in shaping the union impact on rewards. The union mark-up, the dispersion of pay, the gender pay-gap and union influence over contingent pay are all affected by the structure of collective bargaining. The effect seems most apparent when one considers differences in the union effect on reward between countries. In crude terms, there appears to be a trade-off between a relatively high mark-up for union members secured in countries with fragmented bargaining and a more solidaristic, compressed distribution of pay found in countries with co-ordinated bargaining.

The second constraint that has emerged repeatedly is the system of employment law, though in many respects this should be viewed as an opportunity rather than as a constraint. What is striking is the extent to which there is interaction between union attempts to influence reward through joint regulation and the system of legal regulation of pay and benefits. Thus, in many cases the law can operate as a lever for union influence, with unions using equal pay or other legislation to open up negotiations on the shape of pay structures, the operation of pay systems and employee benefits. The direction of influence can flow the other way, however, and it is apparent that unions can play an important mediating role by informing, advising and representing employees when their legal rights are contravened. Unions can use the law to promote joint regulation, therefore, but they can also help enforce the law and ensure legal regulation has genuine effect.

Although much of the review points to the continued effectiveness of unions in shaping reward, it has also pointed to declining influence. It is for this reason that we have examined non-union institutions of worker voice. An important theme that has emerged here is that of the relationship between unions and these newer organisations. In many instances this is based on direct cooperation, such as the coalitions that have been formed to press for equal treatment in reward practice for minority workers and those on non-standard contracts and for family-friendly benefits and flexible working. In other cases, the pressure emanating from non-union institutions acts in the same broad direction as that from unions, with both types of institution seeking to raise pay for low earners, reduce inequality and make reward management more formal and transparent. Nevertheless, there can also be conflict and rivalry and this is most apparent in the activities of solicitors representing women workers in equal pay cases, who have on occasion attacked trade unions and the collective agreements to which they are party.

The other theme that emerges from the review of non-union institutions is that of their effectiveness. Examples have been given of civil society organisations campaigning for living wages and for more equal and family-friendly benefits and of legal representatives securing major changes in the pay of women workers in public services. In other cases, however, the effectiveness of non-union representation seems rather limited and this appears to be particularly the case with employer-sponsored systems of participation, which generate few discernible reward effects. Moreover, even when non-union bodies have been effective the scale of their action has often been modest, confined to particular localities, categories of worker or economic sectors. The great historical achievement of trade unions has been to shape the broad pattern of reward outcomes within the economy and it remains to be seen if other institutions of worker voice can generate equivalent effects. Perhaps the best outcome for the future is for these non-union institutions to continue to expand and work cooperatively with unions but for unions themselves to undergo a process of renewal that will enhance the positive effects on reward management described above.

Note

1 The observations on CSOs in this chapter are informed by joint research undertaken with Brian Abbott and Stephen Williams on 'Civil Society Organisations and Worker Representation', funded by the Nuffield Foundation.

References

Arrowsmith, J., Marginson, P. and Gray, M. (2008) 'Variable pay: undermining collective bargaining?', *IRRU Briefing*, 16: 1–3.

Arulampalam, W. and Booth, A. (1998) 'Training and labour market flexibility: is there a trade-off?', *British Journal of Industrial Relations*, 36 (4): 521–36.

Baddon, L., Hunter, L., Hyman, J., Leopold, J. and Ramsay, H. (1989) *People's Capitalism? A Critical Analysis of Profit-Sharing and Employee Share Ownership*, London: Routledge.

Bennett, J.T. and Kaufman, B.E. (eds) (2007) *What Do Unions Do? A Twenty-year Perspective*, New Brunswick and London: Transaction Publishers.

Bernstein, J. (2005) 'The living wage movement: what is it, why is it, and what is known about its impact?', in R.B. Freeman, J. Hersch and L. Mishel (eds) *Emerging Labor Market Institutions in the Twenty-First Century*, Chicago and London: University of Chicago Press.

Bewley, H. (2006) 'Raising the standard? The regulation of employment and public sector employment policy', *British Journal of Industrial Relations*, 44 (2): 351–72.

Bewley, H. and Fernie, S. (2003) 'What do unions do for women?', in H. Gospel and S. Wood (eds) *Representing Workers: Union Recognition and Membership in Britain*, London: Routledge.

Blanchflower, D. G. and Bryson, A. (2002) *Changes Over Time in Union Relative Wage Effects in the UK and US Revisited*, NBER Working Paper No. 9395.

Blanchflower, D. G. and Oswald, A. (1990) 'The determinants of white collar pay', *Oxford Economic Papers*, 42: 356–78.

Blanchflower, D. G., Bryson, A. and Forth, J. (2007) 'Workplace industrial relations in Britain, 1980–2004', *Industrial Relations Journal*, 38 (4): 285–302.

Booth, A. L. (1995) *The Economics of the Trade Union*, Cambridge: Cambridge University Press.

Briscoe, F. and Safford, S. (2008) 'The Nixon in China effect: activism, imitation and the diffusion of domestic partner benefits', *Administrative Science Quarterly*, 53 (3).

Brown, W. (1973) *Piecework Bargaining*, London: Heinemann.

Brown, W., Deakin, S., Hudson, M., Pratten, C. and Ryan, P. (1998) *The Individualization of Employment Contracts in Britain*, Employment Relations Research Series 4, London: Department of Trade and Industry.

Bryson, A. (2007) 'The effect of trade unions on wages', *Reflets et Perspectives*, XLVI (2/3): 33–45.

Bryson, A. and Forth, J. (2008) 'The theory and practice of pay-setting', in N. Bacon, P. Blyton, J. Fiorito and E. Heery (eds) *The Handbook of Industrial Relations*, London: Sage.

Budd, J. W. (2007) 'The effect of unions on employee benefits and non-wage compensation: monopoly power, collective voice, and facilitation', in J. T. Bennett and B. E. Kaufman (eds) *What Do Unions Do? A Twenty-year Perspective*, New Brunswick and London: Transaction Publishers.

Budd, J. W. and Mumford, K. (2004) 'Trade unions and family-friendly policies in Britain', *Industrial and Labor Relations Review*, 53 (1): 204–22.

Calmfors, L., Booth, A., Burda, M., Checchi, D., Naylor, R. and Visser, J. (2001) 'The future of collective bargaining in Europe', in T. Boeri, A. Brugiavini and L. Calmfors (eds) *The Role of Unions in the Twenty-First Century*, Oxford: Oxford University Press.

Card, D., Lemieux, T. and Riddell, W. C. (2007) 'Unions and wage inequality', in J. T. Bennett and B. E. Kaufman (eds) *What Do Unions Do? A Twenty-year Perspective*, New Brunswick and London: Transaction Publishers.

Charlwood, A. and Terry, M. (2007) '21st century models of employee representation: structures, processes and outcomes', *Industrial Relations Journal*, 38 (4): 320–37.

Colling, T. and Dickens, L. (1998) 'Selling the case for gender equality: deregulation and equality bargaining', *British Journal of Industrial Relations*, 36 (3): 389–411.

Crouch, C. (1982) *Trade Unions: The Logic of Collective Action*, Glasgow: Fontana.

Cully, M., O'Reilly, A., Millward, N., Forth, J., Woodland, S., Dix, G. and Bryson, A. (1998) *The 1998 Workplace Employee Relations Survey: First Findings*, London: Department of Trade and Industry.

Davies, P. and Freedland, M. (2007) *Towards a Flexible Labour Market: Labour Legislation and Regulation Since the 1990s*, Oxford: Oxford University Press.

Dickens, L. (1989) 'Women – a rediscovered resource?', *Industrial Relations Journal*, 20 (3): 167–75.

Eaton, A. E. and Voos, P. (1992) 'Unions and contemporary innovations in work organisation, compensation and employee participation', in L. Mishel and P. Voos (eds) *Unions and Economic Competitiveness*, Armonk, NY: M.E. Sharpe.

Edwards, C. and Heery, E. (1989) *Management Control and Union Power: A Study of Labour Relations in Coalmining*, Oxford: Clarendon Press.

Falkner, G. (1998) *EU Social Policy in the 1990s: Towards a Corporatist Policy Community*, London: Routledge.

Firestein, N. and Dones, N. (2007) 'Unions fight for work and family policies – not for women only', in D. S. Cobble (ed.) *The Sex of Class*, Ithaca and London: ILR Press.

Forth, J. W. and Millward, N. (2000) *The Determinants of Pay Levels and Fringe Benefit Provision in Britain*, NIESR Discussion Paper 171, London: National Institute of Economic and Social Research.

Freeman, R. B. (1992) 'Is declining unionisation of the US good, bad or irrelevant?', in L. Mishel and P. B. Voos (eds) *Unions and Economic Competitiveness*, Armonk, NY: M.E. Sharpe.

Freeman, R. B. (2005) 'Fighting for other folks' wages: the logic and illogic of living wage campaigns', *Industrial Relations*, 44 (1): 14–31.

Freeman, R. B. (2007a) *America Works*, New York: Russell Sage Foundation.

Freeman, R. B. (2007b) '*What Do Unions Do?* The 2004 M-Brain stringtwister edition', in J. T. Bennett and B. E. Kaufman (eds) *What Do Unions Do? A Twenty-year Perspective*, New Brunswick and London: Transaction Publishers.

Geddes, L. and Heywood, J. S. (2003) 'Gender, piece rates, commissions and bonuses', *Industrial Relations*, 42 (3): 419–42.

Gilbert, K. and Secker, J. (1995) 'Generating equality? Equal pay, decentralisation and the electricity supply industry', *British Journal of Industrial Relations*, 33 (2): 191–207.

Grainger, H. and Crowther, M. (2007) *Trade Union Membership 2006*, London: Department of Trade and Industry.

Heery, E. (1997a) 'Performance-related pay and trade union derecognition', *Employee Relations*, 19 (5): 208–21.

Heery, E. (1997b) 'Performance-related pay and trade union membership', *Employee Relations*, 19 (5): 430–42.

Heery, E. (2006) 'Bargaining for balance: union policy on work-life balance in the United Kingdom', in P. Blyton, B. Blundon, K. Reed and A. Dastmalchian (eds) *Work-Life Integration: International Perspectives on the Balancing of Multiple Roles*, Basingstoke: Palgrave Macmillan.

Heery, E. and Conley, H. (2007) 'Frame extension in a mature social movement: British trade unions and part-time work, 1967–2002', *The Journal of Industrial Relations*, 49 (1): 5–30.

Heery, E. and Warhurst, J. (1994) *Performance-related Pay and Trade Unions: Impact and Response*, Kingston Business School Occasional Paper, Kingston-upon-Thames: Kingston University.

Heery, E., Conley, H., Delbridge, R., Simms, M. and Stewart, P. (2004) 'Trade union responses to non-standard work', in G. Healy, E. Heery, P. Taylor and W. Brown (eds) *The Future of Worker Representation*, Basingstoke: Palgrave Macmillan.

Heywood, J. S. and Jirjahn, U. (2006) 'Performance pay: determinants and consequences', in D. Lewin (ed.) *Contemporary Issues in Employment Relations*, Champaign IL: Labor and Employment Relations Association.

Heywood, J. S., Seibert, W. S. and Wei, X. (1997) 'Payment by results systems: British evidence', *British Journal of Industrial Relations*, 35 (1): 1–22.

Holgate, J. and Wills, J. (2007) 'Organizing labor in London: lessons from the campaign for a living wage', in L. Turner and D. B. Cornfield (eds) *Labor in the New Urban Battlegrounds: Local Solidarity in a Global Economy*, Ithaca and London: ILR Press.

Jackson, M. P., Leopold, J. W. and Tuck, K. (1993) *Decentralisation of Collective Bargaining: An Analysis of Recent Experience in the UK*, Basingstoke: Macmillan.

Kersley, B., Alpin, C., Forth, J., Bryson, A., Bewley, H., Dix, G. and Oxenbridge, S. (2006) *Inside the Workplace: Findings from the 2004 Workplace Employment Relations Survey*, London: Routledge.

Kessler, I. (1994) 'Performance-related pay: contrasting approaches', *Industrial Relations Journal*, 25 (2): 122–35.

Kessler, I. (2001) 'Reward system choices', in J. Storey (ed.) *Human Resource Management: A Critical Text*, 2nd edn, London: Routledge.

Lawler III, E. E. (1990) *Strategic Pay*, San Francisco: Jossey-Bass.

LGE (2006) *Unblocking the Route to Equal Pay in Local Government*, London: Local Government Employers.

Luce, S. (2007) 'The US living wage movement: building coalitions from the local level in a global economy', in L. Turner and D. B. Cornfield (eds) *Labor in the New Urban Battlegrounds: Local Solidarity in a Global Economy*, Ithaca and London: ILR Press.

Marsden, D. and Belfield, R. (2005) 'Unions and performance related pay: what chance of a procedural role?', in S. Fernie and D. Metcalf (eds) *Trade Unions: Resurgence or Demise?* London: Routledge.

McGovern, P., Hill, S., Mills, C. and White, M. (2007) *Market, Class and Employment*, Oxford: Oxford University Press.

McNabb, R. and Whitfield, K. (2007) 'The impact of varying types of performance-related pay and employee participation on earnings', *International Journal of Human Resource Management*, 18 (6): 1004–25.

Metcalf, D. (1994) 'Transformation of British industrial relations? Institutions, conduct and outcomes 1980–1990', in R. Barrell (ed.) *The UK Labour Market*, Cambridge: Cambridge University Press.

Metcalf, D. (2005) 'Trade unions: resurgence or perdition?', in S. Fernie and D. Metcalf (eds) *Trade Unions: Resurgence or Demise?*, London: Routledge.

Millward, N., Stevens, M., Smart, D. and Hawes, W. R. (1992) *Workplace Industrial Relations in Transition*, Aldershot: Dartmouth.

Slichter, S. H., Healey, J. J. and Livernash, E. R. (1960) *The Impact of Collective Bargaining on Management*, Washington DC: The Brookings Institution.

Stonewall (2008) *Workplace Equality Index 2008. The Best 100 Employers for Lesbians, Gays and Bisexuals*, London: Stonewall.

Visser, J. (1998) 'Two cheers for corporatism, one for the market: industrial relations, wage moderation and job growth in the Netherlands', *British Journal of Industrial Relations*, 36 (2): 269–92.

White, M., Hill, S., Mills, C. and Smeaton, D. (2004) *Managing to Change? British Workplaces and the Future of Work*, Basingstoke: Palgrave Macmillan.

Wills, J. (2004) 'Organising the low paid: East London's living wage campaign as a vehicle for change', in G. Healy, E. Heery, P. Taylor and W. Brown (eds) *The Future of Worker Representation*, Basingstoke: Palgrave.

4 Grading systems, estimating value and equality

Sue Hastings

Summary

This chapter examines the background to modern grading systems and the influence of cultural, social and legal factors. The first section considers the origins of British grading systems for 'manual' and 'non-manual' workers and the legacy of these distinct histories for present-day structures. The second section outlines current grading techniques, reviewing competence-based pay (CBP) systems and job evaluation schemes.

The impact of equal value legislation on the measurement of job worth is identified through descriptions of a number of key equal pay claims. The implications of these Tribunal decisions for the design and implementation of job evaluation schemes and the development of grading structures is considered, with analysis of recent systems in the health service and local government sectors, and an assessment of the continuing importance of the concept of equal value for grading and pay in the UK. The chapter concludes with a comment on the future of grading, suggesting that job evaluation is the approach most obviously consistent with equal pay legislation, but developed in more flexible forms than was historically the case.

Introduction

Classical economists argue that wage rates represent the price at which the supply and demand for labour coincide (Sapsford and Tzannatos 1993). Whilst organisations may position their pay structures in relation to the (perceived) 'going rate' for the relevant types of work, and structural shortages are likely to lead to increases in salaries for the group in question, the theory is inadequate as a means of explaining pay practice. It does not tell personnel practitioners how to deliver a stable pay structure, nor how to allow for the serious lags and imperfections in the market. Nor does it provide personnel managers with a satisfactory way of grading and paying jobs that are unique to the organisation (Sapsford and Tzannatos 1993; Jacobsen 1998: 203–342). Macro-economic theorists also have difficulty explaining how economic forces result in discrimination in favour of some and against other groups of employees, apparently regardless of the relative efficiency of these groups. The reality is that the labour market provides only part of the explanation for pay determination. Individual pay rates are set, not only against the labour market, but also by reference to a system of micro-economic internal relativities – the organisational grading structure.

This chapter examines the background to modern grading systems and the influence of cultural, social and legal factors. In the first section we consider the origins of British grading systems; the second outlines current grading techniques, reviewing competence-based pay (CBP) systems and job evaluation. We then discuss the impact of equal value legislation and its continuing importance for job evaluation. The chapter concludes with a comment on the future of grading.

The historical development of modern British grading systems

British grading systems for 'manual' and 'non-manual' groups have existed and developed, until recently, quite separately – a separation that has been perpetuated by collective bargaining systems.

The origins of manual pay structures

Manual work, for men at least, was broadly divided into skilled and unskilled, with the skilled work being reserved for those who served apprenticeships, or an equivalent form of work-related training. Pay rates were determined according to this broad, skill-based banding system. In many organisations a semi-skilled band was also created and subsequently subdivided into numerous rates, negotiated individually or collectively, as they were needed. The social construction of skill discriminated against women. Female workers in manufacturing establishments did not usually have access to guild or craft training. Their jobs were, for the most part, regarded by employers and by skilled male workers as unskilled. Women were therefore paid less than unskilled men, regardless of the tasks on which they were actually employed. These lower rates became institutionalised into separate women's rates, usually for different or distinctly separate jobs. Skill-based grading structures prevailed until the 1970s and 1980s, and can still be seen in some smaller organisations. However, large-scale industrialisation led to the introduction of more sophisticated techniques, for example, payment by results (PBR) systems. Such systems generally retained the old skill-based classifications but allowed workers to earn more than the standard rate for their grade of work, essentially by completing designated tasks in a lower time than that allocated.

Women's jobs, notably in the textile and clothing sectors, were also subjected to payment by results. Although some women proved adept at increasing their levels of dexterity and co-ordination, and thus their rate of work and pay, this did not alter the underlying pattern of discrimination.[1]

The origins of non-manual structures

Significant numbers of non-manual jobs developed only with industrialisation and with the accompanying growth of employment in the retail and finance sectors, in office and administrative jobs and in state employment. Wages for clerical staff were generally low compared with those for production employees.

Incentives to remain with the employing company were provided by seniority or age-related scales, whereby employees received a small increase on their birthday or on the anniversary of starting with the firm. The underlying assumption was that clerical employees higher up an age-related scale would have more knowledge of the organisation's procedures and thus be able to undertake more demanding work, including supervising less experienced clerical staff. Such service – or age-related – pay scales provide the origins of traditional annual incremental scales for non-manual employees, just as skill-related rates of pay provide the origins of flat 'rate for the job' pay systems for manual workers once entry training was completed.

Large corporations and the development of job evaluation systems

Techniques of job evaluation were originally developed in the United States of America before and immediately after the Second World War. The aim was to find methods that would provide for non-manual administrative and managerial jobs in large public corporations a systematic basis for grading and pay similar to that provided by work study techniques for manual and production-related jobs. Practitioners were also interested in identifying the job features that determined labour market rates for white-collar employees – as levels of skill were seen as doing for manual workers (Benge *et al.* 1941; Patton *et al.* 1964). One of these early practitioners was Edward Hay, whose Guide Chart Profile system of job evaluation was refined into its present form in the years immediately following 1945 (Hay and Purves 1954).

Some job evaluation (JE) systems involve developing a job hierarchy, either by putting them in rank order on the basis of information about the jobs as a whole, or by matching them against criteria in a job classification system. Such whole-job rank order and classification systems of JE are much less common than they used to be. They cannot deal with the complexities of modern organisations and may be open to challenge on discrimination grounds, although they are still described in current JE textbooks (Armstrong and Baron 1995: 51–64; Pritchard and Murlis 1992: 51–55; Armstrong *et al.* 2003: 18–23).

However, what the Hay System and most other job evaluation techniques had in common, then as now, was (a) the analysis of jobs under a set of factor headings agreed to be suitable for the job population in question; and (b) the assessment of each job against factor scales (usually but not always predetermined) to give a total score for each job. The third feature of these techniques was the weighting of factors, initially to reflect the perceived value placed by the labour market on each, but subsequently modified to reflect organisational values (ILO 1986).

Job evaluation techniques were introduced to Britain in the early 1950s – in the insurance sector and subsequently in other large, predominantly white-collar companies in the private sector, and to managerial groups in many organisations.

JE for manual workers

The use of JE for manual worker groups was rare in Britain until the mid-1960s. Around this time some management consultants, notably in Urwick Orr (subsequently part of Price Waterhouse) and Inbucon (now part of PE), began adapting the techniques for manual jobs – as Urwick Orr did for Ford production workers in 1967.

In 1968 the National Board for Prices and Incomes (NBPI) published a report specifically on job evaluation (National Board for Prices and Incomes 1968). The report recommended the adoption of JE as a mechanism for rationalising the very complex structures that had developed for manual groups in the public sector. As a direct result of this and similar recommendations in sectoral reports, JE schemes were developed and implemented, for example, for ancillary workers in the National Health Service and manual workers in local government (both Urwick Orr schemes).

Following these initial public sector exercises, separate schemes were designed during the 1970s to cover non-manual groups in the public sector – for example, the Administrative, Professional, Technical and Clerical (APT & C) group in local government.

These schemes were developed to match traditional collective bargaining groups. So a single company in the private sector might, by the 1980s, have three or four different JE schemes in operation to cover its distinct bargaining groups. Alternatively they might use JE for some groups and other grading and pay systems for others. In the banking sector, for example, there was a sector-wide JE scheme covering clerical, secretarial and administrative staff. Each major bank had its own grading and pay structures for what were known as the appointed grades (professional, financial and managerial jobs), often using the Hay Guide Chart System of JE; and all had non-evaluated, skill-related structures for their messenger (and other manual) employees.

Current grading techniques

These historical developments have influenced current grading techniques. Within this section we focus on competence-based payment systems and JE, first mentioning briefly market rate systems of internal relativities.

Market rates as the basis for internal relativities

All organisations aim to set their pay structures at a level at which they can adequately recruit and retain employees to their mainstream functions, even if it then means paying more to 'hard to recruit' groups (see Chapter 2, Determining Pay).

Some organisations go further and use market rates as the basis for determining internal relativities. They are thus allowing the external market to determine their internal relativities. There are advantages to such systems for organisations employing high proportions of specialist jobs and low proportions of generalists. They are simple to operate, as benchmarking data is usually bought in, and they avoid the high administrative costs of JE or competence-based systems for determining internal relativities. They generally deliver good rates of pay to specialists, who therefore accept the system and the secrecy that tends to go with it.

The use of external market rates as the sole basis for internal wage relativities can be problematic in a number of respects:

- Such systems are not as objective as they sound. The concept of a market rate is elusive (Armstrong 2002: 162–81) and without scientific foundation (Gomez-Mejia and Balkin 1992). Market rate data is reliant for its quality on its sources, other organisations, and these are difficult to control.
- Pay benchmarking for individual job rates also relies heavily on the information used for job matching against the market data. Job titles can be misleading and short pen portraits only a little better.

Market rates may incorporate historic gender pay discrimination from the provider organisations. Moreover, the data is not always applied in the same manner to men and women.

Competence-based payment systems

There has been growing employer interest in competence-related frameworks to cover all employees (often referred to as skills-based pay for manual workers), as the basis for recruitment, redundancy, promotion and training policies, in order to secure the best return on investment in human resources. Some organisations have linked their competence frameworks to pay. What these have in common is that they reward individuals for the broad competencies (not just traditional skills, or formal qualifications) required for the work, and often also for the acquisition of additional competencies.

Competence as the basis for grading

Where competence is used as the basis for grading, jobs are graded by reference to the overall competencies required, usually by reference to an objective standard, such as National Vocational Qualifications (NVQs) or the Scottish equivalent (SVQs). The difference between this type of grading structure and a traditional skills-based structure is that the former encompasses a wider range of skills. Competencies may include written and oral communication skills, information technology and record-keeping skills, as well as technical and manual skills. They can, therefore, accommodate non-manual as well as manual jobs.

Competence as the basis for both grading and pay progression

Here jobs are graded by reference to the competencies required, as defined by an objective standard, as for the previous category. However, progression up the pay scale or within the pay range also depends on the acquisition of additional competencies, often within modules leading towards the next broad competence band. One example is the Scottish Power's Generation Wholesale Division (GWD), covering all its power station and associated head office staff, from industrial and clerical assistants through craft-trained electricians and qualified electrical engineers to power station managers (Adams 1993). All roles were assimilated into one of six bands according to reference to SVQs for technical, professional and administrative occupational groups (with some additional modules specifically designed for unique power generation roles). Progression within the band salary range for individuals depends on the acquisition of additional competence modules along pre-determined pathways for particular occupational groups.

The Scottish Power example illustrates the advantages of competence-based pay (CBP). Management wanted a more flexible workforce, able to increase production without the need to employ more people. Employees and their union representatives wanted the opportunity to acquire additional skills, and to be paid for doing so. This example also illustrates the potential disadvantages and possibly explains why few organisations have adopted comprehensive competence-based pay systems (CBI/Hay Group 1995: 22–3). Linking competence to pay requires substantial investment in training facilities and competence assessment systems, so that all employees have the opportunity to increase competence and pay levels. Even with this investment, a rationing procedure is required, as not all employees can be released for competence-related training at the same time.

Other obstacles for employers, however, to a CBP system are the difficulties of making accurate assessments of competencies (Sparrow 1996); and concerns over whether competency-based pay systems can meet with legal equality requirements (Adams 1996; Gilbert *et al.* 1996). The result is that there are relatively few examples of competence-based basic pay structures to be found, but the ideas behind them have influenced changes to JE techniques.

JE

By the 1980s, traditional job evaluation techniques were appearing outmoded because of changes in technology and work organisation (Grayson 1982 and 1987).

The 2004 Workplace Employment Relations Survey found job evaluation recorded in 20 per cent of the surveyed workplaces, 25 per cent of those with over 25 employees. This is similar to the proportions in 1990, the main difference being a significant increase in the percentage of public sector workplaces with JE, from 27 per cent in 1990 to 44 per cent of those with over 25 employees in 2004 (with a corresponding decrease in use in the private sector). There also appears to have been an increase in the incidence of points rating, as opposed to whole job, systems of job from around 45 per cent to 60 per cent of JE users. JE systems were more commonly found in workplaces where women were in the majority, than the reverse, 24 per cent compared with 17 per cent (Kersley *et al.* 2006: 244–7). There are a number of possible reasons for the spread of JE, particularly in the public sector.

First, changes in technology and work organisation have in practice led to JE becoming more flexible. Second, JE systems are no longer restricted to traditional collective bargaining groups, but have become broader in coverage, a development which has necessitated re-thinking some of the techniques, for example, making factor-level definitions more generic to cover different families or types of jobs. Third, instead of evaluating tightly defined sets of tasks, JE techniques have been adapted to cover more flexible, sometimes multi-skilled roles (Pritchard and Murlis 1992).

Additionally, JE techniques have been adapted to incorporate the concepts of competency by, for example, placing increased emphasis on broad skill-related factors. An example of this is the Higher Education Role Analysis (HERA) system, developed by a consortium of higher education institutions to cover all jobs in their sector, 'from porter to professor', as their publicity material says (Education Competences Consortium 1998). The HERA scheme elements for analysis are set out in Figure 4.1.

1. Communication
2. Teamwork and motivation
3. Liaison and networking
4. Service delivery
5. Decision-making processes and outcomes and organising resources
6. Initiative and problem solving
7. Investigation, analysis and research
8. Sensory and physical co-ordination
9. Work environment
10. Pastoral care and welfare
11. Coaching, development and instruction
12. Teaching and training
13. Knowledge and experience

Figure 4.1 Higher educational role analysis elements

Equal value legislation has encouraged employers to adopt JE for all employees, and, arguably, is increasingly influencing the nature of modern job evaluation.

Because this has major implications for grading structures, it is considered in more detail in the next section. However, the debate on the merits or otherwise of JE as a basis for internal relativities continues. For example, McNabb and Whitfield demonstrate that organisations with both analytical job evaluation and a high performance system are less likely to have above average financial performance than those with either of these on a single basis and suggest that this means that there is a potential incompatibility between some types of JE and high performance approaches (McNabb and Whitfield 2001: 293–312). Sliedregt *et al.* argue that there is only partial correlation between job evaluation scores and market pay rates (2001: 1313–24). Arnault *et al.* find that different evaluators, using the same job information and evaluation system, come up with different outcomes (2001). This result will be of no surprise to evaluation practitioners and illustrates the need for trained panels, rather than individuals, and thorough consistency checking.

The impact of 'equal value'

As we have seen, jobs typically undertaken by women, whether manual or non-manual, were historically often categorised as unskilled or less skilled than those of men. This became institutionalised in separate, and lower, women's rates of pay, which prevailed in many sectors until the mid-1970s – particularly in the private sector and among manual groups in the public sector in Britain. Although women's average earnings are lower than men's in most countries for which statistics are collected, most other European Union (EU) member states have equal pay provisions written into their constitutions or other fundamental legal framework; and in many member states the gender earnings gap is significantly smaller than in Britain (Jacobsen 1998: 350–3).

So, for example, at the Ford Motor Company before a new job-evaluated structure was introduced in 1967, there were effectively four grades for production workers, if account is taken of the separate grade for women (Friedman and Meredeen 1980: 44; see Figure 4.2).

The largest single group of female Ford production workers at that time comprised sewing machinists, who earned 92 per cent of the basic rates of men undertaking unskilled jobs and 80 per cent of the male semi-skilled rate

Male – Skilled
Male – Semi-skilled
Male – Unskilled
Female

Figure 4.2 Ford grading structure pre-1967

(*Report of a Court of Inquiry under Sir Jack Scamp* 1968: paras 13–5). Similar grading and pay structures prevailed in many other manufacturing companies.

British equal pay legislation

The principle of 'equal pay for work of equal value' was embodied in Article 41 of the Constitution of the International Labour Organisation at the end of the First World War (*Report of the Royal Commission on Equal Pay* 1946). However, in the UK there was little progress until Herbert Morrison, then a Minister in the National Government, set up a Royal Commission on Equal Pay in 1944. The Royal Commission concluded that equal pay for equal work, in the sense of the same rate for the job, could be introduced in what they termed 'overlap areas' (where men and women worked interchangeably) for non-industrial civil servants, teachers, and local government officers (*Report of the Royal Commission on Equal Pay* 1946: para. 563). As a result of these recommendations equal pay for the same work in the non-manual public sector was achieved gradually and by negotiation with recognised trade unions during the early 1950s. Women teachers, female civil servants and local government employees all received equal pay for the same work as men during this period.

The moves towards equal pay for the same work did not extend into the private sector, nor did they cover manual women workers in the public sector. One of the reasons for this was the very high degree of occupational segregation, and thus absence of 'overlap', in these areas. But the absence of equal pay legislation was a cause for concern amongst the emerging women's and civil liberties groups of the late 1950s and early 1960s. Their campaigning contributed to the inclusion in the Labour Party Manifesto in 1964 of a commitment to introduce legislation on equal pay.

The Equal Pay Act (EPA) became law in 1970. It might never have been passed had it not been for the Ford sewing machinists. In 1966–7, the Ford Motor Company commissioned consultants, Urwick Orr & Partners, to develop and implement a job evaluation scheme covering production and craft jobs (*Report of a Court of Inquiry under Sir Jack Scamp* 1968). The resulting grading structure, introduced from July 1967, had five broad grades, as set out in Figure 4.3.

The job of sewing machinist was one of 56 benchmark jobs used as the basis for designing the system. It came out in grade B; however, as this was before the 1970 Equal Pay Act, the machinists were not paid the full grade B rate,

E – Most skilled craft jobs
D – Less skilled craft jobs
C – More skilled production jobs
B – Less skilled production jobs
A – Unskilled jobs

Figure 4.3 Ford grading structure from July 1967

but only 85 per cent of it. The sewing machinists were incensed, first because they received only 85 per cent of the rate for men doing work in the same grade as themselves, but second on account of the grade of the job. They thought their jobs should have been in grade C. They took industrial action and, as cars cannot be sold without seat covers, rapidly brought production to a halt (*Report of a Court of Inquiry under Sir Jack Scamp* 1968).

The dispute was resolved in 1968 following a meeting with Barbara Castle, at the Department of Employment and Productivity, which hastened the introduction of legislation (Friedman and Meredeen 1980). The agreement awarded the sewing machinists 100 per cent of the male grade B rate phased in over two years; and established a public court of inquiry to examine the grading of the job. By 1971 they were receiving the full grade B rate, but the Court of Inquiry concluded that the dispute was 'about the grading of sewing machinists, not about equal pay', and recommended an internal review committee with an independent chairman, which ultimately confirmed the grade B rate (*Report of the Proceedings of a Special Ad Hoc Joint Committee under the Chairmanship of J. Grange Moore Esq.* 1968: para. 6).

By introducing an implied equality clause into the contracts of all employees, the 1970 Equal Pay Act (EPA) had the effect of making separate women's rates of pay illegal.[2] The EPA also provided for those not receiving equal pay for 'like work' to be able to take claims to an industrial tribunal (IT).[3] Employers were allowed until 1975 to eliminate separate lower rates. The response of many was to raise the women's rate to the lowest male rate, regardless of the comparative skill levels. Some employers introduced job evaluation schemes, which often weighted highly factors such as physical effort and traditional skills, thus achieving a similar effect by a supposedly objective means (Ghobadian and White 1995: 9–10).

European equal pay legislation

In the meantime, the original members of the European Economic Community had signed the Treaty of Rome in 1957. Article 119 provided for 'equal pay for equal work' between men and women.[4] This was amplified in the Equal Pay Directive of 1975,[5] to require 'equal pay for work of equal value', although without definition of the concept, except to say that job classification systems (which are taken in European terminology to encompass job evaluation schemes) should be free from discrimination. This was expanded and consolidated as Article 141 of the Treaty of Amsterdam (sometimes referred to as the Treaty of Maastricht), effective in the UK from May 1999. The Equal Pay Directive of 1975 also required member governments to have legislation to provide for national enforcement of its provisions.

The European Commission decided to take the UK government to the European Court of Justice (ECJ) on the issue of 'equal value'. In spite of the 'work rated as equivalent' clause of the EPA, the ECJ was satisfied that a significant proportion of women fell outside the scope of 'equal value' (IRLR 1982). The result was the Equal Pay (Amendment) Regulations of 1983,[6] which, from 1 January 1994, added a third ground for a complaint to an industrial tribunal – where an applicant considered that her work was of 'equal value' to that of a male comparator in the same employment. The concept of 'equal value' is not defined in the amended Act, except to say that the jobs of applicant and comparator should be compared 'under such headings as effort, skill and decision'.

The impact of the 'equal value' clause of the EPA has been delayed and diluted by the cumbersome procedures enacted for determining the question of equal value, and by the legal issues raised on behalf of employers apparently aimed at thwarting the intentions of the legislation. However, there have been a number of successful cases, which illustrate how work typically undertaken by women has been historically undervalued.

Hayward v. Cammell Laird

Julie Hayward was a cook employed by Cammell Laird in the canteen at their Birkenhead shipyard. Supported by her union, the GMBATU (now GMB), she claimed equal pay for work of equal value with male craft workers – a shipboard painter, a joiner and a thermal insulation engineer – who received higher craft rates of basic pay once they had all completed their apprenticeships. The case continued for many years through the appeal courts. The House of Lords eventually decided in her favour (IRLR 1988). The key issue for the purpose of this chapter was that the work of a City & Guilds qualified cook had been found to be of equal value to that of male apprentice trained craft workers.

Enderby v. Frenchay Health Authority

Dr Pam Enderby was the legal test case for around 1,200 speech therapists, who in 1987 claimed equal pay for work of equal value with clinical psychologists and hospital pharmacists. The Health Service employers argued that, because the pay of the three groups was determined under separate collective bargaining arrangements (separate Whitley Council sub-committees), this provided a 'genuine material factor' defence to the equal pay claims. This argument was eventually turned down by the European Court of Justice (IRLR 1993: 591).

The question of 'equal value' was not considered by any IT until 1995, when 20 'lead cases' were referred to a team of independent experts. The first report to be considered by the IT was in the case of *Evesham v. West Hertfordshire*. The applicant, Margaret Evesham, was in 1987 a district speech therapist, responsible for the speech therapy services for the District Health Authority (DHA) and with additional responsibilities for co-ordination of para-medical services, including clinical psychology. Her comparator was a district clinical psychologist, responsible for the clinical psychology services for the DHA and with additional specialist responsibilities for personally providing psycho-therapy services. The IT found the applicant's work to be of equal value to that of her comparator.[7] More radically, in another claim, the industrial tribunal considered the question, previously avoided by most tribunals, of 'what is equal value' and effectively found that 'almost equal value' is 'equal value', if the jobs would have come in the same grade 'in the real world'.[8] The tribunal concluded (para. 31):

> The Tribunal ... finds that there is no ... measurable and significant difference in the demands made upon Mrs. Worsfold as compared to her comparator. It is supported by this in the evidence of [the Independent Expert] to the Tribunal that if he as a manager were grading the job for job evaluation purposes the difference would not lead to a difference in grading in the real world. The Tribunal therefore concludes that the Applicant was engaged on work of equal value with that of her comparator.

The Employment Appeals Tribunal subsequently confirmed this decision.

In these speech therapist cases, the IT found equal value in relation to specialist and professional management posts in a typically female caring occupation, which had traditionally been paid substantially less than the male-dominated medical and related Health Service professions. It is clear that these cases have major implications for all the female-dominated care professions, and indeed for future grading and pay determination for professional groups in the Health Service (Department of Health 1999).

Hayes and Quinn v. Mancunian Community NHS Trust

The applicants in this case were dental surgery assistants, who having tried and failed to secure regrading to the highest relevant grade, in 1993 submitted tribunal claims for equal pay for work of equal value. Their comparators were a senior dental technician, a senior mortuary technician and a technical instructor, employed by an occupational therapy department to provide and supervise woodworking and upholstery activities to assist in-patient/client rehabilitation. Of these, the best paid was the senior dental technician, followed by the technical instructor and then the senior mortuary technician. The applicants and the three comparators were covered by four separate collective bargaining agreements.

The claims were referred to an independent expert whose report concluded that the applicants' jobs were of equal value to that of the technical instructor, but not to those of the other named comparators. The tribunal confirmed the independent expert's findings and awarded equal pay with the technical instructor.[9]

Wilson and Others v. Carlisle Hospitals NHS Trust

Mrs Wilson and her colleagues occupied a range of lower paid jobs in the health service. They were cooks, catering assistants, domestic assistants on wards and in theatres and laboratories, domestic supervisors, sewing room assistants, sterilising department assistants, clerical assistants, telephonists, nursing assistants and some lower graded nurses. They compared themselves with higher paid craft workers and supervisors, maintenance labourers and a medical electronics technician.

The claims were referred to Independent Experts in 2000. The Independent Experts found that, for example, the jobs of the domestic assistants and clerical assistants were of equal value to those of the maintenance labourers; the nursing assistants and domestic supervisors were of equal value to the craft workers; and the qualified nurse claimants' jobs were of equal value to craft supervisors and the medical electronics technician. Their findings largely confirmed those coming out of the Agenda for Change exercise (see p. 92).

Mrs M. McKechnie & Others v. Gloucestershire County Council

The applicants were nursery nurses employed by the County Council in a number of settings, for example, a special school for children with severe physical disabilities, a family centre, a pre-school opportunity centre for children with communication delay or disability, and an infant school class assisting the class teacher. Under the terms of a national agreement they were employed on a scale equivalent to 2/3 on the local government APT & C structure. The applicants, supported by their union UNISON, claimed equal pay for work of equal value, on a rate per hour basis, with a waste technician, in the Environmental Health Department, graded and paid on scale 6 of the APT & C structure; and an architectural technician, graded and paid on the next higher grade, Senior Officer (SO) 1. After hearing expert evidence, the tribunal effectively re-assessed the jobs themselves. They found the work of the applicants to be of equal value to both their named comparators.[10]

Once again, an IT had found in favour of applicants in a female-dominated caring occupation, whose work has traditionally been undervalued and under-paid. The decision was significant because of the large numbers of women working as qualified nursery nurses in both the public and private sectors, and the consequent cost implications.

Bailey & Others v. the Home Office (Prison Service)

These claims concerned Prison Service administrative staff at different levels, who sought to compare themselves with men in operational grades – prison officers and prison support officers. The starting point for the claims was the 1990 Woolf Report into the prison service, which recommended, among other things, that the pay and conditions of administrative staff should be reviewed.

Benchmark jobs from across the service, including operational and governor grades as well as administrative grades, were used for the review. Some of the claimants' jobs were found to be of equal value to previously higher-paid operational and governor roles.

It was originally envisaged that the job evaluation outcomes would be implemented in two phases. Phase 1 would cover the highest of the administrative grades (HEOs) and governor grades; phase 2 would cover the rest of the prison staff. Phase 1 was completed with non-benchmark jobs in these grades being scored and placed into pay bands. Phase 2 was never completed.

In January 1999 the union for the administrative grades, the Public and Commercial Services union (PCS), submitted on their behalf the first of 2,000 equal pay claims. The first group of 'work rated as equivalent' claims were for those whose jobs had been evaluated as part of the benchmark exercise; the rest were 'equal value' claims based on similar principles. The equal value claims were eventually referred to a member of the ACAS panel of Independent Experts and settled on the basis of his findings.

These claims followed others, for example, against both WH Smith and John Menzies retail distribution divisions, which involved administrative and clerical claimants comparing their work with male-dominated manual warehouse roles. They all challenged the traditional view implicit in relative pay rates, described in the introduction to this chapter, that male jobs, involving physical effort, must be of greater worth than sedentary female jobs.

Most of the above cases were taken against public sector organisations. Between them they shattered the trade union myth that equal pay had been achieved in the public sector in the early 1950s. They were followed by a series of grading and pay structure reviews covering much of the public sector.

JE and 'equal value': recent developments

There are a number of ways in which the concept of equal value, as applied in the UK, is associated with, and has impacted on, JE in this country. The first is in relation to the law. The obvious legal connection between 'equal value' and job evaluation is that the EPA requires a comparison 'under such headings as effort, skill and decision' – headings which are also often factors, or characteristics, in job evaluation systems. The legislation provides that the existence of a fair and non-discriminatory JE scheme, covering the jobs of both applicant and comparator, would provide a 'no reasonable grounds' defence to an 'equal value' claim.[11]

The consequence of this provision is that, where both applicant and comparator jobs have been evaluated under a reputable JE scheme, the applicant has first to demonstrate that the scheme is fundamentally flawed, either in design or implementation, or both. To date, no JE scheme has been found to be flawed in this way, but some applicants have got round this JE defence by showing that their work has not been correctly analysed or evaluated under the scheme.

The first job evaluation scheme to be considered by an IT was that covering Ford production workers. A number of sewing machinists had submitted 'equal value' claims almost as soon as the Equal Pay (Amendment) Regulations were effective, from 1 January 1984. The preliminary hearing, on the company's 'job evaluation study' defence, took place in April 1984 (IRLR 1984). The majority decision of the tribunal was that there was no evidence of bias or discrimination in the Urwick Orr JE study. Similar conclusions were reached by ITs in other cases where a JE scheme was challenged.

None of the cases in which JE schemes have been accepted by tribunals as providing 'no reasonable grounds' for equal value claims to be pursued has reached an appeal hearing. There are, however, grounds for considering that these decisions may not meet European requirements.

A number of equal value claims have been defeated at this preliminary stage, without consideration being given to the question of whether the jobs were of equal value. It seems likely that many more claims will have been deterred. The decision in the case of speech therapist Margaret Evesham is notable for the tribunal's comments on the equal value assessment methodologies adopted by the expert commentators. The respondents' experts, who were employed by Hay Management Consultants, used a version of the company's Guide Chart Profile system of JE to make their comparative assessments. The tribunal accepted the criticism made on behalf of the applicant that the scheme was not sufficiently modified properly to reflect the key demands of jobs, especially in relation to interpersonal skills. They also expressed concerns about how the internal scoring constraints within the Hay system impacted on the jobs in question.[12]

The impact of the JE study defence has been to contribute to the extension of JE, both in the private and in the public sector. Following claims against Lloyds Bank by clerical and secretarial employees who claimed equal pay with higher-paid messenger grades, this bank and all except one of the other major English clearing banks implemented the Hay job evaluation system to cover all employees.

This extension of JE would be no problem if job evaluation schemes were fair and non-discriminatory, and thus delivered equal pay for work of equal value. However, there is considerable evidence that this is not the case. When in 1984 the industrial tribunal rejected the equal value claim of the Ford sewing machinists, they did so on the grounds that there was a fair and non-discriminatory job evaluation scheme in place. The Transport and General Workers' Union (TGWU) appealed against this decision, on behalf of the applicants. The sewing machinists also submitted a further internal grading appeal, in accordance with company procedure, at the time of the annual pay negotiations in late 1984. The grading appeal was again rejected by the company; and again the sewing machinists took industrial action.

The dispute was resolved by an agreement to refer the matter to an independent job evaluation panel.[13] The terms of reference required the panel to 're-profile' the sewing machinist job, using the original job evaluation system. The panel effectively re-evaluated the sewing machinist job. This process placed the job in grade C, the grade that they had claimed, and, in fact, quite close to the grade D boundary. The company accepted the panel's report and re-graded the sewing machinists. The view of company representatives appears to have been that the panel's conclusion arose because so many of the original benchmark jobs had changed or ceased to exist. An alternative interpretation would be that the scheme had been implemented in a discriminatory way in 1967. There was growing awareness of the ways in which factors can be interpreted in a sexually discriminatory way. The characteristics for which the panel changed the original benchmark assessment included the following:

- 'visualisation of shapes and spatial relations' (originally the job had been scored 'low' because the machinists did not use engineering drawings or patterns, but they did have to work 'inside out' and were assessed by the panel at 'high');
- 'paced muscular effort' (increased from 'moderate' to 'high' because of the pace of the work, even though it did not require as great a physical exertion as many of the benchmark jobs);
- 'hand/eye co-ordination' (where the panel judged the degree of hand/eye co-ordination to be higher than that of even the highest level benchmark job).

(*Equal Opportunities Review* 1985: 8–12; Industrial Relations Services 1985: 15–17)

The non-discriminatory finding on the Ancillary Staffs Council JES is also open to question, as the employers subsequently agreed to a review of the JE scheme, which resulted in significant changes to the scheme. However, these were never implemented because of the introduction of local collective bargaining into the NHS, following the Conservative government's NHS reform legislation.

Concerns about traditional job evaluation schemes have led to reviews, even where schemes have not been formally challenged, as the following case demonstrates. A 1987 report was critical of the Greater London Whitley Council (GLWC) job evaluation system on a number of grounds:

- the 'education' factor, based on qualifications, was 'too narrow' and 'not sensitive to knowledge, skills and expertise acquired in ways other than by formal education';
- the 'experience' factor reflected typically male, managerial career patterns;
- the 'supervisory' responsibility factor was 'outdated' in giving more points to those managing professional staff than to those managing

technical or clerical employees, and the scheme failed to measure the supervisory responsibilities of many care jobs for clients or residents;

- the scheme over-rewarded professional status, managerial roles and the position of jobs in the status hierarchy (all more likely to be associated with male-dominated roles);
- it under-rewarded caring and other interpersonal skills, difficult or demanding contacts, work pressures, stress, creativity, skills less likely to be recognised through professional qualification, knowledge gained through experience (e.g. of other cultures), language skills, and supervision of clients (all more likely to be associated with female-dominated roles) (London Equal Value Steering Group 1987: 6–10).

Following this report, this scheme was replaced by another which dealt with most, but arguably not all, of the defects.

The legislation has led to the development of a small number of schemes designed specifically to move towards 'equal pay for work of equal value', rather than simply providing the employer with a defence to 'equal value' claims. One of the first of these was a scheme covering all employees at the Save the Children Fund (SCF) charity (IRS 1989: 9–10).

JE and equal value in the public sector

Another early 'equal value' JE system was the Local Authorities' Manual Workers' Job Evaluation Scheme (IRS 1987). The features of this scheme are summarised in Table 4.1. The major differences between this scheme and the early predecessor scheme are the 'Responsibilities for People', that is, clients, children and members of the public; and the specific inclusion of references to 'caring skills' in the 'skills factor' level definitions.

With hindsight, there are criticisms to be made of this scheme. The measurement of the 'responsibility for supervision' factor, in terms of numbers of

Table 4.1 Local authorities' manual workers' job evaluation scheme: summary, 1987

FACTOR	LEVEL					WEIGHT
	1	2	3	4	5	%
Skill/responsibilities	36	72	180	306	360	36.0
People	12	30	90	120		12.0
Resources	12	30	90	120		12.0
Supervision	6	12	54	108	120	12.0
Initiative	6	18	36	60		6.0
Mental effort	8	24	48	80		8.0
Physical effort	8	24	48	80		8.0
Working conditions	6	18	36	60		6.0
						100.0

staff supervised, proved problematic in times of competitive tendering (when staff numbers and hours tended to decrease). The scheme undervalued the more extensive work allocation and team-leading responsibilities of school cooks (compared with caretakers supervising cleaners, for example). The 'skills' factor would nowadays probably be sub-divided, to avoid under-valuation of interpersonal and/or physical skills. And the uneven scoring system is difficult to justify. However, of its period it was progressive and certainly raised the basic pay of large numbers of female employees (notably home helps, care assistants, school catering staff, and school crossing patrols) relative to that of traditional male groups, such as gardeners, refuse col-lectors, roadworkers and roadsweepers. It also influenced other schemes developed to cover groups of manual jobs (IRS 1989).

Some of the key features, of both design and implementation, from the Manual Worker Scheme, are also to be found in the more recent job evalu-ation scheme designed to support the 1997 local government agreement bringing together manual and APT & C jobs, the Single Status Agreement (IRS 1998).

The local government experience following this agreement highlights the difficulties with JE and equal value in the public sector – scale, cost and the need for changes in cultural perceptions of jobs undertaken by men and women in highly segregated occupational groups. The 1997 Agreement placed the obligation on individual local authorities in England and Wales to carry out grading reviews – a process that proceeded slowly. Seven years on, in 2004, the Local Government Services Agreement required all local author-ities in England and Wales to complete their grading reviews by April 2007, but the hiatus had allowed 'no win, no fee' lawyers to exploit the situation by encouraging thousands of women to submit 'work rated as equivalent' equal pay claims, based primarily on the 1987 manual worker scheme (see above) and the fact that they were not eligible for bonus payments, unlike their male comparators as refuse collectors, grounds maintenance workers and street sweepers.

The Local Government Services NJC ('Single Status') JE scheme was innovative because it includes a relatively large number of knowledge and skills factors – intended to ensure that, for example, caring, other inter-personal skills and physical skills, such as dexterity and co-ordination, are all fairly measured. This is in addition to the more conventional knowledge demands. An emotional effort factor is incorporated (to complement the more conventional mental and physical effort factors) and an arithmetic scoring system, with equal numbers of points per level per factor (to avoid introducing an unjustified hierarchical effect into the system). The scheme factor plan, scoring and weighting are summarised in Table 4.2.

The Local Government Services JE experience can be contrasted (Hastings 2001) with the parallel exercise in the health service, called Agenda for Change after the Government Green Paper (Department of Health 1999) which insti-gated it. Although developed by different joint groups with different remits,

Table 4.2 Local government NJC (single status) job evaluation scheme, 1997

FACTOR	LEVEL								WEIGHT
	1	*2*	*3*	*4*	*5*	*6*	*7*	*8*	%
Knowledge and skills									
Knowledge	20	40	68	80	100	121	142	163	16.3
Mental skills	13	26	39	52	65	78			7.8
Communication skills	13	26	39	52	65	78			7.8
Physical skills	13	26	39	52	65				6.5
Effort demands									
Initiative and independence	13	26	39	52	65	78	91	104	10.4
Physical effort	10	20	30	40	50				5.0
Mental effort	10	20	30	40	50				5.0
Emotional effort	10	20	30	40	50				5.0
Responsibilities									
People	13	26	39	52	65	78			7.8
Supervision	13	26	39	52	65	78			7.8
Financial resources	13	26	39	52	65	78			7.8
Physical resources	13	26	39	52	65	78			7.8
Environmental demands									
Working conditions	10	20	30	40	50				5.0
									100.0

there are clear similarities in the design of the scheme (Department of Health 2004) – set out in Table 4.3 in a manner in which it can be compared with the Local Government NJC JES.

The main differences between the two exercises are practical and political:

- The Local Government exercise was initiated under a Conservative government keen to decentralise pay bargaining in the public sector. The NHS exercise was carried out under a Labour government which had become convinced that, for the health service at least, centrally controlled grading and pay structures were essential.
- No additional funding was ever provided for single status reviews in local government. Extensive additional funding, although still insufficient, was injected into the health service to cover Agenda for Change.
- The above two points resulted in delays in implementation in the local government sector. In the health service in England and Wales, following agreement in October 2004, the Department of Health set a target for implementation by end September 2005 (the devolved assemblies in Scotland, Wales and Northern Ireland allowed more time for implementation).
- In local government training materials and assistance through a team

of associate consultants were provided to local authorities through the NJC. In the health service, the Departments of Health funded extensive cascade training programmes and ongoing support to trusts implementing all aspects of Agenda for Change (Table 4.3).

Table 4.3 Health Service Agenda for Change job evaluation scheme, 2004

FACTOR	LEVEL								WEIGHT
	1	2	3	4	5	6	7	8	%
Knowledge and skills									
Communication and relationship skills	5	12	21	32	45	60			6.0
Knowledge, training and experience	16	36	60	88	120	156	196	240	24.0
Analytical and judgemental skills	6	15	27	42	60				6.0
Planning and organizational skills	6	15	27	42	60				6.0
Physical skills	6	15	27	42	60				6.0
Responsibilities									
Responsibility for patient/client care	4	9	15	22	30	39	49	60	6.0
Responsibility for policy and service development and implementation	5	12	21	32	45	60			6.0
Responsibility for financial and physical resources	5	12	21	32	45	60			6.0
Responsibility for human resources	5	12	21	32	45	60			6.0
Responsibility for information resources	4	9	16	24	34	46	60		6.0
Responsibility for research and development	5	12	21	32	45	60			6.0
Freedom to act	5	12	21	32	45	60			6.0
Effort and working conditions									
Physical effort	3	7	12	18	25				2.5
Mental effort	3	7	12	18	25				2.5
Emotional effort	5	11	18	25					2.5
Environmental demands									
Working conditions	3	7	12	18	25				2.5

The future of grading

There seems little doubt that large organisations will continue to need to value and grade jobs relatively for the foreseeable future. Individual market rates provide an alternative for small numbers of managerial or specialist jobs, but have so far proved impractical for larger numbers and are open to anomaly, legal challenge and upward drift.

CBP systems, or at least competence-oriented JE schemes, seem likely to provide the main alternative to conventional JE. They fit well with the current emphasis on increasing skill levels and role flexibility. However, the investment in comprehensive training and assessment, and the implied additions to the pay bill if the system is effective, may render such CBP systems impracticable for most organisations, other than those with specific skill requirements.

That leaves JE. But as we have seen, JE techniques can be used in a variety of ways for a variety of purposes. There are signs that JE schemes in the future will have to accommodate all the roles in an organisation, rather than being restricted to those within the purview of traditional collective bargaining. A number of questions arise: Will this affect the structure of JE schemes? Will traditional schemes be shoe-horned into organisations and made to fit specialist and indirect roles? Or will new JE techniques be developed, using the sorts of approaches of the local government NJC scheme? Will JE be used only to provide a defence to equal value claims from predominantly female groups? Or will it be developed into a tool for implementing equal pay for work of equal value? JE and other grading systems appear to be at a crossroads.

Notes

1 See, for example, Specialarbejderforbundet I Danmark v Dansk Industri, acting for Royal Copenhagan a/s [1995] IRLR 648, where the European Court of Justice said that it was open for employers to explain pay differentials between men and women undertaking work of equal value in terms of 'choice by the workers concerned of their rate of work and to rely on major differences between total individual pay within each of these groups'.
2 Equal Pay Act 1970 (c 41 1970): s. 1(1) states: 'If the terms of a contract under which a woman is employed at an establishment in Great Britain do not include (directly or by reference to a collective agreement or otherwise) an equality clause they shall be deemed to include one.' s. 1(2) of the Act goes on to describe the situations where the equality clause should apply. In 1970 these were when the 'woman is employed on like work with a man in the same employment'; and where the 'woman is employed on work rated as equivalent with that of a man in the same employment'.
3 Equal Pay Act 1970 (c 41 1970) s. 2 (1) states:

> Any claim in respect of the contravention of a term modified or included by virtue of an equality clause, including a claim for remuneration of arrears or damages in respect of the contravention, may be presented by way of a complaint to an industrial tribunal.

From August 1998 industrial tribunals became employment tribunals.

4 Treaty of Rome, 1957, Article 119 states: 'Each Member State shall during the first stage and subsequently maintain the application of the principle that men and women should receive equal pay for equal work.'

For the purposes of this Article, 'pay' means the ordinary basic or minimum wage or salary and any other consideration, whether in cash or kind, which the worker receives, directly or indirectly, in respect of his employment from his employer. Equal pay without discrimination based on sex means:

(a) that pay for the same work at piece rates shall be calculated on the same unit of measurement;

(b) that pay for work at time rates shall be the same for the same job.

5 Equal Pay Directive, Council Directive No. 75/117, Article 1 states:

The principle of equal pay for men and women outlined in Article 119 of the Treaty, hereinafter called 'principle of equal pay', means, for the same work or for work to which equal value is attributed, the elimination of all discrimination on grounds of sex with regard to all aspects and conditions of remuneration.

In particular, where a job classification system is used for determining pay, it must be based on the same criteria for both men and women and drawn up so as to exclude any discrimination on grounds of sex.

6 Equal Pay (Amendment) Regulations 1983 SI 1983/1794.

7 Margaret Evesham v. North Hertfordshire Authority and the Secretary of State for Health: case no. 17844/87: Decision sent to the parties 9 September 1997: 'The Tribunal finds that the Applicant was engaged on work of equal value with that of her male comparator.'

8 Mrs S. Worsfold v. Southampton District Health Authority and the Secretary of State for Health: case no. 18296/87: Decision sent to the parties 10 March 1998. Mrs Julie Lawson v. South Tees District Health Authority and the Secretary of State for Health: case no. 17931/87.

9 Hayes and Quinn v. Mancunian Community Health NHS Trust and South Manchester Health Authority: case nos 16977/93 and 16981/93: Decision of the Manchester Industrial Tribunal of August 1996.

10 Mrs M. McKechnie & Others v. Gloucestershire County Council: case nos 12776/96; 1400205/96; 1400207/96; 1400208/96: Decision sent to the parties 9 September 1997.

11 Equal Pay Act, op. cit.: s. 2A(1) provides that where there is a dispute over an 'equal value' claim, the tribunal may either:

(a) proceed to determine that question; or

(b) unless it is satisfied that there are no reasonable grounds for determining that the work is of equal value as so mentioned, require a member of the panel of independent experts to prepare a report with respect to that question.

s. 2A(2) explains that there are no reasonable grounds for determining the question if

(a) . . . [the woman's] work and the work of the man in question have been given different values on a study such as is mentioned in section 1 (5) above [a job evaluation study]; and

(b) there are no reasonable grounds for determining that the evaluation contained in the study was (within the meaning of subsection (3) below) made on a system which discriminates on grounds of sex.

Subsection (3), rather meaninglessly from a job evaluation perspective, states that An evaluation contained in a study such as is mentioned in section 1(5) above [a job evaluation study] is made on a system which discriminates on grounds of sex where a difference, or coincidence, between values set by that system on different demands under the same or different headings is not justifiable irrespective of the sex of the person on whom these demands are made.

12 Evesham v. North Hertfordshire HA, op. cit.: paras 36–8.
13 ACAS: Independent Job Evaluation Panel Report and Award on a Dispute between the Ford Motor Co. Ltd. and the Transport and General Workers' Union: ACAS 2C/ 107/85:25 April 1985: 1, para. 3.

References

Adams, K. (1993) 'Scottish Power post-privatisation: using competencies to achieve top performance', *Competency* 1 (2) Winter: 13–20.

Adams, K. (1996) 'Competency: discrimination by the back door?', *Competency* 3 (4) Summer: 34–9.

Armstrong, M. (2002) *Employee Reward, third edition*, London: Institute of Personnel and Development.

Armstrong, M. and Baron, A. (1995) *The Job Evaluation Handbook*, London: Institute of Personnel and Development.

Armstrong, M., Cummins, A., Hastings, S. and Wood, W. (2003) *Job Evaluation, A Guide to Achieving Equal Pay*, London: Kogan Page.

Arnault, E.J., Gordon, L., Jones, D.H. and Phillips, G.M. (2001) 'An experimental study of job evaluation and comparable worth', *Industrial and Labour Relations Review* 54 (4) July.

Benge, E.J., Burk, S.L.H. and Hay, E.N. (1941) *Job Evaluation Manual*, New York: Harper Brothers.

Boston, S. (1987) *Women Workers and the Trade Unions*, London: Lawrence & Wishart.

CBI/Hay Group (1995) *Trends in Pay and Benefits Systems, 1995 CBI/Hay Survey Results, 1995*, London: CBI.

Daniel, W.W. and Millward, N. (1983) *Workplace Industrial Relations in Britain. The DE/PSI/ESRC Survey, 1983*, London: Heinemann Educational Books.

Department of Health (1999) *Agenda for Change, Modernising the NHS Pay System*, London: Department of Health.

Department of Health (2004) *NHS Job Evaluation Handbook, second edition*, London: Department of Health.

Education Competences Consortium Ltd (ECC) (1998) *Higher Education Role Analysis (HERA): Submission to the Independent Review of Higher Education Pay and Condition*, London: ECC.

Equal Opportunities Commission (January 1997) *Code of Practice on Equal Pay*, EOC: Manchester.

Equal Opportunities Commission (December 2003) *Code of Practice on Equal Pay*, EOC: Manchester.

Equal Opportunities Commission (2003) *Guidance Notes for the Equal Pay Review Kit*, EOC: Manchester.

Equal Opportunities Review (1985) no. 2 July/August: 8–12.

Equal Pay (Amendment) Regulations (1983) S1 1983/1794, London: HMSO.

Equal Pay Task Force (2001) *Just Pay*, EOC: Manchester.

Figart, D. (2001) 'Wage setting under Fordism: the rise of job evaluation and the ideology of equal pay', *Review of Political Economy* 13 (4).

Friedman, H. and Meredeen, S. (1980) *The Dynamics of Industrial Conflict. Lessons from Ford*, London: Croom Helm.

Ghobadian, A. and White, M. (1995) *Job Evaluation and Equal Pay*, Policy Studies Institute, Research Paper no. 58, London: Department of Employment.

Gilbert, K., Lawrence, V. and Mitchell, J. (1996) 'Equality and competency in payment systems'. Paper presented to Conference on Equal Pay in a Deregulated Labour Market, 7 June, Middlesex University, London.

Gomez-Mejia, L.R. and Balkin, D.B. (1992) *Compensation, Organisational Strategy, and Firm Performance*, Cincinnati: Southwestern Publishing.

Grayson, D. (1982) 'Job evaluation and changing technology'. ACAS Work Research Unit, Occasional Paper no. 23, September, London: ACAS.

Grayson, D. (1987) 'Job evaluation in transition', ACAS Work Research Unit, Occasional Paper no. 36, January, London: ACAS.

Hastings, S. (2001) 'Ways of moving towards equal pay for work of equal value in the public sector in the UK', in E. Ranftl, B. Buchinger, U. Gschwandter and O. Meggeneder, (eds) (2002) *Gleicher Lohn für gleichwertige Arbeit*, München und Mering.

Hastings, S. and Dixon, L. (1995) *Competency: An Introduction*, Oxford: Trade Union Research Unit.

Hay, E.N. and Purves, D.D. (1954) 'A new method of job evaluation – the guide chart profile method', *Personnel (US)* 31 (1) July.

ILO (1986) *Job Evaluation*, Geneva: International Labour Organisation.

Industrial Cases Reports (ICR) (1985) *Hayward v. Cammell Laird Shipbuilders Ltd*, London: Incorporated Council of Law Reporting for England and Wales.

Industrial Relations Law Reports (IRLR) (1982) *Commission of the European Communities v. United Kingdom of Great Britain and Northern Ireland 333 ECJ*.

Industrial Relations Law Reports (IRLR) (1984) *Neil and Others v. Ford Motor Company Ltd 339 IT*.

Industrial Relations Law Reports (IRLR) (1988) *Hayward v. Cammell Laird Shipbuilders Ltd 25 7 HL*.

Industrial Relations Law Reports (IRLR) (1993) *Enderby v. Frenchay Health Authority and Secretary of State for Health 591 ECJ*.

Industrial Relations Law Reports (IRLR) (2005) *Bailey & Others v. The Home Office (Prison Service) 369 CA*.

Industrial Relations Services (IRS) (1985) 'Ford and Smales', *Industrial Relations Review and Report* 345 (4) June: 15–18.

Industrial Relations Services (IRS) (1987) 'Equal value in local authority job evaluation', *Industrial Relations Review and Report* 388 (17) March: 8–12.

Industrial Relations Services (IRS) (1989) 'Job evaluation: the road to equality?' 'Employment Trends' section of *Industrial Relations Review and Report* 448 (26) September: 8–10.

Industrial Relations Services (1998) 'From status quo to single status: job evaluation in local government'. 'Employment Trends' section of *Industrial Relations Review and Report* 663 September: 4–11.

Jacobsen, J. (1998) *The Economics of Gender*, 2nd edn, Oxford: Blackwell.

Kersley, B., Alpin, C., Forth, J., Bryson, A., Bewley, H., Dix, G. and Oxenbridge, S. (2006) *Inside the Workplace: Findings from the 2004 Workplace Employment Relations Survey*, London: Routledge.

London Equal Value Steering Group (1987) *Job Evaluation and Equal Value – A Study of White-collar Job Evaluation in London Local Authorities*, September, London: LEVEL.

McNabb, R. and Whitfield, K. (2001) 'Job evaluation and high performance work practices: compatible or conflictual?', *Journal of Management Studies* 38 (2) March.

Millward, N. and Stevens, M. (1986) *British Workplace Industrial Relations 1980–1984, the DE/ESRC/PSI ACAS Surveys, 1986*, Aldershot: Gower.

National Board for Prices and Incomes (NBPI) (1968) Job evaluation report no 83. Cmnd 3772. London: HMSO.

National Joint Council for Local Government Services (2005) *National Agreement on Pay & Conditions of Service, Part 4, Joint Advice*. Local Government Employers, London.

Neathey, F., Willison, R., Akroyd, K., Regan, J. and Hill, D. (2005) *Equal Pay Reviews in Practice*, EOC Working Paper Series no. 33, Manchester.

Patton, J.A., Littlefield, C.L. and Self, S.A. (1964) *Job Evaluation – Text and Cases*, 3rd edn, Homewood, IL.: Richard D. Irwin, Inc.

Pritchard, D. and Murlis, H. (1992) *Jobs, Roles and People: The New World of Job Evaluation*, London: Nicholas Brealey.

Quaid, M. (2000) 'Job evaluation as institutional myth', *Journal of Management Studies* 30 (2) March.

Report of a Court of Inquiry under Sir Jack Scamp into a dispute concerning sewing machinists employed by the Ford Motor Company Limited (1968) (the Scamp Report). Cmnd. 3749, August, London: HMSO.

Report of the Independent Expert, case number 5979/84 (1984): Miss J.A. Hayward (Applicant) v. Cammell Laird Shipbuilders Limited (Respondent), attached as appendix to Decision of Industrial Tribunal, available from Central Office of Industrial Tribunals.

Report of the Royal Commission on Equal Pay 1944–46, (1946) Cmd. 6937: October, Appendix II. London: HMSO.

Report of the Proceedings of a Special Ad Hoc Joint Committee under the Chairmanship of J. Grange Moore Esq. TD (1968) 5 September. London: Ford.

Sapsford, D. and Tzannatos, Z. (1993) *The Economics of the Labour Market*, London: Macmillan.

Schafer, S., Winterbotham, M. and McAndrew, F. (2005) Equal Pay Reviews Survey 2004, Working Paper Series No. 32, EOC: Manchester.

Sliedregt, T. van, Voskujil, O. and Thierry, H. (2001) 'Job evaluation systems and pay grade structures: do they match?', *International Journal of Human Resource Management* 12 (8) December.

Sparrow, P. (1996) 'Too good to be true', *People Management*, 5 December: 22–7.

5   Wages and low pay

Janet Druker

Summary

There is a historic division between waged workers (with wages typically calculated on the basis of an hourly rate and paid weekly or fortnightly) and those receiving salaries (calculated on a monthly or annual basis). This distinction in the form of wages is more fully reflected in the reward package and in the job control of waged and salaried employees. The traditional differences between them are being eroded and the contrast in conditions of work between waged and salaried employees, including the additions to basic pay, is now less significant than in the past. The expansion of employment in the service sector has reinforced the ranks of waged workers in areas such as retail and hospitality and in employment agencies. New forms of incentive payment are developed in these work situations to meet different business needs. The National Minimum Wage (NMW) was introduced from April 1999 and has risen more rapidly than average earnings since that date with an increasing number of workers covered by its provision. Its impact is greatest in female-intensive sectors. However there is little evidence so far that the NMW has reduced the gap between the highest and the lowest earners.

Introduction

This chapter explores the position of 'waged' workers – defined here as those whose pay is calculated on an hourly basis, paid weekly or fortnightly – asking how their position is differentiated from those who are 'salaried'. Manual employees in manufacturing, construction and agriculture, lower-paid employees in the retail, hospitality and cleaning industries as well as lower-grade clerical or sales roles are all commonly paid 'wages'. So too are many workers with employment agencies, who are placed with host organisations, most commonly (but not exclusively) on a short-term basis. Workers who are receiving 'wages' are more likely than salaried employees to fall within the ranks of the low paid (White 1999) and so the chapter considers both the position of hourly-paid employees and the position of the low paid. The NMW had only recently been introduced when the first edition of this book was written and it is timely now, some ten years since that legislation was enacted, to review the impact and implications of the NMW.

Employers have significant discretion in the choices that they make about pay. Those choices are, of course, constrained by legislation affecting wages and salaries – notably in relation to equal pay and statutory minimum rates of pay (see p. 110). Apart from the exigencies of statutory compliance, employer decisions are shaped by other influences including product and labour markets and by the weight and influence of trade union membership. Changes in global competition, in social values and in management theories and trends all play a part. The influence of situational context and historical legacy – how things have traditionally been done – are significant, since changes to reward systems are not easily made and the risks associated with change may be high. Employees cannot be assumed to be acquiescent or compliant and change may well be made at some cost since the level and frequency of payment will be specified in the individual employment contract. The form and content of wage systems has been of central interest to trade unions and, whilst union organisation has diminished, employers will be aware of the scope for resistance.

Debates about human resource management (HRM) in the 1980s and 1990s revealed differences in perspective between and within practitioner and academic groups as to the meaning and significance of human resource management. Key features of HRM were identified within the strategic nature of the contribution that could be made; in the significance of line managers and the importance of key 'levers' for change (for a summary review of these debates see Storey 2007). 'New Pay' theories, presented by Lawler (1990) and Schuster and Zingheim (1992), seemed to be particularly relevant in this context, echoing as they did the universalistic perspectives of some of the HRM writers and emphasising the importance of aligning rewards to performance in order to realise strategic business objectives. These shifting perspectives concerned with the theories and practices of management have impacted only partially and gradually so that there is evidence of innovation as well as of remarkable continuity in the position of waged work and the composition of wages over the last twenty years. The decline in manufacturing industry, the impact of information and communication technologies and the growth and transformation of service sector industries have re-shaped the world of employment and the value that is placed upon work – including the work of lower-paid and manual workers. In the public sector the impetus toward pay modernisation involving single-status working and equal-pay-proofed job evaluation have provided an additional impetus for change.

The chapter is divided into three sections. The first section considers the status divide between waged and salaried workers, a distinction that has changed, becoming blurred but retaining much of its traditional salience in terms of the form and level of pay of these groups. The second section highlights the nature and extent of change in the composition of earnings for waged workers. It points to the diminished significance of payments over and above basic time rates of pay and considers whether manual workers are excluded from the 'New Pay' approaches that have been advocated. This section points to the emergence of bonuses at establishment or enterprise level. The final section discusses the question of statutory intervention in relation to pay, focussing particularly on the NMW, introduced with effect from April 1999. It considers the impact of the NMW, the scope of its coverage and also the continuing gap between the highest earners and those on the adult minimum wage.

The status divide

The demarcation between 'salaried' and 'waged' workers marks a division within the enterprise which signifies and reinforces differences in the way in which people are managed. Workplace rules tend to be stricter and working hours more closely defined for waged workers. Wages systems are intended to reinforce industrial discipline by associating pay with controls over time to assert workplace discipline – for example over attendance or time-keeping. Notice periods between salaried and waged workers differ too, with the former having a longer notice period whilst the weekly or hourly paid employee is more tenuously positioned and more vulnerable to termination of the employment contract. Waged workers are also less likely to have access to organisational benefits such as sick pay or pension schemes.

Labour market and economic changes have significantly affected the status divide. There has been a growth in employment in sections of the waged workforce – in the service sector – in retail, hospitality, tourism and the leisure sectors, for example, and in customer call centres. Manufacturing industry is less significant as an employer now than it was a quarter of a century ago and the payment systems devised to enhance productivity in a manufacturing context are inevitably less significant too. Between 1978 and 2006 the total number of jobs in the manufacturing sector in the UK declined from 7.1 million to 3.3 million. Service sector jobs – including employees and the self-employed – rose from 16.5 million to 25 million over the same period (Brook 2008). The rise in service sector employment has reinforced a waged workforce in areas which, historically, have been low paid. This provides at least a part of the overall explanation for shifts within forms of payment since the workforce controls and disciplines of the service sector are associated with different payment arrangements than those which characterised manufacturing.

The differentiation between wages and salaries marks a form of labour market segregation which has changed in many ways but has not yet been eroded. Many of the disadvantages of 'waged' work continue. As in the past, under wages systems, earnings are unlikely to rise significantly with length of service and there may be little opportunity to benefit from pay progression over time. Whilst earnings of both waged and salaried employees may be enhanced by additions to pay, employers are likely to apply more than one incentive scheme, with a recent survey suggesting a mean of 3.68 cash-based or incentive-bonus schemes for each employer (Chartered Institute of Personnel and Development (CIPD) 2008: 12). This means that waged and lower paid workers are likely to be remunerated by different systems than more senior employees – notably by payment by results, shift pay and over-time – components that may vary from week to week. Waged workers often lack the benefit of longer-term consolidation of additions to pay, whereas salaried employees may benefit from increases within broad payment bands or incremental pay structures.

In some cases employers have turned to enterprise-based approaches to 'total reward', with the intention of fostering a culture of engagement across the whole of the workforce. Interest in 'harmonisation' of terms and conditions of different groups of employees seemed to be especially marked toward the end of the twentieth century, encouraged by changing technolo-gies that rendered obsolete some traditional skills but created new skills and new occupations based on emerging technologies (Druker 2000). The nature of work was re-shaped so that lean production and sophisticated and rapidly changing technology required a substantially different approach to workforce management. The skills or competencies of some manual employees, who might in the past have been paid 'wages', were substantially re-adjusted to meet these demands. In this way manual employees were assimilated into the salaried workplace hierarchy, carrying responsibility for quality assurance, for innovation and for process development, and rewarded in line with their peers in non-manual occupations. These changes, especially relevant in the context of manufacturing, were accompanied in some cases by adjustments in working hours, in notice periods and in access to related workplace bene-fits. The decline of trade union organisation may be seen both as cause and effect and employer interest in fostering commitment from all the workforce rather than from salaried employees alone has further encouraged this trend.

The rhetoric of human resource management seemed to lend itself to an approach to workforce management which encouraged harmonisation in the treatment of different groups within the workforce. American 'New Pay' advocates championed alternative approaches to reward, suggesting that payment for the person, rather than payment for the job, is more likely to encourage learning, development and motivation appropriate to the modern organisation (e.g. Lawler 2000). Some of these precepts seem to have found their way into practice as payment structures for waged workers have been adjusted over time, with evidence of a stronger focus on rewarding behaviours that contribute to organisational strategies and priorities.

Yet the pace and significance of innovation through 'harmonisation' seems to be attracting less attention now than in the last decade of the twentieth century and the wave of interest of the 1990s is past. The term 'harmonisa-tion' is now less used – or is used with a different meaning to describe the process changes associated with organisational merger or acquisition – for example bringing together two organisations or sometimes two different departments within one organisation (see, for example, Incomes Data Services (IDS) 2006a: 7–11).

An analysis of 'wages' must focus then on a diminished group within the manufacturing sector and on employees – both full-time and part-time – in the service sector whose work is especially exposed to low pay.

The composition of earnings

The significance of salaries – as compared to wages – can be readily understood when we take account of the very simple fact that salaried workers are likely to earn more than those who are in receipt of wages. Salaries are calculated on an annual basis, often paid in monthly instalments, whereas many lower-paid workers are rewarded with hourly rates of pay for a specified number of weekly hours, paid at weekly or sometimes at fortnightly intervals. Nearly three-quarters of higher-paid employees are paid on a calendar month basis, but less than a third of low-paid employees receive their pay each calendar month. By contrast, 42 per cent of low-paid employees are paid weekly (Annual Survey of Hours and Earnings (2006 (ONS)).

From the employer perspective, hourly rates of pay are easily understood and straightforward to administer. An hourly-based-payment system provides that weekly earnings are calculated on the basis of the hourly rate, according to the number of hours worked. Earnings based upon an hourly rate may comprise a range of additional elements and bonus or incentive payments are the most significant.

A grading structure may provide for differentials in hourly rates, rewarding the perception of skill so that higher time rates are paid to those who are perceived to be more highly skilled with lower rates for the semi-skilled or unskilled. Historically, the social construction of skill placed a lower premium on trades or occupations that were filled by women. Men's claims to skilled status were often reinforced by trade union organisation; moreover women's skills, particularly interpersonal and caring skills, have tended to be undervalued (Edwards and Gilman 1999; Hastings, this volume). Despite the provisions of the Equal Pay Act, passed in 1970 and brought into effect from 1975, and the requirements ten years later that there should be equal pay for work of equal value, the difference between women's pay and men's is being eroded only very slowly. Women's labour force participation is higher than ever before, yet in July 2007 women working full-time earned, on average, 17 per cent less than men. This compared with a gender pay gap of 20.7 per cent in 1997 (Equal Opportunities Commission 2007). Although the gap had diminished over the previous decade, progress was slow and the Equal Opportunities Commission estimated in July 2007 that the difference might take a further 20 years to erode. For women working part-time the gap was wider – standing at 38 per cent per hour, with closure requiring a further 25 years (Equal Opportunities Commission 2007). A more critical approach to the criteria underpinning job evaluation has played a part in laying the foundations for new approaches to grading in the public services – through Agenda for Change in the National Health Service, the Local Government Job Evaluation Scheme and the Higher Education Role Analysis for universities. Yet the costs of implementation for the public services are high and progress has been slow.

The continuing differences between men's and women's pay can be accounted for by occupational distribution, being widest for managers, senior officials and skilled trades and lowest in professional occupations. It is affected by the pattern of working hours, since women are more likely to work part-time and less likely to be rewarded by additions to pay in the form of payment by results (pbr) or overtime premia. However the nature of the workplace and gender segregation between different establishments is also important with women in female-dominated workforces being more likely to be low paid.

At the core of debates about pay and earnings is the question of variability – to what extent should earnings reflect performance and output? To what extent can the prospect of high earnings be used as a motivational tool? The relationship between pay and performance has been a long-standing theme in management thinking and from the employer's perspective there is customarily an expectation that the cost of such schemes should be self-financing and contribute overall to business objectives.

A visible and tangible link between pay and performance was advocated by Taylor (1913) as one of the fundamental principles informing 'scientific management'. Taylor argued with 'firm conviction' that the interests of the employer and employee are 'one and the same' (1913: 10). Yet he also acknowledged the widespread perception of 'antagonistic' interests, recognising that, both individually and collectively, employees might manipulate wage systems and working arrangements to their advantage. He commented particularly on 'soldiering' – a form of deliberate slow working. Drawing in part on his own experience and citing examples from other industries, he argued for the benefits of payment by results.

Conflict over pay, piecework pricing and bonus has been a core theme within the history of British industrial relations conflict and this is perhaps one reason why employers have sought alternative arrangements. Without some sort of bonus there is no obvious incentive for employees paid on a simple hourly basis to improve productivity or performance. Yet because of the ambiguities inherent in individual motivation and because business processes differ significantly the benefits of payment by results have never been universally accepted even amongst employers. Some observers have argued that it is the process of organising the business effectively that yields benefits – not simply the payment system in itself (e.g. Behrend 1959). From this perspective effective work organisation and workplace communication, rather than incentive payment, are viewed as the key to high performance. Improvements in work method may precede or accompany the introduction of payment by results and productivity gains may mistakenly be attributed to the payment system, rather than to work organisation, it is argued. Conversely, pbr may have a negative impact on quality.

Job analysis – involving the measuring and timing of tasks – is central to the operation of individual pbr. Job analysis is often seen as 'scientific' but there is, inevitably, an element of subjective judgement involved in the measurement of performance. Work-measured schemes construct a 'standard time' for particular tasks. This may be done on the basis of observation – an approach that may seem to be scientific but is open to manipulation and to conflict. Under such schemes incentive pay is linked to the time saved against the 'standard'. There are questions about the choice of subjects which should be measured; in what conditions and over what time period; what allowances are to be made – for example for learning new tasks or for handling interruptions? How should an 'average' performance be defined? Inconsistencies and discrepancies undermine the scientific credibility of measurement. Some individuals may hold back on effort when they are under observation, with a view to ensuring that targets can be met without undue difficulty. Whether the scheme is to be based upon individual or group performance, decisions about performance norms are open to question and challenge. Group norms may be established to govern output and the close link between work organisation and payment arrangements may, in some circumstances, become an impediment to change.

Alternatively a time may be constructed according to data held on physical movements, with extra time built in for contingencies. Again this can be a source of conflict where data-based times give insufficient attention to the human realities of the work situation. Work-measured schemes have predominated on routine, repetitive work where downtime is rare. They are less relevant where work processes must be regularly updated to take account of changing product requirements or technological innovation – for example in the case of a production worker who is running a programmable machine tool or engaged in statistical process control.

The choice of wage form has been seen as 'control by incentives' or 'control by foremen' (National Board for Prices and Incomes 1968: para. 87, quoted in Fernie and Metcalf 1998). In general it seems that large establishments are more likely than smaller firms to use incentives (Brown 1990). In part this is explained by the economies of scale that can be achieved when incentive schemes are applied to a large number of people (Heywood *et al.* 1997). Incentive pay is more common in routinised jobs which can be performed without direct supervision or where supervisors have a wide span of control. Not surprisingly, there is less use of incentive pay and greater use of standard rates where duties are variable (Brown 1990).

Under time-based-payment systems, employer control over pace and performance is reliant on direct supervisory controls or on the willingness of the employee to engage fully with the task or tasks to be performed on the basis of 'responsible autonomy' (Friedman 1977). Time-based pay is most likely to be deployed where the machine or the process can determine the pace of work; it may be used where workflow is uneven (so that incentive payments would be unsuitable), where output is difficult to measure; or where the pace of work is outside of the individual's control – as in parts of the service sector. Time-based payment may also be preferred because the pace of work is less important than other factors – for example quality of service delivery – and is likely to provide the base for payment systems in many areas of service sector employment.

The 'New Pay' advocates, writing toward the end of the twentieth century, stressed the benefits of variable pay and the importance of aligning pay structures and rewards with business objectives – principles that led to the notion of a 'new logic of organizing' for the business (Lawler 2000: 24–39). This requires attention to employee business involvement, to the use that is made of human capital, to team-based organisation, and to products and customers. Within this approach, reward systems must reflect and reinforce the focus on strategic objectives of the business, it is argued. During the last decades of the twentieth century, it seemed that there was some evidence of the influence of the ideas of New Pay theorists, at least for managerial and salaried employees. Yet whilst performance- and profit-related pay for these groups was becoming more common-place, payment by results schemes have been diminishing in significance and in value as a proportion of overall earnings for waged workers. It would be simplistic to suggest that the New Pay is linked very simply to the deployment of variable payment arrangements. Rather, evidence for the significance of 'New Pay' thinking would have to be found in holistic approaches to reward, challenging some of the traditional divisions and authority relations within the workplace. It is interesting to note in this respect the different experiences of salaried and professional groups as contrasted with waged employees, but also the growing body of evidence of consistency in approach.

Data from the Government's New Earnings Survey (NES), published annually until 2003, indicated a steady diminution in the proportion of employees in receipt of pbr. The British Workplace Employment Relations Survey 2004 reported that pbr alone was used in 23 per cent of workplaces surveyed but that where pbr and other forms of incentive payment were made, they applied solely to non-managerial employees and not to other groups in 34 per cent of participating organisations (Kersley *et al.* 2006: 194). Unfortunately the Annual Survey of Hours and Earnings (ASHE) which replaced the NES from 2004 does not provide comparable data to that previously published, since it does not distinguish between pbr and incentive pay and reports, simply, on incentive pay. This means that it is no longer possible to track over time the use that is made of pbr. However there is no evidence to suggest since 2004 that the well-established trend away from pbr has been reversed.

There is evidence though that changes in occupational structure, increased employment in the service sector and the accompanying shifts in workforce composition have encouraged more complex and sophisticated approaches to bonus arrangements affecting waged employees. Whereas pbr schemes have tended to emphasise time saved in performing a particular task, new-style bonus schemes are more likely to be constructed in relation to a range of organisational and behavioural factors that are deemed to be important to company performance. These may include productivity and output, financial performance, quality, safety, customer service and attendance. Here it seems that Lawler's 'new logic of organizing' has some resonance. In the engineering industry, for example, firms have moved to measuring plant or company productivity, for example by reference to output or profits or focus on factors such as quality and safety. An example is Nissan where manufacturing staff receive merit awards (IDS 2007a). An employee's progression within a salary range depends upon individual performance from 'outstanding' to 'below average'.

New style bonus schemes are more sophisticated in structure and may be more generally applicable to the service sector as well as to manufacturing. Such schemes can focus on one single issue – single-factor schemes – and they can be more complex, with multiple factors. Single-factor schemes relate pay to one determining factor – for example sales – as in Boots within the retail sector. Increasingly though schemes are constructed by management to encourage and to reinforce employee behaviours around a range of business objectives through a multi-factor approach (IDS 2005: 2). A multi-factor scheme may relate pay to financial performance, productivity, sales, quality and safety. The most commonly used factors in engineering were found by IDS (2006b: 12) to be company financial performance, output and attendance. Multi-factor schemes may also be multi-level – that is reflecting performance at establishment and enterprise level, combining company-wide objectives with those for the team, the department or the establishment (IDS 2007b: 4). A scheme may measure performance at team level with a team-based or group bonus scheme in order to facilitate a mutually supportive group of people, encouraging self-management.

The frequency and timing of bonus payments will depend in large measure on the way in which the bonus is constructed. Where payment by results or bonus is paid weekly or monthly, practitioners are advised to ensure that it can be readily understood in relation to effort so that there is continuing motivation to improve performance. For more complex schemes, bonus may be payable on an annual basis and the connection may be less readily apparent. Nearly two-thirds of the organisations whose practices were reviewed by IDS in 2005 were making bonus payments on an annual basis (IDS 2005). In other cases bonus may be triggered only where minimum levels of performance are reached across a range of issues. Employee attendance, for example, may be a factor in determining eligibility within a particular period. Where a shorter performance period applies, bonus will be paid more regularly (IDS 2007b). Shorter measurement times may be more readily understood and more motivational as an annual payment may be forgotten later in the year. In order for a scheme to be effective it is important that it is understood and that there is communication to employees about the basis on which the bonus scheme is constructed. It is also significant that there should be feedback so that they know how bonus is progressing if it accrues over a long period – a process in which trade union representatives may play a part (IDS 2007b).

Hourly paid employees can normally expect that additional hours worked attract additional payments for overtime, although this is not necessarily or automatically the case. Overtime payments are more commonly received by full-time than part-time employees and by men rather than women. According to the Annual Survey of Hours and Earnings 2006, 22.8 per cent of full-time employees worked paid overtime in 2006, down 1.1 per cent compared with 2005. By comparison only 20.7 per cent of part-time employees worked paid overtime in 2006. The number of overtime hours averaged 1.5 hours per week for full-time employees and 1.0 hour per week for part-time workers. Here too earnings reflected differences in gender experience with a marked contrast in the experience of full-time men and women, with 27.6 per cent of full-time men working paid overtime with an average of 2 hours a week worked, whilst only 15.5 per cent of full-time women did so and averaged only 0.7 hours per week. The difference was less significant for part-time workers, although here too men were more likely than women to work paid overtime (ASHE 2006).

Normally overtime working attracts premium pay once normal full-time hours have been reached, with manual employees and lower-grade workers more likely to receive premium rates (IDS 2006c). Typically, paid overtime might be time and a half for overtime worked between Monday and Friday – and this rate often applies on Saturday too with the majority of organisations paying for overtime on a Sunday and on bank holidays at double time. However this is not uniformly the case and there is evidence of employers seeking to eliminate or to control the cost of overtime working – either by ending premium rates for overtime, by introducing stricter criteria or by introducing annualised working hours schemes. These may involve a basic number of rostered hours with provision for some of the annual hours to be delivered flexibly in a way that meets periods of peak demand in workflow (IDS 2006c). Overall then, the trend is toward a reduction in the number of employees receiving paid overtime and a reduction in the level of premium pay that is awarded for overtime hours. Accompanying these changes are complaints from many employees of a 'long-hours culture' where overtime hours are worked on an unpaid basis (IDS 2006c).

In concluding this discussion about the composition of wages, it is relevant to note the continuing decline in collective bargaining over pay and the diminished role of trades unions at workplace level within the private sector. The WERS survey of 2004 reported that 34 per cent of employees belonged to trade unions or independent staff associations, compared with a figure of 37 per cent in 1998 (Kersley *et al.* 2006: 109). However there was a marked difference between the private and the public sector. In the private sector some three quarters of workplaces had no trade union members, although in the public sector, by contrast, the position was reversed. The proportion of workplaces setting pay through collective bargaining has been in decline for the last twenty years and this decline was confirmed in the most recent WERS report (Kersley *et al.* 2006: 180–7), notably within the private sector where bargaining incidence fell from 17 per cent of workplaces in 1998 surveyed to 11 per cent in 2004. Pay bargaining continued to be more commonplace within larger workplaces and marked differences were evident between industries. In hotels and restaurants, in the wholesale and retail sector as well as in 'other business services' collective bargaining coverage was particularly weak and the composition of earnings – as well as the level of earnings – was unlikely to be affected by trade union representation. In manufacturing – the traditional locus for negotiation over incentive payments – the level was higher. Collective bargaining coverage was reported at 35 per cent by 2004 – down from 38 per cent in 1998 (Kersley *et al.* 2006: 187).

Low pay and the national minimum wage

Perhaps the most significant change of the last decade in considering wages and low pay within the UK is the introduction of the National Minimum Wage Act, passed in 1998. The National Minimum Wage (NMW) came into effect in April 1999, creating a new legal minimum for adult workers (those aged 22 or over), for younger employees and those in training. This training or development rate, for those aged 22 and over, was established in 1999 but was abolished with effect from 1 October 2006 since it had been little used.

Tax credits have operated alongside the NMW with the intention of reducing the disincentive through the benefits system for people to accept paid work. They provide a minimum threshold encouraging employment whilst the NMW prevents employers from lowering wages to bring employees within the scope of Government subsidies to incomes through working benefits.

The introduction of the NMW was not, of course, the first time that employers in the UK had encountered some form of statutory wage regulation. Low-paid workers in particular occupations and sectors were protected by Wages Councils for most of the twentieth century (between 1909 and 1993), setting minimum standards on pay and working conditions. The Wages Councils covering the largest groups at the time of abolition were the Licensed Non-Residential, Licensed Residential & Licensed Restaurants, Retail Food and Allied Trades and Retail Trades non-Foods.

Minimum employment standards had also held statutory support through the Fair Wages Resolution, a measure which had its origins in the late nineteenth century. Essentially the Fair Wages Resolution, as revised after the Second World War, required Government contractors to apply the terms and conditions of relevant collective agreements. Schedule 11 of the 1975 Employment Protection Act (EPA) further extended that principle so that workers who did not engage in collective bargaining could claim the rates of comparable workers who did. The changes of the 1980s and 1990s were premised on free market principles, fostering deregulation and encouraging unfettered competition. The EPA provisions relating to the extension of collective bargaining were abolished in 1980. The Fair Wages Resolution was abolished in 1983 and the Wages Acts were reduced in scope and, finally, were abolished, in 1993. Whilst their applications had been uneven and enforcement problematic, in the mid-1980s they had covered about 2.5 million workers – over 10 per cent of the workforce (Rubery and Edwards 2003: 454). In a climate of de-regulation, there was no statutory minimum level for wages until the introduction of the NMW.

The NMW hinges around an hourly rate and is of greatest relevance to women workers and to part-time workers, who feature disproportionately within the ranks of the low paid. Unlike the Wages Acts which were applied to sectors where collective bargaining had limited significance or was non-existent, the NMW is general rather than sectoral or occupational in its application. It was recognised at the outset that its impact would be felt more keenly in some sectors than in others. In the hotel and catering industry, in retail employment, in the care sector and in hairdressing – sectors with many small workplaces and very little trade union representation – the NMW is of particular importance. Since the rate is national in scope – and since the cost of living varies regionally – its impact is inevitably greater in some parts of the UK than in others.

Set initially at a rate of £3.60 for adult workers, that is those aged 22 or over, it provides a 'youth rate' for 18 year olds and above, applying – controversially – up to and including the age of 21 (Low Pay Commission 1998: 11; IDS 1998: 3). Initially the NMW did not apply to the youngest in the workforce but a lower rate for 16–17 years of age was established with effect from October 2004. The rates between 1999 and 2008 are set out in Table 5.1.

Table 5.1 The national minimum wage, 1999–2008

Date	Adult workers	% Change	Youth rate (those aged 18–21)	% Change	Aged 16–17
April 1999–May 2000	£3.60		£3.00		
June 2000–Sep 2000	£3.60	0	£3.20		
Oct 2000–Sep 2001	£3.70	2.8	£3.20	0	
Oct 2001 Sep 2002	£4.10	10.8	£3.50	9.4	
Oct 2002–Sep 2003	£4.20	2.4	£3.60	2.9	
Oct 2003–Sep 2004	£4.50	7.1	£3.80	5.6	
Oct 2004–Sep 2005	£4.85	7.8	£4.10	7.9	
Oct 2005–Sep 2006	£5.05	4.1	£4.25	3.7	
Oct 2006–Sep 2007	£5.35	5.9	£4.45	4.7	£3.30
Oct 2007–Sep 2008	£5.52	3.2	£4.60	3.3	£3.40
October 2008–	£5.73	3.8	£4.77	3.7	£3.53

Source: Data drawn from LPC 2007: 11, Table 2.1 and LPC 2008: xviii

The NMW is up-rated on the basis of recommendations from the Low Pay Commission, recommendations which may be accepted by Government. For the last eight years through until 2007 this resulted in regular increases above the rate of inflation, so that the NMW has become increasingly significant over time. There was an increase in the adult minimum wage of 27.4 per cent between October 2002 and October 2006, with a corresponding increase in average earnings of 17 per cent (LPC 2006: v–vi). However there is no requirement for Government to implement regular increases. The principles underlying the NMW are now well established and endorsed by politicians from all of the main political parties. Interestingly, it was the Liberal Party which, historically, had championed the cause of a national minimum wage. Although the NMW Bill was opposed by the Conservative opposition in the 1990s, the current Conservative leadership have indicated to us (2008) that they will retain the NMW if they were to be elected to government. This does not mean that there is necessarily agreement on the regularity or level of adjustment, which remains dependent upon Government willingness to accommodate recommendations of the LPC.

The key question is, how effective has the NMW been in improving the position of the lowest paid employees? How was it implemented and how effectively is it now policed? Constructed on the basis of an average hourly rate, the NMW is calculated over a specified pay period. For waged workers this is likely to be weekly or fortnightly. This average includes some of the other components in the wage package – for example payment by results and output-based payments. Where workers receive incentive payments or where they are paid tips or gratuities, distributed centrally through payroll, these payments can be taken into account in calculating the NMW. The cost of accommodation – up to a maximum of £4.46 per day in October 2008 – provided by the employer can be off-set.

In terms of coverage, the evidence concerning the impact of the NMW is positive, with the NMW rising more rapidly than average earnings and an increasing number of workers in scope. Early research suggested widespread compliance with the NMW, leading to some impact on differentials (Dickens and Manning 2004). The adult minimum has increased over time and its 'bite' – defined by the LPC as the ratio of the adult minimum wage to the median hourly wage – has risen from 47.6 per cent in April 1999 to over 50 per cent in October 2006 (LPC 2007: xi and 21). Set at a single figure to apply nationally, the NMW is most likely to impact in the regions with lower pay – the North-East, the East Midlands and Northern Ireland – and is of less significance overall in London and the South-East where earnings are higher and where the notion of a 'living wage' remains an important campaigning issue. It benefits women particularly, since two-thirds of minimum wage jobs are held by women and part-timers – with 47 per cent of minimum wage jobs being held on a part-time basis. The NMW has narrowed the gap between women's pay and men's at the lower end of the pay range (LPC 2007: xvi). It has also improved the income of lower-paid ethnic minority workers. In terms of occupation, the impact is most likely to be felt in female-intensive sectors such as hairdressing, hospitality, cleaning and retail sectors. The NMW has been reported as having a 'huge effect' in the care home sector, raising the wages of 30 per cent of the workforce (Dickens and Manning 2003).

Has the gap between rich and poor (or between high earners and those on the adult minimum wage) been reduced as a consequence of the NMW? The data presented by the LPC and the Office for National Statistics (ONS) suggest that it has not. Earnings of full-time employees in the top 10 per cent of the distribution rose more rapidly than those in the bottom 10 per cent for six of the eight years between 1997 and 2005 with the upper decile experiencing an increase of 33.8 per cent compared with an increase of 30.2 per cent for the bottom decile (Dobbs 2006: 50). Subsequently the highest earners have benefited from increases above the average. The adult NMW, expressed as a percentage of the upper decile of earnings, actually fell in 2000 and 2001, rising only slightly in subsequent years. Analysis is complicated because of discontinuity in the data series provided by the Annual Survey of Hours and Earnings so that direct comparisons before and after 2004 cannot be reliably made. Nonetheless the figures from 2004 to 2006 suggest a very slight shift in the position with the NMW representing an increased percentage of upper decile earnings with a rise from 22 per cent to 22.6 per cent over that period. This is a marginal change and, given the difficulties of comparison identified above, it does not seem that we can yet justify the view that the NMW has closed the gap between the top and the bottom of the earnings spectrum. Moreover ONS data point unequivocally in the opposite direction. Between 1998 and April 2007 the top decile of earners saw an improvement in earnings of 42.5 per cent against an increase for the bottom decile of 39.7 per cent (Daniels 2007).

Moreover some groups remain disadvantaged, despite the legislation. There is evidence that some migrant workers, for example, whose numbers have grown since 2004, have been disadvantaged by excessive deductions from pay, for example for accommodation provided (LPC 2007: xviii). Migrant workers and those in the informal economy are less likely to be aware of their entitlements, or to be in a position to seek redress. Although there is some encouraging evidence with respect to employer compliance from specific studies (e.g. French and Mohrke 2006, cited in LPC 2007: 225; Datta *et al.* 2007), nonetheless migrant workers are less likely than others to be aware of their entitlements and still less to have the knowledge and confidence to raise complaints about their rates of pay or about recurrent problems such as unauthorised deductions. One change which has been effected relates to gangmasters, whose operations were licensed with effect from 2006. As a consequence, workers engaged through gangmasters must be paid the NMW or the agricultural minimum wage. It is still rather early to evaluate the impact of the new Licensing Standards yet the LPC believes that 'the evidence of exploitation of migrant workers is compelling' (LPC 2007: 230) and recommended a targeted NMW campaign focussing on a low-pay sector with a high proportion of migrant workers. Home workers too, often paid on a piece rate basis, have also experienced problems.

Similarly, workers engaged through employment agencies and placed with a 'host' organisation, paid on an hourly basis, may be disadvantaged both in terms of pay levels and in access to some of the benefits of employment. Whilst employees with an 'employment business' have employed status, workers with an employment agency are more precariously situated and at the time of writing have no rights to equality in treatment with their counterparts within the host company.

Trade union organisation and recognition remains important in protecting the position of the low paid, despite the advances in the NMW. The WERS survey, 2004, supports earlier research indicating that workplaces in which some collective bargaining took place reduced the percentage of low-paid employees in the workforce (Kersley *et al.* 2006: 198–9). The survey found that four fifths of the employees who were low paid were working in workplaces with no collective bargaining.

Trade union protection is the more important because enforcement mechanisms for the NMW remain relatively weak (Croucher and White 2007). Responsibility rests formally with Compliance Officers from Her Majesty's Revenue and Customs (HMRC). In practice enforcement relies largely on low- paid workers themselves reporting problems to HM Revenue and Customs. This requires individuals to understand their rights and to have confidence that the steps that they will be required to take to redress problems will yield positive results. Since employees in this situation are unlikely to be unionised and may have difficulty in accessing reliable information, they may, understandably, be reluctant to take action. Penalties for non-compliance remain inadequate, with only a partial response by Government to LPC recommendations (LPC 2007: 216). Where an employer is found not to have complied with the NMW, the arrears owing must be paid – and only if they are not paid is there any specific penalty. The penalty itself is low – only £5,000 – and to date only one criminal prosecution has been taken. Whilst there is widespread awareness of the existence of the NMW, knowledge of the rates that apply is, unsurprisingly, more patchy. Complaints of under-payment rose between 2003 and 2007, with more workers affected over time (LPC 2007 and 2008). The accommodation off-set has been a particularly difficult area with reports that migrant workers being charged sums far in excess of those permitted. Targeted enforcement campaigns offer a response to enforcement problems, with hairdressing – a sector with many women and part-time employees – being the first. The hairdressing campaign has been partially successful, although awareness of the NMW within the sector is uneven and further initiatives are required to ensure that workers are aware of their rights. Employers could be required to carry information about the minimum wage on wage slips – a suggestion first made by the LPC (1998) but rejected by Government (Croucher and White 2007).

Critics were initially concerned about the potential impact of the NMW on prices and business stability, particularly for smaller firms which might struggle to meet increased wage levels. Concerns are still voiced most particularly about sectors where low pay is more commonplace and where job losses are feared. Until recently, research commissioned by the LPC has suggested that the NMW is unlikely to be a determining factor in job loss or business failure. However reports during 2006 and 2007 suggest a more ambiguous position, noting job losses in the retail sector and in hospitality. Concerns have increased in 2008 in the face of a deteriorating economic position. Conversely though, it had been suggested when the NMW was first introduced that it might bring about a shift in thinking, 'encouraging firms to compete on the basis of quality as well as price' (LPC 1998: 15 quoted in Grimshaw and Carroll 2006) yet this seems to be the case only for a minority of firms (Druker *et al.* 2005; Grimshaw and Carroll 2006).

Responses to the NMW are more complex than might be anticipated by classical economic theory, which suggests that increasing the price of labour will necessarily lead to a reduction in employment. Card and Krueger's studies of minimum wage schemes in the USA found that firms were more diverse than this in their responses to wage regulation (Card and Krueger 1995, cited in Lam *et al.* 2006: 72). Whilst employer response might be brought about through reductions in staffing levels or in staff hours, in some cases the response might be a deliberate choice to maintain wages above the level of the NMW. There is evidence that increases in the NMW have led to concomitant increases in wage rates to maintain differentials. In developing the notion of a 'company minimum wage' Lam *et al.* argue that, whilst the most common 'company minimum' is set at the NMW, this actually accounts only for a small proportion of companies. Their evidence points to companies clustering their company minimum wage at 'round' salaries – e.g. £5.00 or £5.50. Wages then move up in parallel, rather than differentials being compressed over time as they show in the retail sector (Lam *et al.* 2006).

The NMW has been in place now for several years. There is just one set of rates – set centrally through Government, on the basis of recommendations from the Low Pay Commission – whereas Wages Council rates were set through sectoral Wages Boards. There is significant evidence of employer compliance with the NMW. Its influence is felt because companies use the NMW as the minimum rate and there may be as many as one million employees who are affected in this way by the NMW. Its influence is also significant because companies may refer to it as they seek to position themselves slightly above the minimum and this may double the number of employees whose earnings are influenced as a result (IDS 2006d: 2).

The principles underlying the NMW, like the Wages Councils and the FWR in the past, are now widely accepted and relatively uncontroversial. David Cameron's Office has confirmed that a Conservative Government will keep the minimum wage (Office of David Cameron email, 14th January 2008). Labour and Liberal Democrat politicians are committed and the Confederation of British Industry (CBI) as well as the Trades Union Congress

(TUC) remain committed, although employer representatives lay increasing stress on the need for caution in the level of increases in the face of economic uncertainty.

The NMW is clear in terms of its coverage and simpler in terms of the wage structures that it sets out than the sectorally based Wages Council rates. It has a more limited application in terms of coverage than did the Wages Councils in (say) the mid-1980s – before they were reduced in scope. Like the Wages Councils the enforcement mechanisms remain problematic and awareness of the rates themselves is currently rather limited. Moreover the level is vulnerable to change in Government policy with no automatic provision for upward adjustment. The qualified progress of the past is not guaranteed to continue in the future if governments do not ensure continued up-rating in the level at which the rates are set.

In conclusion

This chapter sets out to review the position of waged and low-paid employees. The transformation in economic and labour market context has been a major driver for change yet there is remarkable continuity in arrangements governing pay. Hourly-based pay rates, weekly (or fortnightly) pay, and additions to basic pay through payment by results and overtime remain commonplace. The erosion of the pay differential between women and men is slow, hampered by continuing occupational gender segregation, with women disproportionately represented in the lower-paid service sector. Although a 'floor' has been set to adult wages by the NMW, there is little evidence as yet that the differentials between the highest paid and the lowest paid within the workforce have been eroded. Interest in single status and harmonisation of working hours and in terms and conditions seems to have diminished.

There are signs of change too, reflecting re-alignments of the workforce within a segmented labour market rather than a fundamental challenge to the principle of labour market segmentation. Pbr and overtime – the traditional additions to hourly-based pay – are now less important as a component in earnings overall than they were in the past and new style bonus arrangements emphasise a more complex array of factors linking individual earnings to business performance. These trends to a more strategic and holistic approach to reward – echoing the precepts of the New Pay writers – seem set to continue. Statutory constraints constitute an important development, both with respect to equal pay and low pay. Yet progress toward equal pay remains slow. The NMW is well established and widely accepted. It has impacted positively on the earnings of the lowest paid but the compliance regime remains weak and there is no mechanism for automatic adjustment to rates. The wide differentials between the lowest and the highest paid remain.

The weighting between change and continuity must be affected by considerations of gender and grade, by women's historic exclusion from many areas of skilled manual work and by the growth of women's labour-market participation. The status difference between the waged workforce and salaried employees in the UK has not disappeared. The account of changes in payment arrangements that tend to accompany discussions of human resource management and 'New Pay' initiatives must be tempered by a reference to lower-paid work and to continuity in the experience of many waged workers.

References

Behrend, H. (1959) 'Financial incentives as the expression of a system of beliefs', *British Journal of Sociology*, 10 (2): 137–47.

Brook, K. (2008) 'Developments in measuring the UK service industries, 1990 to 2006', *Economic and Labour Market Review*, 2 (1), Jan: 18–32.

Brown, C. (1990) 'Firms' choice of method of pay', *Industrial and Labor Relations Review*, 43, special issue, February: 165-S–182-S.

Card, D. and Krueger, A. (1995) *Myth and Measurements: The new economics of the minimum wage*, Princeton University Press. Cited by Lam *et al.* 2006.

Chartered Institute of Personnel and Development (CIPD) (2008) *Reward management survey report*, 2008, London: CIPD.

Croucher, R. and White, G. (2007) 'Enforcing a National Minimum Wage: the British case', *Policy Studies* 28 (2): 145–61.

Daniels, H. (2007) *Patterns of Pay: Results of the Annual Survey of Hours and Earnings, 1997–2007*, London: ONS.

Datta, K., McIlwaine, C., Evans, Y., Herbert, S., May, J. and Wills, J. (2007) 'From coping strategies to tactics: London's low pay economy and migrant labour', *British Journal of Industrial Relations*, 45 (2) June: 404–32.

Dickens, R. and Manning, A. (2003) 'Minimum wage, minimum impact', in R. Dickens, P. Gregg and J. Wadsworth (eds) *The Labour Market Under New Labour: The state of working Britain*, Basingstoke: Palgrave Macmillan.

Dickens, R. and Manning, A. (2004) 'Has the national minimum wage reduced UK wage inequality?', *Journal of the Royal Statistical Society*, 167 (4): 613–26.

Dobbs, C. (2006) 'Patterns of pay: results of the Annual Survey of Hours and Earnings 1997 to 2005', *Labour Market Trends*, February: 45–55.

Druker, J. (2000) 'Wages systems', in G. White and J. Druker (2000) *Reward Management: A critical text*, London: Routledge: 106–25.

Druker, J., White, G. and Stanworth, C. (2005) 'Coping with wage regulation: implementing the National Minimum Wage in hairdressing businesses', *International Small Business Journal*, 23 (1) February: 5–23.

Edwards, P. and Gilman, M. (1999) 'Pay equity and the national minimum wage: what can theories tell us?', *Human Resource Management Journal*, 9 (1) Special Issue: 20–38.

Equal Opportunities Commission (2007) *Completing the Revolution*, Manchester: Equal Opportunities Commission.

Fernie, S. and Metcalf, D. (1998) '(Not) hanging on the telephone: payment systems in the new sweatshops', Centre for Economic Performance, Discussion paper 390, London: Centre for Economic Performance.

French, S. and Mohrke, J. (2006) 'The impact of "new arrivals" upon the North Staffordshire labour market', Research Report for the Low Pay Commission,

Centre for Industrial Relations, Institute of Public Policy and Management: Keele University. Cited in the Low Pay Commission Report, 2007: 347.

Friedman, A. (1977) *Industry and Labour: Class struggle at work and monopoly capitalism*, London: Macmillan.

Grimshaw, D. and Carroll, M. (2006) 'Adjusting to the National Minimum Wage: constraints and incentives to change in six low-paying sectors', *Industrial Relations Journal*, 37 (1): 22–47.

Hastings, S. (2009) 'Grading systems: estimating value and equality', in G. White and J. Druker (2009) *Reward Management: A critical text*, 2nd edn, London: Routledge.

Heywood, J., Seibert, W.S. and Xiangdong, W. (1997) 'Payment by results systems: British evidence', *British Journal of Industrial Relations*, 35 (1) March: 1–22.

Incomes Data Services (IDS) (1998) *Report* 771 October, London: IDS.

Incomes Data Services (2005) 'Bonus Schemes', *IDS HR Studies* 794 March 2005, London: IDS.

Incomes Data Services (2006a) *IDS Pay Report*, 953, May 2006, London: IDS.

Incomes Data Services (2006b) *IDS Pay Report*, 963, October 2006, London: IDS.

Incomes Data Services (2006c) 'Overtime', *IDS HR Studies*, 813, January 2006, London: IDS.

Incomes Data Services (2006d) *IDS Pay Report*, 967, December 2006, London: IDS.

Incomes Data Services (2007a) *Pay and conditions in engineering 2006/07*, London: IDS.

Incomes Data Services (2007b) 'Bonus schemes', *IDS HR Studies*, 843, April 2007, London: IDS.

Kersley, B., Alpin, C., Forth, J., Bryson, A., Bewley, H., Dix, G. and Oxenbridge, S. (2006) *Inside the Workplace: Findings from the 2004 Workplace Employment Relations Survey*, London: Routledge.

Lam, K., Ormerod, C., Ritchie, F. and Vaze, P. (2006) 'Do company wage policies persist in the face of minimum wages?', *Labour Market Trends*, March 2006: 69–81.

Lawler, Edward E. (1990) *Strategic Pay: Aligning organisational strategies and pay systems*, San Francisco: Jossey-Bass.

Lawler, Edward E. (Edward E. Lawler III) (2000) *Rewarding Excellence*, San Francisco: Jossey-Bass.

Low Pay Commission (LPC) (1998) *The National Minimum Wage: first report of the Low Pay Commission*, June 1998, Cm 3976, Norwich: HMSO.

Low Pay Commission (2003) *The National Minimum Wage. Fourth report of the Low Pay Commission: Building on success*, March 2003, Cm5768, Norwich: HMSO.

Low Pay Commission (2006) *National Minimum Wage: Low Pay Commission Report 2006*, Cm 6759, Norwich: HMSO.

Low Pay Commission (2007) *National Minimum Wage: Low Pay Commission Report 2007*, Cm 7056, Norwich: HMSO.

Low Pay Commission (2008) *National Minimum Wage: Low Pay Commission Report 2008*, Cm 7333, Norwich: HMSO.

National Board for Prices and Incomes (1968) 'Payment by results systems'. Report 65, Cmnd 3627, May, London: HMSO.

Office for National Statistics (ONS) (various years) *Annual Survey of Hours and Earnings*. Published online at http://www.statistics.gov.uk

Rubery, J. and Edwards, P. 'Low Pay and the National Minimum Wage', in P. Edwards (ed.) *Industrial Relations, Theory and Practice*, Oxford: Blackwell.

Schuster, J.R. and Zingheim, P. (1992) *The New Pay: Linking Employee and Organizational Performance*, New York: Lexington Books.

Storey, J. (2007) 'Human resource management today: an assessment', in J. Storey, *Human Resource Management: A critical text*, London: Thomson.

Taylor, F.W. (1913) *The Principles of Scientific Management*, New York and London: Harper & Brothers.

White, G. (1999) 'Pay structures of the low paid and the national minimum wage', *Labour Market Trends*, 107 (3): 129–35.

6   Salary progression systems

Marc Thompson

Summary

This chapter critically reviews theoretical and empirical evidence to consider developments in salary progression systems in the UK over the last two decades. At a theoretical level, it outlines the key economic and psychological frameworks, arguing that both need to be considered together to enrich our understanding of salary progression systems in practice.

The empirical data suggests that, whereas the 1980s and early 1990s were characterised by a shift to performance-based salary progression, convoluted pay structures and high levels of management control in the context of looser labour markets, the last 10 years or more have been marked by the combination of skill shortages with equal value concerns to challenge this model and re-establish more transparent salary progression systems. A key trend has been the emergence of 'hybrid' salary progression schemes combining behavioural and output-based metrics.

The research evidence on salary progression systems and pay systems in general reveals a field that is not in good health. There is a need for more rigorous, in-depth, longitudinal research on change in reward systems in order to develop more robust theory that can be useful to practitioners.

Introduction

The concept of pay progression originates in the development of salaried employment in the late nineteenth century. In contrast to wage workers, salaried status implied a long-term employment relationship and the potential for career development. Employees therefore tended to be rewarded for seniority and their growing experience and hence value to the organisation.

Salary progression payment systems, in these traditional terms, consist of a number of basic elements; a number of levels of work organised around a grade structure, often determined by a job evaluation methodology, together with a series of steps or pay points enabling incremental progression within these grades. The means of progression through these scales was traditionally based upon length of service or age. When an employee's skills or potential outgrew the limits of the grade, there was often an opportunity for promotion to a higher grade. In addition, salaried (or white-collar) employees also enjoyed a range of employee benefits that differentiated them from manual (or wage) employees. Typically white-collar employees have occupational or company pension schemes, shorter working hours, longer holidays and access to a range of perks dependent on their grade and status. Given the long-term growth in the relative share of white-collar jobs in the economy such payment systems have increased their coverage, particularly in large public- and private sector organisations (Institute for Employment Research 2006).

When these bureaucratic systems emerged in the late nineteenth and early twentieth centuries, they were seen by social scientists (Weber 1978; Schumpeter 1950) as progressive, rational and an expression of the emergence of industrial society. However, the discourse on these payment systems in the last two decades has not continued in the same vein. Rather, such payment systems have been seen as constraints on business and no longer efficient in the light of contemporary competitive dynamics. A new discourse has emerged using terms such as 'new pay', 'paying for contribution', 'pay for competence', and this has challenged the assumptions underpinning traditional salary progression systems.

The 'New Pay'

The so-called 'New Pay' paradigm, most commonly linked with the work of Lawler (1994) and Schuster and Zingheim (1996), argues that pay should be more closely aligned with the strategic objectives of the organisation. Rather than reward being seen as a heavily institutionalised system, often seen as outside of managers' control, these authors argue that it is a strategic lever that can enable managers to shape the skills, competencies and performance levels required to deliver the organisation's strategic goals.

The new pay is characterised not only by an emphasis on a new way of thinking about pay but also by an association with a specific set of new pay practices: linking pay to performance or competencies, using team-related bonuses and, in terms of grading systems, adopting new approaches such as broad banding or job families for example.

Because the concept of the new pay elides two ideas (that of thinking strategically and the introduction of new pay practices), it can be criticised for lacking clarity and precision. This, in turn, can create problems in researching the nature, purpose and impact of adopting a so-called 'new pay' approach.

A hypothetical example serves to illustrate this point. Take two organisations in the same sector. Both may use broadly the same set of traditional reward practices but one may be defined as adopting the new pay if it invests more managerial time in aligning these practices to the strategic objectives of the firm. In one interpretation it is the process of strategic alignment that is critical. On the other hand, take two other firms in the same sector. One has adopted a set of new pay practices (competency-based pay, broadbanding, team incentives) but fails to link these to the strategic goals of the organisation. Another deploys existing traditional compensation practices but takes great care to continually review these pay practices to ensure that they deliver strategic organisational objectives. On the surface the first firm may be regarded as operating in the new pay domain because of its deployment of new pay practices. However, the second firm may in fact deliver much higher performance without significant change to the actual reward practices being used. Which firm can be considered to have adopted the 'new pay' model?

The story of Lincoln Electric in the USA illustrates this dilemma. While the example refers to a payment scheme for manual employees, the implications can be generalised to other payment forms. Lincoln Electric has been operating the same piece-work payment system for its manual employees since 1934. Research suggests that over 70,000 piecework changes have been made over 60 years and less than 1 per cent of these have been challenged by employees (Wiley 1993). These changes have been made to address the changing nature of markets and technologies, what we might think of as strategic alignment. The firm has not introduced new reward practices in this period but its process of aligning the reward system to the changing operational context has ensured that it can adapt to change. Can this be regarded as a 'new pay' organisation even though its reward practices are more than 70 years old?

This feature is recognised by one of the leading exponents of strategic reward. 'The New Pay is not a set of compensation practices at all but rather a way of thinking about the role of reward systems in a complex organisation' (Lawler 1995: 15). His stress on 'thinking about' implies that a cognitive shift by those managing and managed underpins the new pay, not necessarily the adoption of new practices. Consequently, an important differentiating characteristic is that the new pay seeks to align employee interests with those of the firm. This is often seen to operate through the closer integration of organisational performance, individual performance and rewards. Taking this line of argument, it is perfectly reasonable to interpret Lincoln Electric as an example of the 'new pay'.

The discussion above has important implications for how we research and understand research on payment systems. If the new pay is about the managerial processes of aligning and adapting existing payment systems to contingencies then most survey research on pay in organisations fails to provide us with much data or insight on this process dimension. Furthermore, if the new pay is based on a new cognitive framing of the role of reward, as Lawler suggests, few, if any, studies explore this dimension either. As a result, surveys that record the incidence of new pay practices (which is the bedrock of much research in the field to date) may fundamentally under-report or over-report the extent of strategic pay as this is embedded in the organisational processes that managers use to align pay with strategic contingencies (market, technology, etc.). As the Lincoln Electric case illustrates, these aspects are revealed through more detailed longitudinal case studies. Unfortunately, few of these types of studies exist.

In a further contribution to the new pay debate, Gomez-Mejia (1993:14) argues that:

> The emerging paradigm of the field is based on a strategic orientation where issues of internal equity and external equity are viewed as secondary to the firm's need to use pay as an essential integrating and signalling mechanism to achieve over-arching business objectives.

This observation underscores a considerable shift in the logics driving the reform of pay systems. Whereas traditional payment systems have been characterised by their focus on meeting the equity concerns of employees, often articulated through collective bargaining and union philosophy, the new pay is characterised by the primary focus on business strategy.

Reflecting this shift in thinking in relation to the use of performance-pay in the 1990s, Kessler and Purcell (1992) argued that organisations' use of performance-related pay is being shaped by objectives that are no longer traditional (i.e. the desire to recruit, retain and motivate labour). Their detailed case-study work in both public and private sector organisations found that managerial strategies for performance-pay schemes reflect motives such as culture change or organisational transformation. As such, this study confirmed some of the premises underpinning the new pay debate with performance-related pay seen to play a symbolic role, communicating to employees a new strategic intent and a new business model for the future. Performance-related pay was therefore part of moulding attitudes and behaviours amongst the workforce and management in an attempt to realise strategic objectives.

In summary, the new pay debate raises a number of challenges to the traditional salary progression model. The emphasis on seniority and not performance as a basis of pay progression questions seniority as one of the fundamental values underpinning traditional schemes. As Heery (1998) has noted, the new pay has challenged prevailing notions of equity. Should employees be rewarded for loyalty and long-term commitment to the organisation by incremental progression based on length of service (one model of equity?) or should their pay progression be regularly reviewed in line with their contribution to the organisation (another model of equity?)? This question of equity is one that we return to as we review empirical evidence on salary progression systems, particularly in the public sector.

Another important issue relates to the evidence base itself. The primary focus in this chapter is to review developments in salary progression systems over the last decade or so taking account of newly published theoretical and empirical material. However, if the new pay can be interpreted as a managerial mindset or embedded in a set of processes that link reward practices to the strategic objectives of the organisation, it makes many of the cross-sectional, employer-based surveys that dominate the field rather limited in their ability to capture such phenomena.

Given the importance of mindsets and new ways of thinking about reward and in particular developments in salary progression systems, these systems will now be considered within a broader theoretical context. This is not irrelevant to our understanding of practice and one example serves to underline this point. Principal-agent theory, which is discussed shortly, forms the intellectual bedrock of the UK government's approach to reform (including reward systems) in the public sector. As the review of public services productivity (HM Treasury 2003) observed: 'Principal-agent theory is an established body of economic literature that provides a number of insights into institutional design that have informed the government's framework for raising public services productivity' (p. 41). This theory and its implications for salary progression systems are returned to in due course.

Safe to say, there are many strands of thought in the social science literature that can shed light on organisations' use of salary progression systems, of which principal-agent theory is but one. These main theories are reviewed and their implications for pay progression systems in practice discussed. Next, trends and developments in salary progression systems in the UK are considered, outlining important differences between the public and private sectors. Here, particular attention is drawn to changes in public sector pay progression systems. Lastly, some observations on the research, policy and managerial implications of this review are made.

Theoretical perspectives

Salary progression systems are an important feature of the employment relationship but how can we explain their existence from a theoretical perspective? Given that employment is both an economic and psychological relationship, these two main literatures are drawn upon to deepen our understanding of salary progression systems.[1] Answers to this question can be found in two main literatures – economics and psychology – which both bring different assumptions and perspectives to bear. While it could be argued that the assumptions underpinning both perspectives are fundamentally incommensurate because of their different models of human behaviour, considering both together can provide a richer interpretation of the rationale for such pay systems. Furthermore, each theory emphasises different aspects and therefore provides new insights on the operation of pay systems, including salary progression systems in practice.

Economic perspectives

Internal labour market theory

Doeringer and Piore (1971) developed internal labour market theory as a means of explaining why classical economic theory failed to explain why jobs that are, to all intents and purposes, similar, can attract vastly different wages between firms. Their path-breaking contribution was to posit that administrative rules and procedures within firms might explain these variations. They defined an internal labour market (ILM) as:

> . . . an administrative unit within which the pricing and allocation of labor is governed by a set of administrative rules and procedures. ILMs interact with external labor markets (ELMs) through certain ports of entry or exit, with the remaining jobs within the ILMs being filled by promotions or transfers. In consequence, the jobs are shielded from any direct influence of the ELMs.
>
> (Doeringer and Piore 1971: 9)

While the firm with an ILM is connected to market mechanisms at key ports of entry jobs, once in employment internal rules shape the wages of employees. The main focus of these rules is on progression and promotion through the various job ladders. ILM rules determine the number of progression points, the rate of progression and also the criteria that determines who progresses. Typically, seniority or age has been the most widely used criteria for progression but, as we will see later, both managerial and institutional factors have played an important part in reshaping these criteria. Progression between grades is possible when vacancies are available at higher levels, which implies that such systems depend on growth or reasonable levels of staff turnover (in a steady state environment) in order to open up opportunities and thereby maintain the incentives of the reward structure.

In practice these structures have existed primarily in large organisations in the public and private sector, where there is scope for such progression. Internal labour markets are much weaker outside of these types of business (Eyraud *et al.* 1990). Therefore, most of the discussion of salary progression systems and internal labour markets relates to large organisations.

The employment relationship in an ILM is essentially long term in nature and Doeringer and Piore (1971) identified these systems as conferring a number of benefits for organisations, namely:

1 reducing turnover costs by providing incentives for employees to remain with the firm;
2 building firm specific skills which enable the organisation to extract higher rents;

3   enabling firms to align jobs with technologies and specific customer demands;
4   providing the opportunity to monitor employee quality and performance.

More recently, writers from the 'new personnel economics' perspective (e.g. Lazear 1999) have argued that ILMs provide an opportunity for firms to gather more information on worker quality and thereby reduce their risks in future employee investments through promotions. Furthermore, the incentive structures inherent in salary and grading structures associated with ILMs could serve to reduce employee 'shirking' and stimulate employee performance.

Internal labour markets are also seen as beneficial by human resource theorists who argue that they enhance employee commitment through increasing employee identification with the firm (Benson 1995; Cappelli 1995). Furthermore, this increased commitment leads to positive economic benefits for the firm in the form of higher levels of productivity, better quality and customer service, as well as lower levels of employee turnover. Therefore, internal labour markets are seen as integral to a high commitment and high performance organisation (Pfeffer 1998).

Another important dimension of internal labour markets is that the administrative rules that govern their operation contribute to a set of expectations and psychological behaviours amongst employees. These rules underpin and help develop customs and norms about wage structures, promotion and progression arrangements as well as other aspects of work (Doeringer and Piore 1971). Internal labour markets can therefore help create a stable environment of mutual expectations and obligations – a high trust environment. As a consequence, any change in the administrative rules will potentially have a serious knock-on effect for the psychological dimension of the employment contract.

The reshaping of bureaucratic rules in ILMs is returned to later when reviewing the empirical evidence on developments in salary progression systems, particularly within the UK public sector. Here, social norms enshrined in legislation combating discrimination on the basis of age and gender has played an important role in the restructuring of salary progression systems. To some extent, the economic forces that focused on flexibility and minimising the costs of bureaucracy in internal labour markets have been reined in by societal concerns with equity and justice. This trend, to a large extent, could be seen to characterise developments in reward in the public services in the last decade.

The emphasis on administrative rules in ILM theory leaves open the possibility that these rules can be reformed, renegotiated and reshaped in new ways. In focusing on rules, customs and norms, the theory is important in helping us understand the dynamic nature of these systems. In a recent review of research on ILM, Piore (2002), one of the originators of the concept, argued that while it had come under significant pressure from new management strategies such as outsourcing, network and project-based organisational forms, it is still a resilient and significant labour market institution shaping employer and employee behaviour. In particular, he argued that:

> We will, in other words, continue to have internal labour markets in the broad sense of the term. But the particular forms these internal labour markets will take are extremely varied. No single form will be dominant in the way in which bureaucratic organisation was dominant in the post-war period.
>
> (Piore 2002: 273)

One implication is that we may see much more heterogeneity in payment systems, a point returned to when assessing the empirical evidence.

Transaction Cost Economics (TCE)

In Williamson's transaction costs theory (Williamson 1975), firms rationally choose seniority-based pay systems because the information and system costs of specifying and monitoring individual performance contracts are considered too high. While Doeringer and Piore emphasised the importance of economic efficiency and the role of social custom in shaping the development of ILMs, Williamson's theory was driven by economics alone. Williamson, building on Coase (1937), addressed the question as to why firms (and internal labour markets) exist. He explained this phenomenon by reference to the 'transaction costs' associated with market mechanisms. Quite simply, the idea of transaction costs is based on the insight that the cost of discovering the best deal outweighs the benefits gained. When it comes to ILMs, Williamson developed the concept of 'small numbers bargaining' wherein the idiosyncratic nature of jobs in the ILM means that there may not be a competitive market for these skills in the external labour market. Furthermore, the task mix in these idiosyncratic jobs which have been developed by internal training and custom are affected by shifts in demand, new technology, market regulation and so on. The risk inherent in these 'small numbers bargaining' situations is that they can promote opportunistic behaviour since the market mechanism is not available to discipline both parties. In these cases, it is more efficient for the firm to develop longer-term, often open-ended, contracts with workers. Bounded rationality (Simon 1957) also creates conditions that support such contracts because it is impossible for firms to specify ex ante all the possible future outcomes that may arise in the labour contract. Consequently, it is economically efficient for firms to develop arrangements whereby workers are prepared to accept direction from managers in return for obligations on the part of the employer. In the context of the ILM, this would typically include promotion from within, seniority-based pay progression and some protection from arbitrary dismissal.

Efficiency wage theory

Efficiency wage theory was developed in order to explain why some firms in identical market situations opt to pay much higher salaries for their employees in what to all intents and purposes might be regarded as similar types of jobs. Economists could not understand why there should be steep earning curves in these firms when they could pay much less.

Efficiency wage theory suggests that the higher wages available in the organisation's internal labour market will have two main effects. First, it will prevent turnover because employees will not be able to command the same salary levels in the external market. Therefore, the financial losses associated with leaving the firm will encourage employees to exert more effort on behalf of the organisation. This is based on the assumption that an employee's skills are generally firm specific, such as familiarity with a particular working environment, a group of colleagues and the organisation's systems and processes (Stevens 1999). In return for the 'gift exchange' (Akerlof and Yellen 1986) of higher wages, the organisation hopes to achieve high levels of co-operation from the employee in which they would work 'beyond contract' to meet the changing needs of the firm.

Higher wage levels may also minimise supervisory costs as increased work effort and motivation by employees may mean less managerial supervision. Lazear (1999) and Yellen (1984) also argue that higher wage levels will prevent 'shirking'. This view, based in a neo-classical economic model, sees workers as making daily trade-offs between work and leisure with the risk to employers that without appropriate supervision or incentive schemes they will inevitably prefer leisure (i.e. shirking).

This perspective tends to ignore the intrinsic motivational nature of work itself, which features more highly in psychological perspectives. A second key benefit is the firm's ability to attract higher-quality or more conscientious employees (a sorting effect). This is based on the assumption that high-ability employees are less likely to be attracted to lower-wage employers.

The issue of efficiency wages, turnover and shirking is returned to when the available empirical evidence is reviewed.

Principal-agent theory

Principal-agent or agency theory has become the most important framework informing the design of executive compensation reward schemes, but the general principles can be applied to any situation in which delegation of decision-making happens and hence is relevant for the design of reward systems more generally. The fundamental problem agency theory seeks to address is the lack of alignment between the interests of owners and managers in the modern corporation.

In agency theory terms owners are 'principals' and managers or employees are 'agents'. The theory developed amongst others by Holmstrom and

Milgrom (1991), Jensen and Meckling (1976) and Mirrlees (1972) is rooted in the neo-classical view of human behaviour where the fundamental assumption is that employees or managers are driven by self-interest which is characterised by manipulative behaviour to serve their own interests. This self-interest means there is 'goal incongruence' between the principals and agents and this in turn can lead to or be shaped by other classical contracting problems in economics such as 'moral hazard', 'information asymmetry' and 'adverse selection'.

Information asymmetry is where principals have less information than agents either about the decisions made by agents or their ability. These problems can be exacerbated by 'adverse selection' decisions by principals before an employment (or other contract) is finalised. These might include people overstating their previous accomplishments in CVs or using inside knowledge of company performance that might affect negotiation over the measures to be used in rewarding performance (e.g. market share versus profitability).

Moral hazard problems can arise post-contract when an executive, for example, might manipulate financial information for personal gain against the interests of the owners and shareholders. These practices are very hard to uncover by principals who are often reliant on agents for information and mitigating such risks can lead to significant agency costs. Agency theory explores how the risks associated with moral hazard, information asymmetry and adverse selection amongst others can be mitigated by designing an appropriate contract. The theory posits that principals can design two main types of contractual arrangement: one based on outcomes and the other on behaviours. Outcome-based contracts are seen to be preferable as they can minimise monitoring costs and have the potential to align interests between principal and agent more closely. Behaviour-based measures bring with them considerable information-monitoring costs and are complex where the principals are not experts in the particular field which makes judgements of effective behaviours difficult to make. In practical terms behaviour-based approaches might include better systems of work design and measurement such as performance-management systems which are aimed at improving the correlation between effort and performance (Milgrom and Roberts 1992).

In the context of salary progression systems where line manager assessment is important for pay progression, the individual manager will play an important role in renegotiating performance expectations, as Marsden (2004) has suggested. Introducing new forms of assessment and performance measurement can set new norms around work performance and can therefore be critical in responding to external competitive pressures. The extent to which these aspects of agency theory are reflected in the empirical evidence on developments in performance-based salary progression systems are returned to later.

Psychological perspectives

There are at least three main psychological theories that are relevant to under-standing salary progression systems: expectancy theory, goal setting and finally equity theory. It should be stressed that economic theories and psycho-logical theories tend to be shaped by quite different models of human nature. Before his untimely death Sumantra Ghoshal argued that the 'dismal' science of economics taught in business schools tended to stress the one-dimensional, self-interested and narrow economic aspects of human nature and that this has become a self-fulfilling prophecy leading to managerial malfeasance much in evidence at Enron and Tyco (Ghoshal and Moran 1996).

Psychological theories, by and large, take a much broader view of human motivation and goals, looking beyond narrow monetary dimensions. Psycho-logists also tend to focus on understanding the cognitive processes and dis-positions associated with motivation and developing theories that model these processes. Expectancy theory is a key building block in work psych-ology and its conditions inform the design and evaluation of pay systems, often implicitly. The theory (Vroom 1964; Porter and Lawler 1968) sees performance as the product of an individual's ability and motivational force to engage in one type of behaviour rather than another. Three factors are important in shaping this motivation force: expectancy (the perceived link between effort and behaviours), instrumentality (the perceived link between behaviours and outcomes such as incentive pay) and valence (the value attached to the incentive by the individual). High levels of motivation are possible when these three conditions are met but if one or more of the condi-tions is absent the motivational force is likely to be much reduced. Despite this there is little empirical research that has found support for the model. However, the main tenets of the theory have been widely accepted in the design and reform of payment schemes.

Goal-setting theory

Goal-setting theory predicts that higher levels of effort and performance are the result of individual commitment to specific and attainable goals (Locke 1968). In subsequent empirical work Locke and Latham (1984) were able to specify certain other supporting conditions for the model, particularly in relation to the role of pay. First, they cautioned that incentives can only support goal setting when they are supported by a rigorous and consistent process of goal choice and commitment. Such commitment can be achieved by involving employees in the setting of their goals. Furthermore, and in line with expectancy theory, employees need to perceive the goals as attainable. If goals are seen to be too difficult employees are unlikely to be motivated to commit to their attainment. The challenge for managers is to get the right balance between goal commitment and difficulty in order for rewards to act as performance incentives. From this perspective, goal setting is a critical mediator between incentives and performance. Empirical research has shown that there is a strong and positive relationship between goal difficulty, commitment and performance (Klein *et al.* 1999). A major criticism of goal setting is that employees tend to focus solely their attention on what is rewarded and ignore other factors that may be important in contributing to performance. A study by Wright *et al.* (1993) found that difficult goals combined with incentives could work against 'prosocial helping behaviours' important in team production contexts. Thus, 'bad measures' could drive out other beneficial behaviours in the goal setting process.

Equity and justice theories

Equity theory is perhaps one of the most relevant theories to developing an understanding of salary progression systems in practice. The question that an employee will ask in a reward system where one individual achieves faster pay progression than another is whether the decision made has been fair in relative terms. Equity theory, quite simply, is based on the proposition that people make judgements about the fairness of their pay on a comparative basis. People in the same job role, doing similar work under a pay progression system determined by systems such as merit or appraisal, will make assessments about whether the effort-reward outcomes are fair.

Equity and justice theories make distinctions between procedural and distributive justice. It is possible for an employee to be dissatisfied with their pay outcome in relation to others (distributive justice) but also theoretically possible that they may feel that the way this decision was arrived at was broadly fair (procedural justice). Research has tended to show that where firms pay attention to both dimensions of justice perceptions employee dissatisfaction is likely to be minimised. Brockner and Wiesenfeld (1996), for example, found that where there are high levels of distributive justice (i.e. when people feel they have been well rewarded) they are less likely to worry about the processes that led to this outcome.

However, if they received low levels of outcome they were more likely to be dissatisfied with the procedures used to make the distribution decision. Put simply, the outcome tended to override procedural equity concerns. Interestingly, in cases where there was perceived to be low distributive justice, high levels of procedural justice moderate negative satisfaction outcomes. Treating people in a fair and consistent manner is important in terms of their pay satisfaction. In a study of scientists and engineers in R&D-based organisations, Thompson and Heron (2005) explored the role of the line manager in this process and found that what they termed 'interactional justice' (i.e. the quality of the relationship between the manager and employee) moderated the negative outcomes of distributive and procedural justice in relation to employee commitment. Consequently, merit- and appraisal-based pay systems are likely to trigger equity and justice concerns amongst workers but these downsides might be moderated by good procedures and high-quality relationships between line managers and employees.

However, for pay scheme designers one of the issues unresolved by the theory is what constitutes equity or justice? Many motivation studies have shown considerable variation in the incentives or rewards valued by individuals and that these rewards are not stable over the life-cycle. Designing effective individualised pay for performance schemes is likely to depend on several co-related factors which can interact to produce either more or less negative outcomes.

In brief, a number of theories based in either economic or psychological epistemologies that provide different perspectives on salary progression systems have been presented so far. These are summarised in Table 6.1 which sets out the underlying design principles or empirical fact that theory is trying to understand. So, for example, with Transaction Cost Economics it is why idiosyncratic jobs exist and with goal setting it is defining objectives for employees. The table then looks at the management implications of the theories and finally their impact or benefit.

Performance-based pay progression: empirical evidence

Incremental, seniority-based salary progression systems rely on the assumption that performance improves with length of service and that age and seniority are as good proxy measures for performance improvement as any. As we have outlined, the story of pay progression systems over the last two decades has been to move away from this principle and focus on individual behaviours, skills and competencies as the main criteria for progression. This shift in focus towards individualisation and a greater emphasis on flexibility and adaptability on behalf of the employee has reshaped the psychological contract for many white-collar employees (and increasingly manual employees too). But how widespread is the use of performance-based progression systems?

There are surprisingly few large-scale representative and reliable studies that can help us understand the evolution of salary progression systems. A major problem in assessing the growth of salary progression systems linked to performance is the lack of data using consistent measures. The Government's Annual Survey of Hours and Earnings (ASHE) provides information about the composition of employee earnings (i.e. overtime pay, shift pay, payment by results and profit-related pay) over time for different occupational groups. Unless an employee receives a separate merit payment (which can be identified as payment by results), there is no way of determining how an employee is paid. The category called 'all other pay' (which includes basic pay) does not distinguish between the method of progression for salaried workers (seniority, age, performance, skills acquisition or competence). This does not help to understand the extent to which salary progression systems for white-collar employees have shifted from using rules based on seniority to rules based on performance.

Table 6.1 Theoretical implications for salary progression systems

THEORY	IMPLICATIONS FOR SALARY PROGRESSION SYSTEMS		
ECONOMIC	PRIMARY FOCUS	MANAGEMENT	EFFECT/BENEFITS
Internal labour market theory	Administrative rules	• Rules can be negotiated • High-trust, stable environment critical	• Lower turnover costs • Firm-specific skills • Strategic alignment • Employee commitment • Monitor employee quality
Transaction cost economics	Idiosyncratic jobs	• Long-term, open-ended contracts • Employees accept management direction • Promotion and seniority rules	• Lower turnover costs • Firm-specific skills • Employee flexibility
Efficiency wage theory	Steep earning curves/high wages	• Lower management/employee ratios	• Lower supervisory management costs • Lower turnover • Attract better quality labour • Commitment and motivation
Principal agent theory	Alignment of interests in devolved decision-making contexts	• Renegotiation of performance norms • Outcome- and behaviour-based contracts	• Minimise goal incongruence • Minimise 'shirking' • Improve labour quality
PSYCHOLOGICAL	PRIMARY FOCUS	MANAGEMENT	EFFECT/BENEFITS
Expectancy theory	Motivation force	• Clarity of objectives • Reward valued by employees • Skills and ability of employees	• Motivation • Job satisfaction • Labour turnover decreased
Goal setting theory	Goal definition	• Goal choice • Employee involvement in process • Goal difficulty	• Motivation • Lower turnover • Commitment
Equity theories	Procedural and distributive justice rules	• Fair procedures • Feedback mechanisms • Open information	• Motivation • Lower turnover • Commitment

This material is taken from the CIPD annual survey report Reward Management (2007) with the permission of the publisher, the Chartered Institute of Personnel and Development, London (www.cipd.co.uk)

To understand these more subtle questions we need to turn to other sources of data. The most representative source of data on work and employment issues in the UK is the Workplace Employment Relations Survey (WERS). The latest available data comes from the 2004 survey. However, this survey also presents problems in trying to understand the coverage of salary progression systems based on either seniority or performance rules. First, the survey does not collect data on pay structures or pay levels which are important data in building a picture of salary progression systems, particularly if we are interested in rates of change. Second, while the survey does ask questions related to the basis for determining pay these are at a level of abstraction that make it difficult to understand the micro-level processes at firm level and how these might be changing. The best that we can do, as is the case with much survey data, is to make some inferences on trends based on the limited data available.

WERS 2004 (Kersley *et al.* 2006) gathered data on 'performance related payment schemes'. These covered two principal types of scheme. The first, payment by results (PBR), is an output-based payment system related to the level, quality, value or other output measure. The second is merit pay in which pay is related to a subjective assessment of performance by a supervisor.

Of these two types of performance-payment system, merit pay is the one most closely associated with our definition of a performance-based salary progression system. However, this interpretation needs some caveats. WERS does not provide information on whether these merit payments were consolidated and formed part of a pay ladder or were simply one-off incentive payments. This is important. If we do not know whether merit payments are linked or detached from salary progression it is difficult to understand the extent to which these payments are substituting for, or additional to, seniority-based progression rules. Workplaces using only merit payment systems accounted for 9 per cent of the sample and 30 per cent used a combination of both merit and PBR (Kersley *et al.* 2006). In total, 40 per cent of all workplaces had some incidence of performance-related pay. Further complications arise when trying to understand change over time as the measures used by the survey in 2004 were different from those used in 1998. However, panel data estimates do provide some level of comparative analysis and show that workplaces using incentive payments (merit or PBR) had increased from 20 per cent in 1998 to 32 per cent in 2004.

The WERS data show that the most popular approach to performance-based pay is to combine objective and subjective methods of assessment to form hybrid or what is now being termed 'contribution'-based pay systems (Brown and Armstrong 1999). The empirical evidence challenges the tenets of principal agent theory that suggests that firms will make choices between output-based and behaviour-based schemes depending on context. The theory does not sufficiently take account of hybridised approaches. Furthermore, the transaction cost perspective may also have difficulty in reconciling the increased monitoring costs associated with deploying both incentive forms simultaneously. Psychological theories, on the other hand, such as expectancy and goal setting, are more able to deal with hybridised models.

The WERS data, while indicative of a trend towards relating pay to performance, are less helpful in understanding the extent to whether performance rules are replacing seniority rules in salary progression systems. One can infer that there may be some link but WERS does not provide sufficient evidence. The Chartered Institute for Personnel and Development's (CIPD) Reward Management survey, albeit less rigorous and representative, can help address this gap. The survey is based on responses from 466 organisations from across public and private sectors. The 2007 survey repeats questions first asked in 2005 on performance pay and includes valuable information on salary progression but also gathers data on other aspects of pay structures relevant to salary progression systems such as the use of job evaluation and different types of grading structures (e.g. broad bands).

Job evaluation and pay structures

One of the building blocks of traditional salary progression systems is a job-based pay structure underpinned by a job-evaluation system. Job evaluation provides a means of not only providing an internal logic to the job structure but also a way of monitoring pay levels with external labour markets. One interpretation of the 'new pay' literature (Schuster and Zingheim 1996; Lawler 1994) is that organisations will move away from such systems as they are perceived to introduce rigidities and inflexibilities that prevent firms from recognising individuals' contribution. In other words, individual productivity should drive pay rather than jobs and markets. The CIPD survey (Table 6.2) reveals that job evaluation is used by around three-quarters of respondents employing more than 1,000 staff. Furthermore, around one in six organisations plan to introduce a new job evaluation system or change their existing one with this rising to nearly one in four public sector organisations. On this evidence, the job-based pay structure is far from dead and, if anything, looks as if it is enjoying a renaissance.

Table 6.2 Pay structure management by occupational group, 2007

Type of pay structure	Senior management	Middle/1st line Mgr	Technical/ professional	Clerical/ manual
Individual pay rates/spot salaries/ranges	44	26	25	23
Broadbands	33	40	40	35
Narrow-graded pay structures	12	14	14	22
Pay spines	10	14	15	16
Job families/career grades	22	30	31	26

Source: CIPD 2007

This rediscovery of job evaluation does not appear to be linked to discontent with the 'new pay' ideology. Rather, it appears to be driven by three factors. First, as a pragmatic response to legislative changes, second as a means of addressing employee and organisational dissatisfaction with more fluid structures, such as broadbanding, and third as a way of ensuring pay structures are competitive in a much tighter labour market. Organisations have adapted their reward systems in order to respond to developments in the legislative environment. In both the public and private sectors, organisations have been 'equality-proofing' their pay since the introduction of the EOC Code of Practice on Equal Pay (EOC 1997) and coming into force of the Employment Equality (Age) Regulations in October 2006. These regulations require that pay scales with increments extending for more than five years need to be justified objectively to show that they do not discriminate on age or indirectly on gender.

The response in both public and private sectors is to shorten pay scales not only for protection against legal claims but also to rebuild career structures and retain skills. The much tighter labour market context has put the 'war for talent' at the top of the HR Directors' agenda and in an effort to recruit and retain staff, many organisations have rediscovered career ladders and rebuilt their internal career structures to make them more transparent. In particular, there has been an increase in the use of job families where firms bundle together jobs with similar competencies to form career ladders and also support market rate tracking. This has seen a move away from broad-banded systems that lacked clarity and exposed them to the risk of equal value claims (IDS 2007a).

An example of the effect of legislation on salary progression systems comes from the public sector. The Advisory and Conciliation Service (ACAS) moved to shorter pay scales in 2001 after losing an equal pay case brought by one of its female employees. In Crossley and Others v. ACAS (Birmingham Employment Tribunal, 1304744/98 20.12.99), the Tribunal found in favour of the Applicants. The Applicants' case was that the ACAS pay system, which rewarded length of service, was indirectly discriminatory and therefore contrary to the Equal Pay Act. Within ACAS the pay structure incorporated a system which automatically awarded incremental pay increases to staff each year. Even though the incremental system had since been abandoned in favour of performance-related pay, nonetheless the old increments remained embedded in the system. The female member of staff earned £3,000 less than her male counterpart because of his longer service in the service-related pay structure.

More recently, the Cadman ruling on equal pay at the European Court of Justice has further emphasised the need for pay progression systems to be objectively justified (IDS *Employment Law Brief* 2006). The Cadman case arose when an employee of the Health and Safety Executive (HSE), Bernadette Cadman, brought an equal pay claim to an employment tribunal. She was paid £9,000 less than four male counterparts employed on the same band. The main reason for the pay difference was that the men had longer service periods.

At a theoretical level, the role of legislation in shaping organisational practice around salary progression systems appears to support the original arguments of Doeringer and Piore (1971) that social custom and norms are reflected in the structuring of internal labour markets. In other words, societal values around equity and fair treatment, articulated through legal codes, have shaped the administrative rules governing salary progression systems. Furthermore, the ongoing campaigns by unions in the public services in the UK which have raised concerns about the potential for discrimination in these payment systems have also shaped norms and values amongst staff and managers. As a result, unions have an increasingly important role in influencing the design of payment schemes in the public sector through their involvement in equal pay audits. This level of involvement is not as widespread in unionised workplaces in the private sector where many firms prefer to focus union-management dialogue on total paybill figures (often percentages) rather than the detail of the pay schemes that generate these paybills. Consequently, norms around equity and fair treatment may not be as well embedded in the private sector as in the public services which are now explored in more depth.

Public services and pay progression

There has been a revolution in pay in the public services. According to IDS,

> between 2002 and 2006 we have seen the biggest transformation of public sector pay structures and systems for more than a generation. This has involved moves to single status, equal-proofed job evaluation, new progression arrangements to retain staff and the building of modern career structures.
>
> (IDS 2007b: 15)

But what has driven these changes, many of which relate to salary progression? First, concerns have been expressed about the motivational claims made in relation to the introduction of performance-related pay schemes during the 1990s. The Makinson Report (Makinson 2000) reviewed the UK Civil Service experience with performance pay in the 1990s after complaints from staff of slow pay progression, lack of incentives and the possibility of discrimination in performance-assessment processes. The report, based on an analysis of incentive payment systems in four major government departments, recommended that they should return to a 'rate for the job' model and design salary progression systems that enable staff to achieve this level in four to five years maximum. In some cases, Makinson discovered it could take an individual up to twenty years to progress to the scale maximum.

Makinson also advised that any discussion of pay progression should be kept separate from performance-based rewards:

> the appraisal review, and indeed any general discussion of pay progression, should involve a more subjective discussion of an individual's strengths and weaknesses. To confuse the two would throw into question the legitimacy of the performance-pay scheme.
>
> (Makinson 2000: 25)

As IDS commented, 'effectively this has meant a severing of the link between basic salary and individual performance which has been the touchstone of civil service pay systems through the latter half of the 1990s' (IDS 2007b). The Makinson recommendations on separating career and development issues from performance pay reflects observations made by Bevan and Thompson (1992) in their research on performance management systems in the UK.

The Makinson recommendations, combined with concerns with equality proofing and tightening labour markets, have stimulated profound changes in salary progression systems in the public sector. The main change has been the shortening of pay scales and the move away from broadbanding which was seen to exacerbate transparency and equity issues. These shorter pay scales have been accompanied by new progression rules which mean that an average performer will move to the 'rate for the job' (i.e. the scale maximum) in four to five years whereas for good performers this might take two to three years. Part of the reason for these new pay structures has been to make pay progression more transparent and state more explicitly the time and requirements needed to progress to the top of their scale.

These changes have also been driven by the realisation that equal value claims could place considerable costs across the public sector. This is a particular challenge in Local Government where it is estimated the cost could be in the region of £3bn and this may rise as the deadline for implementing equal pay audits for March 2007 is unlikely to be met (IDS 2007c).

From a theoretical perspective, the new changes address some of the issues raised by expectancy, equity and goal-setting theory which place an emphasis on clarity of reward levels, fairness and transparency of reward systems and clear expectations and goals. The previous broadbanded systems with long pay grades and lack of consistency regarding performance criteria failed many of the theoretical tests set out by these models. Principal-agent theory has been explicitly cited as a key theoretical underpinning to government strategies to reform the public services and achieve higher levels of productivity. However, this theory fails to take account of wider institutional and societal level factors that may shape the evolution and effectiveness of devolved decision-making in areas such as reward practices. As such, the theory is insufficient in its ability to explain correctly the reason for the reform of salary progression systems over the last decade. These changes have been largely made in response to social Europe rather than driven by markets, technology and the need for the principals' and agents' interests to be aligned – economic Europe. As such, agency theory and other economic and psychological theories, while methodologically rigorous, fail to give sufficient weight to the social context in which this rational behaviour is embedded (Muller-Jentsch 2004).

Salary progression

The CIPD Reward Survey of 2007 (CIPD 2007) provides one of the few sources of data in the UK on salary progression practices. The study covered several modes of progression (see Table 6.3). In practice, the study found that most organisations (79 per cent) tended to use a combination of criteria to determine pay progression rather than just one. The most widely used progression criteria are 'individual performance' followed by 'market rates' and 'individual competence'. There are variations by sector with 41 per cent of public-sector respondents using 'length of service' compared to just 9 per cent of private services.

In a review of organisation practice on pay progression for the Office of Manpower Economics (OME 2005), IDS identified at least seven types of pay progression system: service-related; performance-related; competency-related; skills-related; market-related; promotion and, finally, hybrid schemes. The final category of scheme, which the CIPD survey found to be the most numerous, is a combination of two or more of the other criteria – for example, service and performance or market and competency. These hybrid or mixed methods of determining salary progression have been described as 'contribution-based' pay by Brown and Armstrong (1999) who argued that organisations would increasingly move away from 'one size fits all' approaches to pay for performance to more blended approaches that combine both behavioural and output-based measures.

Table 6.3 Pay progression criteria (within a hybrid approach) by sector

Progression based on:	All	Manufacturing/ Production	Private Services	Voluntary Sector	Public Services
Individual performance	80	78	88	63	66
Market rates	65	57	76	79	24
Competency	47	34	52	46	44
Organisational performance	42	48	48	42	15
Skills	33	26	35	42	27
Team performance	16	17	17	17	10
Length of service	14	9	9	17	41

Source: CIPD 2007

The picture emerging from these data appears to support this view and points to the presence of reasonably complex systems for determining salary progression. It could be argued that this is empirical evidence of firms being more strategic about their pay systems in that they are selecting criteria that are most relevant to their strategic needs. However, it is very difficult to ascertain whether these choices are ad hoc, responding to waves of fad and fashion in the world of reward management or the strategic choices made on an understanding of the business goals of the organisation. Given the dominance of consultancy firms in the reward management area, the influence of fads and fashions is likely to be important (Abrahamson 1991) but so is the classic British management approach of 'muddling through'.

The limited research evidence we can draw upon to understand the changing nature of reward systems in organisations in both public and private sectors points to the need for more rigorous research. At a theoretical level, more work is also required to explain the simultaneous use of output- and behaviour-based reward approaches for certain categories of employee.

Managing salary progression systems

The 'principal-agent' model (influential in government policy on public sector productivity) suggests that there is an important role for the clear specification and measurement of the performance output required if incentive schemes are to be effective (Holmstrom and Milgrom 1991). Managers have two options when setting reward measures – outcome-based or behaviour-based. Outcome-based systems tend to place considerable risk on the employee and the risk-aversion behaviour of employees limits the extent to which such contracts are used. The second option is to use behavioural-based measures and the organisation might use inputs such as effort, attitude or length of service. Both approaches require managers to assess performance in some way and the CIPD survey evidence suggests that many firms have developed hybrid schemes incorporating behavioural and output measures. As ACAS (2003: 10) makes clear in their guidance on appraisal-related pay schemes, 'it's the line manager who has to set and explain the standards of performance and behaviours required, clarify the aims of the scheme, make decisions about assessment, communicate the decision to staff and defend any judgements made between levels of performance'.

This renegotiating of performance standards has been argued by Marsden (2004), building on principal-agent theory, to be one of the defining features in the development of performance-based pay systems in the public services and has contributed significantly to productivity improvement. Managers combined appraisal with incentives and goal setting in order to establish new performance norms for staff. In particular, managers' ability to set performance objectives at the start of an annual cycle is seen as important in this process. Marsden argues that this renegotiation of performance norms explains the paradox of performance pay in the public services wherein incidences of low employee motivation went hand-in-hand with productivity increases. However, Marsden's work may underestimate other factors that can play an equally important role in productivity improvements such as outsourcing, reductions in employment and new capital investment. Consequently, it is difficult to establish the relative contribution of these performance-setting practices to the overall productivity increase. On the other hand, their absence may equally undermine these other investments as suggested by Milgrom and Roberts (1992). Assessment and the setting and reviewing of performance standards does bring with it other sets of issues which are now considered.

Assessing performance

A growing body of work questions the ability of managers to correctly specify and assess individuals' performance. The work psychology field has produced a strong body of evidence to suggest that manager-subordinate assessments of employee performance can be influenced by a broad range of non-job-related factors (such as gender, race, age, etc.) which may carry disproportionate weight in performance evaluations. Furthermore, various studies of managers' appraisals have demonstrated low levels of inter-rater reliability when evaluating the performance of the same employee. For example, a review by King *et al.* (1980) found that the upper limit for the correlation between appraisals by different supervisors of the same employees was 0.6 per cent. This suggests that the information and assumptions on which performance assessments are based can diverge quite widely.

The potential influences on inter-rater reliability have been identified as falling into three broad categories: organisational factors, managerial characteristics and individual (recipient) characteristics (Landy and Farr 1983). Whilst organisational characteristics such as the profitability and nature of its product market may determine the size of the pot available for performance pay increases, it may also indirectly shape managerial assessment behaviour through the imposition of quotas and a consensus that salary costs need to be contained.

Managers' decisions can also be shaped by other factors. For example, a manager may award higher assessment ratings because the employee has similar characteristics to them or their own appraisal rating may influence their evaluation of subordinates (i.e. a low personal rating of themselves may encourage them to be harsher on their own staff). Similarly, the supervisor's affiliation needs might encourage them to make little or no differentiation between the performance of their employees for fear of not being viewed positively by subordinates.

As for employees, age, gender and ethnicity may all play a role in influencing appraisers' evaluations. In a review of gender bias in 24 appraisal-based systems, Nieva and Gutek (1980) found that 16 demonstrated pro-male bias. Research by Bevan and Thompson (1992) found that managers both look for and value different traits and characteristics in men and women subordinates. For example, they found that women were often rated highly if they conformed to stereotypical behaviour traits (i.e. being dependable, perceptive and committed) and not against male-traits (i.e. dynamic, aggressive, ambitious). Evidence of both race and gender bias in assessment have been found across the Civil Service. The union IPMS found that appraisal results showed 'ethnic minority staff to have been marked significantly lower than white staff; and women to have been marked significantly higher than men' (LRD 1992). These concerns about gender, race and more recently age discrimination have played an important role in the reform of salary progression systems in the UK public services.

This research and the broader body of evidence from the psychology field suggest that it is difficult to eradicate the potential for bias although the better development of performance criteria, the training of supervisors and close monitoring of the process can all play a part. Organisations have responded to these concerns about the effectiveness and reliability of the measurement of individual performance by introducing more sophisticated processes (thereby increasing monitoring costs of the employment system). Consequently, there has been a growing interest in peer assessment as a way of broadening out the information taken into account when assessing an individual's performance. Typically this has developed in professional organisations where senior managers are too removed from the day-to-day activities of their subordinates to have a rounded picture of performance. At managerial level 360-degree assessment processes are becoming increasingly popular as a means of management development. Many organisations have shied away from making a direct link between these more rounded measures of performance and pay awards, understandably concerned that it may encourage dysfunctional behaviours. Furthermore, these practices also increase the costs of using such systems and would appear to contradict some of the tenets of transaction cost theory (Williamson 1975).

Managerial skills and abilities

As researchers have attempted to understand the lack of success of many new reward practices they have increasingly focused on the capability of line managers who have the responsibility to implement these schemes. A study of line-managers' role in reward practices found that 'front-line managers' skills and abilities are perceived to be the main inhibitor to the successful implementation of a reward strategy' (Purcell and Hutchinson 2007). This research also argued, based on evidence from The John Lewis Partnership, that one of the most effective ways of building these capabilities, as well as commitment to manage these new pay systems, is to involve line managers in the design and implementation of new reward practices. This insight builds upon the rigorous work carried out by Bowey *et al.* (1982) which explored the effectiveness of different payment schemes. However, this earlier research also found that the most effective reward systems not only involved managers but also employees in their design and implementation. Given the individualisation of the employment relationship, weakening of employee representation in the workplace and negative management attitudes towards involvement and consultation that have characterised developments in organisations over the last two decades or more, our deep knowledge of the process and practice of reward systems today leaves a lot to be desired. Some areas where a future research agenda might be developed are outlined below.

Future research

Research on reward systems generally, and salary progression systems in particular, is not in good health. There has been little significant published work in this area beyond studies of performance pay in the public sector (see Marsden 2004 for an example) or scientists and engineers in high technology firms (see Thompson and Heron 2005, for an example). The bulk of evidence on developments in reward systems in the UK is provided by niche consultancy and practitioner research organisations such as IDS and IRS or professional bodies such as the CIPD. While these studies are valuable in providing snapshots on current practice, by their nature they are unable to address in depth some of the issues raised by developments in reward practice. Furthermore, large-scale surveys such as WERS are also limited in the extent to which they can address these issues despite their longitudinal advantages.

Future research needs to be much more in-depth to understand the practical and theoretical challenges related to new developments in progression systems. For example, equal pay pressures have encouraged many organisations to redesign their progression systems to be much shorter in range with people moving to scale maximum within five years. What are the implications of these new systems on motivation, skill acquisition, flexibility and knowledge sharing, amongst other factors? The 'new pay' stresses the cognitive aspects of strategic pay wherein managers designing reward systems take a more strategic perspective on aligning reward with corporate objectives. To what extent is this true? Our current evidence base is very weak and we do not know whether shifts in managerial cognition result in different outcomes. This also raises questions about shared cognition within and between managerial levels when designing and implementing new reward practices.

The issues raised in this review also point to the need for more studies of change in reward systems. Such studies can reveal the contingent factors that shape design decisions and how new pay practices such as competency-based pay are actually embedded within different organisational contexts. They can also help us understand why some practices are discontinued whereas others exist for long periods of time (as in the Lincoln Electric case). Detailed, longitudinal and mixed methods studies such as Bowey *et al.* (1982) are required. Further research is needed to understand the hybrid, more heterogeneous progression systems that combine outcome- and behavioural-based metrics. To what extent are these systems re-shaping our understanding of what we mean by internal labour markets? What are the implications for principal-agent theory? Detailed case research that can trace the evolution and impact of these new systems is required.

Finally, the importance of social norms (Scott 2007) may need to be embraced in further research as developments over the last decade have illustrated how institutional pressures regarding equity have had a dramatic impact on salary progression systems. There is a rich agenda for future research in this area.

Conclusions

The last decade can be characterised, in salary progression terms, as the rediscovery of the internal labour market. Whereas the 1980s and early 1990s were characterised by the shift to performance-based payment systems, convoluted pay structures with high levels of management control in the context of loose labour markets, the last ten years or more have been dominated by skills shortages where recruitment and retention has combined with equity concerns to challenge management control and re-establish more transparent salary progression systems. The 'new pay' discourse which has been largely defined by its focus on the strategic alignment of rewards with business priorities which emphasised internal, business logics has had to adapt to pressures imposed by the so-called 'war for talent' and wider societal pressures to tackle discrimination on gender, age and race. The pendulum has swung back somewhat and notions of 'fairness at work' which characterised New Labour's first term would appear to have had some impact on salary systems, at least in the public services.

From a theoretical perspective, developments over the last decade have shown that over-commitment to one perspective can simplify our understanding of the operational complexity of salary systems. Rather, taking both economic and psychological theories together can provide a much richer insight into the rationale and operation of reward practices.

Finally, there is a need for more rigorous and in-depth, longitudinal research on change in salary systems. Only through this can we hope to build and develop more robust theory that can be useful to practitioners.

Note

1 This section draws upon Gerhart and Rynes (2003) and Rynes and Gerhart (2000).

References

Abrahamson, E. (1991) 'Managerial fad and fashion: the diffusion and rejection of innovations', *Academy of Management Review*, 16 (3): 586–612.
ACAS (2003) *Guide to Appraisal Related Pay Schemes*, ACAS: HMSO.

Akerlof, G. (1984) 'Labour contracts as partial gift exchange', *Quarterly Journal of Economics*, 97: 543–569.

Akerlof, G. and Yellen, J. (1986) *Efficiency Wage Models of the Labour Market*, Cambridge: Cambridge University Press.

Benson, J. (1995) 'Future Employment and the Internal Labour Market', *British Journal of Industrial Relations*, December, 33 (4): 603–608.

Bevan, S. and Thompson, M. (1992) *Performance Management in the UK*, London: Institute of Personnel Management.

Bowey, A., Thorpe, R. and Mitchell, F. (1982) *Effects of Incentive Payment Systems*, London: Department of Employment.

Brockner, J. and Wiesenfeld, B. M. (1996) 'An integrative framework for explaining reactions to decisions. The interactive effects of outcomes and procedures', *Psychological Bulletin*, 120: 189–208.

Brown, D. and Armstrong, M. (1999) *Paying for Contribution*, London: Kogan Page.

Cappelli, P. (1995) 'Rethinking Employment', *British Journal of Industrial Relations*, December, 35 (4): 563–602.

CIPD (2007) *Reward Management Survey 2007*, London: Chartered Institute of Personnel and Development.

Coase, R. (1937) 'The nature of the firm', *Economica*, November: 386–405.

Doeringer, P. and Piore, M. (1971) *Internal Labor Markets and Manpower Analysis*, Lexington: Heath Lexington Books.

Equal Opportunities Commission (1997) Code of Practice on Equal Pay (Appointed day) Order 1997 (no 131 (C.6)), London: HM Stationery Office.

Eyraud, F., Marsden, M. and Silvestre, J.J. (1990) 'Occupational and internal labour markets in Britain and France', *International Labour Review*, 129 (4): 501–517.

Gerhart, B. and Rynes, S. (2003) *Compensation:Theory, Evidence and Strategic Implications*, Thousand Oaks, CA: Sage.

Ghoshal, S. and Moran, P. (1996) 'Bad for practice: a critique of transaction cost theory', *Academy of Management Review*, 21 (1): 13–47.

Gomez-Mejia, L. (1993) *Compensation, Organisation Strategy and Firm Performance*, Brookhaven, USA: Southwestern Publishers.

Heery, E. (1998) 'A return to contract? Performance related pay in a public service', *Work, Employment and Society*, 21 (1): 73–95.

IIM Treasury (2003) *Public Services: Meeting the Productivity Challenge*, London: HM Treasury.

Holmstrom, B. and Milgrom, P. (1991) 'Multi-task principal agent analysis: incentive contracts, asset ownership, and job design', *Journal of Law, Economics and Organization*, 7: 24–52.

IDS (2006) *Employment Law Brief*. October 2006: 815.

IDS (2007a) 'Age discrimination and reward', *IDS Pay Report 977* May.

IDS (2007b) 'Pay in the Civil Service', *IDS Pay Report 972* March.

IDS (2007c) 'Equal pay in local government', *IDS Pay Report 969* January.

Institute for Employment Research (2006) *Review of the Economy and Employment 2006*, IER: University of Warwick.

Jensen, M. C. and Meckling, W. H. (1976) 'Theory of the firm: managerial behavior, agency costs, and ownership structure', *Journal of Financial Economics*, 3: 305–360.

Kersley, B. C., Alpin, J., Forth, A., Bryson, A., Bewley, G., Dix, G. and Oxenbridge,

S. (2006) *Inside the Workplace: Findings from the 2004 Workplace Employment Relations Survey*, Department of Trade and Industry, London: HMSO.

Kessler, I. and Purcell, J. (1992) 'Performance-related pay: objectives and applications', *Human Resource Management Journal*, 2 (3): 34–59.

King, L., Hunter, J. and Schmidt, F. (1980) 'Halo in a multi-dimensional forced choice performance scale', *Journal of Applied Psychology*, 65 (2): 507–516.

Klein, H. J., Wesson, M. J., Hollenbeck, J. R. and Alge, B. J. (1999) 'Goal commitment and the goal setting process: Conceptual clarification and empirical synthesis', *Journal of Applied Psychology*, 84: 855–896.

Landy, F. and Farr, J. (1983) *The Measurement of Work Performance*, New York: Academic Press.

Lawler, E. E. (1994) 'From job-based to competency-based organisations', *Journal of Organisational Behaviour*, 15 (1): 3–15.

Lawler, E. (1995) 'The New Pay: A Strategic Approach', *Compensation and Benefits Review*, July, 27 (4): 14–20.

Lazear, E. P. (1999) 'Personnel economics: past lessons and future directions', *Journal of Labor Economics*, 17: 199–236.

Locke, E. A. (1968) 'Toward a theory of task motivation and incentives', *Organizational Behaviour and Human Performance*, 3: 157–189.

Locke, E. A. and Latham, G. P. (1984) *Goal Setting: A motivational technique that works!* Englewood Cliffs: Prentice Hall.

LRD (1992) 'The Perils of Performance Pay', *Bargaining Report*, 191: 7–13.

Makinson Report (2000) *Incentives for Change*, London: HMSO.

Marsden, D. (2004) 'The role of performance-related pay in renegotiating the "effort bargain": the case of the British public service', *Industrial and Labor Relations Review*, 57 (3): 350–370.

Milgrom, P. and Roberts, J. (1992) *Economics, Organisation and Management*, Englewood Cliffs, NJ: Prentice Hall.

Mirrlees, J. A. (1972) 'The optimal structure of incentives and authority within an organisation', *Bell Journal of Economics*, Vol. 7 (1): 105–131.

Muller-Jentsch, W. (2004) 'Theoretical approaches to industrial relations', in B. E. Kaufman (ed.) *Theoretical Perspectives on Work and the Employment Relationship*, USA. Industrial Relations Research Association Series.

Nieva, V. F. and Gutek, B. A. (1980) *Women and Work: A psychological perspective*, New York: Praeger.

Office of Manpower Economics (OME) (2005) *Organisational Practices on Pay Progression*, London: OME.

Pfeffer, J. (1998) *The Human Equation: Building profits by putting people first*, Boston: Harvard Business School.

Piore, M. J. (2002) 'Thirty years later: internal labor markets, flexibility and the new economy', *Journal of Management and Governance*, 6: 271–279.

Porter, L. W. and Lawler, E. E. (1968) *Managerial Attitudes and Performance*, Homewood, IL: Dorsey.

Purcell, J. and Hutchinson, S. (2007) *Rewarding Work: The vital role of line managers*, CIPD.

Rynes, S. and Gerhart, B. (2000) *Compensation in Organisations: Current research and practice*, San Francisco: Jossey-Bass.

Schumpeter, J. A. (1950) *Capitalism, Socialism and Democracy*, New York: Harper & Row.

Schuster, J. R. and Zingheim, P. K. (1996) *The New Pay: linking employee and organizational performance*, San Francisco: Jossey-Bass.

Scott, W. R. (2007) *Institutions and Interests*, 3rd edn, Thousand Oaks, CA: Sage.

Simon, H. A. (1957) 'The compensation of executives', *Sociometry*, 20: 32–35.

Stevens, M. (1999) 'Human capital theory and UK vocational training policy', *Oxford Review of Economic Policy*, 15 (1): 16–33.

Thompson, M. and Heron, P. (2005) 'The difference a manager can make: organisational justice and knowledge worker commitment', *International Journal of Human Resource Management*, 16(3): 383–404.

Vroom, V. H. (1964) *Work and Motivation*, New York: Wiley.

Weber, M. (1978) *'Economy and Society: An Outline of Interpretive Sociology'*, in G. Roth and C. Wittich (eds), University of California Press.

Wiley, C. (1993) 'Incentive plan pushes production', *Personnel Journal*, 72 (8).

Williamson, O. (1975) *Markets and Hierarchies*, New York: Free Press.

Wright, P. M., George, J. M., Farnsworth, R. and McMahan, G.C. (1993) 'Productivity and extra-role behaviour: the effects of goals and incentives on spontaneous helping', *Journal of Applied Psychology*, 78: 374–381.

Yellen, J. L. (1984) 'Efficiency wage models of unemployment', *American Economic Review*, 74: 200–205.

7   Executive reward

Stephen Perkins

Summary

Executive reward and its management have become increasingly complex and controversial; the area may also be perceived as replete with contradictions. These three c-factors form a framework for the discussion in this chapter. Executive reward and corporate governance are positioned as inseparable. But, it is argued, dominant theoretical assumptions guiding policy and practice may be appraised and found incomplete, drawing on commentary beyond the mainstream, surfacing complementary lines of inquiry and action.

Introduction

A chapter on executive reward management prompts the question: why devote space in a collective volume on reward management to the issue of executive reward? The question may be addressed by reference to three 'c-factors': complexity, controversy and contradiction. Taken together, these serve as an organising frame for the discussion that follows. First, executive reward management – as a field attracting considerable attention among practitioners, as well as academic commentary – has become very complex, incorporating aspects not ordinarily seen in reward arrangements applicable to employees generally. This complexity applies in the case of design, operation and, more significantly than other reward management areas, reporting in compliance with externally imposed standards. Second, executive reward and its management are controversial. Over the past decade and a half, considerable attention has focused on the topic of 'exploding increases for senior executives' (Reilly and Scott 2005: 34) and alleged 'excess' (Crystal 1992) benefiting executive 'fat cats', so that what might nominally be seen as a rather mundane topic of limited interest to the non-specialist has entered popular consciousness, requiring politically motivated intervention in response to calls for 'something to be done'. Glancing back to state incomes policy initiatives intended to address Britain's perennial 'pay problem', McCarthy (1993) notes with some irony the refocusing of calls for pay restraint from shop floor workers and trade unions during the 1960s and 1970s, towards the 'captains of industry' themselves in the 'deregulated' millennium era. Third, there is the contention articulated here that executive reward is replete with contradictions. Theoretical perspectives have been drawn on explicitly or implicitly in describing and prescribing on executive reward and its management, including in a succession of corporate governance regulatory initiatives. But this theory, and what its users may assume in terms of individual behaviour and organisational outcomes, may be contrasted with alternative theory on organisational effectiveness. The terrain is thus contested, prompting critical appraisal.

Key terms

Definition is needed of some key terms used to guide subsequent analysis. An obvious starting point is what do we mean when referring to 'executive' employees compared with other workers? Is this a function of where employees are located, to whom they are answerable, how their terms of employment are set, who has to account for the decisions made, or the functions they perform? In turn, what is 'executive reward'? Is there something specific about executive pay and benefits and how they are managed?

For the purpose of this chapter, an executive is defined as someone in an organisation's senior management group employed at corporate level. A lot of 'top pay' commentary focuses on the Chief Executive Officer (CEO), probably the result of securing access to published data prior to the movement in the 1990s for greater transparency in reporting on top pay and related employment benefits (Reilly and Scott 2005). And while there are reasons, discussed later, for continued attention specifically to the CEO, remuneration committees of corporate boards of directors generally determine the pay and benefits of all executive board members, not just the CEO. Often referred to collectively as the Executive Committee, executive employees are charged with oversight of strategy implementation at corporate level and constitute a prime source of input to corporate strategy making. In fact, the Executive Committee often comprises individuals who may not be appointed main board directors (e.g. Chief Technology Officer, HR Director, although they *may* be on the board) as well as the Chief Operating Officer, Finance Director, etc. The criterion for Executive Committee membership may be direct line of reporting to the CEO,[1] who in turn is answerable to the board and may take direction from a board chair, now generally independent of the CEO (FRC 2006).

Pepper (2006: 5) describes executives as 'responsible for defining and executing a company's strategy, who through their actions are capable of directly affecting (positively or negatively) the company's profits, share price, reputation, market positioning, and so on'. Of course, the role of 'outside' or 'non-executive' directors in this regard should not be discounted but their status as board appointees (who ultimately sanction strategy, including board appointments) without the employment contracts enjoyed by the executive group, makes non-executives distinctive in reward terms.

The sum of elements comprising senior executive rewards symbolises a particular form of employment relationship. From the individual's vantage point, reward may be measured in terms of securing an acceptable return on the investment of human capital (i.e. the individual's experience and skills, in addition to a willingness to contribute these on the employer's behalf). Nominally, this may be approached from both an objective and subjective standpoint. Whether or not the individual's view of self-worth is shared and warranted depends on who may be asked to pronounce and against what criteria. From the employer's viewpoint, the search is for a resource that will demonstrably contribute to the employer's aim to create profit through the application of other corporate resources (or in the case of a publicly owned or voluntary sector body to satisfy efficiency and effectiveness criteria in this task). Thus what has been referred to as the effort-reward bargain between employer and employee (Baldamus 1961) applies to executives, but with a distinctive character as will be discussed below. Briefly, executive reward may be examined from the dual perspectives of 'amount', on the one hand, and 'mix', on the other. The primary dimensions along which the mix varies are '(1) fixed compensation independent of firm performance, versus variable reward [tied to a performance measure], and (2) current compensation accruing at the end of the year, versus deferred compensation accruing in later years' (Veliyath 1999: 124). Beyond the bargain agreed between two parties, increased public scrutiny of executive reward has come to influence both substance and process.

But to what extent does the relationship offer guarantees on either side? The search for an executive employment relationship to meet the aims of the employer (as the 'principal' in the relationship) and the employee (or 'agent'), as well as the need to comply with standards of public reporting, has led to the establishment of norms around an executive reward 'package'. These are constructed from three elements either directly in cash or ultimately convertible to cash: a) the salary traditionally afforded to a 'staff' employee (someone whom it is assumed the employer anticipates hiring beyond the hour or the day);[2] b) a 'bonus' payment for meeting short-term performance requirements beyond contributing attendance and capability to perform; and c) forms of deferred reward – specifically long-term incentives for meeting objectives of strategic significance over an extended period (generally beyond one year), and a retirement pension. An additional element of the executive reward package comprises 'perks' and other non-cash benefits such as insured benefits, company-funded cars, etc.[3]

The remainder of the chapter is organised as follows: To begin, the detail of contemporary executive reward and its management is reviewed, highlighting the complexity decision-makers and other interested parties face in this area of people management, interfacing with corporate governance considerations. Next, the various ways in which action and outcomes at that nexus have resulted in ongoing controversy surrounding executive reward and its management are discussed. Finally, attention turns to perceptible inherent contradictions prompting executive reward outcomes that may be judged theoretically and practically perverse – or at least apparently out of kilter with the express intentions of policy makers.

Complexity

An increasingly pro-active orientation on the part of decision makers is evident in designing executive reward 'packages', apparently inspired by the combined pressure of 'competition for scarce talent in an international market' (House of Commons Trade and Industry Committee 2003: 17) and corporate governance regulatory developments (e.g. Cadbury 1992; Greenbury 1995; Hampel 1998; HMSO 2002; DTI 2003; Higgs 2003; FRC 2006). While specialists may continue to pay attention to the constituent parts, those required to sanction and account for executive reward packages are looking for a compound instrument to order the employment relationship with executives. Changing conditions and notions surrounding what the package should involve, and what conditions should apply to its application (Buck *et al.* 2003), to simultaneously satisfy the multiple goals and interests involved mean the process is not straightforward.

The basic salary continues to be the foundation for executive reward package design, but its relative position has been subordinated. 'Good practice' guidelines have shifted the focus increasingly towards 'at risk' rewards in order to align executives' interests with shareholders – sharing the risk and potential reward (Norris 2005; Pepper 2006). This has been further refined so that executive reward combines not only short-term incentives to perform individually but also a longer-term element to retain executives in post and to focus their attention on creating value over the longer term. While it is true to say that 'at risk' remuneration has become increasingly common across all employee groups, in the case of executives it is perhaps even more common, as this group is viewed as most able to impact positively or negatively on corporate performance. Pepper (2006: 14) posits 'a strong prima facie case' for keeping the three elements in balance. The conclusion drawn is that, at least in theory, decision-makers anticipate that the combined reward elements will motivate executives, acting together to represent shareholder interests and sometimes those of wider stakeholders (Jensen *et al.* 2004), beyond the separate effects of the elements comprising the package taken singly. The evidence discussed later in this chapter as to whether this aim is achieved in practice suggests a need for caution, however.

An illustration of the complex nature of executive reward and its management may be found in accounts provided by board remuneration committees. The following worked example demonstrates not only complexity in design but also the resource effort necessary to account to shareholders for the actions taken by board remuneration committees. Remuneration committee reports have become a sizeable part of the documentation publicly quoted companies now regularly produce for reporting purposes. Running to several pages in length, these make explicit connections between executive reward and corporate commercial performance.

Table 7.1 is a modified version of part of the remuneration committee report of a FTSE-100 company's annual report and accounts, published in 2007. Details are provided of the various elements making up the executive reward package applicable to members of the firm's corporate level Executive Committee. Details are given of the reasons why the various elements are included and over what period performance is recognised in the form of remuneration, as appropriate. The various contingencies to which remuneration is linked are also specified. In the report itself, a detailed (audited) statement is provided as well as giving specific information on the levels of pay and other employment benefits named individuals covered by these arrangements have received. This includes details of the timing of the exercise of outstanding share options, 'incentive' share vesting, individual shareholdings and trading in company shares. This detailed reporting is intended to 'tell the story' behind actions taken to order the relationship between the executive directors and their employers. The aim is to demonstrate objectively how the financial gain individuals make through their employment, which might otherwise pass to shareholders, represents a legitimate share in the value created by the individual and the executives on behalf of the shareholders.[4]

The total remuneration available to the executives is therefore anchored in a basic guaranteed amount, taking account of comparisons with other employees inside and outside the firm at peer level and below and the individual executive's perceived contribution potential. Individuals are targeted to receive just over double the basic pay element of remuneration, as an additional reward, from the combination of short- and long-term 'at risk' elements based on performance against goals determined by reference to standardised corporate accounting measures. Part of this additional remuneration is a bonus available to be earned as a non-consolidated amount each year. Another part is long-term, based on the allocation of shares. Vesting of these shares is contingent on corporate performance outcomes and, as a further discretionary element, individuals may benefit provided they invest in company shares recognised in kind by the company. It is possible that, provided performance targets are exceeded, basic remuneration may be extended by approximately a further 400 per cent.

There is a range of potential outcomes from operation of an executive reward framework such as the one illustrated in Table 7.1, taking into account the combination of fixed and variable elements intended to recognise how 'executive team' members create value for shareholders over the short- and longer-term. Complex calculations often attach to the estimated value arising from incentive plans, forming part of the information companies are expected to disclose in accordance with regulatory standards. In practice, however, wide deviations are reported between estimates and eventual outcomes, a

Table 7.1 Overview statement of FTSE-100 company executive reward framework

Element	Objective	Performance period	Performance conditions
Salary	Recognise base-line 'market value' of role and post holder's experience and skills	Not applicable	Reviewed annually, following external benchmarking and taking into account post holder's performance and salary increases awarded to other employees
Annual Incentive Plan	Provide an incentive for achievement of performance goals over a year	One year	Awarded subject to achievement of revenue and 'economic profit' (EP)* targets for the year
Voluntary Bonus Share Investment/ Retention Plan	Provide an incentive for sustained annual growth, aid retention of executives, and actively support share ownership by executives	Three years	Basic award and an additional match subject to continued employment and to achievement of compound annual growth in aggregate EP
Long-Term Incentive Plan	Provide an incentive for long-term value creation and help retain executives	Three years	Half of award subject to total shareowner return (TSR)* ranking relative to a company peer group; half of award subject to achievement of compound annual growth in aggregate earnings per share (EPS)*

* EP is defined as profit from operations, less a charge for the weighted average cost of capital, and growth in revenue. TSR is defined as the product of the share price plus reinvested dividends. EPS is defined as the net after tax profit attributable to each ordinary share. EPS is calculated using the formula net profit after taxation divided by the total number of ordinary shares.

situation further complicated by corporate concern about making public commercially sensitive operating plans during executive performance target setting (Deloitte 2004). In the FTSE-100 case, authority to review and approve the package of rewards for executive directors has been delegated by the board to its remuneration committee. The report states that, in accordance with 'best practice', the committee is tasked with ensuring that individual rewards are linked to performance and aligned with shareholder interests. The requirement is for 'cost effective' packages suitable to attract and retain highest calibre individuals and to motivate them to perform to the highest standards. The Committee also oversees remuneration arrangements applicable to non-board member senior executives to the same end. Changes in the nature of long-term incentive arrangements have been common recently among stock market listed companies (Deloitte 2004; IDS 2006). A rise in incentive scheme potential payments at the maximum, justified in terms of action to align directors' and shareholders' interests, is reported by IDS (2006). This is leading to a shift in the balance between fixed and variable pay towards performance-related remuneration (albeit not at the expense of salary rises). The controversy around share options, leading to a move away from this previously popular long-term incentive, is discussed in the next section of the chapter.

Complexity arises not only in the composition of reward packages such as that illustrated using the FTSE-100 company details summarised in Table 7.1. Maintaining and accounting for a sophisticated executive reward portfolio has become an increasingly demanding undertaking. Detailed statements such as the one referred to above would not have featured in companies' annual reports and accounts only a few years ago. State regulation and stock market listing requirements, drawing on the governance 'codes', have triggered enhanced transparency in executive reward administration. And this activity, including the time invested by remuneration committee members and their internal and external advisors, incurs a significant transaction cost for a minority segment of the workforce. In their government-commissioned review, consultants Deloitte note that shareholder representatives consulted by them reported that the requirement in the Directors' Remuneration Report Regulations (HMSO 2002), to vote on whether or not to accept the remuneration committee report, has had a 'very significant impact upon [shareholder] attitudes and behaviours' (Deloitte 2004: 19). More comprehensive disclosure is perceived as having been vital in enabling informed review and decision taking. Moreover, the complex task facing boards in reporting, and shareholders in acting on, this detailed information is unlikely to recede.

Controversy

At the time this chapter was first drafted, controversial developments were being reported in the media concerning proposed changes to a bonus plan applicable to senior executives in communications company Cable and Wireless. The situation was labelled as 'among the most contentious shareholder votes this year' (Burgess 2007). Newspaper reports linked this with the failure of the company's chairman to win backing for his re-election from more than 11 per cent of votes cast, and the unwillingness of almost 10 per cent of investors to support re-election of the Cable and Wireless senior independent director (Wray 2007). While it may rate highly in the 'contention' stakes, this is not an isolated case. Despite application of the complex amalgam of regulation and associated 'good practice' guidance over a 15-year period in the UK, executive reward continues to attract controversy. 'Shareholder activists' have argued that corporate governance problems on both sides of the Atlantic have become so acute as to represent a systemic problem (Monks and Sykes 2002). While the most serious effects are being felt in the USA, Sykes (2002) argues, executive remuneration in Britain is demonstrating the same underlying weaknesses.

Something regarded as subject to controversy tends to be understood as open to discussion and/or debate; it may be perceived as questionable, perhaps actively disputed – evidentially the case with executive reward (Benz and Frey 2007; *Economist* 2007). Gomez-Mejia and Wiseman (1997: 291) cite Taussig and Baker (1925): 'one of the earliest empirical studies on this issue'. The lack of consensus is especially pronounced in relation to 'equity incentives' – i.e. stock options or share-based long-term incentive plans (Core *et al.* 2003). Sykes (2002: 256) contends that 'dangerous pressures' governing the determination of executive reward are 'perhaps the most egregious illustration of the debilitating [corporate] governance weaknesses that need to be urgently addressed to restore public trust'. Reilly and Scott (2005) point to the end of the economic boom in the 1990s, as well as the coincidence of questionable reward practices in prominent corporations, making executive pay highly controversial. But what is at issue here? Is it the absolute or relative size of executive reward? Is it determinants of executive pay, where views appear to vary around the role of labour market factors, institutional prescription, and/or performance (of individuals correlated with the performance of firms whose operations they oversee)? And what defines 'acceptable performance'? Is the problem the nature of the relationship between executives and their employers (assuming clarity on the mediated employment relationship can be obtained)?

Point (2005) suggests that the 'fat cats' debate may extend back to concerns surrounding UK corporate scandals during the 1980s, such as Blue Arrow, Guinness, and Maxwell. He argues that guidance emerging from the 'highly influential' 1992 Cadbury Report, followed in 1995 by Greenbury, was 'theoretically designed to . . . make high pay levels acceptable' (2005: 61). The guiding principle behind the governance enshrined in the Combined Code is 'comply or explain': companies are required to disclose aspects with which their executive reward practices do not match (or may not fully comply with) the governance standards and give reasons why. Ogden and Watson (2004: 35) add that governance regulations from Cadbury onwards have set out to enshrine the principle that remuneration committees, comprised of 'independent' (non-executive) directors, will incorporate into executive reward 'strong incentives for executives to act in shareholder interests'. While aimed at creating transparency and legitimacy, governance prescriptions 'were never intended specifically to hold down pay levels' (Ogden and Watson 2004: 35). In a parliamentary statement then Secretary of State for Trade and Industry, Patricia Hewitt, was clear on this point: 'All can agree that directors deserve high rewards for good performance' (Hewitt 2004). But she did emphasise the 'need to think creatively about the design of remuneration packages' and vigilance on the part of shareholders 'to ensure that situations where directors enjoy rich rewards whilst companies perform poorly and shareholders and employees suffer are challenged' (Hewitt 2004).

Tyson (2005: 20) argues that reliable data are not hard to find in the surveys such as those produced by the major HR consultancies to help assess whether or not the 'almost frenzied [media] attention' to executive reward is factually based. Findings from a survey of FTSE 350 directors published in autumn 2006 by Incomes Data Services (IDS 2006) reveal that just over a half of all FTSE 350 chief executives earned over £1 million with five receiving total packages grossing more than £10 million. Total earnings for FTSE 100 CEOs increased on average by 43 per cent (from £2,014,665 in 2005 to £2,886,324 in 2006), with corresponding figures for mid-250 chief executives of £1,083,163 and £1,191,427. Reporting reaction to the IDS evidence, journalists Robert Watts and Dan Roberts (2006: 1) quote 'senior City figures' as concluding that: '. . . the astonishing figures for the first time laid bare how, after three years of more modest rises, executive pay was once again spiralling out of control'.

Rather than being related to absolute levels of executive reward, however, controversy seems to derive from relative earnings between the different employee segments. In the same survey, IDS (2006) reports FTSE 100 CEOs earning on average 98 times more than all full-time UK employees over the year to July 2006, which it judges to be the biggest pay gap recorded since the beginning of the decade. Adding a temporal dimension, IDS (2006) refers to an ever-widening pay gap between executives and other employees. To evidence this situation the survey findings show that, since 2000, average FTSE 100 CEO total earnings have increased by 102.2 per cent, compared to an equivalent rise for all UK full-time employees recorded at 28.6 per cent. Findings from another survey the previous year confirm the trend, adding additional comparative indicators. In 2005 CEO pay in a UK listed company had risen 208 per cent since 1998, against average all-employee earnings increases over the same period of 33 per cent and with a fall in the FTSE Index of 13 per cent (IRS 2005). And the gap is not confined to variable remuneration levels. IDS (2006) reports further that FTSE 350 directors' salary increases also outpaced those received by shop floor employees. Over the year surveyed, directors' salaries increased on average by 9.6 per cent, contrasting with IDS Pay Databank figures showing wage settlements for employees generally across the UK economy running at 3 per cent (IDS 2006).

Tyson (2005: 21) calls for 'a sense of proportion' when evaluating issues around the scale of UK executive reward. Although FTSE 350 executive pay levels reported in survey evidence such as that presented by IDS 'may seem beyond the dreams of most ordinary working people', again adopting a relativist stance, rewards achieved by the top ten earners among US executives reported by Forbes, illustrate a large transatlantic disparity. 'The lowest of the top ten earners was Seibel System's CEO on $88 million' (Tyson 2005: 22).

Conyon and Murphy (2000) show that, controlling for size, sector, and other firm and executive characteristics, CEOs in the USA earn 46 per cent higher direct cash remuneration and 190 per cent higher total reward (accounting for share options, etc.). Moreover, Tyson (2005) points to two weaknesses in popular debate: first, a tendency to generalise from particular cases; and second, a failure to recognise the complexities involved (such as those described in the previous section).

Context is helpful when seeking to understand controversy connected with executive reward. The coincidence of corporate leaders' actions impacting adversely on other groups of employees or on the public at large, at a time when executive rewards appear to be on an upward trend, may have triggered sensational media coverage and the perceived need for government intervention on public interest grounds. For example, perceived funding liabilities associated with corporate all-employee pension schemes based on a 'defined benefit' promise has led to widespread action to close or restrict these types of arrangements that may be interpreted as a significant worsening of emoluments available to the majority of employees (IDS 2007). This action has coincided with some executives retaining the benefits of so-called 'top hat' pension arrangements. According to IRS (2007), CEOs in the top nine UK companies have benefited from increased individual pension fund accrued values of 137 per cent, on average, and across the ten largest UK plcs average accrued pension transfer values increased by almost £1.2m between 2002 and 2003.

A number of widely reported 'severance' payments, including lump sum pension funding enhancements, to executives at the time of leaving office have fuelled an already controversial area of concern. Reilly and Scott (2005) report concerns too over laxity on the part of remuneration committees where executives have been able to exercise large stock option grants just prior to a share price collapse, nominally attributable to the underperforming executive who is being replaced. In the UK, although cautious regarding generalisation from a small number of cases where 'rewards for failure' have been made to executives, the Association of Chartered and Certified Accountants (ACCA) argues that 'such payments reflect an inappropriate culture at the top of organisations and can have a strong influence in wider society, making the issue one in the public interest' (ACCA 2005: 1). In the foreword to the 2003 DTI consultative paper (DTI 2003) on this controversy, concerns were expressed that compensation granted to departing executives seen to be over-generous might damage the image and reputation of British business as a whole. However, rather than introduce further legislation for the time being, the government has opted to rely on 'increased activism by institutional investors, and the promotion of best practice' to remedy the situation (Hewitt 2004: *Hansard* Column 51–52 WS). The Combined Code, as revised in 2006 under the auspices of the Financial Reporting Council, includes an express statement that remuneration committees should as a rule not set directors' notice or contract periods at one year or less. They also should carefully consider what compensation commitments (including pension contributions and all other elements) their directors' terms of appointment would entail in the event of early termination. They should take a robust line on reducing compensation to reflect departing directors' obligations to mitigate loss.

(FRC 2006: 12)

As will be discussed in the third section of the chapter, such intervention may produce arguably perverse outcomes. The problem is that interpreting what shareholder interests – and, even more problematically, stakeholder interests – maybe puts managers in a position where they may be 'damned' whatever they do (Tyson 2005: 15). Complexity in operational issues, set in a wider stakeholder context, may amplify the controversy factor in executive reward debates, with an accent on the ethical issue of 'equity' or 'relative fairness' (Bender and Moir 2006). As will be discussed below, the position may be further clouded however when considering equity with whom, and against which measures.

Controversy surrounding the issue of executive reward determinants features not only in state-sponsored 'reform' initiatives (Dahya and Travlos 2000); contestation in theorising executive pay contingencies is also marked in the literature. Consistent with classical economic theory, 'market forces' have been cited by those seeking to defend as well as to explain executive reward management practice. Company directors have been reported as judging 'market factors' as 'very important in determining executive pay' and 'a central factor in recruitment, retention and motivation' (Stiles and Taylor 2002: 76). And the CEO of a large UK stock market listed company has been quoted, responding to a question at a shareholders' meeting, as declaring: 'My remuneration is determined by market forces' (Pepper 2006: 15). More carefully, the Hampel Report (1998: 4.3) states that to attract business executives 'of the required calibre' their remuneration will be 'largely determined by the market' – inclusion of the word 'largely' implying a qualification in the market forces rationale, expressly stated in the earlier Greenbury Report (1995). Market 'imperfections' mean that: 'While market forces set a broad framework . . . remuneration committees for the most part have quite a wide range of discretion in setting levels and forms of remuneration' (Greenbury 1995: 6.4).

Explaining 'why the market doesn't work' in relation to executive reward determination, Pepper (2006: 15) argues that 'practically none' of the conditions for a perfect economic market to operate are visible. Rather than free market entry and exit, there are limitations on the numbers of executive jobs open and suitable candidates to fill them at any one time. Executive 'commodities' are not homogeneous: no two individuals are the same. The same difficulty applies to systematic comparative evaluation of 'unique' executive roles to be filled (Hijazi and Bhatti 2007). And while (proxy) market comparisons have been encouraged by more comprehensive disclosure of total executive rewards, information on how to 'price' executive experience and skills is far from perfect. A sample of FTSE 100 remuneration committee members interviewed by Perkins and Hendry (2005) expressed themselves constrained in calibrating price-value norms objectively due to idiosyncrasies that require 'artful' assessments of individuals and roles (Noldeke and Samuelson 1997). The price-value placed on a specific executive may depend more on the characteristics and preferences of the purchasers (company) than on the 'commodity' itself. Institutional factors and socially contextualised decision taking thus appear to require attention too.

If markets are unreliable as determinants of executive reward, to what extent does the accent that has been placed by institutional regulators on 'performance' help to address the controversy? Conyon and Sadler (2001: 141) contend that executive rewards and measures of 'company performance' represent 'a central theme within the UK debate'. The same analysts add that 'intuitively' an appropriate indicator of company performance is 'total shareholder return' – i.e. share price appreciation and dividend yield (2001: 146). The conclusion from a wide-ranging review of the evidence is that even where a statistical link, calculated using econometric models, was identifiable between direct (cash and incentive bonus related) rewards and a firm's stock market performance, this was small. Company size and pay level was found to demonstrate a more robust correlation (Conyon 1998). Using data from large UK companies over the period 1986–1994, Conyon (1998) found the threat of dismissal was also a source of discipline motivating, especially younger, executives to perform in the long-term interest of shareholders. Dahya *et al.* (2002: 469) posit a similar connection between 'forced turnover, in the CEO position' and adoption of the Cadbury principles. Conyon and Sadler (2001) examined evidence that reflected the changing composition of executive reward packages in the late 1990s and indicated the shift from 'current cash compensation' (2001: 146), to an emphasis on share-based related incentives. There is a practical reason for incorporating a wider definition of executive reward: data available for this kind of analysis has only begun to include the wider reward portfolio elements as disclosure has required companies to release this information into the public domain.

There is evidence from these later, typically US, studies suggesting that, taking account of a reward portfolio calibrated in favour of 'changes in the value of the stock and equity options held by the CEO ... the pay-performance link may be becoming stronger' (Conyon and Sadler 2001: 151). Conyon (1998) develops the idea that talent increases in its impact on performance the higher it is situated in the organisational hierarchy. So, he reasons, the CEO who oversees the performance of other executives is part of a cascade effect where the talent exercised at the top projects positively on to the performance of executive subordinates. In economics jargon 'the marginal product of the CEO is reproduced at successively lower levels of the hierarchical organization' (Conyon 1998: 488). Using late 1990s data on 100 UK stock market listed companies, covering over 500 individual executives,

Conyon *et al.* (2001) found, however, that variation in executive team pay had little role in determining company performance.

Jensen *et al.* (2004) are, however, critical of equity-based reward policies, which they believe compound the problem of over-valued corporate equity they say executives know is not sustainable. This recognition leads to action to manipulate short-term equity prices – when under pressure to sustain artificially inflated levels – resulting at worst in the sorts of outcomes witnessed at Enron, for example, and subsequently played out in the courts. But even in less high profile cases, the ultimate result for shareholders is 'value destruction' over the long run. Jensen *et al.* (2004) allege a form of collusion between executives and financial investment market managers, to the detriment of the beneficial owners of the financial equity. For Jensen *et al.* (2004: 239), a 'key concern is that many institutional investors are not acting as shareowners'. In the UK the Myners Report, published in 2001, sought to promote greater shareholder activism – especially in the stance taken towards under-performing companies, 'exercising their votes in a considered way' (Mallin 2004: 239). And, as observed in the previous section, eschewing further legislation, recent regulatory action on the part of the UK government has been to place the onus on institutional shareholders to play the more 'engaged' role advocated by 'activists' such as Monks and Sykes (2002).

Controversy, then, is not related just to how much executives earn absolutely or relatively, or to technical debates around the merits of market- or performance-based economic determinants. The reference to control in reported reactions to 'spiralling' executive reward levels surfaces the issue of who is and/or should be 'controlling' executive pay, indicating the need for attention to the relationship between executives and those who employ them – or at least determine their reward on behalf of the 'employer', to which attention now turns.

The 'interpretative gap' (Knights and McCabe 2000) experienced by executives and those tasked with overseeing their activities has social and psychological as well as economic characteristics. Again, there is no shortage of controversy in academic debate on this problem. Theoretical argument emphasises, respectively, 'agency' considerations (Jensen and Meckling 1976; Jensen *et al.* 2004); power-dependency factors (Pfeffer and Salancik 2003; Wright and McMahan 1992); 'tournament'-based interaction between actors close to the top of corporate hierarchies (Conyon *et al.* 2001; Conyon and Sadler 2001); and more relativist accounts (Roberts 2001).

Jensen and Meckling's (1976) theorisation of 'principal-agency' relations has dominated the analysis of corporate governance for over 30 years (Buck *et al.* 1998). An agency relationship is defined as a contract: a principal (owner/shareholder) engages an agent to perform some service on the principal's behalf. Under this perspective, 'shareholders are seen as the focal group whose interests are furthered through crafting executive pay arrangements that cause a top management team motivated by self-interest to maximize shareholder value' (Bruce *et al.* 2005: 1493). Agency problems arise for investors, however, in assessing whether they are getting the best value return from the executives to whom corporate management is delegated. If it were easy to assure alignment between payments (inputs) to executives and performance (outputs), shareholders could simply pay their executives a fixed salary (in effect, a form of insurance payment), and then assess whether that agent is supplying optimal effort in the shareholders' interest (Perkins and Hendry 2005). Jensen *et al.* (2004) are firmly of the opinion that the agency problem cannot be eliminated, only mitigated. But they argue that executive reward and how it is determined offers a source of mitigation. The downside is that inappropriately governed executive reward policies and practices risk value-destroying agency on the part of executives entrusted with the running of the firm. Thus, pay design cannot successfully be considered independent of corporate governance considerations (Jensen *et al.* 2004).

The mediated agency relationship is a further source of disquiet. Sykes (2002: 256) alleges 'widespread conflicts of interest', derived from the complicated sets of interrelations involving institutional investment managers concerned with widely dispersed share portfolios managed on behalf of beneficiaries and non-executive directors. Sykes' (2002) criticism is aimed at 'largely passive shareholders' and 'complacent and ineffective non-executive directors' (2002: 256). There are the executives' own roles too: while formally delegating administration to a remuneration committee, 'directors have power to influence their own rewards and to affect the performance of their firms, probably to a greater extent than other employees' (Tyson and Bournois 2005: 7). This is the issue to which analysis and codes of practice have been especially directed. Introducing the consultative document on directors' remuneration, then Secretary of State for Industry, Patricia Hewitt, observed that this is 'the issue above all others, on which directors face a conflict of interest' (DTI 2001: 4). Hence the legal obligation placed on UK publicly traded companies, under the Directors' Remuneration Report Regulations (HMSO 2002), to require extensive disclosure in a remuneration committee report accompanying company annual reports and accounts. The report must also be submitted for approval at the annual general meeting, creating scope for the kinds of controversial interactions between corporate leaders and shareholders reported at the start of this section of the chapter.

In a pragmatic counterpoint, Tyson argues that the separation of ownership from control of organisations requires managers to be afforded some latitude to make decisions – authority must accompany accountability. And senior managers are not just acted on by institutions – they are themselves actors with intentions and wants, he argues, as they seek to 'orchestrate the affairs of the corporation' (2005: 16). The problem for boards is stark. 'No one stakeholder can speak with unchallenged authority for the corporate interest', so this latitude includes the freedom for managers 'to align [their] interests with the "interests" of the corporation' (2005: 16). Pfeffer and Salancik (2003) draw attention specifically to the impact of power in relations between organisational actors, arguing that, if organisations are to be controlled and managed (as well as understood), account needs to be taken of the actions of core interest groups. Emphasising context, they argue that academic literature tends to overlook – or take as a given in modelling economic transactions – the apparently obvious point that behaviour in organisations is behaviour that adapts to the environment. Using the language of agency theory, organisational principals must acquire and maintain the resources necessary to develop and enact strategy and operations. And the more the principal depends on the resources, the more leverage the resource-holder may exercise in the transaction around whether or not and to what extent to perceive their interests as aligned with the principal interest-holders.

Applying this reasoning to executives, Molm *et al.* (1999) argue that the relative power of principals and their agents in determining the effort-reward contract is derived from their mutual dependence. The extent to which behavioural adaptation occurs with outcomes that more or less favour principals or agents is moderated by existing power relationships within the firm (Festing *et al.* 2007). The relationship between the parties to corporate governance relationships therefore becomes 'the product of ongoing interaction and discussion' (Roberts 2001: 1549). While Conyon (1998) finds that the threat of dismissal may discipline young CEOs, he argues that executives may be able to mobilise embedded power resources to 'entrench themselves in their positions, making it difficult to oust them when they perform poorly' (Bebchuck and Fried 2003: 72). Regulatory initiatives are meant to address such controversy. But faced with the annual shareholders' meeting media story and continuing 'pay gap' survey data reported earlier, some commentators remain unconvinced regarding efforts to achieve equilibrium in the executive-shareholder power balance. The charge sheet lists: remuneration committees lacking independence; management choosing the consultants to advise on their pay setting; managerial action motivated by pressures to produce 'shareholder value' over impossibly short time periods – and stock option gains to be made – leading to value destruction (Sykes 2002).

Using published data from FTSE companies over the period 1990–2004, O'Connell (2006) shows that the marked and growing gap between executives and other employees widens still further at the top of the organisational hierarchy. He discovers a 42 per cent increase in the share of relative executive cash reward paid to CEOs compared with non-CEO executives on the board. O'Connell (2006) argues that the evidence may illustrate increasing CEO power not held in check by remuneration committees. It may be that remuneration committees are uncritically accepting 'benchmark' practice elsewhere and/or are simply not paying attention to the fact that, while pay increases have been steady, over the entire period the cumulative consequences are significant. O'Connell (2006) notes arguments that CEOs receive the highest relative reward due to the increased level of responsibility they shoulder, with demand for CEOs outstripping supply, and due to the relatively stronger association between CEO performance and that of the company they head. However, he finds no strong case supported by the FTSE data to suggest that responsibility at CEO level has become relatively greater since 1990. Moreover, he can offer no obvious reason why fewer CEO candidates are available to fill the jobs available. Also, when looking at performance alignment it seems that the rate of increase in CEO cash reward has continued to run ahead of increases in corporate performance. Additionally, there is no obvious sign that CEO pay and performance are more forcefully aligned compared with other board executives.

Another proffered explanation is 'the tournament effect', with the ultimate 'prize' limited to the CEO. Whether the need for the prize to have increased over the past decade and a half to the extent that CEO pay has remains an open question. In theory, locating a distinctive 'prize' at the top of the organisation may be predicted to motivate agents in contention for CEO positions, for example, to compete by out-performing fellow executives, with the result that the organisation and its principals benefit from the sum of individual contributions. The line of reasoning may falter, however, once there are 'no tomorrow aspects of the final stage of the game' (Rosen 1986: 701). Few empirical tests of tournament theory in general have been reported, and 'only a handful in the context of executive compensation' (Conyon and Sadler 2001: 155). Conyon *et al.* test tournament predictions using data on 100 large stock market companies, finding 'some confirmatory evidence' that 'the ratio of pay increases as one moves up the hierarchical level . . . Moving from the level just below the CEO to the Group CEO job position generates an approximately 60% increase in pay' (Conyon *et al.* 2001: 155). They observe a positive relationship between the CEO reward premium and the number of tournament contenders. Greater support for hypotheses derived from tournament theory has been found in sporting settings (e.g. racing drivers, jockeys, professional golfers). However, increased transparency not only in terms of rewards obtained but also levels of performance attainment makes the pay-performance linkage easier to observe in sport than in business settings (Conyon and Sadler 2001).

Calling for a return to first principles, Roberts (2001) challenges the dominant agency orientation in corporate governance literature and policy. Agency theory, he argues, is predicated on an essentialist perspective of human nature: accordingly, employment relationships are no more than a series of implicit and explicit socio-economic contracts with associated rights. A more relativist perspective, on the other hand, introduces the possibility of learned and reinforced trust. Buck *et al.* (1998), for example, extend agency theory beyond its 'traditional financial version' to propose a Stakeholder Agency Theory (SAT). As a heuristic for structuring corporate governance analysis, SAT hypothesises the existence of organisational cultures in which trusting relationships encourage stakeholders to suspend opportunistic actions in favour of an ethic of cooperation (Buck *et al.* 1998).

The evidence discussed here is indicative of the lack of consensus justifying the quantum of executive reward – how it should be set and who should take the lead role in controlling this controversial aspect of corporate governance.

Critically inclined commentary may go a stage further, however: the problem with the range of interpretations and 'solutions' is the scope not only to create complexity and possible confusion among interested parties. Inherent in the assumptions and consequential initiatives observable in attempts to regulate executive reward is the scope for contradiction potentially leading to perverse outcomes. Due to space restrictions, the issues can only be briefly sketched in the section that now follows. However, mainstream theory on executive reward governance may usefully be contrasted with alternative theories on routes to organisational effectiveness.

Contradiction

Mainstream efforts to regulate the executive effort-reward bargain risk overlooking alternative routes to releasing resource-embedded capabilities to achieve sustainable (profitable) enterprise. In some cases, criticism is directed as a matter of principle against introduction of a 'visible hand' in economic decisions impacting on executive reward determination (Zajec and Westphal 1995). Focusing on the ethics of executive reward management, Bender and Moir (2006) observe that regulatory initiatives informed by agency theory prevail in the face of alternative commentary arguing against this 'Economic Man' orientation (e.g. Bruce *et al.* 2005; Roberts 2001). Agency theory takes an essentially negative view of the relationship between principal and agent, which may be assumed to extend to non-executives as boardroom intermediaries. Little or no account is taken of 'the differing attitudes of managers, nor of the different conditions under which they operate' (Morris and Fenton-O'Creevy 1996: 709), which might assuage this negative assumption. While a robust response to calls to abandon agency theory is offered by Gomez-Mejia *et al.* (2005), this is not to say that possible contradictions should not be exposed.

Based on data from proxy statements in the USA over 15 years, Zajec and Westphal (1995) found that agency explanations, rather than what they label 'HRM explanations', have become more prevalent in considering executive pay. Calling for an analysis that goes beyond economics and politics, they argue that substantive disclosure is inadequate. Symbolic considerations are of equal importance in understanding what is going on. Responses to the 'comply or explain' requirements for remuneration committee decisions are likely to reflect context-specific interpretations of the prevailing beliefs among opinion formers regarding the socially legitimate purpose of executive reward. Agency theory may be viewed as a *symbolic* basis for justifying the rise to prominence of long-term incentives in executive reward packages, as 'interest-alignment mechanisms', shifting from the previous dominant HR logic of attracting and retaining scarce managerial resources 'by raising the potential total compensation levels' (Zajec and Westphal 1995: 285). Using incentive reward to achieve organisational effectiveness in pursuit of corporate value over the long term implies skilful goal setting and performance appraisal. Executive incentive goal management is however regarded as the most difficult, as well as a central problem for principals (Gomez-Mejia and Weisman 1997). The scope for contradictory outcomes is large. Misalignment will not lead to sustained added value derived from executive behaviour; and goals must be set so they are not too low, so under-performance is tacitly signalled, or too high so as to demotivate performance. Communicating the assumptions accompanying an agency relationship may run contrary to the conditions needed for trust-based 'give-and-take' under complexity.

The resource-based view (RBV) of the firm and HRM-inspired commentary have become well-established perspectives on strategy and people planning. For the purpose of the present short discussion, two seminal statements are cited. Barney (1991), departing from the business economics orthodoxy of the 1960s, outlined a framework for considering the basis on which firms might obtain sustainable competitive advantage. And in 1987, Guest (1987) wrote an article aimed at tightening up the then loosely defined references to 'HRM' which had been put forward (originally in the USA) as a distinctive approach for managing the employment relationship.

Previously assumed as a given common to all firms, Barney (1991) argues that firm resources are heterogeneous with constrained inter-organisational mobility. Given these assumptions, RBV theorising holds out the prospect for strategy, conception and execution to create organisationally specific, sustainable, competitive advantages difficult for competitors to replicate. Firm resources under this perspective are not only valuable; they are rare, inimitable and not easily substituted by alternative resources (Barney 1991: 101). Among the resources to which Barney refers, human capital resources are defined in terms of the training, judgement, experience, intelligence, and relationships managers possess. Barney's (1991) conclusion is that firms cannot expect to 'purchase' sustainable competitive advantage on open markets. This, he says, must be found in the valuable, rare, inimitable and non-substitutable resource already controlled by a firm.

Barney (1991) refers to top management teams as a specific illustration of the necessary conditions for RBV application. Each of the four operational traits referred to must apply as a bundle. While a top management team may be rare and valuable, another firm may develop an equivalent resource using different people with alternative talents so that the first firm does not have strategic advantage as a function of the top team's characteristics. Barney (1991) cites relationships as one of the features to be factored-in. Positive, trusting and open, rather than cautious and compliance oriented, relations between executive agents and their shareholder principals (and non-executive intermediaries), for example, may be a potential source of non-substitutable top management resources, creating advantage that cannot simply be competed away. Executive reward regulatory compliance requirements, premised on agency assumptions running contrary to the kinds of relationship basis Barney is advocating, may conspire to frustrate efforts to build sustainable competitive advantages from RBV type managerial resource bundles.

Similar to the 'bundling effect' associated with RBV-informed strategic planning,[5] Guest (1987) situates the notion of 'integration' at the heart of HRM theorising. The goal is to align business and HR strategies, HR and other functional aspects – marketing, finance, operations, etc. – and also the portfolio of HRM practices (including reward). This represents a break with piecemeal and reactive 'personnel administration'. Getting employees to display a high intrinsic motivation allied to commitment, Guest (1987) argues, 'the aim is to obtain an identity of interest, so that what is good for the company is perceived by employees as also being good for them' (1987: 512): HRM in Guest's model is 'unitarist and individualistic in focus' (1987: 518). It seems reasonable to assume that intrinsic motivation allied to commitment to the organisation and its corporate purpose is critical in the case of the executives to whom a principal chooses to delegate managerial control. Such reasoning conflicts with the assumptions underlying corporate governance 'best practice' applied to executive reward, under which alignment of apparently disparate interests in realising corporate value must be stimulated by extrinsic incentives. An accent on 'administrative efficiency and cost minimization' (Guest 1987: 518) may prevail, contrary to HRM/RBV norms. Due to a values system emphasising 'financial issues and often short-term financial issues imposed by the City', Guest (1987: 519) found the UK corporate governance environment not conducive to HRM-oriented strategy planning. Two decades on, corporate governance standards for executive pay regulation may be interpreted as an indication that the position is little altered.

Kessler (2001) criticises deficiencies in RBV commentary, largely because there is little evidence on how complex bundles of competencies emerge. He suggests that exploration guided by new institutional theory might help, taking cognisance of how the actors interpret the organisational setting, as well as the firm's and their own history as an influence on what they do. Guest (1987) too counsels against generalisation of HRM prescriptions as though all contexts and all employees are the same. Contexts and individuals vary: some settings are more 'adversarial' than others and people come with values and experiences that orient them to organisation and work in a variety of ways. Taking this view into account, exclusively external disciplinary provisions to control the negative potential in managerial agency may be flawed due to under-socialised foundational assumptions (Bruce *et al.* 2005). For example, Combs *et al.* (2007) suggest that, rather than relying solely on institutional investors and non-executives to keep CEOs in check, control by fellow executives may be a potential avenue to pursue. Citing power circulation theory, they suggest that CEOs may be potentially vulnerable leaders of a dominant management coalition. The argument is that 'other executives are highly motivated to detect and react to shortcomings of the CEO because each of them may have the potential to become CEO and accrue greater prestige and wealth if the incumbent is replaced'. But this is not a tournament theory variant. 'Given that the stain of poor performance tarnishes all of a firm's executives, not just the CEO, power circulation theory asserts that other executives are driven to scrutinize the CEO and form a coalition to oppose the CEO if necessary' (Combs *et al.* 2007: 1302).

So principals creating the conditions for an exclusively economic and negative agency relationship with executive agents, as well as regulators advocating this position, may either find their strategic management capability limited by ignoring this line of reasoning or find themselves surprised when, having apparently embraced HRM and resource-based strategy, outcomes contradict those predicted. Scope for interests to conflict between organisational stakeholders may be more a function of context – high trust/low trust assumed – than an essential condition of human nature (Roberts 2001).

The second possible contradiction is discernible in Jensen *et al.*'s (2004) reflections on contemporary problems in regulating executive reward. Tyson (2005, citing Clarke 1998) warns that developments in executive incentive plans may be no more than what economists have in the past referred to as a 'satisficing' move. Regulatory compliance is *seen* to be achieved but executives recognise that sustained success depends not only on rewarding shareholders, but also in attending to the needs of wider enterprise stakeholders. Popular over the past decade or so, 'balanced scorecard' approaches reinforce this multidirectional orientation for 'translating strategy into action', as Kaplan and Norton (1996) put it. A new requirement features in the 2008 Regulations on Large and Medium-sized Companies and Groups (Accounts and Reports) that the directors' remuneration report should contain a statement of how pay and employment conditions elsewhere in the organisation have been taken into account in determining directors' remuneration for the financial year in question. Adopting a 'stakeholder' orientation and basing incentives on balanced scorecard targets represents one of the ways that Jensen *et al.* (2004) argue executive reward management may exacerbate rather than overcome the agency problem.

Jensen *et al.* (2004) argue that 200 years of economics research makes it clear that unless corporate leaders have a singular goal – increasing the long-run value of the company – then it will not be possible to hold management to account in a principled way. The aim is to make effective use of socially valuable resources. In a company competing to make a profit, a range of stakeholder interests needs to be satisfied. But Jensen *et al.* (2004) contend that ambiguity enters when using a range of factors or relying on internally generated measures. There is a risk of confusing managerial energies at best, and encouraging manipulation of 'performance' indicators, at worst. The Balanced Scorecard is rejected: a score, as in a sports contest, to see who has 'won' and who has 'lost' is the only way management can be transparently held to account. Managerial stewardship should be judged according to value creation (not maximisation as it is impossible to ascertain when value has been maximised) based on how a firm is valued in the capital markets. This does not translate into advocacy for maximisation of short-run stock market prices – quite the reverse. Executives are privy to information denied to stock market investors; therefore investors' short-run assessments of corporate worth may be inadequate. To avoid the risk of contradictory messages, Jensen *et al.* (2004) advocate that remuneration committees should design and apply reward policies to attract executive resources at the lowest price, and retain the 'right' executives at the lowest price while encouraging the 'right' executives to leave at an appropriate time. During their tenure organisationally effective reward should motivate executives to secure the greatest long-run value for the firm; it should act to discourage shareholder value destroying the agency. The accent seems to be on keeping the focus 'simple not simplistic'.

None of the positions sketched above is presented with prescription in mind. The object here is to draw attention to the room for missed opportunities as well as unintended outcomes observable in the controversy surrounding executive reward management over the past decade and a half. As a final example of perversity, following the populist campaign over relative top executive reward levels in the USA that featured as a 1992 presidential election campaign issue, legislation was introduced defining non-performance-related compensation as unreasonable and therefore not deductible as an ordinary business expense for corporate income tax purposes. Ironically,

> although the populist objective was to reduce 'excessive' CEO pay levels ... the ultimate outcome was a significant increase in executive compensation. It appears from the data that once the Act defined $1 million compensation as reasonable many companies increased cash compensation to $1 million, and then began to add on the [stock option] based [performance] pay that satisfied the act.
>
> (Jensen *et al.* 2004: 30)

As with the c-factors of complexity and controversy, plenty of room exists for contradiction in executive reward management policy and practice.

Conclusion

In this chapter, a range of contemporary literature has been drawn on to defend a decision to devote space specifically to executive reward. Three factors – complexity, controversy, and contradiction – have been applied as lenses through which commentary ranging from scientifically oriented exploration to polemic may be interpreted and critically appraised.

Complexity in executive reward design and administration may be judged a function of observable efforts to specify, maintain, and account for the executive effort-reward bargain. Accentuating 'this' or 'that' approach reflects the perspective adopted to weigh choices – micro level cost-effectiveness, return on human capital invested, at one point, and transparency and accountability against a range of meso and macro level economic, political and social considerations at the other end of the spectrum.

The ever-increasing complexity for which executive reward and its management may be judged distinctive is not only subject to controversy, as the interested parties debate approaches and underlying assumptions. Complexity itself creates the conditions for controversy, particularly among simplistically inclined commentators. And complexity may exacerbate concerns about a lack of transparency, fanning the flames of suspicion. Interest in executive reward is not merely objective – the assessor's standpoint gives rise to a subjective dimension too. Further, the symbolic nature of executive reward – as it links not only with reward at lower organisational levels, and principal-agent interaction, but with wider 'stakeholder' considerations – augments the scope for a range of viewpoints and 'interpretative gaps'. Agency-based assumptions appear to underpin the regulatory policy that has emerged to date. A risk arising from complexity and controversy in executive reward management is that possible contradiction in underlying assumptions and prescriptions may lead to perverse outcomes.

It would be unwise to consider executive reward management and corporate governance in isolation from each other and the wider environment in which they continue to evolve. Given scope for sending out contradictory messages to the actors, more detailed specification of organisational effectiveness aims grounded in particular contexts may be sensible. While not overlooking their limitations, HRM and RBV may be helpfully factored-in to the mix by researchers and policy makers. Future investigation may thus include more contextualised reflection on the systematic interplay of complexity, controversy, and contradiction around executive reward and its management: phenomena that appear likely to prevail for the foreseeable future.

Notes

1 In some cases the term 'Chief Executive's Committee' is used underlining this point.
2 In the USA employment contracts that extend beyond an 'at will' basis on which individuals and the organisation may sever the relationship tend to be restricted to executive level.
3 Some 'flexible benefits' schemes do permit conversion between certain benefits and cash.
4 The roots of the controversy lie in the separation of firm ownership and control, long ago highlighted by business economists (Berle and Means 1991 [1932]), accompanying the rise of professionally managed giant industrial corporations whose capital is widely dispersed among shareholders.
5 Purcell (1999) specifically articulates a 'bundling effect' emerging from more sophistication as HRM theorising evolves beyond the earliest iterations.

References

ACCA (2005) 'Executive pay', Policy Briefing Paper, June, London: Association of Chartered and Certified Accountants.
Baldamus, W. (1961) *Efficiency and Effort*, London: Tavistock.
Barney, J. (1991) 'Firm resources and sustained competitive advantage', *Journal of Management*, 17 (1): 99–120.

Bebchuck, L. A. and Fried, J. M. (2003) 'Executive compensation as an agency problem', *Journal of Economic Perspectives*, 17 (3): 71–92.

Bender, R. and Moir, L. (2006) 'Does "best practice" in setting executive pay in the UK encourage "good behaviour"?', *Journal of Business Ethics*, 67 (1): 75–91.

Benz, M. and Frey, B. S. (2007) 'Corporate governance: What can we learn from public governance?', *Academy of Management Review*, 32 (1): 92–104.

Berle, A. A. and Means, G. C. (1991[1932]) *The Modern Corporation and Private Property*, Somerset, NJ: Transaction Publishers.

Bruce, A., Buck, T. and Main, B. G. M. (2005) 'Top executive remuneration: a view from Europe', *Journal of Management Studies*, 42 (7): 1493–1506.

Buck, T., Bruce, A. and Main, B. G. M. (2003) 'Long term incentive plans, executive pay and UK company performance', *Journal of Management Studies*, 40 (7): 1709–1727.

Buck, T., Filatotchev, I. and Wright, M. (1998) 'Agents, stakeholders and corporate governance in Russian firms', *Journal of Management Studies*, 35 (1): 81–89.

Burgess, K. (2007) 'C&W wins approval for senior pay plans', *Financial Times*, 22–23 July: 15.

Cadbury, Sir A. (1992) *Report of the Committee on the Financial Aspects of Corporate Governance*, London: Gee Publishing.

Combs, J. G., Ketchen Jr, D. J., Perryman, A. A. and Donahue, M. S. (2007) 'The moderating effect of CEO power on the board composition–firm performance relationship', *Journal of Management Studies*, 44 (8): 1299–1323.

Conyon, M. J. (1998) 'Directors' pay and turnover: an application to a sample of large UK firms', *Oxford Bulletin of Economics and Statistics*, 60 (4): 485–507.

Conyon, M. J. and Murphy, K. J. (2000) 'The prince and the pauper? CEO pay in the US and UK', *Economic Journal*, 110 (467): 640–671.

Conyon, M. J. and Sadler, G. V. (2001) 'Executive pay, tournaments and corporate performance in UK firms', *International Journal of Management Reviews*, 3 (2): 141–168.

Conyon, M. J., Peck, S. I. and Sadler, G. V. (2001) 'Corporate tournaments and executive compensation: Evidence from the U.K', *Strategic Management Journal*, 22 (8): 805–815.

Core, J. E., Guay, W. R. and Larcker, D. F. (2003) 'Executive equity compensation and incentives: a survey', *Federal Reserve Bank of New York Economic Policy Review*, 9 (1): 27–50.

Crystal, G. (1992) *In Search of Excess: The overcompensation of American executives*, New York: W. W. Norton & Company.

Dahya, J. and Travlos, N. G. (2000) 'Does the one man show pay? Theory and evidence on the dual CEO revisited', *European Financial Management*, 6 (1): 85–98.

Dahya, J., McConnell, J. J. and Travlos, N. G. (2002) 'The Cadbury committee, corporate performance, and top management turnover', *Journal of Finance*, 57 (3): 461–483.

Deloitte (2004) *Report on the Impact of the Directors' Remuneration Regulations: A Report for the Department of Trade and Industry*, London: Deloitte & Touche LLP.

DTI (2001) *Directors' Remuneration: A Consultative Document*, URN 01/1400, December, London: Department for Business Enterprise and Regulatory Reform.

DTI (2003) *'Rewards for Failure' Directors' Remuneration – Contracts, Performance & Severance: A Consultative Document*, URN 03/652, June, London: Department for Business Enterprise and Regulatory Reform.

Economist, Business (2007) 'The politics of pay: executive salaries', *The Economist*, 24 March.

Festing, M., Eidems, J. and Royer, S. (2007) 'Strategic issues and local constraints in transnational compensation strategies. An analysis of cultural, institutional and political influences', *European Management Journal*, 25 (2): 118–131.

FRC (2006) *The Combined Code on Corporate Governance*, London: Financial Reporting Council.

Gomez-Mejia, L. and Wiseman, R. M. (1997) 'Reframing executive compensation: an assessment and outlook', *Journal of Management*, 42 (7): 291–374.

Gomez-Mejia, L., Wiseman, R. M. and Johnson Dykes, B. (2005) 'Agency problems in diverse contexts: a global perspective', *Journal of Management Studies*, 23 (3): 1507–1517.

Greenbury, Sir R. (1995) *Report of the Study Group on Directors' Remuneration*, London: Gee Publishing.

Guest, D. E. (1987) 'Human resource management and industrial relations', *Journal of Management Studies*, 24 (5): 503–521.

Hampel, Sir R. (1998) *Committee on Corporate Governance: Final Report*, London: Gee Publishing.

Hewitt, P. (2004) 'Trade and Industry statement: directors' remuneration, contracts, performance and severance', *Hansard*, 25 February, Column 51–52 WS.

Higgs, D. (2003) *Review of the Role and Effectiveness of Non-executive Directors: Consultation Paper*, London: Department of Trade and Industry.

Hijazi, S. T. and Bhatti, K. K. (2007) 'Determinants of executive compensation and its impact on organizational performance', *Compensation and Benefits Review*, March–April: 58–68.

HMSO (2002) *Statutory Instrument 2002 No. 1986: The Directors' Remuneration Report Regulations 2002*, London: The Stationery Office.

House of Commons Trade and Industry Committee (2003) *Rewards for Failure: Sixteenth Report of Session 2002–2003*, London: The Stationery Office.

IDS (2006) *Directors' Pay Report 2006*, London: Incomes Data Services.

IDS (2007) *Benchmarking Review of Pension Schemes 2007*, London: Incomes Data Services.

IRS (2005) *Executive Directors Total Remuneration Survey 2005*, London: Independent Remuneration Solutions and Manifest.

IRS (2007) *Executive Directors Total Remuneration Survey 2007*, London: Independent Remuneration Solutions and Manifest.

Jensen, M. C. and Meckling, W. H. (1976) 'Theory of the firm: managerial behavior, agency costs and ownership structure', *Journal of Financial Economics*, 3 (4): 305–360.

Jensen, M. C., Murphy, K. J. and Wruck, E. G. (2004) 'Remuneration: where we've been, how we got to here, what are the problems, and how to fix them', ECGI Working Paper No. 44/2004. Social Science Research Network Electronic Paper Collection: http://ssrn.com/abstract=561305 (accessed 27 August 2007).

Kaplan, R. S. and Norton, D. P. (1996) *The Balanced Scorecard: Translating strategy into action*, Boston, Mass.: Harvard Business School Press.

Kessler, I. (2001) 'Reward system choices', in J. Storey (ed.) *Human Resource Management: A critical text*, 2nd edn, London: Thomson.

Knights, P. and McCabe, D. (2000) ' "Ain't misbehavin' "? Opportunities for resistance under new forms of "quality" management', *Sociology*, 34 (3): 421–436.

Mallin, C. (2004) 'Trustees, institutional investors and ultimate beneficiaries', *Corporate Governance*, 12 (3): 239–241.

McCarthy, W. (1993) 'From Donovan until now: Britain's twenty-five years of incomes policy', *Employee Relations*, 15 (6): 3–20.

Molm, L. D., Peterson, G. and Takashini, N. (1999) 'Power in negotiated and reciprocal exchange', *American Sociological Review*, 64 (6): 876–890.

Monks, R. and Sykes, A. (2002) *Capitalism without Owners will Fail: A policymaker's guide to reform*, London: CSFI Publications.

Morris, T. J. and Fenton-O'Creevy, M. (1996) 'Opening up the black box: a UK case study of top managers' attitudes to their performance related pay', *International Journal of Human Resource Management*, 7 (3): 708–720.

Noldeke, G. and Samuelson, L. (1997) 'A dynamic model of equilibrium selection in signaling markets', *Journal of Economic Theory*, 73 (1): 118–156.

Norris, P. (2005) 'Shareholders' attitudes to directors' pay', in S. Tyson and F. Bournois (eds) *Top Pay and Performance: International and Strategic Approach*, London: Elsevier.

O'Connell, V. (2006) 'The CEO's share of total directors' cash compensation: U.K. evidence', *Compensation and Benefits Review*, 38, Sep/Oct: 28–34.

Ogden, S. and Watson, R. (2004) 'Remuneration committees and CEO pay in the UK privatized water industry', *Socio-Economic Review*, 2 (1): 33–63.

Pepper, S. (2006) *Senior Executive Reward: Key models and practices*, Aldershot: Gower.

Perkins, S. J. and Hendry, C. (2005) 'Ordering top pay: interpreting the signals', *Journal of Management Studies*, 42 (7): 1443–1468.

Pfeffer, J. and Salancik, G. R. (2003) *The External Control of Organizations: A resource dependence perspective*, Stanford, CA: Stanford University Press.

Point, S. (2005) 'Accountability, transparency and performance: comparing annual report disclosures on CEO pay across Europe', in S. Tyson and F. Bournois (eds) *Top Pay and Performance: International and Strategic Approach*, London: Elsevier.

Purcell, J. (1999) 'Best fit and best practice: chimera or cul-de-sac?', *Human Resource Management Journal*, 9 (3): 26–41.

Reilly, M. and Scott, D. (2005) 'An inside look at compensation committees', *World at Work Journal*, second quarter: 34–40.

Roberts, J. (2001) 'Trust and control in Anglo-American systems of corporate governance: the individualizing and socializing effects of processes of accountability', *Human Relations*, 54 (12): 1547–1572.

Rosen, S. (1986) 'Prizes and incentives in elimination tournaments', *American Economic Review*, 76 (4): 701–715.

Stiles, P. and Taylor, B. (2002) *Boards at Work: How directors view their roles and responsibilities*, Oxford: Oxford University Press.

Sykes, A. (2002) 'Overcoming poor value executive remuneration: resolving the manifest conflicts of interest', *Corporate Governance*, 10 (4): 256–260.

Taussig, F. W. and Baker, W. S. (1925) 'American corporations and their executives: a statistical enquiry', *Quarterly Journal of Economics*, 40 (1): 1–51.

Tyson, S. (2005) 'Fat cat pay', in S. Tyson and F. Bournois (eds) *Top Pay and Performance: International and strategic approach*, London: Elsevier.

Tyson, S. and Bournois, F. (2005) 'Introduction', *Top Pay and Performance: International and strategic approach*, London: Elsevier.

Veliyath, R. (1999) 'Top management compensation and shareholder returns:

unravelling different models of the relationship', *Journal of Management Studies*, 36 (1): 123–143.

Watts, R. and Roberts, D. (2006) 'FTSE pay spirals out of control', *Sunday Telegraph*, 24 September, City Section, p. 1.

Wray, R. (2007) 'C&W bosses to get unlimited bonuses', *The Guardian*, 21 July: 40.

Wright, P. M. and McMahan, G. C. (1992) 'Theoretical perspectives for strategic human resource management', *Journal of Management*, 18 (2): 295–320.

Zajec, E. J. and Westphal, J. D. (1995) 'Accounting for the explanations of CEO compensation: substance and symbolism', *Administrative Science Quarterly*, 40 (2): 283–308.

8 Benefits

Angela Wright

Summary

The development of employee benefits has been changing and is likely to continue changing as a result of the effects of a combination of a growing and competitive insurance market, demographic and labour market changes and social regulation within the EU. There have been cutbacks in the most costly benefits and at the same time a growth in low-cost lifestyle and voluntary benefits. These seem to fit with a changing employment scene in which women, particularly mothers, have increased their labour market participation. While recruitment and retention arguments may be made by employers, in support of their benefits policies, the evidence of the motivational value of benefits is slight. Some of the literature focuses on organisational outcomes such as employee retention and productivity effects, tempered by other research, which stresses the importance of employee knowledge about benefits in affecting their estimations of the value of their benefits package. The future for benefits is uncertain in light of rising costs and the ageing of the workforce, although continued incremental change seems more likely than radical revisions of benefits provisions.

Introduction

The UK has a long tradition of employer-provided benefits. Although they remain a durable feature of the reward package there have been changes of emphasis in the make-up of the package in recent years. Smith (2000) identified benefits as substantial elements of remuneration. This chapter draws attention to the withdrawal of more costly benefits and to the growth of low or nil cost 'voluntary' or 'lifestyle' benefits. It asks whether employers do this for strategic reasons. Developments suggest there may be a departure from a traditional definition of 'benefits' to ensure value for money for employers (Moonman 1973). This chapter charts the principal changes taking place. It begins by examining theoretical perspectives. It turns then to influences from the international as well as the national context. European legal and social developments are important here – as are demographic trends. An analysis of the development of benefits is followed by a discussion of their costs and value.

Theoretical perspectives

Two theoretical perspectives contribute particularly to understanding benefits – first from economics and second from psychology. From the economic perspective it might be argued that benefits are used by employers in competitive labour markets as a way of compensating for low cash pay. There is little evidence to support such a view since benefits tend to be better in higher-paying companies (Dale-Olsen 2005). Rather it seems that efficiency wage theory may offer a more fruitful framework since higher wages and generous benefits might go together, either as part of a policy designed to engender employee loyalty and effort, or as a result of unions successfully pressing for benefits as well as higher wages (Forth and Millward 2000). Another perspective identified in relation to flexible benefits – but arguably just as relevant to benefits more generally – derives from institutional theory which suggests that managers may want to be seen as 'modern' or 'professional' and are willing to bear extra costs in order to do that, arguing recruitment and retention objectives (Barringer and Milkovich 1998).

From the psychological perspective, motivation theory including expectancy theory and organisational justice theory offer the greatest potential for an understanding of benefits. Assumptions that employee benefits do not motivate employees (Milkovich and Newman 2004) and may be better viewed more as a 'hygiene' factor (Hertzberg 1968) have underpinned much of what has been written. Although assumptions about the motivational value of benefits are widespread there is little evidence of a positive relationship between motivation and benefits. Within organisational justice theory the concepts of procedural and distributive justice are potentially relevant. Procedural justice relates to the perceived fairness of organisational decisions, in this context on benefits, while distributive justice relates to the perceived fairness of the outcomes of such decisions. There is rising interest in applying procedural justice theory within the reward field (Newman and Milkovich 1990). A study by Cole and Flint (2004) which uses organisational justice theory compares aspects of traditional benefits programmes with flexible benefits. It concludes that employers who offer a flexible plan may be able to increase employee perceptions of procedural justice without any reduction in perceptions of distributive justice. They suggest that some diminution of distributive justice perceptions might have been expected under a flexible scheme in which people choose certain benefits and do not choose others.

Expectancy theory has been used in research relating to reward from the early twentieth century (Latham 2007) but tends to focus on cash-based rewards, rather than benefits. Employers might cite recruitment and retention arguments for the provision of benefits and it might then be argued that if employees value the benefits offered by their employer then such benefits could have a positive motivational impact. Nonetheless, there is a lack of systematic evidence that employee benefits, which are inevitably only a small part of the overall employment experience of employees, have such a strong effect in practice.

The total rewards model forms a useful way of conceptualising recent developments. The concept of total rewards emerged in the 1990s as a new way of thinking about pay and benefits, combined with the other aspects of the employment experience, such as training and career development and also including less tangible issues concerning management style and organisational climate. One of the principal proponents of the model (WorldatWork 2007) contends that both the monetary and non-monetary rewards provided by the employer should be seen in a strategically integrated way by employers. The nature of reward is drawn widely, in this account, to encompass five separate elements – pay, benefits, work-life balance, performance review/ feedback/recognition and employee/career development. While there is evidence of employer initiatives in all of these areas there is less evidence of strategic coherence as prescribed by the model (Chartered Institute of Personnel and Development (CIPD) 2007). Nonetheless, nearly a third of employers believe that training and development and flexible working are benefits and 28 per cent of employers now claim to use the total reward approach.

Legal and government policy developments

The influence of the law and government policy was felt from the 1960s and 1970s when benefits provision grew in response to (or in order to bypass) Government Statutory Incomes Policies and higher marginal rates of income tax. Fiscal and government policies continue to influence benefits provision but of course once in place benefits are not easily removed. Some of the most valued benefits introduced in the Incomes Policy period, like company cars, have remained popular subsequently in spite of more recent fiscal measures to reduce their appeal. In practice the benefits package (particularly at senior levels) has proved remarkably durable.

Company tax charges now reflect Government policy so that benefits are fiscally neutral in relation to equivalent sums paid to buy cars. Company car taxation rules were revised from April 2002 but subsequent surveys of executive packages show that while the attractiveness of the car as a benefit has diminished, it remains prevalent (Monks Partnership 2005) as does the provision of private use petrol by employers to senior executives. Nevertheless Her Majesty's Revenue and Customs (HMRC) (2006) reported that the number of company cars fell from 1.6 million in 1999 to 1.2 million in 2005. Incomes Data Services (IDS) (2006a) review of company cars suggests that while cars remain the benefit of choice for many employees, employers are beginning to revise policies in line both with environmental concerns and with tax changes. Many are now offering cash alternatives to eligible executives.

There continue to be small National Insurance savings from voucher-based benefits. Salary sacrifice schemes in which employees sacrifice pay for benefits, which may be provided in voucher form – for example, childcare vouchers are shown by CIPD surveys to be growing in popularity (2005a, 2006, 2007). Indeed, the home computer scheme, whereby an employer could provide a tax-free loan to employees, proved so popular the Government ended the fiscal advantage offered by the scheme, under which there were National Insurance savings to be made by employers and employees. Childcare vouchers and bicycles have, to date, escaped the cutback in tax breaks.

European and national law is important in prompting the development of certain benefits – such as maternity, paternity and adoption provisions and paid holidays. It has also triggered new attention to some existing benefits – for example based on age. The incoming Labour Government from 1997 enacted a series of enhancements to individual rights to provide measures that would help working parents to combine work and parenthood. Some of these were initiated as a direct response to European Union (EU) law, while others stemmed from the Government's domestic policy agenda on equality.

The Employment Act 2002 introduced a new statutory framework of parental rights which came into force on 6 April 2003, enhancing statutory maternity pay provisions and giving parents new rights on flexible working, paternity and adoption. These rights have been increased and rights to paid adoption and paternity leave extended as of April 2007, under the Work and Families Act 2006. This legislation increased maternity and adoption pay from six to nine months and extended the right to request flexible working (already in place for parents) to carers of adults from 6 April 2007. The least popular element of the legislation for employers, according to the CIPD (Hilpern 2007), is the provision in the Act to introduce further parental rights, to extend maternity pay to 52 weeks and allow mothers to 'pass on' to fathers up to 26 weeks of their paid leave.

The Working Time Regulations 1998, enacted in response to European health and safety legislation, introduced into UK law, for the first time, a right to paid holidays. The minimum period of 20 days paid holiday was extended from October 2007 to 24 days, to ensure full compliance with the EU Directive and rises again to 28 days from 2009.

Also made under EU law, the Age Discrimination Regulations 2006 ban discrimination on grounds of age. The regulations affect benefits, particularly age-linked or length of service provisions, such as service-related holiday entitlement, limiting lawful service-based provision to a maximum of five years.

Demographic and labour market developments

Demographic and social changes affect the approach that employers take to benefits too. Three changes are particularly relevant for this discussion.

First, women's increased participation in the labour market is one of the most significant changes in the past 20 years. Drawing on the Labour Force Survey, the Women and Work Commission (2006) shows that women with young children have been the group that has increased its participation in the labour market more than any other over that period. Some 56 per cent of working-age women whose youngest child is under five are now in employment and the UK has one of the highest labour market participation rates for women in the EU. However, as women continue to have the main responsibility for childcare, unpaid care of the elderly and domestic work there are challenges for employers who wish to provide benefits which help employees to balance their commitments outside work with those in the workplace (Women and Work Commission 2006).

Second, one of the most profound trends that could impact on the benefits that are offered by organisations in the future is the ageing of the workforce. The Government estimates that the number of people aged below 50 will fall by 2 per cent by 2016, while numbers in the 50 to 69 age group are projected to increase by 17 per cent. By about 2018 there will be more people above 40 years than below and by 2031 the proportion of people over the age of 65 years will increase from 16 per cent of the population in 2004 to almost a quarter (23 per cent). From times of mass redundancies in the 1980s until the early 2000s, the employment rate of men aged 55 to 65 dropped. In recent years the employment rates of both older men and women have increased (Department of Work and Pensions (DWP) 2005).

Third, at the same time as the population is ageing, medical advances mean people are living longer and today's employees have a much longer life expectancy than their own parents. In addition as the post-Second World War 'baby boomer' generation ages a slowing birth rate means fewer younger people available to replace them in the labour market. The ageing workforce could have an impact not only on which benefits employers offer, but also on whether they can afford to offer a benefits package in its current form (Furness 2007). The specific concern here is over insured benefits, particularly if insurance premiums rise in line with age.

International comparisons

The modern day provision of benefits by employers has its origins in the State-provided sickness, accident and 'old age' insurance and pensions first provided by Bismarck's Germany in the late nineteenth century (Callund 1975). The State remains an important provider of certain benefits in many European and other countries. However, in some states employers have either taken on part of the funding burden for State-provided insured benefits or are expected to provide certain benefits, such as sick pay, directly to eligible employees.

Comparative analyses between countries are fraught with difficulties. First, for any benefit that is linked to health it is difficult to compare like with like since a fundamental factor is the very different level of State funding of health services. World Health Organisation (2007) data show substantial differences between countries in the balance of health funding which comes from the private sector (including employer) sources and from Government. More than 80 per cent of healthcare is Government funded in countries such as Denmark, Norway, Sweden, Luxembourg and in the UK. The private sector is more significant in the USA where the State funded just 44 per cent of health expenditure in 2004. Because of these contextual differences, comparative analyses of health-linked benefits in the UK in comparison with mainland Europe and with the USA are complex and may be at best treated as estimates. There is nevertheless an interest in making meaningful comparisons of benefits between countries. The literature in this comparative area is not very well developed, with the focus most often on terms and conditions for expatriates. There is a distinct gap in research, which offers comparative analyses on perceptions of benefits as well as on other aspects of the reward package, which Lowe *et al.*'s research (2002) aimed to fill. However, the conclusions, which can be drawn from their study are limited, partly because of the lack of contextualisation. They find that a sample of managers and engineers in the USA and Canada believe that benefits are more important in the reward package than do managers in Australia, Japan and some other Asian countries, and that these benefits were considered 'generous' in the USA, Canada, Latin America and Taiwan.

Table 8.1 offers a summary of provisions in a number of European countries and in the USA.

Although it is difficult to generalise too much from such comparisons it is apparent that the USA has less generous leave entitlements than many European countries. In the USA there is no legal right to annual holiday and the Family and Medical Leave Act 1993 covers a wide span of circumstances in which employees might need time off work. Under its terms employees may take up to a total of 12 weeks of unpaid leave during any 12-month period for the birth and care of a newborn child, for placement with the employee of a son or daughter for adoption or foster care; to care for an immediate family member (spouse, child, or parent) with a serious health condition; or themselves to take medical leave when the employee is unable to work because of a serious health condition. Such terms seem much less generous than in EU countries.

Comparisons can however be informative both for policy makers and for employers wishing to be ahead of domestic legal developments and to draw on knowledge of other countries with more generous legally-based provisions. The proposal contained in the UK's Work and Families Act 2006 for mothers to be allowed to assign to their baby's father up to 26 weeks of their own paid maternity paid leave, draws on – but does not go as far as – provisions in Sweden and other EU countries.

Table 8.1 International comparisons: public and statutory holiday entitlement, maternity leave and maternity pay, paternity leave and parental leave

Country	Public holiday days p.a.	Statutory entitlement to annual leave days p.a.	Maternity leave and maternity pay	Paternity leave	Parental leave
Austria	13	25	N/a	N/a	N/a
Belgium	10	20	15 weeks: Full pay public sector; 75%–82% pay private	3 days full-pay (employer) plus 7 days (insured)	3 months, up to child age 6 years, part paid
Denmark	9.5	30	18 weeks full pay (capped)	2 weeks full pay (capped)	32 weeks per family until child is 4, pay capped
Finland	12	24	105 working days, average pay 66% of full pay.	18 days, plus 12 bonus days for fathers who take last 2 weeks of parental leave, average pay 66% of full pay.	185 working days per family, average pay 66% of full pay.
France	11	30	16 weeks, full pay capped	2 weeks, full pay capped	Until child is 3
Germany	9–12	20	14 weeks, full pay	No general entitlement	Until child is 3
Great Britain	8	20 incl. public hols	52 weeks; 90% of earnings for 6 weeks; flat rate payment for 20 weeks; 26 weeks unpaid.	2 weeks at time of the birth, flat rate payment	13 weeks per parent per child, unpaid
Greece	10–12	20	17 weeks, full pay	2 days at time of the birth	Three and a half months leave, unpaid
Ireland	9	20	34 weeks, 70% of earnings (capped) for 22 weeks then 12 weeks unpaid	No general entitlement	14 weeks per parent per child, unpaid

Italy	12	20	20 weeks, 80% of earnings	No general entitlement	Six months for fathers and for mothers, up to child age 3, pay is 30% of earning, otherwise unpaid
Netherlands	8	20	16 weeks, full pay (capped)	2 working days at time of birth, full pay	13 times the number of working hours per parent per child, to be taken up to child age 8, tax break
Portugal	12–14	22	120 days, full pay	20 days, full pay	3 months per parent, unpaid
Spain	12–14	30	16 weeks, full pay (capped)	2 days at time of the birth full pay	Can be taken until child is 3
Sweden	11	25	Subsumed under parental leave	10 days at time of birth, at 80% of earnings	480 days paid leave, 60 only for mother and 60 only for father, remaining 360 days is family entitlement
USA	14		No statutory minimum	12 weeks unpaid for childbirth, care of newborn child, care of a seriously ill child, spouse or parent, or for a serious health condition of employee	

Sources: Adapted from CIPD (2005), Moss and O'Brien (2006), Kersley *et al.* (2005)

Development of benefits

Benefits practice is influenced by legal, fiscal and labour market developments, but also by collective bargaining and pay determination practice.

In the UK, the development of organisational benefits policies and practices in recent decades runs in parallel with the broader trend towards the increasing individualisation of pay determination, and the decline of collective bargaining activity (Kersley *et al.* 2005). There has tended to be a separation of determination in respect of pay on the one hand and benefits on the other in which collective bargaining has played a variable role. Forth and Millward's study (2000) found that unions continue to have a limited role in encouraging employers in the private sector to offer enhanced benefits, but their analysis was confined to pensions and sick pay. Employer policies, underpinned by a paternalistic style of personnel management (Russell 1991), tended to shape company-provided benefits policies, which were focused on sick pay and welfare, rather than the wider array of benefits now evident.

Surveys of employer benefits show a fairly uniform picture of provisions by occupation or seniority, suggesting that employers continue to treat employees as groups (as they did when collective bargaining was stronger). There continues to be a fairly standardised approach by employers, even though collective bargaining with trades unions is now less widespread than in the past (Brown *et al.* 1998). Practitioner surveys show that some benefits such as holidays and other types of leave are more likely to be subject to collective bargaining than pension schemes and insured schemes of one sort or another (e.g. IDS 2006 b, c and d).

Traditional welfare-based benefits policies are under pressure with cutbacks in healthcare provision, reflecting both increases in health costs and employer measures to manage absenteeism to raise performance (CIPD 2005a and 2006). In the survey undertaken by the CIPD in 2005, the incidence of private healthcare, long-term disability cover and occupational sick pay schemes was reduced (CIPD 2005a). In the following year, company cars and allowances were the benefits most likely to be cut or scaled back although sick pay and permanent health insurance were also down (CIPD 2006).

Yet whilst some benefits have diminished in scope, others have been introduced or extended in significance.

Two areas have shown most growth in recent years. The first concerns family-friendly benefits, responding to the diverse needs and lifestyles of today's workforce (Sparrow 1998). Employers have recognised that many employees have child care responsibilities outside the workplace and understand the business advantages for the employer of offering benefits to facilitate the combining of parenthood with work (IDS 2003 and 2007). However legislation has also been influential in the growth of more family-friendly terms and conditions. In 2003 Incomes Data Services reported that all the employers they reviewed had implemented the (then new) statutory maternity provisions but had improved on the legal minimum requirements in some respect. Many had done so in the context of a broader framework of family-friendly or work-life balance policies. Not all employers adopt generous policies, however. Table 8.2 includes data from the Workplace Employment Relations Survey 2004 which finds that paid leave of all types for parents is much more likely to be provided in the public than in the private sector.

Childcare is a crucial benefit for working parents. Although workplace nurseries are provided by a few employers as is out-of-school care (IDS 2007) the growth in recent years has been in the use of childcare vouchers, both employer-paid and voluntary schemes using a salary sacrifice mechanism.

Parents or carers may need additional leave over and above maternity, paternity and parental leave, to provide for emergencies when their caring circumstances mean they cannot be at work The Employment Rights Acts 1996 and 1999 gave a legal right to employees to take unpaid time off for emergencies but there is currently no entitlement to paid leave. The WERS 2004 survey (Kersley *et al.* 2005) asked a series of questions of employers about their leave arrangements to support employees with caring responsibilities, focusing on provision beyond the statutory entitlement. They were given the opportunity to identify provision of unpaid parental leave, paid parental leave, special paid leave, sick leave and some other leave arrangement. The answers showed that only a minority of employers make such provision. Ten per cent of workplaces cited paid parental leave and 19 per cent cited special paid leave.

The second major area of change is evident where employers initiate low-cost 'lifestyle' and voluntary benefits, the provision of which seems to fulfil some social purpose (CIPD 2007). These cover a wide range of 'benefits' from travel and pet insurance to retail and child care vouchers, which can

Table 8.2 Extra statutory leave arrangements to support employees with caring responsibilities, by sector

Benefit	Private sector (% of workplaces providing)	Public sector (% of workplaces providing)	All workplaces (% of workplaces providing)
Fully-paid maternity leave	51	84	57
Fully-paid paternity or fully-paid discretionary leave for fathers	49	84	55
Paid parental leave or special paid leave for parents	21	47	25
Special paid leave for family emergencies	43	80	49
Leave for carers of older adults	4	16	6

Source: Adapted from Kersley *et al.* (2005)

be paid for under a salary sacrifice arrangement, with savings both for employers and employees. These arrangements in which employers provide third-party goods and services at a discount are on the increase (CIPD 2006 and 2007). Some of the driving force to implement such low or nil cost 'benefits' seems to come from increasing competition between benefits and insurance providers, in effect developing their respective product markets (IDS 2004). IDS suggests that developments in voluntary benefits are driven not only by suppliers but also by employers keen to explore a potentially cost-free way of extending what they offer to employees. Employers use their purchasing power to secure discounts from a benefits provider, and employees are either provided with the insurance at a discounted rate through a salary sacrifice mechanism or they may (under a flexible benefits plan) choose the insurance as one of their benefit options, which are paid for by the employer (IRS 2005).

Flexible benefits programmes respond to diverse lifestyles in the context of a more individualised approach to pay and benefits. These schemes have been in existence in a small number of organisations for some years. The pace of growth of schemes seems to have been modest with an estimated 8 per cent of employers using them (CIPD 2005a, 2007; Employee Benefits 2003). Such schemes range from small-scale schemes, similar to voluntary benefits schemes (IRS 2005) – whose cost and extent is minimal and which may entail salary sacrifice – to much more substantive schemes in which employees get a significant level of choice as to the benefits they receive. This might be 'buying' or 'selling' holiday entitlement, extending health benefits as well as the possibility of choosing a range of lower-cost benefits.

Status still matters

In spite of a trend to harmonisation of terms and conditions for different groups of workers (Price and Price 1994) differences in benefit entitlement between occupational group and level in the organisation remain significant. 'Single status' arrangements, where different groups in a given workplace had the same entitlements, were found in the Workplace Employee Relations Survey 2004 data in around half (48 per cent) of workplaces (43 per cent in the private sector and 73 per cent in the public sector) (Kersley *et al.* 2005). The corresponding figure for the previous (1998) survey was lower at 41 per cent, suggesting some continuing moves to harmonise. Table 8.3 drawing on data from WERS 2004 shows the benefits in which there were substantial differences in entitlement between managers and 'core' employees. Managers were more likely than core employees to have access to costly benefits such as cars and medical insurance. They are also, according to executive surveys of the private sector (e.g. Monks Partnership 2005), more likely than other employees to have access to the increasingly costly Permanent Health Insurance and long-term disability cover.

Table 8.3 Status differences: managers and 'core' employees

Benefit	% of managers	% of core employees
Company car	45	15
Private health insurance	38	16
Employer pension scheme	71	64
More than four weeks of paid annual leave	67	59
Sick pay in excess of statutory requirements	62	54

Source: Adapted from Kersley *et al.* (2005)

Cost and value

Overall non-wage costs account for between 15 and 40 per cent of total labour costs in the larger countries within the Organisation for Economic Co-operation and Development (OECD 1997) and are rising. These figures include benefit costs but the nature of funding of the healthcare systems of the respective countries is relevant in interpreting overall aggregate costs.

The CIPD (2006) reports that as a percentage of the pay bill, the median cost of benefits for employers in Britain is 15 per cent, within an inter-quartile range of between 10 per cent and 24 per cent. The question of who provides and who pays for benefits, as the populations of western countries age and the large 'baby boomer' generation retires, is increasingly pressing. Provision of the most costly benefits such as pensions and health care has become increasingly contentious (Rousseau and Ho 2000). Questions about who should be responsible for funding have surfaced in the UK in relation to pensions (Pensions Commission 2004) but not – to a great extent – about the funding of other benefits, as yet. In the USA, where employers make substantial contributions to health care through insured schemes, cost questions are being hotly debated. Olson and Terry (2007), drawing on Towers Perrin's survey of employees in the USA, found that 55 per cent of the employees surveyed viewed the provision of high-quality health care as an individual or shared responsibility. This suggests that employees may be more willing than is widely believed to share the costs and risks of health care funding with their employers (Olson and Terry 2007). Towers Perrin's (2004) international survey found that the escalation of medical costs remains a key concern for employers not only in the USA, but also in other countries where companies provide medical benefits schemes which are supplementary to extensive State provision, as in the UK. They point out that as publicly-funded healthcare systems in several countries struggle with growing costs burden, the cost of supplemental employer-sponsored medical coverage is increasing in many parts of the world. With cost increases continuing well above inflation, the issue of affordability for both businesses and employees could become considerably more challenging in the future as the Baby Boomer generation ages and chronic diseases (such as diabetes and obesity) proliferate (Towers Perrin 2007).

While in the UK pensions might be the costliest benefit, the sum of employer expenditure on the range of other benefits can be substantial, and it seems likely that employer attention could be drawn to other expensive 'employee protection' benefits (Confederation of British Industry (CBI) 1995) in the longer term. Perhaps somewhat paradoxically, the benefits employees want as they age, such as private medical insurance (PMI) or income protection insurance, might be just those which employers may judge have become too expensive for them to provide. However, an ageing workforce could result in lower costs for some benefits – for example life insurance, which tends to end at retirement age – since employers' group life insurance premiums should reduce as people live longer (Furness 2007).

The quest for value from benefits may lead employers in the UK increasingly to withdraw from health-linked benefits in the future, but first and foremost employers must know just how much such benefits are costing them. Thomson Online (2007) report that their survey of 522 employers showed almost half of respondents (45.3 per cent) did not know how much they were spending on employee benefits as a percentage of payroll.

Evaluating the impact of benefits

What do employers hope to gain from providing benefits? Some benefits may seem merely to be a tax-efficient form of remuneration. To what extent does the benefits package enable employers to recruit and retain employees? In the context of rising costs and demographic changes some fundamental questions have begun to be asked as to whether or not employers should be providing benefits. What are the bottom line effects of providing them? If efficiency wage theory or expectancy theory are relevant in understanding employee reaction to benefits then the quantity or quality of work should rise when people have benefits they value and this should in turn lead to greater productivity.

Various case study-based and quantitative analyses (Hong *et al.* 1995; Baughman *et al.* 2003; Tsai and Wang 2005; Dale-Olsen 2005) establish some associations between benefits and certain positive organisational outcomes such as productivity measures. They also give encouragement to the notion that benefits are provided to help employers recruit and retain the best staff. Most of the quantitative studies indicate that benefits programmes may have positive effects on productivity, motivation and/or employee retention, but the evidence is limited and the effects may be limited too.

The issue of employee awareness of benefits is relevant in this context and leads to a cautious interpretation of the relevance of these studies. As Hennessey *et al.* (1992) argue, unless employees intending to leave or those thinking about joining an organisation have a reasonably detailed knowledge of the relative merits of the benefits packages of the old employer and the potential new one there are unlikely to be pronounced competitive advantage effects. An employer survey (Thomson Online 2007) in the UK found that less than five per cent of respondents (3.9 per cent) thought that their employees valued their benefits highly. Since employees placing a relatively high value on benefits is a starting point if organisational outcomes are to be achieved such findings are not encouraging. It may also put into perspective the findings of surveys such as that of *HR Focus* (2000) which show that employees may value low-cost benefits such as office social events more highly than more costly benefits such as sabbaticals – perhaps because the former is more widely applicable than the latter. Employees are more likely to value benefits whose relevance is readily apparent and which can be easily understood. Relevance and employee understanding, rather than cost, might be the determining criteria.

Deciding to take benefits away because they do not get an immediately high rating from employees might however be a rather short-sighted strategy. Olson and Terry (2007) warn that reducing benefits provision can seriously undermine employee trust. Although such research does not rely specifically on organisational justice theory, it might be argued that distributive, procedural and interactional justice are all potentially important when a change of benefits is proposed. Distributive justice issues comes into play in terms of the choice of benefits offered; procedural justice in relation to how changes and management decisions are made and interactional justice might be relevant in relation to issues concerning communication with employees on the change.

Context (country and company), demographic factors and specificity of benefit may be important factors. Tsai and Wang's (2005) study of the Taiwan high tech sector, in which a relatively high level of benefits is available, indicates that benefits have some moderating effects on productivity, with the effect being greatest in smaller firms. However the study does not reveal in detail the relationship between the benefits package and productivity. Dale-Olsen's study of Norwegian companies (2005) found that establishments spending more on benefits tended to have certain characteristics – they were larger, employed more highly-educated workers, were more capital intensive, paid higher wages, and produced more. Although value added was seen to increase as benefits provision increases, no causal impact of benefits on productivity was identified.

People at certain stages of life or in different occupations may value benefits differently. Hong *et al.*'s (1995) study of benefit effects on motivation and productivity finds some support for expectancy theory revealing significant differences between people of different ages, genders and occupations. Perhaps it is not surprising if different groups are seen to have different benefit demands.

As well as the risk of neglecting disaggregated results on the basis of demographic patterns, it may be dangerous to over-generalise on the basis of the aggregate or standardised benefits package provided as there could be certain benefits, which have a more profound effect than others. The studies by Baughman *et al.* (2003) and Dale-Olsen (2005) find that benefits, which are related to childcare or other 'family-friendly' terms, may be particularly effective in generating productivity and encouraging employee retention. Incomes Data Services (2007) further suggests that employer-provided assistance with childcare can improve staff retention; repeating employer claims that it enhances the image of the organisation as an employer of choice thereby aiding recruitment; and that staff with employer-provided childcare assistance are likely to be more engaged and less absence-prone.

Conclusion

The development of employee benefits policies in the UK currently shows the effects of both a growing and competitive insurance market, demographic and labour market changes and social regulation within the EU. The growth of voluntary benefits fits with a low-cost, market-driven trend, as the development of more family-friendly terms, spurred on by women's labour market participation and by domestic and EU law, fit a more socially-oriented trend. The critical issue for parents is that of balancing family life with employment or, indeed, being able to work at all. This is all the more important since labour market developments indicate many more mothers as well as fathers are in employment and wanting to work.

An ageing workforce and rising costs are highlighting concerns about health-linked benefits and who should pay for them. A focus in the literature is on organisational outcomes, measured in terms of productivity, motivation and/or employee retention. There is no compelling evidence that benefits in general have a pronounced motivational value, but the organisational justice issues which can arise when employers seek to take benefits away or fail to provide expected benefits seem to suggest that many employers will continue the trend of the past few years and make gradual rather than radical changes. Finally, it may be questioned (drawing on Legge 1995) whether the development of a 'rhetoric' among employers relating to a concern to respond to employees' increasingly diverse lifestyle needs could be counterbalanced against a 'reality' of cutbacks in the most expensive pension and health-related benefits and the substitution of low or nil cost discounts.

References

Barringer, M. and Milkovich, G. (1998) 'A theoretical exploration of the adoption and design of flexible benefit plans: a case of human resource innovation', *Academy of Management Review*, 23 (2) April: 305–324.

Baughman, R., DiNardi, D. and Holtz-Eakin, D. (2003) 'Productivity and wage effects of "family-friendly" fringe benefits', *International Journal of Manpower*, 24 (3): 247–259.

Brown, W., Deakin, S., Hudson, M., Pratten, C. and Ryan, P. (1998) 'The individualisation of employment contracts in Britain', Research Paper for the Department of Trade and Industry, Centre for Business Research Department of Applied

..

Economics, University of Cambridge. Available online http://www.berr.gov.uk/files/file11633.pdf (accessed 13 July 2007).

Callund, D. (1975) *Employee Benefits in Europe: An international survey of state and private schemes in 16 countries*, Epping: Gower Press/Employment Conditions Abroad.

Chartered Institute of Personnel and Development (CIPD) (2005a) *Reward management survey 2005*, London: CIPD.

Chartered Institute of Personnel and Development (CIPD) (2005b) *Reward Review*, Summer 2005, London: CIPD.

Chartered Institute of Personnel and Development (CIPD) (2006) *Reward management survey 2006*, London: CIPD.

Chartered Institute of Personnel and Development (CIPD) (2007) *Reward management survey 2007*, London: CIPD.

Cole, N. and Flint, D. (2004) 'Perceptions of distributive and procedural justice in employee benefits: flexible versus traditional plans', *Journal of Managerial Psychology*, 19 (1): 19–40.

Confederation of British Industry (CBI) (1995) *Employee Protection Benefits: A survey of company attitudes and policies*, London: CBI.

Dale-Olsen, H. (2005) 'Using linked employer–employee data to analyze fringe benefits policies. Norwegian experiences', Institute for Social Research, Norway. Paper presented at Policy Studies Institute seminar, July 2005, London.

DWP (2005) Opportunity Age – Opportunity and Security throughout Life. Department for Work and Pensions, March 2005. http://www.dwp.gov.uk/opportunityage/ (accessed 10 July 2007).

Employee Benefits/MX Financial Solutions (2003) 'Flexible benefits research 2003', *Employee Benefits*, April: 4–9.

Forth, J. and Millward, N. (2000) 'The determinants of pay levels and fringe benefit provision in Britain', *Discussion paper* No. 171, London: National Institute of Economic and Social Research.

Furness, V. (2007) 'The long-term trends likely to affect the future of benefits'. Available online http://www.employeebenefits.co.uk (accessed 2 July 2007).

Heinemann, R., Ledford, G. and Gresham, M. (2000) 'The changing nature of work and its effects on compensation design and delivery', in S. Rynes and B. Gerhart (eds) *Compensation in Organisations: Current research and practice*, San Francisco: Jossey-Bass.

Hennessey, H., Perrewe, P. and Hochwater, W. (1992) 'Impact of benefit awareness on employee and organisational outcomes: a longitudinal field examination', *Benefits Quarterly*, 8 (2): 90–96.

Her Majesty's Revenue and Customs (HMRC) (2006) 'Report on the evaluation of the company car tax reform: stage 2', March 2006. Available online http://www.hmrc.gov.uk/budget2006/company-car-evaluation.pdf (accessed 14 September 2007).

Hertzberg, F. (1968) 'One more time: how do you motivate employees?', *Harvard Business Review*, 46 (1): 53–62.

Hilpern, K. (2007) 'Bumpy road ahead?', *People Management*, 25 January: 30.

Hong, J., Yang, S., Wang, L., Chiou, E., Sun, F. and Huang, T. (1995) 'Impact of employee benefits on work motivation and productivity', *International Journal of Career Management*, 7 (6): 10–14.

HR Focus (2000) '50 benefits and perks that make employees want to stay forever', *HR Focus*, July: S2–S4.

Incomes Data Services (IDS) (2003) 'Maternity and parental leave', *IDS HR Studies Update* 755, August 2003.

Incomes Data Services (IDS) (2004) 'Voluntary benefits', *IDS HR Studies Update* 769, March 2004.

Incomes Data Services (IDS) (2005) 'Benefit trends and provision', *IDS Executive Compensation Review*, 289, March: 8–10.

Incomes Data Services (IDS) (2006a) 'Fewer company cars on the road', *IDS Executive Compensation Review*, 305, July: 7–9.

Incomes Data Services (IDS) (2006b) 'Company cars & business travel', *IDS HR Study*, 817, March 2006.

Incomes Data Services (IDS) (2006c) 'Time off and special leave', *IDS HR Study* 821, May 2006.

Incomes Data Services (IDS) (2006d) 'Hours and holidays, 2006', *IDS HR Study* 830, September 2006.

Incomes Data Services (IDS) (2007) 'Child care', *IDS HR Study* 844, April 2007.

Industrial Relations Services (IRS) (2005) 'Voluntary benefits: saving in the workplace', *IRS Employment Review 818/Pay and Benefits*, 25 February 2005.

Kersley, B., Alpin, C., Forth, J., Bryson, A., Bewley, H., Dix, G. and Oxenbridge, S. (2005) *Inside the Workplace: Findings from the 2004 Workplace Employment Relations Survey* (WERS 2004), Abingdon: Routledge.

Latham, G. (2007) *Work Motivation: History, research and practice*, Thousand Oaks, California: Sage Publications.

Legge, K. (1995) *Human Resource Management: Rhetoric and reality*, London: Macmillan.

Lowe, K., Milliman, J., De Cieri, H. and Dowling, P. (2002) 'International compensation practices: a ten-country analysis', *Human Resource Management*, 41(1): 45–663.

Milkovich, G. and Newman, J. (2004) *Compensation*, Boston: Irwin/McGraw-Hill.

Monks Partnership (2005) *Management Pay UK: Pensions and benefits*, Monks Partnership, Saffron Walden.

Moonman, J. (1973) *The Effectiveness of Fringe Benefits*, Epping: Gower Press.

Moss, P. and O'Brien, M. (2006) 'International review of leave policies and related research', *Employment Relations Research Series* No. 57, London: Department of Trade and Industry.

Newman, J. and Milkovich, G. (1990) 'Procedural justice challenges in compensation: eliminating the fairness gap', *Labor Law Journal*, August 1990: 575–580.

Olson, W. and Terry, M. (2007) 'Benefit strategy report, Towers Perrin'. Available online: http://www.towersperrin.com/tp/getwebcachedoc?webc=HRS/USA/2007/200703/Benefit_Strategy_Study_Report_22807.pdf (accessed 11 July 2007).

Organisation for Economic Co-operation and Development (OECD) (1997) *Employment Outlook, 1997*, Paris: OECD.

Pensions Commission (2004) 'Pensions: challenges and choices'. Available online: http://www.pensionscommission.org.uk/publications/2004/annrep/index.asp (accessed 25 April 2005).

Price, L. and Price, R. (1994) 'Change and continuity in the status divide', in K. Sisson (ed.) *Personnel Management: A comprehensive guide to theory and practice in Britain*, second edn, Oxford: Blackwell.

Rousseau, D. and Ho, V. (2000) 'Psychological contract issues in compensation', in

S. Rynes and B. Gerhart (eds) *Compensation in Organisations: Current research and practice*, San Fransisco: Jossey-Bass.

Russell, A. (1991) *The Growth of Occupational Welfare in Britain: Evolution and harmonisation*, Epping: Gower Publishing.

Smith, I. (2000) 'Benefits', in G. White and J. Druker (eds) *Reward Management: A critical text*, London: Routledge.

Sparrow, P. (1998) 'Can the psychological contract be managed? Implications for the field of rewards management', in S. Perkins and S. Sandringham (eds) *Trust, Motivation and Commitment: A reader*, Farringdon: Strategic Remuneration Research Centre.

Thomson On-line (2007) 'Employee Rewards Watch 2007'. Available online: http://www.thomsononlinebenefits.com/Research (accessed 3 April 2008).

Towers Perrin (2004) 'Worldwide benefits management survey', Towers Perrin. Available online: http://www.towersperrin.com/tp/getwebcachedoc?webc=HRS/GBR/2004/200411/WWBM2004.pdf (accessed 4 September 2007).

Towers Perrin (2007) 'Towers Perrin 2007 Health Care Cost Survey'. Available online: http://www.towersperrin.com/tp/jsp/hrservices_webcache_html.jsp?webc=HR_Services/United_States/News/Spotlights/2007/03192007_spotlight_hccs.htm&selected=leadership&language_code=global (accessed 1 March 2008).

Tsai, K.H. and Wang, J.C. (2005) 'Benefits offer no advantage on firm productivity?', *Personnel Review*, 34 (4): 393–405.

Women and Work Commission (Chair Baroness Prosser of Battersea) (2006) 'Shaping a fairer future'. Available online: http://www.womenandequalityunit.gov.uk/publications/wwc_shaping_fairer_future06.pdf (accessed 23 March 2006).

World Health Organisation (2007) 'World health statistics, 2007: health systems: national health accounts'. Available online: http://www.who.int/whosis/whostat2007/en/index.html (accessed 12 July 2007).

WorldatWork (2007) 'WorldatWork Total Reward model'. Available online: http://www.worldatwork.org/waw/aboutus/html/aboutus-whatis.html#model (accessed 11 July 2007).

9 Occupational pensions

Stephen Taylor

Summary

There is great variation in the arrangements that have evolved in different countries for the provision of retirement pensions. The defining characteristics of the UK system are its considerable complexity and the substantial proportion of retirement funding (40 per cent) which is funded through privately run pension funds, a good majority being sponsored by employers on behalf of their staff (Emmerson 2002: 17). The UK's state pension system is one of the least generous in the world, providing incomes worth just 37 per cent of average earnings, and yet, thanks mainly to the presence of occupational pension funds, retired people in the UK are not significantly worse off than their counterparts in other countries (Pensions Commission 2004: 54, 68).

In most OECD countries there is a far greater reliance on state pensions funded on a pay-as-you-go basis (i.e. funded out of current taxation rather than from invested funds). Occupational pension funds are relatively few and far between, their coverage being limited to senior personnel in private companies. In an era in which the populations of the industrialised world are ageing markedly, the UK system is one which is being imitated by governments elsewhere planning for a future in which established levels of state pension provision will be more difficult to maintain without substantial increases in taxation. Significant expansion of private, funded pension provision is also a central objective for the UK government as it seeks to maintain current levels of spending on state pensions in the face of increases in the proportion of the population which is retired. The aim is to reverse the current ratio of provision so that by 2050 60 per cent of retirement income is privately funded and only 40 per cent provided by the state (Department of Social Security (DSS) 1998). The significance of occupational pensions thus extends well beyond the concerns of the employers providing them and the employees who receive them. This area of reward management practice is the subject of one of the most important public policy debates of our time.

This chapter starts by setting out the major forms that occupational pension schemes take in the UK before focusing on the most significant contemporary trends and their causes. It goes on to debate the extent to which occupational pensions can play a part in meeting organisations' HR objectives and how different types of design may help achieve these. Finally our attention turns to the public policy debates and to the significant ways in which government actions are likely to shape organisational practice in the future.

Occupational pension schemes in the UK

Several million workers in the UK are members of 92,000 separate occupational pension schemes with total combined assets of around £1,370 billion (National Association of Pensions Funds (NAPF) 2007a; NTC 2007: 41). It is not at all uncommon for pension funds to be worth several times more than the companies who run them (Blackburn 2002: 109). 85 per cent of workers in the public sector and 42 per cent of private sector workers are members of schemes from which over five million retired people currently draw an income (Pensions Commission 2004: 62; NAPF 2007a; Government Actuary's Department (GAD) 2006: 41). UK pension funds assets are equal to around 66 per cent of national GDP. Only in the USA, Canada and the Netherlands are there pension funds of comparable economic significance. The figure in Japan is 18.5 per cent of GDP, in Spain 8.2 per cent and in Germany just 3.3 per cent (Munnell 2006: 360–1). UK pension schemes take a number of forms, the central distinction being between those that operate on a defined benefit (DB) and defined contribution (DC) basis.

Defined benefit schemes

DB schemes used to be by far the most common form operated by UK employers. In recent years, however, their coverage has reduced sharply so that by 2006 only 31 per cent of DB schemes were still open to new members (NAPF 2006a). The principle here is that contributions are made by employers, employees or both into a single pension fund, the assets of which are invested on behalf of members in a shifting range of vehicles including equities (i.e. stocks and shares), property and government bonds in order to secure the best long-term collective return. When a member retires their pension is calculated according to a formula which links the benefit to their earnings. Most DB schemes base the pension on the salary being received at the time of retirement or on an average of the salary earned in the last few years immediately prior to retirement. Private sector final salary schemes mostly operate on a 'sixtieths' basis, meaning that the pension is equal to a sixtieth of the final annual salary multiplied by the number of years' pensionable service the retiring member has completed. So someone with 30 years' service under their belt will receive an annual pension worth 50 per cent of their final salary until they die.

Public sector schemes nearly all take the final salary form, but here it is usual for an 'eightieths' formula to be applied, giving a rather lower level of retirement income. By way of compensation, however, public sector workers receive a tax-free lump sum on retirement which can either be spent or invested to give an additional income. These can be quite sizeable. The National Health Service scheme is typical. Here lump sums are worth three eightieths of the final salary multiplied by the number of years' service. So a person with thirty years' service retiring while earning £30,000 a year will receive a payment of £33,750 (tax-free) in addition to a pension worth £11,250 a year. Most DB pensions are not index-linked, so their value can be eroded when inflation rates are high. The Pensions Act 1995, however, requires limited price indexation whereby pensions increase annually by 2.5 per cent or at the rate of the retail price index if this is lower.

The government would like to convert a good proportion of public sector schemes from final salary to career average schemes, a move already being made by a number of larger companies. This reduces the liability for tax-payers because pensions are lower, but there is also a shift in the balance of advantage from higher-paid staff to the lower-paid. People who have been promoted up the ranks do less well than they would under a final salary arrangement, their pensions being closer in value to those of colleagues who have been graded at a similar level throughout their careers.

It is common for DB schemes to have associated with them a range of additional benefits beyond the pension itself. These include death-in-service payments to dependants (an inexpensive form of life assurance) and widows' or widowers' pensions, as well as early retirement and ill-health retirement options. Pensions accrued in DB schemes are portable, but transfer values are calculated in such a way as to favour people who remain for some period of time as scheme members.

A key feature of DB schemes is that, at least in theory, the investment risk is borne by the employer sponsoring the fund. Regular actuarial studies are carried out to ensure that fund assets meet liabilities. Where assets fall below a safe level, the employer is obliged to invest sufficient monies so as to enable a viable level of funding again to be achieved. This helps to secure the level of pensions, but means that the employer's contributions tend to fluctuate markedly from one year to the next and can be both substantial and unpredictable.

Defined contribution schemes

Until the late 1990s DC schemes were only offered to a minority of UK employees (around 6 per cent). Since then coverage has grown rapidly, a majority of new starters now being provided with this type of benefit. DC schemes are also widely known as 'money purchase schemes'. Here employers and employees make contributions, but not into a single organisation-wide pension fund. Instead each member is allocated their own investment account into which these monies are placed. Over time the value of the individual pot increases, but the rate at which this happens varies hugely depending on where the money is invested and how well those investments perform. On retirement whatever sum has accrued is then taken by the retiree and used to purchase an annuity from an insurance company. A pension is then paid until the person concerned dies. The level of benefit is thus unpredictable, being determined partly by the amount of money in the pot and partly on the annuity rates available on the market at the time of retirement. The latter is heavily influenced by the level of interest rates and market expectations about their future likely level. The lower rates are anticipated to be, the lower the level of pension that is achievable. DC schemes thus have the disadvantage, when seen from the employee's perspective, of unpredictability. The investment risk is shouldered by the employee rather than the employer whose liability is restricted to the payment of a monthly sum into each member's pension pot. However, DC schemes are more readily understood and, because each member has his or her own pot, annual statements can be produced setting out what each individual pension is currently worth. Pensions accrued in DC schemes are also more readily portable than is the case with DB schemes, so that the pension can follow the employees very easily when they switch jobs and does not lose value when job switches occur frequently.

A feature of DC schemes which employees sometimes find attractive, but which has been criticised by commentators, is the option for individual members to determine the investment strategy they wish to be adopted for their portion of the fund and to review this from time to time. In most cases the choice is simply between different levels of risk, allowing people to opt for high-risk-high-return investments, low-risk-low-return investments, or something in between. For most people the best way of maximising return is to opt for a higher-risk strategy early in a career, switching the fund into low-risk investments in the years immediately prior to retirement. In practice, however, the majority of people opt for caution when it comes to their pension, the result being a lower level of pension for most than might otherwise have been achieved. Some commentators refer to this problem as one of 'reckless conservatism' and argue that it is not always in the interests of scheme members with their limited understanding of financial markets to be given such a choice.

Hybrid schemes

A small proportion of occupational pension schemes have a design which borrows features from both the DB and the DC forms. The most common is known as a 'money purchase underpin'. This is essentially a final salary scheme, but it also has the individual pension accounts associated with DC pension provision. In most cases it pays a pension based on a final salary calculation, but where a more generous level of benefit would be achieved through the purchase of an annuity using DC principles, that option is available. Portability, of course, is also more straightforward than in a conventional DB scheme. Occupational pension schemes designed for the exclusive benefit of senior executives are the most likely to be hybrid in design.

Group Personal Pensions

The rise of Group Personal Pensions (GPPs) is another significant recent trend. Over a quarter of private sector organisations now provide pensions in this way, their combined funds being worth in excess of £20 billion (NAPF 2003 and 2007a). From the point of view of employees, GPPs look and feel very much like defined contribution schemes operated by their employers. Benefits are determined according to money purchase (i.e. DC) principles, there being individual pension accounts, and pensions are readily portable out of one scheme and into another when people switch jobs. Employers and employees make contributions. They are, however, different in that they are contract-based rather than trust-based. The scheme is entirely administered by an insurance company with whom the employer has a contract. GPPs are thus very different in terms of their governance from conventional occupational pension schemes. They are not set up as trusts and are not overseen by boards of trustees. This has significant implications for individual members if the provider becomes insolvent. Upfront charges also tend to be quite high and are shouldered by employees rather than the sponsoring employer. However, it is still to the advantage of employees to join if it is the only alternative on offer. Charges, while high, are usually lower than conventional personal pensions, while the employer contribution is well worth having.

Stakeholder pensions

Stakeholder pensions are privately provided but tightly regulated by government under the Welfare Reform and Pensions Act 1999. They were introduced in 2001 with the primary purpose of providing private pensions for low- to middle-income earners who did not currently have access to occupational schemes. The target group is those earning salaries in the band just below average earnings (£10,000–£25,000 a year). Stakeholder pensions take the defined contribution form, but they can either be trust-based or contract-based. Various minimum standards are required, the most important of which is a charging structure which limits charges to 1.5 per cent of an individual member's fund for ten years and then to 1 per cent after that. All employers with more than five employees who do not already offer an occupational pension to their staff are required by law to provide access to a stakeholder scheme through the payroll and to publicise this fact to employees, although there is no requirement for employers themselves to make any contributions.

Government ministers claim that the stakeholder scheme has met its objectives, boasting about the fact that nearly three million policies were sold during the first five years of operation (*Hansard* 2006). In truth, however, this figure is misleading because most schemes are still classed as 'designation-only'. Stakeholder pension arrangements have been set up by employers as required under the legislation, but have not been taken up by their employees. According to the Pensions Commission (2004: 92) 'the vast majority are empty shells', the result being a situation in which 'there is little evidence of a net increase in ongoing pension contributions . . . as a result of the introduction of Stakeholder pensions.'

The decline of the established system

Since the mid-1990s major changes have occurred in the occupational pensions sector which have had the effect, at least as far as workers in the private sector are concerned, of eroding the value of pension promises. Two major trends can be observed: the decline of occupational pension coverage generally and the shift from DB to DC plans. In combination, along with the reluctance of UK workers to save into personal private pensions, this means that we are now seeing considerable declines in the amount of money being invested in private pensions.

The extent to which overall coverage of occupational pensions has declined is considerable and is a long-term trend. The figure for the number of people who are members of occupational pension schemes peaked in 1967 at 12.5 million, declining steadily to 10.5 million by 1995. More recently a sharper decline has occurred. In 1995 10.5 million people were members, but by 2005 the figure was only 9.1 million (Pensions Commission 2004: 81; GAD 2006: 9). Expressed as a percentage of the total employed workforce this trend is more marked. Just over 40 per cent of the employed workforce were in membership in 1995, declining to just 31.6 per cent in 2005. This trend is entirely accounted for by the private sector, public sector membership having increased slightly during this period. The net result is a situation in which many more future retirees will be wholly reliant on the state pension system than was the case ten to fifteen years ago. Around 56 per cent of people today have no private pension provision at all, compared to just 44 per cent in 1995 (Pensions Commission 2006: 12). The government's ambition may be to shift the balance of funding away from the state and onto the private pensions sector, but the current trends are strongly in the opposite direction. In short, private sector employers are now far less committed than they were in past decades to set up occupational schemes or to make any contribution at all to their employees' pension plans. This clearly has significant and worrying implications for the level of retirement income that the majority of today's workers will enjoy in old age.

The second trend also relates almost entirely to practice among private sector employers. While DB schemes remain the dominant form in the public sector, the past decade has seen a substantial shift in the private sector away from DB pension provision and towards DC schemes of one kind or another, particularly during the 2001–2004 period. Although there are some examples of companies winding up their final salary schemes altogether, in the main the approach taken has involved closing them to new members. Existing employees thus continue in the established scheme, while new starters are offered membership of a DC scheme. Over time, as people move from company to company, and as new starters replace retirees, the number of people with final salary pensions will decrease while the number with DC pensions will increase. Over two-thirds of private sector DB schemes are now closed to new members (NAPF 2007a), while fewer than 14 per cent of people starting jobs now join DB schemes (Pensions Commission 2004: 84).

There has long been a debate in the pensions industry about the relative virtues of DB and DC schemes when seen from the employees' point of view. Portability is a factor in favour of DC schemes, meaning that for younger employees who intend to move from employer to employer several times in the early parts of their careers a case can be made for the superiority of a typical DC scheme vis-à-vis a DB scheme. In such cases the benefits of higher transfer values can outweigh the requirement for the employee rather than the employer to shoulder the investment risk. Others have argued that the question of which party takes on this risk is of less practical relevance than is often claimed because there are always limits to how far employers are able to fund deficits in DB schemes. If investment performance is poor, pensions will be less than expected whatever the scheme design and whoever carries the risk in theory. Notwithstanding these points, it is fair to conclude that in practice employees who are members of DC schemes are very likely in the large majority of cases to retire on lower pensions than equivalent employees in DB schemes. This is for two reasons. First, in practice, employers do put large sums of money into pension funds in order to keep them solvent (Hills 2006: 116). This is the major reason why contribution levels have increased in recent years (NAPF 2003: 6). Second, and more significantly, employer contributions to DB schemes are in practice a great deal more generous than those that are made to typical DC schemes. On average in the private sector annual employer contributions to open DB schemes are equivalent to 14 per cent of members' salaries. The average employer contribution to an open DC scheme is just 6 per cent (GAD 2006: 100). The result, taking account of similar levels of employee contribution, is that saving into DC pension schemes is falling very considerably short of the 20 per cent of salary required in order to generate a pension equivalent to one provided by a final salary scheme (Hill 2007: 37).

Prior to this period of decline, the UK's occupational pensions system was commonly described as being 'the envy of the world' and likened to the goose that laid the golden egg. The reasons for its deterioration over the past ten to fifteen years have thus been the subject of considerable debate. While there is little question that the major immediate precipitating factor was a serious worsening in the financial position of most occupational funds from the late 1990s onwards, the extent to which other, longer-term causes can be identified and blamed remains disputed.

For some commentators, much of the blame is placed on employers. During the 1980s and 1990s, it is argued, huge fund surpluses were built up but were not put to good use. By 1997 UK occupational pension funds were in combined surplus to the tune of £60 billion, but in most cases the monies were used by employers to take contribution holidays (Blackburn 2002: 127). In some cases organisations spent nothing at all on pensions for several years, finance directors getting very used to this situation. Then, come 2000, when the long period of high returns on investment in equities came to an end and funds began to go into deficit, companies were reluctant to put the necessary additional resources in to keep their funds viable. Instead levels of provision were effectively reduced through the device of switching from DB to DC provision. Had employers refrained from taking contribution holidays during the good times, so the argument runs, there would not have been a need to reduce provision when stock market returns deteriorated in the early years of the twenty-first century.

Employers are also blamed for consistently underestimating the growth in life expectancy during the 1990s, the result being an unnecessarily sharp adjustment in actuarial valuations of fund liabilities after 2000. Further criticism has been levelled at the investment strategies pursued by fund managers, in particular what seems with hindsight a reckless over-reliance on equities. Had more money been invested in less risky investments such as government bonds, there would have been a less spectacular deterioration in the value of funds when the stock market collapsed (Munnell 2006: 374). Finally, a degree of blame is often attributed to pension scandals such as those associated with the collapse of the Maxwell Group of Companies in 1992 and of Equitable Life in 2000, as well as several well-publicised examples of insolvent companies leaving behind funds in serious deficit which could not then pay any pensions (Blackburn 2002: 328–31).

The major alternative view places a greater share of the blame on successive governments who are criticised for over-regulating the occupational sector and for passing measures which were short-sighted, contributing directly to the rapid decline of the established pension system. Adair Turner, chairman of the Pensions Commission, describes the body of regulation dating from the period since 1985 as 'bizarre' in that it told employers that they did not need to provide a pension scheme for their employees, but if they did choose to do so it had to be gold-plated. According to Turner it was equivalent to the government saying that if employers wished to provide company cars to employees they had to be Rolls Royces (BBC TV interview, 5 May 2007). Particular criticism is directed at the Finance Act 1986 which limited over-funding of defined benefit schemes (Munnell 2006: 374), the Social Security Act 1986 which prevented employers from requiring eligible employees to join their schemes (Taylor 2000a: 362), and the Pensions Act 1995 with its raft of new bureaucratic regulation and rigid rules on minimum funding (Pemberton *et al.* 2006). Matters were not helped either by the Finance Act 1997 with its 'reform' of pension dividend taxation which is widely estimated to have cost UK pension funds about £5 billion a year (*The Economist* 1997). More recently Byrne *et al.* (2006) have criticised the Pensions Act 2004 for further heaping costs and bureaucracy on occupational pension funds and, in the process, reducing the likelihood that employers will choose to provide pension schemes for their employees.

Another development which played a role in accelerating the decline in coverage and the switch from DB to DC provision was the decision in 2000 of the Accounting Standards Board to introduce Financial Reporting Standard 17 from 2005. These conventions require organisations to value pension fund assets and liabilities in annual accounts on a market-related basis, meaning that the substantial fluctuations that frequently occur in the value of fund assets are now shown in a company's accounts and may influence investor behaviour and estimates of the market value of companies. Switching from DB schemes, with their unpredictable costs, to DC schemes with their much more predictable and stable annual employer contribution levels has thus been made more attractive.

A third view on the causes of decline blames no party in particular, instead arguing that the system established in the UK had simply become unsustainable and was bound to collapse at some stage. Far from being like a goose that lays golden eggs, commentators such as Adair Turner prefer the metaphor of a house of cards. It is not surprising, he argues, that the collapse occurred. The surprise was that it stayed standing for as long as it did (BBC TV interview, 5 May 2007). Had it not been for the strong growth in equities during the 1980s and 1990s, moves away from DB occupational pension provision would have occurred 20 years earlier instead. The system was designed to meet the needs of employing organisations in the period before and after World War Two. It never was appropriate to the needs of contemporary businesses competing globally by maximising their flexibility and minimising their fixed costs, in the context of rapidly increasing life expectancy.

The HRM perspective

Another area of debate in the field of occupational pensions concerns the role they can and do play in wider employer reward strategies. This is an important subject in its own right, but also plays a role in the wider public policy debates about the state of UK pensions because it relates to the benefits employers gain from sponsoring a fund in the first place.

Historical studies that have focused on the reasons that occupational pensions of the defined benefit form were originally set up in the UK consistently show that HR reasons underlay management motivation. Hannah (1986) and Sass (2006) both stress the significance of employee retention as the chief aim of the organisations which set up the first modern occupational schemes. As white-collar employment expanded from the mid-nineteenth century onwards and internal labour markets were created in larger organisations, it made sense for employers to provide incentives for people to develop their careers within the same corporation, working hard to compete for promotion up the hierarchical ladder. DB schemes are particularly suited to this situation because they reward long service generally, and promotion in particular. They thus serve both to retain staff and to motivate them to perform well. The other principal labour market effect came from the capacity of a good pension scheme to attract large numbers of well-qualified applicants to an organisation, enabling managers to go on to select the most talented people. The coverage of occupational pensions spread in the UK during the twentieth century as employers who did not sponsor schemes realised that they had to if they were to compete effectively for staff with those who did.

A further feature of DB pension schemes that economists see as being significant is the way they make it advantageous for employees to retire at a retirement age set by the employer (Ellwood 1985; Wise 1986; Handa 1994). The economically rational employee will choose to retire at 60 or 65 because this way they maximise the value of the benefit. Having an occupational pension scheme thus helped an employer to deal in a humane way with the personnel problems associated with age-related decline in employees' performance.

It is thus reasonable to conclude that the UK's established occupational pension system took the form it did essentially for HR reasons. While straightforward paternalism and tax breaks clearly played some part too, employers set up their schemes in the main in order to achieve specific employee relations objectives. However, the extent to which this holds true in the early twenty-first century is questionable, and may well in part help to explain the increased reluctance of employers to provide access to DB schemes and indeed to any occupational pension scheme at all.

Numerous econometric studies have been carried out in the UK and the USA which establish clear correlations between employee turnover rates and membership of occupational pension schemes. While the size of the effect varies from study to study, all show clearly that people who are members of employer-sponsored occupational schemes stay longer in their jobs than those who are not members (Mitchell 1983; McCormick and Hughes 1984; Lazear and Moore 1988; Ippolito 1991; Allen *et al.* 1993; Maelli and Pudney 1993; Gallie *et al.* 1998). However, the extent to which this apparently conclusive finding holds true in the UK context at the start of the twenty-first century is questionable. Two major points can be made which shed considerable doubt on the proposition that occupational pensions remain an effective employee retention device.

First, econometric studies show that there is a correlation between pension scheme membership and a propensity to remain loyal to an employer. But they do not prove a one-way causal relationship. It is plausible to argue that employees who intend to remain employed in the one organisation choose to join the pension scheme, rather than remaining employed because they are scheme members. Moreover, it is quite possible that there is some other independent variable which explains the correlation. Gustman and

Steinmeier (1995), for example, have argued that the real correlation is between low turnover rates and the relatively high levels of pay that tend to be prevalent in the organisations which offer pension benefits. But it could more generally be a case of better employers offering pensions as one of a range of strategies designed to attract and retain strong performers.

Second, these studies were all carried out in the USA or in the UK prior to the regulatory revolution referred to above which began in the mid-1980s. The schemes studied were thus, in many cases, likely to have had features built into their designs which served to retain people very effectively, but which are now unlawful in the UK. The chief example is vesting rules which penalise early leavers very heavily. These used to be common in the UK and US schemes, resulting in a complete or major loss of accrued benefits if an employee left after up to seven, ten or even more years of membership were completed. In the UK the current rules require full vesting rights after just two years' membership, hugely reducing the extent to which a scheme can be used as a device to trap employees in the one employment for any length of time.

For the generality of employees, therefore, it is now questionable to claim with any certainty that pensions improve staff-retention rates. The major exception to this relates to people who are nearing retirement and who have built up a considerable pension over a long career. There can be little doubt that they perceive it to be in their interests to see through their employment to retirement age and are deterred from seeking alternative employment in the years leading up to the date they intend to retire (Taylor 2000b; Hales and Gough 2003). For such people occupational pensions remain a powerful retention device. However, the extent to which the employer necessarily benefits is a matter of debate. Surely it is not in the interests of any organisation to continue employing people whose only reason for staying is to claim a pension? If they are not motivated positively by other aspects of the employment experience they are likely to make a limited contribution, and it would be better from a management perspective if they were to leave and be replaced with someone whose commitment is more broadly based.

There is less published evidence about whether the prospect of membership of an occupational pension scheme positively attracts recruits to an organisation. A recent opinion poll survey undertaken by Populus on behalf of the National Association of Pension Funds (NAPF 2007b) suggests that occupational pension provision of some sort is appreciated by most employees. This research involved sampling the attitudes of over 1,000 people of working age. When asked about the importance of 'a pension that comes with your job', 53 per cent said it was 'very important', 22 per cent 'quite important', while only 24 per cent said that it was 'not important'. This finding is broadly in line with studies carried out in the USA (Tetrick *et al.* 1997), who found that pensions were considered to be factors of consequence in general terms when job-seeking, but that people were uninterested in the type of scheme being offered. All they appeared to need to know was that there was some form of pension coverage. Its relative generosity and flexibility as well as the extent to which it carried risk were thus factors of relative insignificance.

Much appears to depend on the particular labour market. Loretto *et al.* (2000) in their study of attitudes to pensions in a large financial services provider reported that the occupational pension was ranked fifth overall in a list of 20 factors that had attracted staff to their jobs. But how far does this finding hold true outside the financial world where a high degree of awareness of pension issues would be expected? Insufficient numbers of studies have been carried out to allow a firm judgement to be made, but it is notable that a further study by Loretto *et al.* (2001), focusing on graduate recruits, found occupational pensions to be much less significant. We also know that a good proportion of employees actively choose not to join their organisation's pension scheme when given the opportunity to do so, particularly lower-paid staff in the private services sector. One would expect financial reasons to play a major part in the decision not to join – employees after all usually have to contribute approximately 5 per cent of their own salary – but interestingly other reasons appear to be more significant. Gough (2004), for example, in her survey of 532 non-joiners in 21 UK companies, found that a reluctance to reduce income was only the fourth most commonly cited reason after 'I have got my own pension', 'I intend to change jobs' and 'I expect my partner to provide for me in retirement.'

Another reason for questioning the true extent of any general attraction effect is the high level of ignorance that employees are consistently shown to have about their schemes. Several studies have shown this to be the case. One was the extensive survey carried out by Towers Perrin Foster and Crosby in 1987 which found that a third of their sample claimed to have 'no idea' of their pension entitlements or the value of their accrued occupational pensions. Research commissioned a few years later by the Goode Committee on Pension Law (Goode 1993) concluded that apart from a 'small well-informed minority' there was a very high degree of ignorance among pension fund members about basic features of their scheme's design and about the likely value of the pension they will receive on retirement. More recently Luchak and Gunderson (2000) found similar levels of ignorance among the generality of Canadian workers, with exceptions among higher-paid people and some older staff.

Perhaps the best general evidence for the view that occupational pensions have a relatively slight role to play in determining labour market behaviour is the high level of employee turnover that has persisted in the UK in recent years. Since 2000 most larger companies have withdrawn from salary-related pension provision by closing their DB schemes to new starters. In the process a clear employee-retention incentive has been created. When people leave to join another company they lose out pension-wise because they are required to switch from a DB to a DC scheme. Yet this does not appear to have had any significant effect on staff reported turnover in the private sector (Chartered Institute of Personnel and Development (CIPD) 2007).

The evidence then is equivocal on the general labour market effects of occupational pension schemes in the contemporary UK context. Overall it would appear to be the case that an employer will benefit in terms of the attraction and retention of staff if it provides an occupational scheme, but that the precise type of scheme or level of benefits offered are unlikely to make much difference except in the case of older and better-informed workers. There is thus an HR-case for occupational pensions, but it is weak in many labour market scenarios and is by no means overwhelmingly convincing. As a result pensions and HR managers are divided about the extent to which their schemes play a serious role in competing for staff and are not now well-placed to advance evidence to support the contention that they do (Taylor 2000b). This is important because unless robust evidence can be provided, finance directors are inevitably going to question the value of continuing pension benefits at a time when costs and the regulatory burden associated with occupational schemes have been increasing rapidly. Strong evidence of scepticism among finance directors and of their central role in determining the future nature of occupational pension practices is provided by Blake *et al.* (2005) in their study of decision-making on pensions issues in small and medium-sized enterprises (SMEs). They found that finance directors were often not just unsupportive of HR arguments in favour of occupational pensions, but in many cases actively hostile to them. FDs tend to see pension schemes as costs for which there is little or no return on investment, but which have serious potential to reduce competitiveness. Indeed, according to Blake *et al.* (2005), senior managers in many SMEs have a policy of providing only the most basic of pension schemes and then take care to ensure that they are not promoted effectively among the mass of the workforce. The fear is that too many employees will join and that the costs will be unsustainable.

Contemporary public policy debates

Since the 1980s public policy towards occupational pensions has focused on issues of regulation. An area of organisational and economic life that was once very lightly regulated has, as a result of a series of statutes, become heavily regulated. There is no question that in the eyes of most working in the pensions industry, occupational pensions and defined benefit schemes in particular have long been over-regulated and that this has had a damaging impact on future retirement income (NAPF 2007c).

In the early 1990s the then government commissioned a review of pensions law under the Chairmanship of Roy Goode. The committee recommended considerable increased regulation, most of which subsequently found its way into the Pensions Act 1995. At the time leading figures in the industry warned that too much red tape would have the effect of reducing employers' willingness to offer occupational pensions. But these warnings appear to have fallen on deaf ears. Professor Goode himself, in giving evidence to the House of

Commons Social Security Select Committee, made it clear that his committee had been unimpressed by such arguments:

> At the same time, we thought it right, where rules were required on the employers, to recommend them and we were not deflected by the thought that any regulation we might recommend would discourage employers from offering pension schemes. It is always said by those who are likely to be regulated that 'if you introduce these regulations we shall move out of the area': one has to take that with a pinch of salt, which we did.
>
> (Minutes from the House of Commons Social Security Select Committee, *Enquiry into the operation of pension funds*, 1994: 393–4)

Professor Goode's view was largely supported by Blake (1995: 248), the leading academic authority on pension funds in the UK. His view was that the threat on the part of employers 'to wind-up their schemes if the government imposes any more restrictions on their actions . . . is not considered to be serious'.

In retrospect it is now clear that these views – influential at the time – were probably profoundly mistaken, and the contemporary public policy agenda reflects a much changed view. Simplification of the regulatory regime and de-regulation where possible are now the focus. Reform of this nature was recommended by the Pensions Commission (2006) in its final report, and is clearly stated as a priority in the government's white paper on pensions published in May 2006:

> Finally we will streamline the regulatory environment. . . . Any such simplifications will be aimed at easing the regulatory burden on employers who provide good occupational pensions. They, and other measures in the proposed reform package, will be taken forward with regard to the Government's wider agenda to promote better regulation and reduce the administrative burdens on business.
>
> (Department of Work and Pensions (DWP) 2006: 19)

Another feature of the current public policy debate which was less evident in the past is an interest in and willingness to face the pensions consequences of long-term demographic trends. Central here is concern about the projected dependency ratio, by which is meant the proportion of people of working age in the population in relation to the proportion who are over retirement age. Predictions can never be entirely accurate because established, long-term trends do reverse from time to time. Significant population ageing, however, has been occurring for some time and can reasonably be expected to accelerate in the future. In 2002 the ratio of people aged 65 and over to those aged 20–64 stood at 27 per cent. Official government projections predict that it will be as high as 48 per cent in 2050, meaning that almost half the UK's adult population will be over the current state pension age in a few decades time.

The main driver is increased life expectancy, but another factor of significance is the low level of the birthrate in the years since the post-war baby
boom came to an end in 1965. A man retiring in 1950 at the age of 65
could expect, on average, to live for a further 12 years. The current figure is
19 years and the projection for 2050 is 22 years. Female life expectancy is
rising too, but is not accelerating quite as quickly. Importantly, however, as
the Pensions Commission Report points out, past official projections have
always underestimated the rate at which life expectancy will increase in the
future, so it makes sense as far as public policy is concerned to prepare for
an even greater rise in the dependency ratio than is currently anticipated
(Pensions Commission 2004: 2). The result is a cross-party consensus around
the broad proposition that the current funding model which places the pre-
ponderance of responsibility for retirement income on the state is unsustainable. Two major policy prescriptions are advanced in response:

1   That the priority must be to expand both the coverage and extent of
    privately funded provision.
2   That the state pension age must increase steadily over time.

By no means everyone, however, is part of this consensus, well-argued cri-
tiques having been published by Blackburn (2002: 16–20) and Hill (2007:
117–34). In both cases the authors accept the evidence on population ageing,
but contend that this does not necessarily mean that dependency will increase.
Hill is concerned that major public policy decisions are being taken in
response to a simplistic analysis. He argues that the 'problem' can be equally
well addressed by increasing the proportion of the UK population of working age which is economically active. The labour force participation rate in
the UK currently stands at 76 per cent, which is higher than that in many
countries, but considerably lower than that achieved in economies such as
Switzerland, Sweden and Denmark. Moreover, in the UK itself some groups
are less likely to participate than they used to, the most important of these
being men between the ages of 55 and 65. Were early retirement rates to be
brought back to their 1980s level and female participation rates raised to
those of Sweden, there would be less need to adjust existing pensions policy.
Blackburn (2002) is stark in his criticisms of the analysis underpinning the
current direction of public policy. His argument is summed up as follows:

> The true dimensions of the ageing population are often misconstrued.
> Thus the 'shortage of workers' argument ignores several major counter-
> veiling circumstances. Firstly, the medical advances which lengthen life
> expectancy also lengthen people's ability to go on working past the
> standard age of retirement. Secondly, if there is a labour shortage in one
> country it can often be met by immigration from another. Thirdly, the
> decline in the birth rate reduces the number of children, which has
> the effect of reducing the number of dependants per worker. Fourthly,

technological advance is continually raising the productivity of labour, meaning that even a reduced workforce could maintain levels of national wealth. Fifthly, it is clear that the problems of modern capitalist economies do not principally centre on labour shortage.

(Blackburn 2002: 18)

A further point which is rarely made in this context concerns the possibility, as a result of low or falling birth rates, for future state resources to be switched from supporting the needs of the dependent young (schools, childcare, child benefit, etc). to those of older people in the form of better-funded state pensions. Population ageing should also mean that substantial reductions are possible in state spending on prisons and the criminal justice system. This is because 14–25 is the peak age for criminal activity, the majority of crime in the UK now being committed by teenage boys. Offending rates decline very substantially after this age and are negligible among the oversixties. It should follow that substantial reductions in crime can be achieved as the proportion of older people in the population increases.

These views are not shared by the ministers and their advisors who currently have responsibility for shaping future public policy. The aim remains to prepare for an increased dependency ratio by maintaining state spending levels on pensions as a proportion of GDP while substantially increasing privately funded pension provision. The Pensions Act 2007, together with further future legislation, intends to achieve these objectives using the following principal measures:

1 By raising the state pension age for men and women after equalisation at 65 has been achieved in 2020. It will increase to 66 from 2024, to 67 from 2034 and to 68 from 2044.
2 By up rating of the basic state pension after 2012 in line with growth in the average earnings of UK workers rather than in line with prices. This commitment, however, is qualified as being 'subject to affordability and the fiscal position'.
3 From 2012 employers who do not provide a superior occupational pension or a GPP will be required to pay a contribution of 3 per cent of all employees' earnings between £5,000 and £33,000 a year into a personal account. Employees will pay a contribution of 4 per cent, a further 1 per cent being paid in as a result of tax relief.
4 Employees will be permitted to opt out, but will be automatically enrolled by their employer either into an occupational scheme or the new personal accounts scheme. The latter will be commercially provided but will operate within strict government regulations.

These proposals mark a significant milestone in the development of the UK pensions system in that for the first time they require employers to make contributions. At present, via the stakeholder pension system outlined above, employers are obliged to provide access to a pension but there is no compulsion to do more. After 2012 this will change. Provided the employee wishes to participate, a contribution worth 3 per cent of salary will have to be made by the employer. To date it is on these proposals that criticism has focused.

First, there is evidence to suggest that employers who do not currently make any pension contributions (mostly SMEs) will seek ways of avoiding starting to do so once the new regime begins operating in 2012. Financial advisors claim that circumventing compulsory contributions will not be difficult to achieve in practice. It simply requires the establishment of systems in organisations which ensure that new employees find it 'quick, easy and attractive to opt out' (Blake *et al.* 2005: 148). Widespread use of such approaches will save employers money, but will undermine a central plank in the government's strategy rapidly to increase pension saving. A second potential fault with the government's plans has been identified by the National Association of Pension Funds (NAPF 2006b). The focus here is on employers who already have DC occupational pension funds into which employer contributions of 5–6 per cent of salary are currently made. This is affordable, it is argued, only because typically just 50–60 per cent of employees join the schemes. Automatic enrolment will mean a substantial rise in the total amount of money such employers will be required to contribute. The fear is that this will be judged unaffordable and will result across the board in a reduction in contribution levels to the statutory minimum level of 3 per cent. The result would be a levelling-down of contributions to the lowest permissible level under the law, rather than in the levelling-up the Government wants to see.

At base all debates about public policy towards pensions in general and occupational pensions in particular are rooted in one major debate: is private or public provision best? At present in the UK establishment opinion is in favour of encouraging private provision, albeit within a tightly regulated framework, employer schemes and contributions playing a central role. This was the central conclusion of the recent Pensions Commission reports (Hills 2006), is the major driver of government policy (DWP 2006) and is a position which enjoys cross-party support in Parliament. Critics remain unconvinced, believing that the result is an overly complex system which incorporates far too many unnecessary transaction costs (Blackburn 2002). They argue that other countries have successful alternative systems which are state-funded, operate on a pay-as-you-go basis, are fairer to all and provide much better value for money. The view that such approaches are unsustainable in the face of rapid population ageing is overstated and has the effect of excluding proper consideration of alternative public policy strategies. Ultimately, as Barr (2006) points out, this debate reflects the political ideology of its participants more than it does the economic reality of future retirement provision. He goes as far as to describe the debate as a 'red-herring' (Barr 2006: 13), arguing that whatever approach is used, future pension provision can be satisfactorily secured provided that macroeconomic stability is maintained, economic growth achieved and retirement ages modestly raised.

References

Allen, S.G., Clark, R.L. and McDermed, A.A. (1993) 'Pension Bonding and Lifetime Jobs', *Journal of Human Resources*, Vol. 28 (3): 463–481.

Barr, N. (2006) 'Pensions: "Overview of the issues" ', *Oxford Review of Economic Policy*, Vol. 22 (1): 1 14.

Blackburn, R. (2002) *Banking on Death or Investing in Life: The History and Future of Pensions*, London: Verso.

Blake, D. (1995) *Pension Schemes and Pension Funds in the UK*, Oxford: Clarendon Press.

Blake, D., Byrne, A. and Harrison, D. (2005) *Barriers of pension-scheme participation in small and medium-sized enterprises*, Discussion Paper PI0505, London: The Pensions Institute, City University.

Byrne, A., Harrison, D., Rhodes, B. and Blake, D. (2006) *Pyrrhic Victory? The Unintended Consequence of the Pensions Act 2004*, London: Institute of Economic Affairs.

CIPD (2007) *Recruitment, Retention and Turnover*, London: Chartered Institute of Personnel and Development.

DSS (1998) *A New Contract for Welfare: Partnership in Pensions*, London: Department of Social Security.

DWP (2006) *Security in Retirement: Towards a new pensions system*, London: Department for Work and Pensions.

The Economist (1997) 'Investment Brown-Out', 5th July: 23.

Ellwood, D. (1985) 'Pensions and the Labour Market: A Starting Point (The Mouse Can Roar)', in D. Wise (ed.) *Pensions, Labor and Individual Choice*, Chicago: University of Chicago Press.

Emmerson, C. (2002) 'Pension Reform in the United Kingdom', *Working Paper WP402*, Oxford: Institute of Ageing.

GAD (2006) *Occupational Pension Schemes: The thirteenth survey by the Government Actuary*, London: Government Actuary's Department.

Gallie, D., White, M., Cheng, Y. and Tomlinson, M. (1998) *Restructuring the Employment Relationship*, Oxford: Oxford University Press.

Goode, R. (1993) *Pension Law Reform*, Volume 2, London: HMSO.

Gough, O. (2004) 'Why do employees, particularly women, reject occupational pension schemes?', *Employee Relations*, 26.5: 480–494.

Gustman, A.L. and Steinmeier, T.L. (1995) *Pension Incentives and Job Mobility*, Kalamazoo MI: Upjohn Institute.

Hales, C. and Gough, O. (2003) 'Employee evaluations of company occupational pensions: HR implications', *Personnel Review*, 32.3: 319–340.

Handa, J. (1994) *Discrimination, Retirement and Pensions*, Aldershot: Avebury.

Hannah, L. (1986) *Inventing Retirement: The Development of Occupational Pensions in Britain*, Cambridge: Cambridge University Press.

Hansard (2006) Answer by James Purnell MP to a question from Gregory Barker MP, Column 24W, October.

Hill, M. (2007) *Pensions*, Bristol: Policy Press.

Hills, J. (2006) 'A New Pension Settlement for the Twenty-first Century? The UK Pensions Commission's Analysis and Proposals', *Oxford Review of Economic Policy*, 22(1): 113–132.

Ippolito, R. (1991) 'Encouraging long-term tenure: wage-tilt or pensions?', *Industrial and Labor Relations Review*, Vol. 44 (3): 520–535.

Lazear, E. and Moore, R. (1988) 'Pensions and Turnover', in Z. Bodie, J.B. Shoven and D.A. Wise (eds) *Pensions in the US Economy*, National Bureau of Economic Research Project Report, Chicago: University of Chicago Press.

Loretto, W., White, P. and Duncan, C. (2000) 'Something for nothing? Employees' views of occupational pension schemes', *Employee Relations*, 22 (3): 260–271.

Loretto, W., White, P. and Duncan, C. (2001) 'Thatcher's children, pensions and retirement: some survey evidence', *Personnel Review*, 30 (4): 386–403.

Luchak, A. and Gunderson, M. (2000) 'What do employees know about their pension plan?', *Industrial Relations*, 39 (4): 646–668.

Maelli, F. and Pudney, S. (1993) Occupational Pensions and Job Mobility in Britain. University of Leicester *Discussion Paper in Economics* (93.19).

McCormick, B. and Hughes, G. (1984) 'The influence of pensions on job mobility', *Journal of Public Economics*, Vol. 23: 183–206.

Mitchell, O. (1983) 'Fringe benefits and the cost of changing jobs', *Industrial and Labor Relations Review*, Vol. 37 (1): 70–78.

Munnell, A.H. (2006) 'Employer Sponsored Plans: The Shift from Defined Benefit to Defined Contribution', in G.L. Clark, A.H. Munnell and J.M. Orszag (eds) *The Oxford Handbook of Pensions and Retirement Income*, Oxford: Oxford University Press.

NAPF (2003) *Pension scheme changes – a snapshot*, London: National Association of Pension Funds.

NAPF (2006a) *NAPF Annual Survey 2006*, London: National Association of Pension Funds.

NAPF (2006b) *More Savers, More Saving? How employer decisions will determine the long term success of pension reform*, London: National Association of Pension Funds.

NAPF (2007a) *Key Facts on Pensions*, London: National Association of Pension Funds.

NAPF (2007b) 'Workplace pensions in demand', Press release, 25th May, London: National Association of Pension Funds.

NAPF (2007c) 'Regulation tops poll of pension scheme concerns', Press release, 6th July, London: National Association of Pension Funds.

NTC (2007) *Pensions Pocket Book*, Henley on Thames, Oxfordshire: NTC Publications in Association with Hewitt.

Pemberton, H., Thane, P. and Whiteside, N. (2006) *Britain's Pension Crisis: History and Policy*, Oxford: Oxford University Press/The British Academy.

Pensions Commission (2004) *Pensions: Challenges and Choices: The First Report of the Pensions Commission*, London: The Stationery Office.

Pensions Commission (2006) *Implementing an integrated package of pension reforms: The Final Report of the Pensions Commission*, London: The Stationery Office.

Sass, S. (2006) 'The Development of Employer Retirement Income Plans: From the Nineteenth Century to 1980', in G.L. Clark, A.H. Munnell and J.M. Orszag (eds) *The Oxford Handbook of Pensions and Retirement Income*, Oxford: Oxford University Press.

Taylor, S. (2000a) 'Occupational Pensions', in R. Thorpe and G. Homan (eds) *Strategic Reward Systems*, Harlow: FT/Prentice Hall.

Taylor, S. (2000b) 'Occupational pensions and employee retention', *Employee Relations*, 22 (3): 246–259.

Tetrick, L., DaSilva, N., Hutcheson, J. and Weathington, B. (1997) 'The effects of compensation packages components on the attractiveness of positions and the relations of individual differences in the relative importance of these components', Paper presented at the American Academy of Management Conference, Boston, 1997.

Towers Perrin Foster and Crosby (1987) *Pension Perception Survey*, London, Towers Perrin.

Wise, D.A. (1986) 'Overview', in D. Wise (ed.) *Pensions, Labor and Individual Choice*, Chicago: University of Chicago Press.

10 Financial participation schemes

Jeff Hyman

Summary

Financial participation schemes aim to provide employees with a stake in the firm for which they work. Schemes can be classified into profit-related pay which offers financial incentives to employees based on organisation profit levels and employee share schemes which offer employees a property interest in the company as well as longer-term financial reward. These forms of financial participation are common in both developed and developing countries. Both approaches aim to enhance productivity through their effects on employee performance. Studies on the impact of profit-related pay are inconclusive, though it appears that its use in tandem with other progressive HR techniques can positively influence employee orientations and performance. The impact of employee share schemes is at worst neutral though positive effects such as reduced labour turnover and expressions of employee commitment are associated with larger allocations of equity and when share schemes are complemented by other forms of employee participation. Nevertheless, under most schemes, share allocations as a proportion of total income are not high and many participants treat their equity as a marginal bonus or dispose of their acquired shares at an early stage.

Introduction

Since the publication of the first edition of this book, the economies of the major developed countries have undergone considerable transformation with widespread adoption of information technologies, deregulation of both product and labour markets, decline of heavy manufacturing, ascendancy of service industries and growing competition for the provision of goods and services, led by new economies such as China and India, which are becoming increasingly prominent globally. Continuous change in product and service markets combined with tightening quality demands require employers to seek more efficient and flexible means of production and for policy-makers to secure international productive competitiveness to ensure rising living standards and to maintain acceptable levels of employment.

Linked to these economic pressures have been corresponding changes in the composition and activities of the workforce. Most obvious has been the decline in trade union membership, activity and influence (Kersley *et al.* 2006). A further shift is that the labour force is becoming increasingly qualified as older staff give way to growing ranks of university and college-educated newcomers to the so called 'knowledge' labour market (Wolf 2002): 'intellectual capital – not natural resources, machinery, or even financial capital – has become the one indispensable asset of corporations' (Little *et al.* 2002: 1). For employers of scarce and highly-qualified labour, gaining employee commitment has ostensibly become the key objective of people management (Walton 1985). The reasons are not hard to find: the labour and outputs of potentially highly mobile, highly skilled and professionalised knowledge workers may be intangible, lack visibility and be difficult for managers to control directly and participation may provide the route for organisations to seek freely-given employee effort and committed service.

Employee participation can be seen as an umbrella title which comprises a broad range of practices. In a widely-recognised classification, Bowen and Lawler (1992) categorise participative or empowerment practice in terms of a hierarchy, ranging from the low-impact informational approaches of suggestion schemes and attitude surveys, through more task-based initiatives such as team-working, to those practices which ostensibly offer employee influence at organisational level. Critically, Bowen and Lawler include employee share ownership (ESO) as an exemplar of organisational-level influence. Under contemporary conditions of comparative trade union weakness, growth of service-led organisations and heightened market competitiveness, it may be expected that managerially-driven participative initiatives would be prominent and it is clear from recent surveys that this is indeed the case. According to the authoritative *Workplace Employment Relations Surveys* (WERS), the proportions of companies using 'new' forms of employee participation has been growing in the UK (Cully *et al.* 1999). With Government tax incentive support, employers have continued to be encouraged to adopt employee share allocation systems. Financial participation incentives have been accompanied by the spread of 'new management' philosophies and strategies. In the 1998 WERS, well over half of workplaces with over 25 employees claimed to have five or more 'new' management and participation practices involving direct communication or consultation with employees. In the 2004 WERS, these practices have been maintained and, indeed, 'seemed to have generally become more prevalent over the period' (Kersley *et al.* 2006: 143). There is little doubt that managers and policy-makers include share ownership among desirable employee initiatives and equate share ownership with employee commitment and organisational performance. With New Labour, this direction was confirmed ten years ago, when the freshly appointed UK Chancellor of the Exchequer, Gordon Brown, made a bold assertion of his desire to 'double the number of firms in which all employees have the opportunity to own shares' (*Financial Times*,

4 November 1998) as a key policy aspiration to capture the commitment of employees.

Ten years of New Labour and 30 years of financial participation practice provide a good opportunity to examine the extent and effects of adoption of financial participation in this country as well as to explore developments elsewhere. The chapter first considers the impact of flexible pay linked to organisational profits, but with no ownership element, commonly known as profit-related pay. We then consider in more depth the rationale for employee share schemes and their recent history in this country. We also have the opportunity to examine recent research findings to see whether, after a generation of active governmental promotion and employer adoption, we are any closer now to providing a definitive understanding of the effects of share ownership on employee attitudes and behaviour.

Profit-related pay

Before focussing on employee share schemes, we consider profit-related pay, a related strand of financial participation, which continues to be attractive to employers in the UK, despite governmental withdrawal of tax concessions for profit-related financial bonuses. Profit-related pay simply means that employees receive a proportion of their income derived from the profits of the organisation. This approach is also common in other countries, notably Japan. In Europe, the highest incidence of profit-sharing is found in France, where 57 per cent of companies were found to use profit-sharing, principally because this approach is legally required in companies with more than 50 employees (Cahill 2000: 6).

Tax-exempt schemes were introduced in the UK in 1987 by the then Conservative Government keen to encourage greater pay flexibility, but these schemes were phased out in 2000, following growing concerns of lost tax revenue and allegations that the concessions were privileging professional and executive management groups rather than providing effective incentives for all employees. Nevertheless, 36 per cent of WERS-2004 respondents in the commercial sectors claimed to offer profit-related bonuses, concentrated in the highly competitive financial (67 per cent of respondents) and utilities sectors (59 per cent) and in half of overseas-owned enterprises (Kersley *et al.* 2006: 192–3). Despite the loss of tax advantages, these figures show little change from the 1998 WERS survey. Unlike employee share schemes, pay supplements based on organisational performance offer purely financial incentives and rewards and do not involve any transfer of ownership to employees. For this reason, profit-sharing schemes are usually viewed as providing a short-term incentive for employees rather than as a means to secure longer-term normative commitment to the enterprise.

For employers, two main benefits have been associated with profit-related pay. First, it may be associated with enhanced employee performance (Kruse 1996; OECD 1995), though direct causal links between the two have been questioned in other studies (Cahill 2000: 11). An American study which identified increased productivity in companies with profit-sharing also acknowledged that research design flaws and an inability to identify the mechanisms through which profit-sharing operates present significant limitations to the analysis (Shepard 1994). A linking strand to the productivity perspective suggests that positive employee behaviour and orientations to the company can be associated with profit-related pay, though empirical studies which test these relationships have again been mixed in their findings (Coyle-Shapiro *et al.* 2002). However, several studies claim that profit-sharing combined with other participative approaches can contribute to employee commitment and organisational performance (Levine and Tyson 1990). Second, through profit-sharing, pay may be more sensitive to organisational performance and thereby can contribute to employment stability. The previous Conservative Government was attracted toward profit-related pay as an attempt to loosen pay rigidity and to encourage flexibility in the labour market, thereby helping product market changes to be met by adjustments in marginal remuneration rather than by labour-shedding. This process was conceptualised as helping to resolve problems of both inflation and unemployment (Weitzman 1984, 1985). However, there is little evidence to suggest that this macroeconomic outcome has occurred in practice (Wadhwani 1985; Blanchflower and Oswald 1986).

Advantages and drawbacks to employees have also been noted. The main potential incentive is based on a visible and tangible link between organisational performance and employee reward, though the incentive effect may be undermined by the free-rider problem that all employees benefit irrespective of contribution. It is also contended that lack of pay stability can adversely affect employee orientations to the enterprise, added to which there is argued to be an inherent transfer of risk from owners to employees under profit-sharing (Cahill 2000).

In summary, from its long history, it is clear that profit-sharing in some form will continue in most countries and that in association with other progressive human resource policies, may well act as a positive incentive and can improve productivity. There is no evidence that profit-sharing has adverse organisational or employment effects.

The rationale and history of employee share schemes

From an employer's perspective, the principal rationale for ESOs is to demonstrate unity of interest, purpose and action between owners, managers and employees and in this way, aim to 'modify employee attitudes and behaviour' (Pendleton 2005: 75) but with less obvious emphasis on employee monitoring and supervision than is encountered in more traditional work settings. For these reasons, historically, ESOs have been opposed in principle by trade unions and their sympathisers and indeed, the earliest schemes were introduced by employers over 100 years ago to deter or deflect collectivist employee pressures at times of economic growth and labour shortages (Ramsay 1977). Unions are also opposed to ESO on grounds of multiple jeopardy in that share schemes can tie up workers' jobs, remuneration and savings, all of which can be put at risk in the event of enterprise falter or failure. There is also a lack of direct link between employees' contribution and reward, potentially exacerbated by the time lag which exists before share income accrues to participants. Moreover, share prices (and therefore employee income) may be affected by factors such as interest rate changes, over which employees exercise no influence. For the trade unions themselves there is the fear of marginalisation as direct communication channels between the company and its staff are established through employee status as shareholders. Notably in the USA, there can be further risk to employees, past and present, in that ESOs often provide a principal source of retirement benefits. A collapse in the share price can leave current and retired staff unprotected, as happened, notoriously, in the Enron case.

Theoretically, ESO has been informed principally from economic and sociological perspectives. These can be summarised as follows:

- Under utility theory, employee enthusiasm for shared ownership can be related to their orientations to risk and to effort. It is argued that less risk-adverse and more effort-conscious employees should be attracted to flexible remuneration and revenue sharing (Pencavel 2001; Oxera Consulting 2007).
- Sautner and Weber (2006) specify more closely the role of individual behaviour in exercising share options or allocations and identify 'a set of rational and psychological variables [such as risk aversion, mental accounting] as factors in whether employees and managers retain or dispose of their allotted shares.'
- Economic theory assumes that employees are instrumentally motivated to work harder if they perceive that their greater efforts can be linked directly to financial reward. For this reason, profit-sharing which provides for financial bonuses to be linked to measures of group performance are associated with short-term incentives, whilst ESO which offers deferred returns can be seen as an indirect and long-term incentive through securing a feeling of company identification (Gregg and Machin 1988; Baddon *et al.* 1989: 12).
- Sociological theory is divided along two main dimensions. On one hand is the unity of interests argument which suggests that ESO helps confirm the essential shared interests of all stake-holders to the enterprise. This unitarist approach is much favoured by free-market advocates and their political sympathisers.
- Conversely there is the 'cycles of control' argument famously proposed by Ramsay (1977, 1983). Ramsay's thesis was that managerial interest in participation, and specifically profit-sharing, could be shown historically to be directly related to threats of collective organisation and action

which could occur at times of tight labour markets. Managerial interest dwindled once these threats passed and economic conditions were again more advantageous to them.

- The 'cycles' thesis has been subject to considerable academic scrutiny, particularly from Marchington and his colleagues in the 1980s (Ackers *et al.* 1992; Marchington 2005: 23) when ESO was resurgent but collective labour posed little or no challenge to management. These authors argued that participation approaches were applied in 'waves' according to a range of management objectives sensitive to market needs and economic conditions, and with schemes ebbing and flowing, replacing and often over-lapping one another depending on management priorities and assessments. Among these, managerial responses to collective labour activity may represent a negligible or unstated factor.

These debates still continue without resolution (Pendleton 2005) though possibly in less urgent terms as ESO has nestled down as an integral part of the organisational policies of considerable numbers of large and economically vibrant companies. Financial participation can be broadly allocated into three different types: those that offer shares to employees; those that provide for employees to buy company shares; and those like profit-related pay or gainsharing that offer no equity but provide additional financial remuneration based on some measure of collective performance.

The remainder of this chapter focuses on share-based financial participation. Performance-related schemes which are established on individual employee performance are also common and are considered in depth in Chapter 6 of this volume. The contemporary sustained policy initiative for allocating company equity to employees began in 1978 with the introduction of so-called *Approved Profit Sharing* (APS), in which Inland-Revenue tax concessions were offered to employers operating share allocation schemes open to all full-time employees who satisfied specified eligibility criteria. APS experienced successively improved tax relaxations over the years, but in 2002 was phased out to be replaced by *Share Incentive Plans* (SIPs) which also incorporate an associated share allocation approach, *Employee Share Ownership Plans* (ESOPs) which allow employees to receive or to purchase higher proportions of shares than are usually associated with APS. For this reason, ESOPs did not prove popular with employers. The option approach, also termed *Save As You Earn* (SAYE), first introduced in 1980, allows all eligible employees the option of purchasing company shares at discounted rates through regular savings made at an approved savings institution, such as a Building Society or of receiving their accumulated cash savings. Options can be exercised at the end of three, five or seven years. A modified approach to SAYE is the company share option plan (CSOP), which provides for employers to select potential participants. Recognising that share schemes were approaching saturation point in large enterprises, so that government policy of doubling the number of participating companies would be near impossible to achieve without further reform, share option arrangements were made more accessible to small and medium enterprises with assets of less than £30 million through *Enterprise Management Incentives* introduced in the 2000 Finance Act. The declared aim of these plans was to help SMEs to recruit and retain high-quality staff.

Numbers of schemes approved by HM Revenue and Customs are shown in Table 10.1 below.

Take-up of employee share schemes

As we have seen the contextual policy and economic conditions for ESO have been favourable in the UK for a number of years. ESO schemes are invariably launched at the initiative of management and in recent years, these have faced little resistance from unions, who, despite their formal opposition, are usually accommodating at enterprise level because their members are usually in favour and provided the schemes do not replace or injure pay bargaining, unions tend to accept them on a pragmatic basis at enterprise level. As shown above, there is clear evidence from successive WERS surveys, that during recent years of economic liberalism, union decline and management ascendancy, employers have enjoyed the freedom to introduce a wide range of enterprise-level 'high commitment' initiatives. As part of the liberalisation process, policy endorsement by both Conservative and Labour governments has been demonstrated in continuing, though limited, relaxation of tax requirements on employee share schemes.

Under these favourable conditions, take up of share schemes has been fairly constant. The 2004 WERS indicates that about one-fifth of trading organisations operate an ESO with SAYE (13 per cent) being the most commonly reported type of scheme. Eight per cent of workplaces operated a SIP, but less than one per cent has an EMI, the scheme designed to encourage SME financial participation (Kersley *et al.* 2006: 191). The main distribution patterns found in the 2004 WERS study were that shared ownership is most likely to be adopted in large enterprises, with ESOs used in two-thirds of

Table 10.1 HMRC-approved financial participation schemes (2005–6)

Name of scheme	Main features	Numbers approved
Share incentive plans	all employee share allocation	760
Savings-related schemes	all employee share options	780
Company share option plans	selective options	2420
Enterprise management incentives	options for SMEs	6880

Source: HRMC Administrative database, June 2007: (http://hwww.hmrc.gov.uk/stats/emp-_share_schemes/companies.pdf)

companies employing more than 10,000 staff. ESOS were also common in large companies that recognise trade unions, in the service sector generally and in specific sectors such as finance. They were also more common in overseas-owned corporations. In all cases, high levels of market competition were also consistent with ESO usage. Notwithstanding the tax concessions and simplified procedures offered to SMEs by *Enterprise Management Incentives*, the adoption size effect is still apparent and there was very little evidence of any significant impact of ESO among SMEs, with less than one per cent of the sample having adopted these schemes. Possible explanations are that larger companies have more sophisticated and well-resourced personnel and especially financial-control systems than their smaller counterparts. Research has shown that chief executives and company finance directors are instrumental in establishing and controlling employee share schemes (Baddon *et al.* 1989: 249). Larger companies also enjoy the attractions of an open market for trading shares. While it is clear that the profiles of companies (in terms of size and sector) deploying share schemes are little different from those of the early days of Brown's chancellorship, not all has remained static in the world of financial participation and employee ownership. There are few signs of decline despite some well-publicised collapses such as Enron and companies which adopt share schemes tend to retain them (Kersley *et al.* 2006). Furthermore, the EU continues to endorse the value of employee share schemes and rapidly developing countries such as India and China are beginning to introduce forms of employee ownership as part of their remunerative practice (see e.g. Cooke 2005).

The attractions of ESO

As indicated above, ESO is invariably encouraged and established through the efforts and direction of senior management. Linked to the theoretical perspectives outlined above, Baddon *et al.* (1989: 81) suggested four main linked objectives sought by management through ESO, namely: motivational, attitudinal, defensive/deterrent against collective employee organisation or action; and ownership as an objective in itself, but through which other objectives may be directly associated. Thus ownership through share acquisition offers a 'stake in the company' (Creigh *et al.* 1981) so that employees may be less inclined to think attitudinally in terms of 'them' (owners) and 'us' (workers) as all contributors will share equal status as property owners. Also, it may be expected that share schemes can offer the means for an equitable resolution for distribution of returns to all stake-holders for their inputs. Rather than disputing the division of the profit 'cake', collective endeavour is focussed on enlarging the cake to the benefit of all participants to the enterprise. Similarly, it may be expected that behavioural divisions between hierarchical superiors and staff will be diffused as the former will be encouraged by senior managers to think of their charges as co-owning colleagues rather than as employees to be controlled. A minority of owners have gone further by adopting a moral position over ownership, believing that producers have the right to equal ownership of their companies and hence provide facilities for complete or majority share distribution among employees. The best-known of these shared enterprises in the UK is the John Lewis Partnership.

Ownership may also provide a platform for more extensive and productive employee involvement with expectations that co-owning employees will be willing to contribute their ideas and suggestions for enhanced performance on the basis of shared benefit. In short, it is expected that ownership of shares will encourage employees to think and behave in unitarist rather than oppositional or obstructive ways to workplace reform for the benefit of all stakeholders to the enterprise and by extension to the economy as a whole.

The consequences of ESO

As can be seen, a substantial number of employers and policy-makers are attracted ideologically and practically to ESO. But what are the benefits of encouraging employees to share in the ownership of their companies? Numerous studies have been conducted in most of the countries where financial participation schemes have been adopted, and from these we can identify two main streams of findings: those that detect a positive effect from their use and those whose findings are less certain. Positive findings are usually associative in their claim that organisational performance tends to be higher in those organisations which adopt ESO compared with those which do not and a causal link between the two phenomena is assumed. Qualitative studies based predominantly on case studies tend to examine specific effects attributed to ESO adoption, such as attitudinal or behavioural changes consequent upon adoption of employee share schemes, but these studies find less convincing evidence of impact. One important conclusion does emerge from both sets of findings: equity sharing *per se* is not sufficient to exert a defined effect, but under appropriate conditions, a positive association with attitudinal, behavioural and performance attributes may be identified.

Positive findings

In a study of 52 UK-located engineering companies, Cable and Wilson (1989) found enhanced productivity associated with profit-sharing. Based on an analysis of the UK WERS 1998, Conyon and Freeman (2004) reported significant productivity effects, especially for share option schemes. Positive productivity impacts have also been reported by Kruse (2002), Fernie and Metcalf (1995) and Perotin and Robinson (2000). A major study commissioned by HLM Revenue & Customs conducted by Oxera Consulting also pointed to positive productivity impacts (2007). Other studies have examined movements in share prices and conclude that share price increases are higher in companies with share-scheme arrangements than those without (Richardson and Nejad 1986; Equity Incentives Ltd 2003).

In North America, a comprehensive range of statistical analyses have been undertaken to examine links between share schemes and company performance (e.g. see Logue and Yates 2001). A recent study by Sesil *et al.* is especially relevant as it examined the role of share schemes in a set of 'new economy' knowledge-based companies, i.e. those enterprises predicted to become dominant in developed economies and ones where it can be assumed that employee behavioural and expertise inputs can directly influence company performance (Sesil *et al.* 2002: 274; Newell *et al.* 2002). Comparing share scheme companies with their non-share counterparts, the authors found greater added value per employee, but not greater new-knowledge generation (Sesil *et al.* 2002: 289). The authors also offered a number of *caveats* to their study: the mechanisms for the higher added-value were not known; also, whilst added value was higher it was not known whether the share scheme was the causal factor. The authors also make a general point which has been raised in previous studies: 'the "arrow of causality" issue plagues research of this type and there are no easy ways to address the issue' (2002: 290). Further, there were data and measurement shortcomings in that the researchers could not be certain that the schemes were broad based, i.e. distributed to a majority of staff.

Other American studies have been conducted by share scheme ideologues, keen to demonstrate associations between equity ownership and performance. Thus Logue and Yates (2001), who dedicate their book to employee owners 'who are building a better way of doing business every day', aim to identify the 'best' employee ownership practices to ensure optimum levels of economic performance. Examining a sample of 270 mainly small companies, positive links between share schemes and company performance were found. There were empirical weaknesses, however: data was gathered from senior managers who were instrumental in the establishment of the scheme and more worrying, perhaps, was that other intervening variables (such as threats of shutdown or takeover) appeared to influence the associations.

A further doubt concerning this generally positive reporting of share schemes is that very few studies have examined their impact on employees in adverse conditions. In the USA, for example, rather than shares enriching employees for their retirement, the Enron collapse effectively impoverished them. Also the collapse of United Airlines, a prominent employee-owned company, prompted serious questions as to whether the levels of employee shareholding actually *contributed* to the company's collapse (Ownership Associates 2003). In recent years, in the UK, company share values have fluctuated considerably. Employees who were facing redundancy at the collapsing Marconi company in 2001 saw the value of their shares dwindle by 97 per cent over the previous year (CIPD 2007). London Bridge Software, a 'knowledge' company, employed 200 people and offered share options to employees. Share values peaked at £10 in August 2000 but by November 2002, had subsided to a value of 35p, provoking a company executive to comment that: 'their options are underwater at the moment ... It is something we are looking at – how do we keep these people incentivised?' (*The Guardian* 2002).

Hodson (2001: 180) cites numerous studies which provide evidence for higher productivity, performance and employee satisfaction because of 'the genuine overlap between the goals of the enterprise and those of employees'. He also suggests that share schemes can help to lubricate communication between the parties, give support to team-working and encourage employees to adopt favourable positions toward task participation. Nevertheless, again, cautious interpretation is needed: Hodson refers to employee-*owned* enterprises, not to the vast majority of conventional companies where employees acquire a small financial stake in the enterprise as part of their overall remuneration. In these cases, there is less evidence of positive associations between share schemes and behavioural outcomes, with the opportunistic selling of shares by employees in conventional schemes and the rating of them primarily for their 'bonus' value both suggesting a less than binding relationship between employees and employers (Baddon *et al.* 1989).

Equivocal findings

A crucial assumption in the management literature is that financial participation can effect changes in employee attitudes and behaviour, thus improving company performance. Numerous studies have failed to demonstrate a direct causal linkage between share ownership, employee attitudes and behaviour and organisational performance (see McHugh *et al.* 2005). Others suggest only a partial or limited impact. Hence, in their 2001 study based on the 1998 WERS, Addison and Belfield (2001) found little evidence of an ESO effect, confirming the findings of earlier studies by Blanchflower and Oswald (1987) and Baddon *et al.* (1989). SenGupta *et al.* (2006) found that ESO is not significantly associated with employee commitment to the organisation, though they did find that ESO helped to restrict labour turnover. There are a number of contended and complex areas along this causal path; the association between ownership and attitude change, between attitude change and changes in employee behaviour, and between attitude change and company performance. Hence, Keef (1998: 73) found that share ownership 'did not result in the expected improvement in attitudes'. It is useful to examine each of these elements and their interaction to gain a better understanding of the dynamics of ESO.

Explanations for absence or weak impact of ESO

Low levels of property rights

Share schemes such as SAYE and SIPS aim to offer stock ownership to employees who are then expected to build up their shareholding over time, increasing their stake and hence personal interest in the fortunes of the company. This raises two main issues. The first concerns the value of the shares allocated to employees and the second the extent to which employees retain their shareholdings. Financial value can be examined along two main dimensions: in terms of the proportion of total individual remuneration represented by equity distributions and second, as a proportion of the aggregate equity distribution made by the enterprise.

We do know that the value of shares distributed to employees under Inland Revenue approved SIPs and their ADST predecessor schemes is not high, though there have been few recent studies which examine in depth the value of shares allocated to employees. Inland Revenue data suggest that there has been little change in equity ownership patterns. In 1995/6 the mean shareholding value per ADST participant was £640. In 2002/3, this figure was £100 less, at £540. For SIPs, the 2005 figure was an average £460 free shares, supplemented by £80 of partnership and £70 of matching shares. Mean SAYE values were higher: in 2005/6, average share values were £3,800 compared with £3,200 ten years earlier (HMRC 2007). However, it should be remembered that SAYE figures do not represent added remuneration but derive from voluntary regular savings contributions made by scheme participants. Perhaps a more useful measure of relative income associated with equity is the proportion of total employee remuneration that share scheme equity represents. This has been calculated at between 2 and 6 per cent of total employee income (IDS 1998; Baddon *et al.* 1989). Writing in 2005, Pendleton estimated that equity transfer to employees is usually less than 5 per cent (2005: 87). As tax relaxations have been marginal over the years and total earned income has increased, it is unlikely that this relatively small proportion will have altered greatly and from the figures given above, as a proportion of total income, the percentage figure represented by shareholdings would have declined. The link to remuneration is important as ESO assumes an alignment in interests between workers and employers and 'for most workers, the amount of capital they own is far less than is necessary to result in a greater return from their assets in the firm rather than their role as workers' (SenGupta *et al.* 2006: 4). It is perhaps not surprising therefore that research indicates that contrary to management hopes, employees may regard their relatively low level of equity as a gratuity or bonus offered to them by their employers (Bell and Hanson 1987; Baddon *et al.* 1989), and not sufficient to create feelings of ownership. A modest proportion of share-holding may also be associated with low levels of organisational identification, a dynamic sometimes referred to as the 'free-rider' problem, in which insufficient congruity of interest is generated by share ownership as individual employees feel unable to exercise any significant influence over performance processes or outcomes and hence are insufficiently motivated to raise their own performance on the utilitarian grounds that so doing would make no difference to organisational behaviour.

The second dimension of employee share ownership concerns employee share allocations as a proportion of aggregate distributed equity, based on the arguable assumption that higher share proportions are linked to greater capacity to influence organisational decisions. It has been contended that the positive motivational effects attributed to share ownership will only be triggered by significant shareholdings (Ramsay *et al.* 1990). Pendleton *et al.* (1998) agree that when the level of ownership is sufficient to produce 'feelings of ownership', higher levels of commitment and satisfaction are observable. It is relevant that employee-owned enterprises and cooperatives do tend to demonstrate a stronger ownership effect, though other factors such as the origins and philosophy of the emergent organisation are also pertinent factors (Carter 1990; Oliver and Thomas 1990). Pendleton and his colleagues found significant positive associations between share ownership and employee commitment in 'companies where significant portions of equity had been transferred to employees and some control had been passed to employee representatives' (2005: 84). A similarly positive finding is reported by Bradley and Nejad (1989) in their evaluation of the effects of employee shareholding in a privatised freight concern where employees, initially at least, held substantial proportions of company stock. Nevertheless, in conventional schemes, employee shares as a proportion of total distributed equity are low. In their study of 108 companies with all-employee schemes Baddon *et al.* (1989: 65) found that over half offered less than 1 per cent of equity to their employees.

A further indication of a sense of ownership among employees is demonstrated by patterns of share retention. Those who see themselves as genuine part-owners of the enterprise might be expected to retain and accumulate their stock, whilst more instrumental or opportunistic motives could be associated with share release, especially after qualifying periods for tax concessions have been attained. Many studies indicate a quick release of equity by employees (Baddon *et al.* 1989: 290–1). A newspaper reported that as many as two-thirds of employees 'cash in their share schemes at the first chance' (*The Guardian*, 4 November 1998: 16). With all-inclusive schemes manual employees are most likely to sell their shares and to do so quickly (Baddon *et al.* 1989: 206–15). Managers are most likely to acquire and retain shares, whether through loyalty to the company or for opportunistic or ideological reasons (Ramsay *et al.* 1990; Nichols and O'Connell Davidson 1992). From the perspective of acquiring shares in option schemes, managers are likely to have more disposable income than manual workers in order to purchase company equity. Nevertheless, managerial behaviour can be closely tied to financial conditions through a complex 'set of rational and psychological variables' (Sautner and Weber 2006: 8). In their study of 70 senior managers in a large German corporation, Sautner and Weber concluded that option schemes offer a very limited incentive effect because their case study managers 'exercise their stock options very early and in a small number of transactions. A larger majority of option recipients sell their shares acquired on exercise' (2006: 26).

It appears then that whilst share schemes do offer employees and managers property rights in the company, levels of ownership are not high. Even with higher levels there may be problems. Hartley (1992: 302) maintains that employee owners may be unwilling to 'make hard decisions' or to discipline colleagues, and furthermore that factionalism will develop. Hartley (1992) continues that employees may also resist taking orders from managers, because owner-employee views formally hold equivalent weight in the decision-making process. Further, where there is a significant element of employee ownership, a manager may feel constrained from exercising authority or from requesting an employee-owner to perform certain tasks. We now look in more depth at the contention that ownership may influence employee behaviour and attitudes.

Ownership, attitudes and behaviour

Of all the assumptions made in the literature of financial participation, the least questioned has been the link between attitude change and behaviour change (Pendleton *et al.* 1998). Pendleton *et al.* point out that positive attitudes towards employee ownership do not necessarily equate with more positive attitudes to work. Guest *et al.* (1993) have also criticised the frequent use of this dubious assumption in the literature. If the validity of this process is questioned, it then casts doubt on the link between financial participation, attitudes and performance. If participation fails to produce attitude changes in employees it may also fail to induce behavioural changes associated with enhancing productivity or reducing company costs, e.g. through reductions in absenteeism and labour turnover. Studies show that links between ownership, employee orientations to work and company, and employee behaviour are complex, dynamic and variable. Attitude and behavioural changes are not uniform and differ between forms of participation used and between different employees. Ben-Ner and Jones (1995) discovered that financial or autonomy rewards affected employees differently; some workers exhibited a more instrumental approach to participation and therefore responded better to financial rewards, others responded more positively when they were offered extra control over their jobs, or a say in company decisions.

Nevertheless, numerous studies point to a direct positive relationship between share schemes and employee behaviour, though for many this relationship can be highly qualified. Thus, in their study by share scheme advocates Hanson and Watson, the performance of 113 publicly quoted share scheme companies was compared with that of 301 non-participating companies and the authors were in no doubt that the share scheme companies out-performed the non-participants over a range of criteria. Moreover, the performance of these companies improved following the introduction of shared ownership (Hanson and Watson 1990). Qualification comes in the authors' comments that the 'apparent correlation between profit-sharing and superior performance may be *entirely* due to any one of several omitted factors' (Hanson and Watson 1990: 180, emphasis added). Further multiple qualification of the relationship is offered in Bell and Hanson's comments that: '*most* managers we have met in profit-sharing companies have said that, *at least* to a modest extent, profit-sharing, as *part* of their total employee participation arrangements, has had *some* effect' (Bell and Hanson 1987: 6, emphasis added).

Other commentators argue that any impact by ESO on attitudes or behaviour depends on the prevailing economic environment (Vaughan-Whitehead 1995) and crucially, on links with processes established for employee influence at work: for, as Strauss (1998: 20) comments on the basis of a review of financial participation studies: 'employee-owned companies are often undemocratic, since employees have few control rights' under financial participation alone. These views are reinforced by a recent study by Michie *et al.* (2002) of 101 companies with extensive employee ownership. The authors found that ownership alone makes little difference to employee orientations to work: the principal impact on motivation and productivity arose when financial participation was associated with genuine employee 'voice' mechanisms which allowed them individually and collectively to exert an influence on organisational affairs.

Similar patterns are demonstrated in North American studies: higher performance in organisations with employee share ownership, coupled with doubts about the identity of the organisational catalysts which contribute to higher performance. Blasi *et al.* (1996) identify 27 studies which examine relationships between employee ownership and measures of performance. The results were mixed with cooperative ventures that have high levels of employee ownership and control offering the most positive signs of impact on employee behaviour. These findings match those from some recent co-operative studies which suggests that producer co-operative participants, i.e. the owners, are less risk adverse than employees in conventionally owned enterprises and are prepared to work harder in order to ensure the co-operative's survival (Pencavel 2001). With more conventional ownership, including ESOPs, Blasi *et al.* conclude that: 'few of these studies have individually found strong and statistically significant effects of employee ownership on performance' (1996: 63).

Conclusions: what purposes do employee share schemes serve?

In the light of the above evidence, we can suggest that under some fairly specific circumstances shared ownership does appear to exert a positive effect on employee behaviour. Further, there is no evidence for any adverse effects of ESO on employees for companies with good share prices and trading profitably (Kruse 2002). Favourable circumstances for ESO are also associated with high levels of employee ownership, and these are usually coupled with organisational mechanisms to ensure that ownership is matched by some measure of employee influence. Nevertheless, as we have seen, many schemes continue to operate with less generous share provisions, so it would be reasonable to enquire what benefits may be expected to accrue from these schemes.

For employers, share schemes can act as a signal to employees, and to prospective employees, that they can expect to share financially in the growth and success of their enterprises. This is especially important in the high-growth profitable sectors, such as finance, where competition for scarce labour is most intense. A second point is that there is evidence that as share options cannot be exercised immediately, schemes may reduce labour turnover and in this way help exert a positive impact upon performance (SenGupta *et al.* 2006). The counter to this of course is the proposition that otherwise disgruntled staff may simply wait until their equity matures before quitting and in the meantime operate at less than optimum performance. Other studies have shown, though, that both labour turnover and absentee-ism were lower in ESO companies than in their non-participating counter-parts (Wilson and Peel 1990). Another potential advantage for companies is that shares are allocated and dividends paid in line with company perform-ance, adding a degree of flexibility to employee remuneration which is independent of direct individual or collective negotiations over pay. Moreover, as ESO is not part of contractual remuneration, scheme managers are free to vary or even withdraw a programme according to their needs and priorities. From an ideological perspective, share schemes may encourage employees to think in terms of the salience of market relations and hence encourage their adaptability to changing economic circumstances and acceptance of sub-sequent organisational policies. From a theoretical point of view, Pendleton (2005: 91) contends that, in contrast to Ramsay's cyclical counter to trade union power, share schemes can be more associated with a reliance on 'market-based rather than relationship-based forms of regulation and governance' and that this growing emphasis provides an explanation for the growth and consolidation of ESO in the UK and USA.

Whilst it is difficult to isolate the effects of financial participation alone on employee motivation and performance, there is convincing evidence that there may be dynamic interaction between ESO and other progressive tech-niques which influence employee orientations to work. McNabb and Whitfield (1998: 171) found that employee involvement schemes could have a negative effect on company economic performance 'when introduced in isolation' from financial participation measures. They go on to add that the benefits claimed for financial participation alone are, however, often 'reflecting the effects of other participation factors' (1998: 172). The combination effect of participation measures is replicated in a number of other important studies (Levine and Tyson 1990; Kochan and Osterman 1994; Ichniowski *et al.* 1994; Fitzroy and Kraft 1995; Logue and Yates 2001). Bryson and Millward's (1997) study of employee involvement in small firms found that a combin-ation of profit sharing and direct employee involvement produced the greatest improvements in company performance. Ben-Ner and Jones (1995) provide evidence that the productivity effects of combination schemes probably require a tailored programme suited to the circumstances of the company, its market and employees.

In all of these studies financial participation provides an integral part of the participative or 'high commitment' cluster of human resource practices. Appelbaum (2002) also found combinations of financial and work-related participation associated with positive performance effects. In a recent study, Bryson and Freeman (2007) found positive associations between ESO and other forms of flexible remuneration. Pendleton (2001: 158) goes further: 'The suggestion that participation in decision-making is an essential accompaniment if share ownership is to bring about attitudinal change has been supported in study after study.'

Notwithstanding the reservations of trade unions, employees may also expect to gain something from these processes. As yet there is no evidence that share schemes undermine or compromise union activity or effectiveness (Pendleton 2005: 88), though of course, union representatives are rarely directly involved in the establishment or subsequent operation of schemes. At the same time, share schemes can enhance communication and information exchange which may serve both unions and employees in their dealings with employers. Also, irrespective of any 'ownership' effect, employees do appreciate the bonus element associated with successful share schemes. Whether the provision of these bonuses has any significant long-term impact on behaviour is still yet to be determined.

References

Ackers, P., Marchington, M., Wilkinson, A. and Goodman, P. (1992) 'The use of cycles? Explaining employee involvement in the 1990s', *Industrial Relations Journal*, 23/4: 268–283.

Addison, J. and Belfield, C. (2001) 'Updating the determinants of firm performance: estimation using the 1998 UK Workplace Employee Relations Survey', *BJIR* 39/3: 341–366.

Appelbaum, E. (2002) 'The impact of new forms of work organisation on workers', in G. Murray, J. Belanger, A. Giles and P. Lapointe (eds) *Work and Employment Relations in the High-Performance Workplace*, London: Continuum.

Baddon, L., Hunter, L., Hyman, J., Leopold, J. and Ramsay, H. (1989) *People's Capitalism? A Critical Analysis of Profit-Sharing and Employee Share Ownership*, London: Routledge.

Bell, D. W. and Hanson, C. G. (1987) *Profit-Sharing and Profitability*, London: Kogan Page.

Ben-Ner, A. and Jones, D. C. (1995) 'Employee participation, ownership and productivity: a theoretical framework', *Industrial Relations*, Vol. 34, No. 4, October: 532–554.

Blanchflower, D. and Oswald, A. (1986) *Profit-sharing – Can it Work?*, LSE Discussion Paper 255, London: London School of Economics.

Blanchflower, D. and Oswald, A. (1987) 'Shares for employees: a test of their effects', Discussion Paper 273, London: London School of Economics.

Blasi, J., Comte, M. and Kruse, D. (1996) 'Employee stock ownership and corporate performance among public companies', *Industrial and Labour Relations Review*, 50 (1): 60–80.

Bowen, D. E. and Lawler, E. E. (1992) 'The empowerment of service workers: what, why, how and when', *Sloan Management Review*, Spring: 31–39.

Bradley, K. and Nejad, A. (1989) *Managing Owners: The National Freight Company Buy-Out in Perspective*, Cambridge: Cambridge University Press.

Bryson, A. and Freeman, R. (2007) *Doing the Right Thing? Does Fair Share Capitalism Improve Workplace Performance?* Employment Relations Research Series 81, London: DTI.

Bryson, A. and Millward, N. (1997) *Employee Involvement in Small Firms*, London: Policy Studies Institute.

Cable, J. and Wilson, N. (1989) 'Profit-sharing and productivity: an analysis of UK engineering firms', *The Economic Journal*, Vol. 99, No. 396: 366–375.

Cahill, N. (2000) 'Profit-sharing, employee share ownership and gainsharing: what can they achieve?', Dublin: National Economic and Social Council, Research Series No. 4, May.

Carter, N. (1990) 'Changing ownership: meaning, culture, and control in the construction of a co-operative organisation', in G. Jenkins and M. Poole (eds) *New Forms of Ownership*, London: Routledge.

CIPD (2007) *Factsheet: Employee Share Ownership*, London: Chartered Institute for Personnel and Development.

Conyon, M. and Freeman, R. (2004) 'Shared modes of compensation and firm performance', in D. Card, R. Blundel and R. Freeman (eds) *Seeking a Premier Economy*, Chicago: University of Chicago Press.

Cooke, F. L. (2005) *HRM, Work and Employment in China*, London: Routledge.

Coyle-Shapiro, J., Morrow, P., Richardson, R. and Dunn, S. (2002) 'Using profit-sharing to enhance employee attitudes: a longitudinal examination of the effects on trust and commitment', *Human Resource Management*, 41 (4): 423–439.

Creigh, S., Donaldson, N. and Hawthorn, E. (1981) 'A stake in the firm', *Employment Gazette*, May: 229–236.

Cully, M., Woodland, S., O'Reilly, A. and Dix, G. (1999) *Britain at Work*, London: Routledge.

Equity Incentives Ltd (2003) London: Field, Fisher Waterhouse LLP.

Fernier, S. and Metcalf, D. (1995) 'Participation, contingent pay, representation and workplace performance: evidence from Great Britain', *British Journal of Industrial Relations*, 33 (3): 379–431.

The Financial Times (1998) 4 November: 4.

Fitzroy, K. and Kraft, K. (1995) 'On the choices of incentives in firms', *Journal of Economic Behavior and Organization*, 26 (1): 145–160.

Gregg, P. and Machin, S. (1988) 'Unions and the incidence of performance-linked pay schemes in Britain', *International Journal of Industrial Organization*, 6 (1): 91–107.

The Guardian (2002) 4 November: 16.

Guest, D., Peccei, R. and Thomas, A. (1993) 'The impact of employee involvement on organizational commitment and "them and us" attitudes', *British Journal of Industrial Relations*, 24 (3): 191–200.

Hanson, C. and Watson, R. (1990) 'Profit-sharing and company performance: some empirical evidence for the UK', in G. Jenkins and M. Poole (eds) *New Forms of Ownership*, London: Routledge.

Hartley, J. F. (1992) *Employment Relations*, London: Blackwell.

HMRC (2007) Available online: www.hmrc.gov.uk/stats/emp_share_schemes

Hodson, R. (2001) *Dignity at Work*, Cambridge: Cambridge University Press.

Ichniowski, C., Shaw, K. and Prennushi, G. (1994) *The Effects of Human Resource Management Practices on Productivity*, Mimeo: Columbia University.

IDS (1998) *Profit-sharing and Share Options*, Incomes Data Services, Study 641, January.

Keef, S. P. (1998) 'The causal association between employee share ownership and attitudes: a study based on the Long framework', *British Journal of Industrial Relations*, Vol. 36, No. 1: 73–82.

Kersley, B., Alpin, C., Forth, J., Bryson, A., Bewley, H., Dix, G. and Oxenbridge, S. (2006) *Inside the Workplace: Findings from the 2004 Workplace Employment Relations Survey*, London: Routledge.

Kochan, T. and Osterman, P. (1994) *The Mutual Gains Enterprise*, Cambridge, Mass.: Harvard Business School Press.

Kruse, D. (1996) 'Why do firms adopt profit-sharing and employee ownership plans?', *British Journal of Industrial Relations*, 34 (4): 515–538.

Kruse, D. (2002) 'Research evidence on the prevalence and effects of employee ownership', *Journal of Employee Ownership Law and Finance*, 14 (4): 65–90.

Levine, D. and Tyson, L. (1990) 'Participation, productivity and the firm's environment', in A. Blinder (ed.) *Paying for Productivity*, Washington DC: Brookings Institute.

Little, S., Quintas, P. and Ray, T. (eds) (2002) *Managing Knowledge*, London: Sage.

Logue, J. and Yates, J. (2001) *The Real World of Employee Ownership*, Ithaca: ILR Press.

McHugh, P., Cutcher-Gershenfeld, J. and Bridge, D. (2005) 'Examining structure and process in ESOP firms', *Personnel Review*, 34 (3): 277–293.

McNabb, R. and Whitfield, K. (1998) 'The impact of financial participation and employee involvement on financial performance', *Scottish Journal of Political Economy*, 45 (2), May: 171–187.

Marchington, M. (2005) 'Employee involvement: patterns and explanations', in B. Harley, J. Hyman and P. Thompson (eds) *Participation and Democracy at Work*, Basingstoke: Palgrave Macmillan.

Michie, J., Oughton, C. and Bennion, Y. (2002) *Employee Ownership, Motivation and Productivity*, Research report for Employees Direct, London: Birkbeck and the Work Foundation.

Newell, S., Robertson, M., Scarbrough, H. and Swan, J. (2002) *Managing Knowledge Work*, Basingstoke: Palgrave.

Nichols, T. and O'Connell Davidson, J. (1992) 'Employee shareholders in two privatised utilities', *Industrial Relations Journal*, 23 (2): 107–119.

OECD (1995) 'Profit-sharing in OECD countries', July, Paris: OECD Employment Outlook.

Oliver, N. and Thomas, A. (1990) 'Ownership, commitment, and control: the case of producer co-operatives', in G. Jenkins and M. Poole (eds) *New Forms of Ownership*, London: Routledge.

Ownership Associates (2003) 'But what about United Airlines? Answering tough questions.' Available online: www.ownershipassociates.com/united_questions.shtm (accessed 10 July 2007).

Oxera Consulting (2007) *Tax-advantaged Employee Share Schemes: Analysis of Productivity Effects*, Appendices to Report 1, HM Revenue and Customs Research Report 33.

Pencavel, J. (2001) *Worker Participation: Lessons from the Worker Co-ops of the Pacific Northwest*, New York: Russell Sage Foundation.

Pendleton, A. (2001) *Employee Ownership, Participation and Governance*, London: Routledge.

Pendleton, A. (2005) 'Employee share ownership, employee relationships and corporate governance', in B. Harley, J. Hyman and P. Thompson (eds) *Participation and Democracy at Work*, Basingstoke: Palgrave Macmillan.

Pendleton, A., Wilson, N. and Wright, M. (1998) 'The perception and effects of share ownership: empirical evidence from employee buy-outs', *British Journal of Industrial Relations*, 36 (1): 99–124.

Perotin, V. and Robinson, A. (2000) 'Employee participation and equal opportunities practice: productivity effect and potential complementarities', *BJIR*, 38/4: 557–584.

Ramsay, H. (1977) 'Cycles of control', *Sociology*, 11 (3): 481–506.

Ramsay, H. (1983) 'Evolution or cycle? Worker participation in the 1970s and 1980s', in C. Crouch and F. Heller (eds) *International Yearbook of Organisational Democracy: Organisational Democracy and Political Processes*, Chichester: Wiley.

Ramsay, H. (1983) 'Recycled waste: response to Ackers *et al.*', *Industrial Relations Journal*, 24 (1): 76–80.

Ramsay, H., Hyman, J., Baddon, L., Hunter, L. and Leopold, J. (1990) 'Options for workers: owner or employee?', in G. Jenkins and M. Poole (eds) *New Forms of Ownership*, London: Routledge.

Richardson, R. and Nejad, A. (1986) 'Employee share ownership schemes in the UK – an evaluation', *British Journal of Industrial Relations*, 23 (2): 233–250.

Sautner, Z. and Weber, M. (2006) 'How do managers behave in stock option plans? Evidence from exercise and survey data'. Available online: http://papers.ssrn.com/sol3/papers.cfm?abstract_id=890177#PaperDownload (accessed 8 July 2007).

SenGupta, S., Whitfield, K. and McNabb, R. (2006) 'Employee share ownership and performance: golden path or golden handcuffs?', Paper presented to the annual meeting of the Labour and Employment Relations Association, January, Boston.

Sesil, J., Kroumova, K., Blasi, J. and Kruse, D. (2002) 'Broad based employee stock options in US "New Economy" firms', *British Journal of Industrial Relations*, 40 (2): 273–294.

Shepard III, E. M. (1994) 'Profit-sharing and productivity: further evidence from the chemicals industry', *Industrial Relations*, 33 (4): 452–466.

Strauss, G. (1998) 'An overview', in F. Heller, E. Pusic, G. Strauss and B. Wilpert (eds) *Organizational Participation: Myth and Reality*, Oxford: Oxford University Press.

Vaughan-Whitehead, D. (ed.) (1995) *Workers' Financial Participation*, Geneva: International Labour Office.

Wadhwani, S. (1985) 'The macro-economic implications of profit-sharing: some empirical evidence', Discussion Paper 220, London: Centre for Labour Economics, London School of Economics.

Walton, R. E. (1985) 'From control to commitment in the workplace', *Harvard Business Review*, March–April: 77–84.

Weitzman, M. (1984) *The Share Economy*, Cambridge, Mass.: Harvard University Press.

Weitzman, M. (1985) 'The simple macro-economics of profit-sharing', *American Economic Review*, 75: 937–953.

Wilson, N. and Peel, M. (1990) 'The impact of profit-sharing, worker participation, and share ownership on absenteeism and quits: some UK evidence', in G. Jenkins and M. Poole (eds) *New Forms of Ownership*, London: Routledge.

Wolf, A. (2002) *Does Education Matter?*, London: Penguin.

11 International reward management

Paul R. Sparrow

Summary

Research on international compensation strategy has extended beyond expatriate compensation, to a larger group of the workforce. The chapter shows how the explanation of international differences in rewards management relies on either institutional or cultural explanations. Narratives around the *Kostenkrise* debate in Germany, and the *Risutora* process in Japan are examined to reveal the depth of knowledge that an in-country HR manager of a foreign multinational needs to understand the institutional web of influences on rewards behaviour. More recently, however, comparative analysis of rewards systems has attempted to understand the role of corporate strategy (across national contexts) and examine the workings of the 'black box' of internal labour markets and rewards behaviour. The chapter explores the theoretical links between national culture and rewards and reviews studies that link country-level national culture patterns to patterns of rewards practice, and studies that link national culture to important decision rules and attitudes within rewards systems.

Introduction

At the beginning of this decade the influence of national characteristics and contexts in the design of rewards systems was a neglected area of research and there were relatively few cross-national studies of rewards systems (Sparrow 2000; Lowe *et al.* 2002). In the first edition of this volume, Sparrow (2000) argued that the issue of international convergence in rewards systems was taking central stage. Research on the convergence and divergence of rewards policy inside organisations revealed pressures to alter the nature of internal rewards markets, the level at which pay determination took place and the institutional arrangements associated with corporate governance of rewards. Examples were provided to show how the collective process in Japan and sector-wide agreements operating in Germany were coming under attack. The original review made it clear that the evidence of international convergence around best practice varied depending on the level at which rewards systems were analysed. It was also argued that analysis of national rewards systems and policy convergence had to be tempered by an increasingly sophisticated awareness of factors, beyond just the institutional differences, that created distinctive individual rewards behaviours across countries. The review drew attention to a number of psychological factors that needed to be understood in a cross-cultural context, such as national value orientations, distributive justice, the concept of socially healthy pay, and the role of pay as a motivator. This chapter, written eight years after the original piece, therefore has three principal aims. It:

- reviews and updates research since 2000 that relates to institutional and cultural explanations of international rewards practice and behaviour;
- provides sufficient detail of study design and methodology to enable readers to make their own assessment of the general quality, strengths and weaknesses of this research;
- assesses the main messages about research methods and priorities that can be derived from recent research.

The pace at which organisations find themselves needing to develop effective international compensation programmes continues to accelerate. In the field of strategic international human resource management (SIHRM) in general, the traditionally separate research traditions that focused on multinationals and internationalisation of the firm, or on comparative differences in human resource management (HRM), have begun to cross-fertilise each other. This observation, it seems, can now also be applied to the field of international rewards. In part this is because compensation strategies have an increasingly important role to play in the delivery of multinational strategy, as argued from either an academic perspective (see for example Festing *et al.* 2007) or a practitioner perspective (see for example Beer and Katz 2003; Watson and Singh 2005):

> For many companies, maintaining a domestic compensation program that supports the strategic goals of the organisation and meets the needs of employees is a difficult challenge. This challenge is intensified when a similar program must be designed to operate in multiple countries with different cultures.
>
> (Watson and Singh 2005: 33)

In addressing these challenges, two trends can be observed:

1   research on international compensation strategy has extended beyond expatriate compensation, to a larger group of the workforce (Festing *et al.* 2007),
2   comparative analysis of rewards systems has attempted to understand the role of corporate strategy (across national contexts) and examine the

workings of the 'black box' of internal labour markets and rewards behaviour.

The problem remains however that simple comparisons of rewards practices across national HR systems are not really possible, or at best are misleading. There have been recent dialogues about international transfer of rewards philosophies, particularly with regard to: individual performance-related, merit pay and employee financial participation (Cin *et al.* 2003, Poutsma and de Nijs 2003; Long and Shields 2005; Brody *et al.* 2006; Ishii 2006; Abe 2007; Bozionelos and Wang 2007); executive remuneration, stock options and incentives (Beer and Katz 2003; Buck *et al.* 2004; Tosi and Greckhammer 2004; Bruce *et al.* 2005); and minimum wage (*The Economist* 2006b). These debates indicate that both the quality of organisational evaluation and the scope of academic research data do not stand up to scrutiny. The transfer of rewards policy and practice may therefore be based on weak assumptions or limited understanding of the likely effects.

Recent research has also witnessed developments in the theoretical bases used to examine international rewards issues. The explanation of international differences has long relied on either institutional or cultural explanations (Festing *et al.* 2007). Parboteeah and Cullen (2003) distinguish these contrasting perspectives as follows. Cultural explanations highlight the role of historically determined notions that are accepted by groups of individuals who share some common historical experience about what is good, right and desirable. Institutional explanations highlight the role of social structures (laws that provide enforcement, educational and training systems that shape socialisation, and economic systems that shape incentives) that help individuals make sense of, and in turn make decisions, that will be deemed legitimate, reasonable and appropriate. The relative importance of both sets of factors in shaping corporate governance has long been debated (Buck and Shahrim 2005) and some of the better recent work attempts to incorporate multiple sets of factors from both perspectives.

Rewards behaviour: what is generic and what is country-dependent?

Before we can make sense of the different impacts that institutional and national culture factors have on the various elements of rewards behaviour, we first need to clarify which elements of rewards behaviour might be deemed generic and which are country-dependent. Psychological analysis of rewards behaviour suggests there are *some* generic cross-cultural processes that relate to both pay satisfaction and the subsequent influence this has on work behaviour (Thierry 1998; Sparrow 2000; Brewster *et al.* 2007). For Thierry (1998) pay has four generic meanings. It:

1   carries motivational properties, in that people differ in the extent to which they see pay as a means of achieving important objectives;
2   signals relative position in relation to performance in comparison with others;
3   carries meaning in relation to the relative level of control an individual has;
4   carries meaning in terms of the utility it creates.

There are also some generic flexibility logics considered to operate at the organisational level, leading to common issues in pay flexibility strategies (Thierry 1998). The desire for greater ease in adjusting employees' or managers' pay has been driven by the desire to create connections between, and flexibility in, four issues: individual pay level and the organisation's success (or otherwise); pay focus and general strategic policy objectives; risk sharing between the organisation and employees' pay level and individual effort. Rewards flexibility delivers greater differentiation between individuals, teams or units within an organisation and greater market sensitivity of rewards.

Here the commonality tends to end. Although there may be some universal principles that relate to the *process* of motivation, the actual *level* of motivation (the willingness to exert effort in relation to the motivator) that is created by rewards and incentives systems is conditioned by a range of comparative factors. These factors have a differential impact on the extent to which effort that is exerted actually satisfies some individual need (Rehu *et al.* 2005). At the level of rewards *practice* (i.e. before one examines relevant institutional and cultural antecedents and functions) the following factors become important (Lawler 2000; Milkovich and Newman 2002; Brewster *et al.* 2007):

- The structure of pay systems: i.e. the different elements of pay (also called pay mix), the forms of payment, and actual pay levels.
- Climate factors, such as level of secrecy or participation.
- The extent to which a pay policy is integrated into the strategic context of the firm.
- The extent to which pay is tailored to other HRM policies such as selection, evaluation and management development.
- Internal and external labour markets. Within internal labour markets, pay structure is an important determinant of individual pay levels, whilst within external labour markets individual pay levels better reflect the value of the job or person in the market place.
- Job- or person-based pay structures. Within job-based structures, pay rates reflect relative internal (value determined by job evaluation) and external (value determined by market pay data) relativities. In person-based pay structures, it is personal performance and attributes (skills, knowledge and behaviour) that determines pay rates.

However, labour economists have long noted their lack of strong evidence about the operation of such internal wage markets (Baker and Holmström 1995; Treble *et al.* 2001; Grund 2005). To address this problem, Grund (2005) conducted a comparative analysis of wage policy in a German and US plant, from two separate firms but both under common ownership and having identical plant technology (i.e. looking at similar firms operating under different institutional frameworks), by analysing personnel records over a 20-year period (1978–98). First, some common principles in wage policy could be observed across country. Both firms had convex wage structure (this is where wage differentials become increasingly large the further up the hierarchy one goes) as predicted by human capital theory, i.e. the further up the hierarchy, the more complex the roles and the greater the potential impact on productivity, and also the greater the multiplier effect (efficiency incentive) on the productivity of lower levels of the hierarchy.

There the commonality ended. Whereas the total amount of wage inequality across hierarchies was similar, wage inequalities within hierarchical levels were larger in the US firm and explained by different factors. In the German firm there was a lower promotion rate and less intense within-grade competition. The effect of Works Councils on wage policy with regard to collective wage agreements and principles of performance-related pay was seen in the fact that '. . . in individual years, either almost every or hardly any employee receives real wage increases in the German plant. In contrast, the group of employees with real wage increases varies between 50 and 80 per cent in the US firm' (Grund 2005: 111). Monetary incentives were smaller in the German firm, and whilst education had a large effect on wages, general ability and effort did not play as important a role in wage levels as in the US firm. In short, the institutional influence on firm-level wage policy was very strong.

As evidence of such international differences in rewards structure, Table 11.1 below shows the percentage of companies adopting a range of four rewards practices from a sample of countries, based on 2004 data from the well-known Cranet survey.

To understand such international differences in reward, we need first to see the inter-dependencies between the institutional web of influences on rewards behaviour.

Understanding international differences in reward in their institutional context

The effect of such an institutional web is often only really understood when you attempt to change it. Two examples are used to exemplify the complex web of institutional factors within which international differences in rewards practice are embedded: the *Kostenkrise* debate in Germany, and the *Risutora* process in Japan. Throughout the two narratives, consider the depth of knowledge that an in-country HR manager of a foreign multinational needs to have to understand the inter-dependent institutional forces at play, let

Table 11.1 International differences in rewards practices based on Cranet data for 2004

Country	Use of individualised pay for performance for clerical employees	Team- or department-based pay for manual employees	Use of employee share ownership	Use of stock options for managers
United Kingdom	19.5	10	15.5	20.8
France	36	15	18.5	27
Germany	38	16	7	13
Sweden	11	14.5	4.5	11
Spain	22	17	0.5	17
Denmark	25	17	17.8	13.8
Netherlands	24	12	7.1	13
Italy	49	30	3.5	26.5
Norway	22	11	11.3	3.8
Switzerland	40.5	17	4.3	13.7
Turkey	18.5	4.5	1.8	4.4
Finland	23	22	2.2	14
Greece	41	13.5	7.8	30
Austria	32	12	4.8	13
Belgium	28	7	10.8	22
Australia	26	13.5	10.7	12.6
New Zealand	24	9.5	6.3	9
USA	23	8	7.5	30.5
Canada	18	5.5	6.7	15.5

After: Brewster *et al.* 2007

alone the likely psychological outcome of suggested convergent rewards processes.

The Kostenkrise *debate in Germany*

Institutional arrangements in Germany have come under a sustained period of pressure for change with the *Kostenkrise* at the centre of attention. The accumulated unit labour cost (ULC) disadvantage for Germany from the period 1989–96 amounted to 18 per cent. Of this disadvantage, 33 per cent was attributed to internal (non-currency value) labour cost factors, and of this, non-wage labour costs (which amounted to 80 per cent of direct wages in Germany) accounted for much of the increase. It was argued that Germany faced an exodus of capital in a globalising market and that this meant that domestic organisations had to reform wage systems. The Bundesverband der Deutschen Industrie (BDI) argued that German enterprise was blighted by high tax, wages and welfare costs. There was pressure to break up the 42,000 *tarifverträge* (conventional contracts that covered wage rates, bonuses and sick pay, training, part-time work, work hours and levels of job security).

These regulated German pay and compensation negotiations and were traditionally negotiated across employers within an industrial sector. However,
the number of firm-specific contracts negotiated with unions was increasing,
and exceptions that allowed pay rates in the east of Germany to be below
national rates were being established. As always, the view that reform was
being driven purely by labour cost and corporate taxation factors was incor-
rect. Qualitative factors such as the skills level of the workforce, density and
tightness of regulatory frameworks, market demand, geo-political location
and national culture all played a role. Only a small proportion of total foreign
direct investment was being driven by wage and related rewards/benefits factors. Moreover, flexibility deals, whilst clearly associated with new flexibilities
in rewards policy, were used to address a complex amalgam of skills, work
hours and employment security issues.

How has this debate in Germany evolved in recent years? The *Kostenkrise*
has been largely resolved, with German industry competitiveness back to pre-
Unification levels. Unit labour costs fell by 20 per cent relative to Italy and
Spain from 2001 to 2007. By 2006 growth in the German economy was 3 per
cent, the highest level since 2000, unemployment was falling, and pay rises
were finally rising. However, labour market reforms throughout the decade
have led to growth in 'mini-jobs', i.e. part-time posts paying no more than
€400 a month regardless of work hours (*The Economist* 2007). Temporary
jobs accounted for more than half of all jobs created in 2006. Wages continue
to be squeezed in the face of jobs export (primarily to Eastern Europe) and
from 2001 to 2007 the share of wages in national income fell from 60 per cent to
55 per cent. Between 1997 and 2004 the proportion of German workers
earning 'low pay' as defined by OECD rose from 16 per cent to 20 per cent.
This has led to a debate about issues such as a minimum wage. Germany does
not have a minimum wage system and has been looking to the UK model,
despite awareness that '. . . it is always risky to import reforms from another
country . . . because in a different environment, they may have unintended
consequences' (*The Economist* 2006b: 44). The unintended consequences that
might result derive from the fact that, even within a single national system,
a range of factors can obscure the officially recorded position and
mask the actuality of behaviour. For example, Croucher and White's (2007)
analysis of the mechanics of the UK minimum wage system highlighted
problems with enforcement arrangements. Moreover, when comparing across
countries, there may be institutional arrangements that provide a functional
equivalent. For example, in January 2006 the minimum wage was €8 an hour
in France, €7.8 in the Netherlands, €7.3 in the United Kingdom, €4.2 in the
United States, €3.8 in Spain and €1.3 in Poland. However, in Germany, the
absence of an official minimum wage is relieved by the benefit system, which
for the long-term unemployed has set up a de facto minimum wage. Benefits
amount to €5 an hour, but the Institute for the Study of Labour estimates
that given illegal employment opportunities, potential employers have to pay
an incentive of €10 an hour to attract labour.

In Germany, wage agreements have become more flexible. The two largest unions, IG Metall and Verdi, have been both militant but flexible, with IG Metall agreeing to exceptions from industry-wide wage deals and Verdi accepting pay for performance for civil servants (*The Economist* 2006a). A package of agreements on pay and job security was signed in November 2004 when the bargaining parties at Volkswagen agreed a deal estimated to save €1 billion per year in labour costs (Dribbusch 2004). This was after six rounds of negotiations and potential strikes involving about 100,000 employees. The compromise included concessions by IG Metall and a pay freeze until 2007 in exchange for a company promise to safeguard employment. Volkswagen agreed to make investments to secure the future of its German plants, in return for a 'collective agreement for the future' (*Zukunftstarifvertrag*) that safeguarded a level of 99,000 jobs plus apprenticeships at German plants until 2011. The Institute for Economic and Social Research considered arrangements at Volkswagen a landmark deal because of the acceptance of a future two-tier pay system which was at odds with traditional trade union principles such as equal pay. In the long run, the agreement will considerably lower pay levels at Volkswagen. Similar agreements have been made at Siemens, DaimlerChrysler and BMW.

Despite economic recovery, a May 2007 settlement with IG Metall was still modest. In a global context questions are still being asked about whether the country's low-qualification jobs are overpaid, with such jobs moving overseas, but at the same time, qualified jobs being associated with globally uncompetitive rewards, leading to a brain drain of professionals (*The Economist* 2007). Wage negotiations have become more idiosyncratic, with specialised professional organisations such as Cockpit (pilots) and Marburger Bund (doctors) growing in influence (*The Economist* 2006a). For example, an OECD study in 2004 showed German physicians earning 15 per cent less than counterparts in the UK, and 40 per cent less than US doctors. Globalization clearly has an indirect influence on the new context surrounding wage systems. The combination of skills shortages and rewards dissatisfaction has been linked to a mini-exodus of doctors moving from Germany to the UK and Scandinavia.

Despite reform labour unrest continues in Germany. Moreover, the economic recovery has been attributed to growth in overseas markets rather than wage reform, with the sobering economic conclusion that '. . . the labour market, for all its improvements, still needs further reform . . . it would be a mistake to get carried away by Germany's revival as it was to write the country off earlier in the decade' (*The Economist* 2007: 88).

The **Risutora** *process in Japan*

In Japan there have also been examples of significant change in rewards systems. Ten years ago Japan had changed from being a role model for HRM policies and practices, to a major target for those who argued that a break-up of national business systems was needed to restore competitiveness. Japan embarked on a restructuring process, called *risutora* (Dirks 1998), to revitalise its economy. Attention was focused on four HRM issues: the introduction of performance-based career and compensation standards; open feedback systems regarding performance evaluation; more differentiated employment tracks between core, specialist and flexible employment groups; externalisation of much corporate welfare; and non-discriminatory hiring practices.

To alleviate labour costs, Japanese firms reduced the level of overtime payments, and transferred more employees between companies. However, the pressures for convergence have been complex, and as with Germany, assumptions about global pressure on relative labour costs oversimplify the situation. Abe (2007) argues that reform was driven by technological innovation and changes in corporate governance. Ishida (2007) suggests wage reform in Japan has occurred as a consequence of business model change and the associated need for active involvement in wage system management by individual firms. Therefore, in parallel to wage system reforms, Japan has witnessed reforms to arrangements for employee and role grading systems, job and performance evaluation.

Some of the rewards problems facing Japanese organisations also reflect structural issues, such as demographic pressures. In Japan earnings vary over age groups, with older employees seeing earnings drop in comparison to middle-aged groups. Despite wage reforms, income distribution by age of household head has remained constant, such that '. . . the rise in the Gini coefficient can mostly be explained as a statistical outcome of Japan's rapidly ageing population' (*The Economist* 2006c: 67). Wage behaviour is intimately connected with demographic factors such as age. The current older generation in Japan experience more inequality as a cohort than they have before and have less to pass on to their children. For the younger generation entering work, the earnings experience over their lifetime is also changing. Historically, and currently, the recruitment process in Japan still emphasises recruitment directly after school or college, so once reaching the age of 30, a part-time worker in Japan finds it increasingly difficult ever to find a full-time job.

Surrounding the complex web of institutional reforms, there has been a development in the nature and definition of the whole Japanese HRM model itself. The key elements have been as follows. Historically there was an annual wage bargaining ritual, known as *shunto* (or spring labour offensive), so that wages increased uniformly across sectors. Awards were made irrespective of productivity. Basic wages in Japan make up about 70 per cent of total compensation but bonuses and overtime could offset wage moderation. In 2000 70 per cent of all tax revenue came from direct taxes on earnings in Japan, so the incentive impact of salaries was diminished, and the top individual tax rate was one of the highest in advanced economies.

Change in labour laws also led to significant change in the Japanese rewards system. From 1996 onwards performance-based pay systems could

242   *International reward management*

be considered and within a year there was some divergence from uniform agreements. Firms like Toyota offered well above the average, whilst Nissan and Honda fell behind. The seniority-based wage system was also coming under threat within organisations. Honda and Sony introduced pay systems placing greater emphasis on performance, Mitsubishi Corporation allowed the pay of managers of the same age to vary by plus or minus 10 per cent, and many firms introduced what on the surface resembled western-style performance-related pay schemes. Matsushita introduced the first tiered wage system in Japan which differentiated between those following a life-time employment 'contract', newcomers who wanted to bring forward and forgo the substantial retirement benefits, and those with specialist skills in demand who wished to contract-out of most age- and service-related benefits.

Japanese pay systems have continued to evolve. Hitachi, having first introduced a merit-based pay system to 5,000 managerial employees in 2000, abolished their seniority-based annual pay increase system in April 2004, implementing a merit-based system for over 30,000 non-managerial employees. Around the same time Matsushita Electric abolished its seniority-based pay system. Until 2002, 90 per cent of salary was determined by age alone, 5 per cent from rank, and another 5 per cent from performance within the rank. Under the new system, bonuses could vary by plus or minus 20 per cent based on performance.

In order to explain the nature of changes in Japanese HRM purely as they relate to rewards management, Suda (2007) teased out a range of comparative factors by contrasting the Japanese (organisation-based) and UK (market -based) rewards systems. In Japan, pay systems are more person and organisation based. Job-related ability pay (*shokumukyu*) is still dominant amongst Japanese employers. Suda (2007) cites a 2002 survey by Nippon Keidanren showing that 72 per cent of firms use this for non-managers and 70 per cent for managers. There is a qualification system that is based on job-related ability (*shokunou shikaku seido*). Qualifications divide employees into grades but are also generally specific to each organisation (internal). External market pay is generally not considered in individual pay determination. Individual factors that are considered also tend to be input factors (job-related abilities, age, service) rather than output factors (performance). Japanese pay systems also work on a stock as opposed to flow principle. In a stock-based system, the personal factors that determine pay progression reflect the sum of appraisal rating points over time or years of service in a grade (progressively developed stock). In a flow-based system, more prevalent in the UK, progression is based more on the current value of the employee.

The UK has a job- and market-based pay system. Suda (2007) cites CIPD survey data that show that in 2005 58 per cent and 54 per cent respectively of manufacturing and service firms link pay structure to individual job worth using either salary or spot rates linked to market rates. Evidence of a flow-based system is reflected in the fact that (in the private sector) 67 per cent of firms in manufacturing and 63 per cent of service firms manage pay progression on the basis of individual performance and skill/competency, whilst 30 per cent and 31 per cent respectively base it solely on individual performance.

However, whilst the UK pay system appears to have remained static, characterised as a job-, organisation- and flow-based system, continued evidence emerges for change in some of the structural and institutional features that surround Japanese HRM along with a shift from organisation-based to more market-based systems. Suda (2007) used analysis of existing large-scale surveys and some case studies to determine the extent of change. A 2002 Ministry of Health, Labour and Welfare survey found that an emphasis on lifetime employment (long seen as only applicable to a minority of firms) had fallen from being important for 32 per cent to 9 per cent of firms from 1993 to 2002. Similarly, pay levels of over 55 year olds compared to 22 year olds used to be six times higher in 1958, but such pay differentials have fallen consistently to a ratio of 4.27 higher by 1970, 3.78 by 1980, 3.46 by 1990 and only 3.06 by 2002. Data from the Japan Productivity Centre for Socio Economic Development (JPCSED) also support the view that '. . . if a broader concept of the job-based pay system is adopted, the use of the job-based pay system can be considered to be increasing' (Suda 2007: 593). JPCSED data also show that by 2002 61 per cent of firms focused most on performance output to determine managerial pay progression, suggesting a transition at this level to a flow-based system.

Developments in Japanese rewards practice have met with mixed success. This is because a number of organisational competencies become important to manage each element of reform. Such organisational competencies rarely form the basis of international rewards system research, but they are important comparative factors. Suda's (2007) analysis of 10 Japanese case studies suggests a phased process of pay system transition, whereby the initial changes shift the emphasis of person-based factors more towards a flow system and performance evaluation, followed by the introduction of more concrete standards to judge job grades, and finally the introduction of market factors to determine the objectivity of pay determination. Similarly, work by the Japan Institute for Labour Policy and Training and other research bodies shows that different competencies become important over time. Attention moves from the ability to demonstrate the logics of the new rewards system itself, to the fairness and competence of job evaluation procedures, the quality of performance appraisal objective setting and management skills, levels of risk avoidance behaviour, adjacent forms of labour market flexibility and also cultural factors such as employee preferences for rewards system design (Ishii 2006; Abe 2007; Ishida 2007).

The case of Japan also shows that international rewards system comparison is not really possible without understanding the wage system within the broader social contract. The social contract in Japan, based on lifetime employment (for a significant cadre, but never for the majority) and seniority-based pay, has slowly broken down as forces of internationalisation, global competition, demography, slowed economic growth, and periodic collapses in investment have put pressure on the HRM system. Takahashi (2006) characterised the old social contract in Japan as one based on slow promotion but low wage inequality. Consequently, the issue of income inequality, which has risen in Japan since the early 1980s, carries important implications. Using the Gini co-efficient, where zero represents equal pay for all households and one represents perfect inequality (a single household taking all income), then World Bank data (*The Economist* 2006c) shows that countries such as Denmark (0.23), Sweden (0.24) and the Netherlands (0.25) have some of the most equal distributions, France (0.27) and Germany (0.28) moderate levels of inequality. Countries such as Australia (0.31), Japan (0.32) and the United Kingdom (0.33) now have high levels of inequality. Japan's Gini co-efficient was 0.27 in 1979, comparable at the time to Scandinavian countries. The United States stands well beyond these countries with a Gini co-efficient of 0.41.

Takahashi (2006) notes, however, that many of the characteristics of Japanese rewards reform, seen as disincentivising in western organisations, still seem to be producing positive behaviours in Japanese organisations. How can this be? He draws upon two theoretical explanations that underpin the existing social contract and that might be used to explain recent firm-level behaviour. Internal labour market theory argues that if the skills and abilities to perform the job are mainly specific to the firm, then promotion through slow development of organisation-wide skills can become the basis for organisational commitment. If, however, changes to rewards systems upset the measurement or assessment of such a concept of ability, then commitment outcomes may be altered. Tournament theory argues that if firms possess imperfect information about or inadequately monitor employees' skills and abilities, then competitions aimed at rewarding winners with prestigious positions (that indirectly have wage premia) produces efficient incentives. The latter system, a tournament, characterises the Japanese social contract, with career incentives being more important than wage incentives.

To understand what is really happening in Japan, Takahashi (2006) surveyed 928 white-collar and 818 blue-collar employees (a 91 per cent response rate) across 75 companies in the Toyota group in order to examine the effects that current wage and promotion incentives have on motivation levels of Japanese employees, and what the social contract appears to be. Both wage and career incentives encouraged employees to work hard, with fair promotion having a greater effect on motivation than wages for both white- and blue-collar workers. In response to this, Japanese organisations have kept the number of managerial positions to a minimum but in the case of insufficient posts, have withdrawn wage increases from post promotion:

> . . . in order to maintain the seniority-based promotion system and avoid a decrease in motivation levels, companies modified their systems to raise the wages in accordance with skill development rather than post

promotion. Wages and promotion were not necessarily related to each other ... when employees sensed that promotion would be difficult they quit pursuing post promotion and changed their orientation to developing skills in order to obtain higher wages.

(Takahashi 2006: 200–201)

Conclusions on the institutional context

So an in-country HR manager of a foreign multinational needs to understand the inter-dependent institutional forces at play in such rewards change processes and to appreciate, the likely psychological outcome. This involves diagnosis of the real pressures for international rewards convergence. These include global labour cost disadvantages, either in terms of wage or non-wage (social cost of employment) factors, but they also include the reasons for foreign direct investment patterns, the skills levels of local workforces, technological innovation patterns, the strategic need for business model changes and even demographic impacts on wage behaviour. The two narratives highlight a broad range of factors involved, the most notable of which include:

- Regulatory arrangements for cross-firm and within-firm wage negotiations: the density and tightness of such arrangements: their scope across flexibility elements (function, reward, time, security); inclusion of monetary and non-monetary elements; the quality of regulatory enforcement
- The role of functionally-equivalent institutional solutions that might produce the same rewards behaviour
- The power of employees in the employment relationship
- Impacts of the benefits system and corporate taxation policies on incentives
- Differentiation in skills levels across the hierarchy
- Performance incentives inherent in the career and compensation systems
- Reliance on stock or flow pay progression systems; the role of job versus personal factors, or input (individual attributes) versus output (performance) in determining pay progression and employee value
- Internal or external qualification systems and labour markets
- Impact of institutional processes on the organisational competencies needed to manage change in rewards processes: such as job analysis and job evaluation; line management performance management skills; risk-avoidance behaviour; the channels for and quality of performance feedback
- Social contract, as evidenced through the trade-offs between security and commitment, income inequalities over careers and lifetime earnings patterns, and social access to different qualities of employment experience.

The cultural perspective on rewards preferences across countries

International HR managers, then, need considerable institutional awareness if they are to advise their organisations effectively. But what about the influence of national culture on individual rewards behaviour? Are there not also differences in the value attributed to money, the response to public, peer and professional recognition, and preferences for intrinsic achievement? Will such factors have different impacts on rewards-relevant outcomes such as employee engagement or productivity? As Rehu *et al.* (2005: 82) point out:

> As multinational corporations enter foreign markets, the question of how to motivate and compensate the foreign employees arises. Merely transplanting performance incentive systems from the home country to the host country might not motivate the foreign employees.

Theoretical links between national culture and rewards

Joshi and Martocchio (in press) developed a theoretical framework to link national cultural values at the individual level to rewards behaviour. Given the challenge of multi-culturalism within single national labour markets within organisations, let alone concerns about the relevance of rewards policies across countries, they argue that we need to treat national culture as a contingency factor against which rewards need to be aligned and the consequence of misalignment can be both affective and cognitive. Using Hofstede's (1980) well-known model, they see two cultural variables acting as important contingencies: individualism-collectivism and masculinity (aggressive goal orientation) – femininity (passive goal orientation). They address two important theoretical questions:

1   How are group cultural concepts reflected in individual rewards behaviour?
2   What specific relationships should be expected?

With regard to the 'how' question, Joshi and Martocchio (2009) draw upon affective events theory, whereby characteristics of the workplace are assumed to constitute discrete events that influence transient moods and emotions and job satisfaction is a consequent judgement made about the work environment as a result of emotional reactions. Workplace practices such as rewards systems act as stressors for employees when not congruent with values. Person-organisation fit theory also argues that characteristics of employees and the context interact to produce a series of proximal outcomes that then become more distally related to rewards behaviour, such as stress, job satisfaction, commitment, intent to stay, willingness to perform, and belief in one's ability to perform effectively. Hofstede's cultural variables are reflected at the individual level of analysis by related individual differences, and it is individual-organisational value congruence (a meeting of expectations driven by the values implicit in a management practice and the values held by the individuals subject to those values) that acts as an important precursor to subsequent rewards-related job attitudes and cognitions.

With regard to the 'what' question, individualism-collectivism is further broken down on the lines argued by Triandis (1995) into a focus on groups and equality amongst their members (called horizontal collectivism) and an acceptance of inequalities within a collectivistic framework (called vertical collectivism). In masculine cultures work is more central, the acquisition of money and things important, and so the focus on career advancement and achievement is high. In feminine cultures quality of life is important and rewards seen on the basis of need and not achievement. This cultural analysis is hypothesised to lead to the following effects. Individuals with individualistic or masculine orientations should prefer individual incentives or merit-based pay rather than seniority-based pay and company-wide incentive plans. They should prefer benefits such as point-of-service, health insurance plans, defined contribution plans, paid time off and flexible schedules rather than health protection, family assistance and defined benefit plans for retirement.

Of course this is theory. Do such hypotheses hold true? Does the existing evidence actually show this to be the case? Lowe *et al.* (2002) examined the role played by pay and benefits in international compensation based on a study of over 2,200 managers across nine countries and one region (Australia, Canada, China, Indonesia, Japan, Korea, Mexico, Taiwan, the USA and a collection of Latin American countries). Current practices (is now) and desired changes (should be) were measured in terms of pay incentives, benefits as part of pay, incentives as a proportion of total earnings, pay contingencies (long term, future focus), pay focus (group or organisation), influence of factors such as seniority or performance. The findings from the study were difficult to interpret since the samples in countries were not comparable, nor could cross-cultural item functionality be assured; and many of the findings were counter-intuitive in relation to assumed cultural hypotheses. However, the study showed that across all cultures few employees from any country felt that a high proportion of salary should be linked to incentives. It would make sense to agree with the authors' conclusion that such research should:

> challenge the notion that 'adopting the status quo' in a given locale is being locally responsive . . . [and that] adopting a lens focused on what employees in a given culture want from a compensation system rather than replicating current cultural norms may help motivate employees to engage in high-performance behaviours.
>
> (Lowe *et al.* 2002: 62)

Studies linking country-level national culture patterns to patterns of rewards practice

There have been two dominant traditions in the national culture – rewards research field. The first major research tradition links (generally abstracted country-level cultural data, but sometimes actual individual values) to particular patterns of rewards practice across countries. Schuler and Rogovsky (1998) conducted one of the earliest systematic explorations of the link between national culture and indicators of national prevalence of pay systems across a dozen nations from across the advanced industrialised world, identifying many relationships that could be understood through the use of a cultural lens. Nations characterised by greater uncertainty avoidance (most commonly Latin nations) tended to feature pay systems in which seniority and some notion of skill weighed heavily. These nations also featured less focus on individual performance-related pay (PRP). Nations with lower uncertainty avoidance (protestant nations and Anglo-Saxon nations) featured less focus on seniority or skill, but more specifically on individual PRP. Nations characterised by greater individualism tended to feature a greater focus on pay for performance generally, and more strongly a focus on individual pay for performance. In contrast, nations with less individualism (for example Spanish- or Portuguese-speaking countries) generally lay at the opposite end of the spectrum. The findings for the focus on share ownership or options were similar. Nations which were materialistic or exhibited greater 'masculinity' in Hofstede's terms focused on individual bonuses. Thus Anglo-Saxon countries, but also Germany and to a considerable extent Japan, featured more individual PRP amongst professional and technical staff, clerical staff and amongst manual employees. In contrast, nations with more personalistic values, such as the Scandinavian nations and the Netherlands, focused less on such payments for non-managerial employees.

In similar fashion, Chiang (2005) recently tested hypotheses linking individual differences in rewards preferences to country-level aggregated cultural scores, along with additional hypotheses that uncertainty avoidance should be associated with a preference for fixed and non-performance-linked rewards systems, and that power distance also be associated with group and non-performance-linked rewards systems (Chiang 2005). Data were collected between 1999 and 2002 from bank employees in the UK (186 employees), Canada (378), Hong Kong (252) and Finland (189). Measurements were made of preferences for 40 types of rewards and the effects of age, gender, position and education were used as controls. Country-level differences in culture failed to support many of the hypotheses and this was used to criticise Hofstede's framework.

Chiang and Birtch (2006) have reported on another analysis from the same dataset, this time examining the rewards preferences of the 441 employees (drawn from 60 companies in the banking industry) from Finland and Hong Kong. Again, highly significant differences in preferences for rewards type and rewards system were reported for the two countries. Hong Kong employees preferred financial rewards to a Finnish preference for non-financial rewards, had a lower preference for job security, preferred performance-based systems compared to a Finnish preference for competency and skill-based rewards systems. Both countries attached a preference for individual-based performance criteria, but also fixed salary over variable incentives. Both countries did not favour seniority-based systems and in both countries individual factors accounted for significant differences in factors. In analysing the package of findings, the authors concluded that:

> the hypotheses tested ... were often not supported or only received mixed support. In fact, the findings were often counterintuitive vis-à-vis the theoretical framework ... culture's impact was apparent on certain reward type preferences ... however, the relationship between national culture and reward preferences is far from straightforward ... its role is far more complex than prior research would have us believe ... the predictive capability of Hofstede's model with respect to reward preferences is therefore limited.
>
> (Chiang and Birtch 2006: 588–9)

Both studies used Hofstede's cultural framework as a basis for specifying hypothesised differences, and in both instances a conclusion was that the evidence was weak.

Rehu *et al.* (2005) noted that one reason for inconsistent findings is that much of this type of cultural research has been divorced from the institutional context that surrounds culture-specific rewards behaviour. They used Hofstede's questionnaire, which assesses satisfaction, with importance of and agreement to 77 work-related goals, along with a ranking of 15 different performance rewards and an assessment of their motivational impact, for 243 US and 336 German employees of a German multinational organisation. Incentive preferences were examined in six categories: earnings and achievements; family-related rewards; fringe benefits; recognition; training, responsibilities and use of skills; and work environment. The motivators and non-motivators were different for the two groups. Motivators for the US employees were stock options, days off, and employee-of-the month awards compared to improvements in working conditions for the German employees. Yet in the US improvements in working conditions was a non-motivator, as was greater responsibilities, training, and retirement plan payments. The non-motivators for German employees were days off and employee-of-the-month awards.

Rehu *et al.* (2005) also argue that in order to understand the utility of a reward to create some individual benefit one has to understand both the value of, and diminishing marginal utility of, a reward (i.e. the potential impact of different economic and formal institutional factors in determining this value) *as well as* the perception of (psychological value) such a benefit. They draw

upon new institutional economic theory to set the frame for their international rewards comparison. This considers the influence of both formal
(legal body of rules) and informal (social, cultural and religious) institutional
frameworks, to examine the nature of motivation through incentive compensation. They concluded that 'institutional differences are found over the six
logical groupings . . . effects of institutional frameworks are not merely an
isolated aspect of one or two compensation items but seem to be present over
a wide range of incentive issues' (Rehu *et al.* 2005: 97). Multinational organisations should only transfer rewards arrangements when they have data that
allows them to understand individual utility of rewards, and this requires an
understanding of satisfaction, preference for and institutional impact of each
aspect of the rewards structure.

Studies linking national culture to important decision rules and attitudes within rewards systems

The second tradition in the national culture – rewards research field – examines
the congruence between important societal values and the principles inherent
in organisational reward systems, in particular by looking at the different
rules that individuals from different countries might use to make rewards
decisions. Such research is underpinned by an assumption that any mismatch
between these two elements has important implications for the perceived
legitimacy of a rewards system and subsequent delivery of productivity. It
has mainly examined the relative role of judgements about equity, equality
and personal need (see for example Hui *et al.* 1991) but has subsequently led
to a stream of research that has looked at how individual managers from
different countries make such rewards policy decisions. For example, Zhou
and Martocchio (2001) used an experimental design to examine how four
competing factors (work performance, relationship with co-workers, relationships with managers and personal needs) influenced award decisions made by
Chinese and US managers (Chinese managers drawn from an executive education course and US graduate alumni) about bonus and non-monetary
rewards. As expected, each set of managers placed different emphases on the
four competing factors, but cross-national differences were relatively small in
magnitude. For US managers the monetary bonus and non-monetary awards
were quite separate decisions but they were much more highly correlated
for the Chinese managers. Chinese managers placed less emphasis on work
performance (but only for monetary bonus, they placed more emphasis on
performance than US managers when it came to non-monetary rewards) and
more emphasis on relationships with co-workers, relationships with managers
and personal need.

For Giacobbe-Miller *et al.* (2003), the issue facing this type of research
is how best to understand the interplay between cultural and institutional
factors. Might variations in the latter enable change in the former? They
examined the convergence, divergence and cross-vergence of distributive

justice values with workplace ideologies in China (113 managers) and Russia (87 managers), as compared to US managers (a previously established sample of 66 alumni from the host university), whilst controlling for different organisation types (joint ventures or foreign-owned versus state-owned enterprises). The results showed that *expressed* pay values (as measured by a beliefs about inequalities survey) did not differ across the sample, but differences were seen in the actual rewards behaviour evidenced by responses to the bonus allocation scenario. In China, irrespective of organisational type, there was more emphasis on equality-driven rather than productivity-driven bonus allocations compared to the USA whilst in Russia (which did not differ from the USA) organisational type did influence distributive justice values. They concluded that:

> [rewards] values adaptation within any organisation is likely to depend on a combination of factors, including cultural distance, cultural propensity for change, and organisational embeddedness as determined by the values at its founding, the amount of time it has been in existence, the extent to which values have coalesced over time as workers self-select into or out of the organisation, and the extent to which the organisation is tightly coupled . . . through regulatory mechanisms, monitoring and compliance activities.
>
> (Giacobbe-Miller *et al.* 2003: 404)

Within this research tradition we can also include work that looks at the link between national cultural values (at the individual level) and pay referent judgements. For example, Bordia and Blau (2003) have shown how individual differences along an individualism-collectivism orientation (allocentrism) are linked to important judgemental processes underlying satisfaction. The social comparisons differed, with collectivist concerns for group norms, interdependence, and sacrifice to help others being more associated with the use of other people as a focus or referent for judgements than when there was an individualist orientation.

Bozionelos and Wang (2007) have examined the attitudes of 106 white-collar employees of a state-owned enterprise to a range of facets of individual performance-related pay systems: equity- and equality-based reward, support for individually-based rewards systems, concern for group harmony, and perceived impact of relationships (*guanxi*) and losing face (*mianzi*). Contrary to expectations, the employees preferred the idea of equity-based systems over equality-based systems and also held quite positive attitudes towards individual performance-related pay systems. However, the latter attitudes were negatively related to the view that Guanxi and Mianzi had an important impact. The findings, then, suggested that some rewards-related attitudes are closer to cultural factors than others.

Brody *et al.* (2006) have also conducted some interesting research looking at how cultural values might impact some specific judgemental mechanisms made within merit pay systems – notably awards given to 'favoured failures' – individuals with whom the individual has had some prior involvement and who still receive favourable treatment despite poor performance. The cultural dimensions of individualism-collectivism and face were considered. They controlled for and looked at the willingness of collectivists to convert merit pay to base salary to enhance harmony, and having controlled for differences in initial preferences for merit pay allocation, manipulated the level of prior commitment in order to test for differences in the willingness to reward the undeserving. Evaluators from each culture had different reward patterns but also reacted differently to their prior commitment to employees. Taiwanese raters sought group harmony and rewarded a greater percentage of employees, with at least some merit pay including failing employees, with a resultant smaller range of merit dollars per employee. American raters followed the performance model more strictly, rewarding high performers much more than lower performers, ending with a greater range.

Conclusions

At the beginning of this chapter it was argued that at the beginning of the decade we knew relatively little about how organisations should take national characteristics and contexts into account in the design of their rewards systems. Far from being a neglected area of research, the challenge now facing the field is the need to unravel the plethora of factors that have been shown to have an important influence. By outlining first the main organisational level factors used to compare and contrast international rewards practice, and then analysing the web of institutional factors that come into play, followed by a separate review of two types of research into the impact of national culture on rewards practice and behaviour, hopefully this chapter has helped bring some order to current understanding.

Returning to the issue of the relative influence of cultural values as opposed to institutional factors as enacted through the social contract, and their relative impact on rewards behaviour, it should be clear that it becomes nigh on impossible to separate out the impact of each. Looking at such differences, Vernon (2005) argues that whilst there are substantial indications of the usefulness of considering national culture when attempting to understand international differences in pay practice, it also has two disadvantages. First, evidence is still patchy in showing that these dimensions help capture and explain either the basis for the incidence of different approaches to reward in different countries, or the typical reactions of a nation's employees to attempts to apply a single system universally. Second, too much emphasis on national culture disregards the autonomous influence of social actors and institutions on pay structures and practices. These may act to shape cultures, cut across a dominant culture or channel cultural influences in a particular way.

Whilst research on national culture frequently assumes long-standing and stable influences on rewards behaviour, a social contract perspective does allow for the creation of relatively new employee behaviours dependent upon the incentives exhibited across the whole employment system. As to which perspective is the most explanatory, the answer clearly depends on which aspect of rewards behaviour is being looked at. Nonetheless, in terms of future research method, some guidance can be found by looking at research on the centrality of work. Parboteeah and Cullen (2003), drawing upon Inglehart and Baker's (2000) observation that cultural and institutional factors have independent effects on values, use individual-level data from the 1990 World Value Survey for 30,270 individuals, along with institutional data from the 26 countries they represented (reflecting socialism, union strength, educational accessibility, social inequality and industrialisation) to assess the relative impact on perceived work centrality. Controlling for age, gender, gender and job satisfaction, and entering country-level data for Hofstede's variables of uncertainty avoidance, individualism and masculinity, 10.5 per cent of variance in work centrality values was between country, of which the social institutions model explained 34 per cent of the variance and the national culture model explained 28 per cent. Excepting industrialisation levels, the institutional and cultural factors were independent of each other. So, with regard to this rewards-related variable, institutions win out over national culture! Would it not be interesting to see such multi-level research models extended to the examination of a broader range of comparative rewards behaviours?

As is evident from the discussion of research on the specific impacts of national culture on rewards, since the previous edition (Sparrow 2000), some more critical views about the culture-rewards literature have emerged. Chiang and colleagues (see Chiang 2005; Chiang and Birch 2006) note that the implicit assumption of work using Hofstede's cultural framework is that rewards policies and practices will be easier to transplant amongst countries sharing similar cultural profiles. They argue, however, that most cultural studies have concentrated on the financial elements of rewards systems, rather than the broader total rewards system (non-monetary elements and intrinsic rather than just extrinsic factors). We still know little about the impact that culture has on *different dimensions of rewards* and need to differentiate its impact on preferences for: different types of rewards; rewards systems; or rewards criteria.

In addressing such questions in the future, we can also expect a more critical eye to be turned on the research methods adopted. In a broader review of the state of knowledge about the link between national culture and employee behaviours, Sparrow (2006) notes that much culture research continues to use Hofstede's framework, even though this has come under increasing criticism as a basis for research. In order for future national culture-rewards research to be of most benefit, a number of methodological refinements are likely to become increasingly important. These issues are generic to much cross-cultural research, but they create particular problems for interpretation in the rewards field, where decisions in real world contexts are often highly pragmatic and contextualised.

The generic issues are: the ecological fallacy problem (using aggregate country-level data measured on group-level constructs) to explain separate individual-level data; convenience samples (students, management course participants, etc.); inferences about convergence based on cross-sectional data; use of decontextualised experimental designs and scenarios that ignore the impact of other proximal variables that might explain decision-making, and confounded measurement that does not balance direct expression (where respondents are influenced by social desirability factors and the temptation to portray themselves in ways they think the experimenter wants to hear) with actual behaviour (which are more reflective of the actuality).

Given the drive noted by Festing *et al.* (2007) towards more standardisation in transnational compensation strategies, a number of important research needs also emerge. To make sense of the emerging research on different national rewards behaviours, international HR practitioners first need a clearer specification of generic rewards functioning at the individual level (for example, is it really just the process of rewards motivation that might be assumed to be generic?). Such generic functioning models also become important in understanding the linkage between rewards behaviour and important antecedent factors or outcomes such as commitment and engagement (Sparrow 2006) that might form the basis of a transnational compensation strategy.

The assertion that national culture influences rewards attitudes and behaviours mainly, but indirectly, through organisational practices also suggests that we need to better understand the processes through which organisational culture and organisational practices mediate the effects that national culture might have. There are also dynamic and two-way (i.e. top-down and bottom-up) processes involved when studying national culture, and this suggests that any modelling of its impacts on specific behaviours (such as rewards) needs to allow for an understanding of not just *how* national culture exerts an influence on work attitudes, but also of how national culture is *enacted within firms and within individuals*. Only this latter understanding enables us to see how there may also be bottom-up influences on the adoption, customisation and redirection of specific rewards practices. There are, then, now a range of highly complex but fascinating questions facing future researchers, and given the increasingly global pressures on compensation strategy, there will be no shortage of practitioners seeking answers.

References

Abe, M. (2007) 'Why companies in Japan are introducing performance-based treatment and reward systems. The background, merits and demerits', *Japan Labour Review*, 4 (2): 7–36.

Baker, G. and Holmström, B. (1995) 'Internal labor markets: too many theories, too few facts', *American Economic Review Paper and Proceedings*, 85: 255–9.

Beer, M. and Katz, N. (2003) 'Do incentives work? The perceptions of a worldwide sample of senior executives', *Human Resource Planning*, 26 (3): 30 44.

Bordia, P. and Blau, G. (2003) 'Moderating effect of allocentrism on pay referent comparison-pay level satisfaction relationship', *Applied Psychology: An International Review*, 52: 499–514.

Bozionelos, N. and Wang, L. (2007) 'An investigation on the attitudes of Chinese workers towards individually based performance-related reward systems', *International Journal of Human Resource Management*, 18 (2): 284–302.

Brewster, C., Sparrow, P.R. and Vernon, G. (2007) *International Human Resource Management*, Wimbledon: CIPD.

Brody, R.G., Lin, S. and Salter, S.B. (2006) 'Merit pay, responsibility and national values: a U.S.–Taiwan comparison', *Journal of International Accounting Research*, 5 (2): 63–79.

Bruce, A., Buck, T. and Main, B.G.M. (2005) 'Top executive remuneration: a view from Europe', *Journal of Management Studies*, 42 (7): 1493–517.

Buck, T. and Shahrim, A. (2005) 'The translation of corporate governance changes across national cultures: the case of Germany', *Journal of International Business Studies*, 36: 42–61.

Buck, T., Shahrim, A. and Winter, S. (2004) 'Executive stock options in Germany: the diffusion or translation of US-style corporate governance?', *Journal of Management and Governance*, 8: 173–86.

Chiang, F.F.T. (2005) 'A critical examination of Hofstede's thesis and its application to international reward management', *International Journal of Human Resource Management*, 16 (9): 1545–63.

Chiang, F.F.T. and Birch, T.A. (2006) 'An empirical examination of reward preferences within and across national settings', *Management International Review*, 46 (5): 573–96.

Cin, B., Han, T. and Smith, S.C. (2003) 'A tale of two tigers: employee financial participation in Korea and Taiwan', *International Journal of Human Resource Management*, 14 (6): 920–41.

Croucher, R. and White, G. (2007) 'Enforcing a natural minimum wage: the British case', *Policy Studies*, 28 (2): 145–61.

Dirks, D. (1998) 'Experimenting with standardisation and individualisation: human resource management and restructuring in Japan', *Management International Review*, 38 (2), 89–103.

Dribbusch, H. (2004) 'Agreements on cost-cutting and job security signed at Volkswagen', *European Industrial Relations Observatory Online*. ID: DE0411203F. Available: http://www.eurofound.europa.eu/eiro/2004/11/feature/de0411203f.htm (accessed: 12 February 2008).

The Economist (2006a) 'German trade unions: there's life in the old dinosaurs yet', *The Economist*, 378 (8485): 41.

The Economist (2006b) 'Germany's labour market: A lesson from Tony Blair', *The Economist*, 379 (8477): 44.

The Economist (2006c) 'Inequality in Japan: The rising sun leaves some Japanese in the shade', *The Economist*, 379 (8482): 67–8.

The Economist (2007) 'Germany's economy: back above the bar again', *The Economist*, 384 (8537): 86–8.

Festing, M., Eidems, J. and Royer, S. (2007) 'Strategic issues and local constraints in transnational compensation strategies: an analysis of cultural, institutional and political influences', *European Management Journal*, 25 (2): 118–31.

Giacobbe-Miller, J.K., Miller, D.J., Zhang, W. and Victorov, V.I. (2003) 'Country and organizational-level adaptation to foreign workplace ideologies: a comparative study of distributive justice values in China, Russia and the United States', *Journal of International Business Studies*, 34: 389–406.

Grund, C. (2005) 'The wage policy of firms: comparative for the US and Germany from personnel data', *International Journal of Human Resource Management*, 16 (1): 104–19.

Hofstede, G. (1980) *Culture's Consequences: International Differences in Work-Related Values*, Beverly Hills: Sage.

Hui, C.H., Triandis, H.C. and Yee, C. (1991) 'Cultural differences in reward allocation: is collectivism the explanation?', *British Journal of Social Psychology*, 30: 145–57.

Inglehart, R. and Baker, W.E. (2000) 'Modernisation, cultural change, and the persistence of traditional values', *American Sociological Review*, 65: 19–51.

Ishida, M. (2007) 'What is the outcome of the wages reform in recent Japan?', *Japan Labour Review*, 4 (2): 55–77.

Ishii, Y (2006) 'Ten years of the performance-based pay system and its merits and demerits', *Japanese Journal of Labour Studies*, September, Report No. 554.

Joshi, A. and Martocchio, J.J. (2008) 'Compensation and reward systems in a multicultural context', in D. Stone, E. Stone-Romero and E. Salas (eds) *Cultural Diversity in Human Resources Practices*, Mahaw NY: Lawrence Erlbaum.

Lawler, E. (2000) *Rewarding Excellence: Pay Strategies for the New Economy*, San Francisco, CA: Jossey-Bass Publishers.

Long, R.J. and Shields, J.L. (2005) 'Performance pay in Canadian and Australian firms: a comparative study', *International Journal of Human Resource Management*, 16 (10): 1783–811.

Lowe, K.B., Milliman, J., De Cieri, H. and Dowling, P.J. (2002) 'International compensation practices: a ten country comparative analysis', *Human Resource Management*, 41 (1): 45–66.

Milkovich, G.T. and Newman, J.M. (2002) *Compensation*, 7th edn, London: McGraw-Hill.

Parboteeah, K.P. and Cullen, J.B. (2003) 'Social institutions and work centrality: explorations beyond national culture', *Organization Science*, 14 (2): 137–48.

Poutsma, E. and de Nijs, W. (2003) 'Broad-based employee financial participation in the European Union', *International Journal of Human Resource Management*, 14 (6): 863–92.

Rehu, M., Lusk, E. and Wolff, B. (2005) 'Incentive preferences of employees in Germany and the USA: an empirical investigation', *Management Revue*, 16 (1): 81–98.

Schuler, R.S. and Rogovsky, N. (1998) 'Understanding compensation practice variations across firms: the impact of national culture', *Journal of International Business Studies*, 29: 159–77.

Sparrow, P.R. (2000) 'International reward management', in G. White and J. Druker (eds) *Reward Management: A Critical Text*, London: Routledge.

Sparrow, P.R. (2006) 'International management: Some key challenges for industrial and organizational psychology', in G.P. Hodgkinson and J.K. Ford (eds) *International Review of Industrial and Organizational Psychology – Volume 21*, Chichester: Wiley.

Suda, T. (2007) 'Converging or still diverging? A comparison of pay systems in the UK and Japan', *International Journal of Human Resource Management*, 18 (4): 586–601.

Takahashi, K. (2006) 'Effects of wage and promotion incentives on the motivation levels of Japanese employees', *Career Development International*, 11 (3): 193–202.

Thierry, H. (1998) 'Compensating work', in P.J.D. Drenth, H.Thierry and C.J. de Wolff (eds) *Handbook of Work and Organizational Psychology. Volume 4: Organizational Psychology*, Brighton: Psychology Press.

Tosi, H.L. and Greckhammer, T. (2004) 'Culture and CEO compensation', *Organization Science*, 15 (6): 657–70.

Treble, J., Van Gameren, E., Bridges, S. and Barmby, T. (2001) 'The internal economics of the firm: further evidence from personnel data', *Labour Economics*, 8: 531–52.

Triandis, H.C. (1995) *Individualism and Collectivism*, Boulder: Westview Press.

Vernon, G. (2005) 'International pay and reward', in P. Edwards and G. Rees (eds) *International Human Resource Management*, London: FT/Prentice Hall.

Watson, B.W. and Singh, G. (2005) 'Global pay systems: compensation in support of a multinational strategy', *Compensation and Benefits Review*, 37 (1): 33–6.

Zhou, J. and Martocchio, J.J. (2001) 'Chinese and American managers' compensation award decisions: a comparative policy-capturing study', *Personnel Psychology*, 54 (1): 115–45.

Index

Note: *italic* page numbers denote references to Figures/Tables.